Private Cloud Computing

T0227211

Private Cloud Computing
Consolidation, Virtualization, and Service-Oriented Infrastructure

Stephen R. Smoot

Nam K. Tan

AMSTERDAM • BOSTON • HEIDELBERG • LONDON
NEW YORK • OXFORD • PARIS • SAN DIEGO
SAN FRANCISCO • SINGAPORE • SYDNEY • TOKYO

Morgan Kaufmann is an imprint of Elsevier

Acquiring Editor: Todd Green
Development Editor: Robyn Day
Project Manager: Danielle S. Miller
Designer: Kristen Davis

Morgan Kaufmann is an imprint of Elsevier
225 Wyman Street, Waltham, MA 02451, USA

© 2012 Elsevier, Inc. All rights reserved.

No part of this publication may be reproduced or transmitted in any form or by any means, electronic or
mechanical, including photocopying, recording, or any information storage and retrieval system, without
permission in writing from the publisher. Details on how to seek permission, further information about the
Publisher's permissions policies and our arrangements with organizations such as the Copyright Clearance
Center and the Copyright Licensing Agency, can be found at our website: www.elsevier.com/permissions.

Designations used by companies to distinguish their products are often claimed as trademarks or registered
trademarks. In all instances in which Morgan Kaufmann Publishers is aware of the claim, the product names
appear in initial capital or all capital letters. All trademarks that appear or are otherwise referred to in this work
belong to their respective owners. Neither Morgan Kaufmann Publishers nor the authors and other contributors
of this work have any relationship or affiliation with such trademark owners nor do such trademark owners
confirm, endorse or approve the contents of this work. Readers, however, should contact the appropriate
companies for more information regarding trademarks and any related registrations.

This book and the individual contributions contained in it are protected under copyright by the Publisher (other
than as may be noted herein).

Notices

Knowledge and best practice in this field are constantly changing. As new research and experience broaden our
understanding, changes in research methods or professional practices, may become necessary. Practitioners and
researchers must always rely on their own experience and knowledge in evaluating and using any information
or methods described herein. In using such information or methods they should be mindful of their own safety
and the safety of others, including parties for whom they have a professional responsibility.

To the fullest extent of the law, neither the Publisher nor the authors, contributors, or editors, assume any liability
for any injury and/or damage to persons or property as a matter of products liability, negligence or otherwise, or from
any use or operation of any methods, products, instructions, or ideas contained in the material herein.

Library of Congress Cataloging-in-Publication Data
Application submitted

British Library Cataloguing-in-Publication Data
A catalogue record for this book is available from the British Library.

ISBN: 978-0-12-384919-9

Printed and bound by CPI Group (UK) Ltd, Croydon, CR0 4YY
12 13 14 15   10 9 8 7 6 5 4 3 2 1

Working together to grow
libraries in developing countries

www.elsevier.com | www.bookaid.org | www.sabre.org

ELSEVIER   BOOK AID
            International   Sabre Foundation

For information on all MK publications visit our website at www.mkp.com

To our wives Marcia Smith and Priscilla Lim Chai Tee,
for their love and support

Contents

Acknowledgments

On numerous occasions, we thought, "Wouldn't it be great if we had something to point people to as they start to get real with the cloud?" After smacking our heads into this wall enough times, we realized that we should write it. We have relied on a large cast of helpers whom we'd like to take the time to acknowledge. Any errors or omissions are the responsibility of the authors alone, given how quickly technology changes we recommend verifying content with up to date manuals from the vendors.

First and foremost, we thank Dr. Mark Day, Alan Saldich, and Dr. Steve McCanne, who provided some of the text we use to lay out the arguments in Chapters 1 and 4. Their perspective and insights dramatically clarified the points that we were trying to make. Karyn Goldstein worked tirelessly to edit the book, helping us express our thoughts, and giving it unity; the book is much better for her work.

We appreciate the technical and other comments we received from our coworkers and friends who looked at the project in its varying stages. We thank Dr. Larry Rowe, Lance Berc, and Kand Ly for their comments on the proposal. Ricky Lin, Joshua Tseng, and Nick Amato were kind enough to look at chapters multiple times for feedback. Finally, we appreciate the technical once-over from Dr. Michel Demmer, Bill Quigley, Bruno Raimondo, Chiping Hwang, Paul Griffiths, Tandra De, Kand Ly, and Phil Rzewski. A special thanks to Emilio Casco for assistance with the figures in Chapter 4 and to Claire Mosher for editing and guidance. The authors appreciate the support from their respective bosses for the time to pull all of this together.

Introduction

There are no rules of architecture for a castle in the clouds.
—G.K. Chesterton

Is "provisioning a web server in 5 minutes for $5" the most interesting thing about the cloud?

Those responsible for IT in their enterprise are quickly discovering that the cloud is a game-changing trend that offers a completely new methodology for service provision. The cloud not only lets you cut IT costs and be greener—it also accelerates innovation within your enterprise. These are the values driving architects to look at how they can build a private cloud for their enterprise.

We are at the start of a decade where network designers will use infrastructure consolidation and virtualization to create next-generation cloud services. Network virtualization is the bedrock for this solution because it can consolidate diverse networks into a single virtual entity, the first step in creating a service-oriented infrastructure. On this foundation, IT resources can be scaled up and down virtually to provision on-demand services (a.k.a. private cloud services) without the addition of new physical devices or entities through server virtualization. From a business perspective, this enables cost savings and increases the ability to rapidly react and adjust to the volatile business climate. This enables more agile balancing of expense reduction with business growth initiatives.

Data centers are the current focus of virtualization because they currently host the largest number of services. To fully realize the cloud vision, one must also look outward to regional and branch offices to find more services eligible for consolidation and to ensure that cloud performance is acceptable to the enterprise. Challenges can come from neglecting the wide area network (WAN) that interconnects the users and services, with inherent delay, packet loss, congestion, and bandwidth limitations. The WAN can be the weakest link in implementing the cloud vision. Broad enterprise cloud computing adoption moves users' computing and storage distant from them; the ensuing latency and bandwidth limitations threaten to reduce performance and thus productivity. WAN optimization is the solution to overcome this obstacle. With WAN optimization, these performance constraints are alleviated, enhancing the performance of a WAN to be nearly that of a local area network.

While there is abundant technical documentation dedicated solely to WAN optimization, next-generation data centers, and virtualization, this book is the first look at all three conjoined as a topic under the mega-trend of cloud computing. This book examines the path toward building a service-oriented infrastructure (SOI) for cloud computing services. It investigates how data center consolidation techniques, and WAN optimization and virtualization (of servers, storage, and networks) enable new structures with increased productivity. Another key factor in data center consolidation is requirements for redundancy to support business availability goals, and we explore the challenges and solutions in data replication for disaster recovery.

Essential to any enterprise cloud is security. We explore it in general for the cloud context and specifically how it applies to the Cisco Unified Computing System. Tying it all together, we provide case studies and examples to demonstrate how enterprises are moving toward a service-oriented infrastructure.

WHO SHOULD READ THIS BOOK

> *One's destination is never a place but rather a new way of looking at things.*
> —**Henry Miller**

This book is intended for network engineers, solution architects, internetworking professionals, IT managers, CIOs, service providers, and everyone else who is interested in building or managing a state-of-art solution for private cloud services. The information in this book enables you to consolidate services from data centers and remote branch offices, leverage WAN optimization to keep performance high, and build a routing and switching platform to provide a foundation for cloud computing services. In general, it is assumed that the reader is familiar with basic TCP/IP networking. As we progress from simple to more complex topics, the book addresses hard-to-understand concepts and difficult areas through each chapter and provides case studies and configuration examples to guide comprehension. If you like really knowing how things work, this is a book for you.

WHO SHOULDN'T READ THIS BOOK

> *"Beware of the man who works hard to learn something, learns it, and finds himself no wiser than before,"* Bokonon tells us. *"He is full of murderous resentment of people who are ignorant without having come by their ignorance the hard way."*
> —**Kurt Vonnegut**

This book is not intended for people who just want to know how to use EC2; it is geared for people who want to learn the underlying concepts required to build their own private cloud infrastructure. Also be warned: we spend the vast majority of our time focused on the technology and market leaders—Cisco for routing/switching, VMware for virtualization, and Riverbed for WAN optimization. Other vendors have relevant products in some cases, but space does not permit more than a nod in their direction. Finally, it is essential to understand automation in building a cloud; that said, it is barely touched upon here.

About the Authors

Stephen R. Smoot, Ph.D., helped start up Riverbed Technology in February 2003, and currently serves as senior vice president of technical operations, running the technical support, technical publications, technical marketing, advanced network engineering, and global consulting engineering groups. He spends his time thinking about where technology is going and helping customers to solve their problems.

Smoot previously worked on acceleration and video at Inktomi Corporation (now a part of Yahoo). He joined Inktomi, following its acquisition of FastForward Networks, which designed overlay network technology for streaming video with millions of viewers over the Internet. Smoot previously worked at Imedia (Motorola), Honeywell, and IBM.

Smoot received his doctorate in computer science from the University of California at Berkeley, working with Lawrence Rowe. His dissertation, *Maximizing Perceived Quality Given Bit-rates Constraints in MPEG Encoding through Content-daptivity,*[1] describes various aspects of creating MPEG video from its original video source. He also holds a master's degree in computer science from the University of California, Berkeley. His undergraduate education was at MIT where he received bachelor's degrees in computer science and in mathematics.

Nam-Kee Tan, CCIE #4307, has been in the networking industry for more than 17 years. He is dual CCIE in routing and switching and service provider and has been an active CCIE for more than 10 years. His areas of specialization include advanced IP services, network management solutions, MPLS applications, L2/L3 VPN implementations, next-generation data center technologies, and storage networking.

Nam-Kee is currently the lead network architect in the Riverbed advanced network engineering team where he designs and deploys cloud computing service infrastructures and virtual data center solutions for Riverbed enterprise and service provider customers. Nam-Kee also advises internal Riverbed engineers in the area of next-generation service provider technologies.

Nam-Kee is the author of *Configuring Cisco Routers for Bridging, DLSw+, and Desktop Protocols*[2]; *Building VPNs with IPSec and MPLS*[3]; *MPLS for Metropolitan Area Networks*[4]; and is co-author of *Building Scalable Cisco Networks.*[5] He holds a master's degree in data communications from the University of Essex, UK, and an MBA from the University of Adelaide, Australia.

Next-Generation IT Trends

Architecture is the reaching out for the truth.
—**Louis Kahn**

INFORMATION IN THIS CHAPTER:

- Layers of Function: The Service-Oriented Infrastructure Framework
- Blocks of Function: The Cloud Modules
- Cloud Computing Characteristics
- Cloud Computing Taxonomy
- Summary

INTRODUCTION

This book is about building a next-generation IT infrastructure. To understand what that means, one needs to start by looking at what constitutes current-generation IT infrastructure. But how did we arrive at the current infrastructure? To get a sensible perspective on that, it helps to back up and look at where computing started.

In the early days of computing, there was a tight connection among users, computers, and applications. A user would typically have to be in the same building as the computer, if not in the very same room. There would be little or no ambiguity about which computer the application was running on. This description holds up when one thinks about the "early days" as referring to an ENIAC, an IBM 360, or an Apple II.

Since those days, enterprise IT organizations have increasingly used networking technologies to allow various kinds of separation. One set of technologies that goes by the name of *storage networking* allows computers and the storage underpinning applications to be separated from each other to improve operational efficiency and flexibility. Another set of technologies called *local-area networking* allows users to be separated from computing resources over small (campus-size) distances. Finally, another set of technologies called *wide-area networking* allows users to be separated from computing resources by many miles, perhaps even on the other side of the world. Sometimes practitioners refer to these kinds of networks or technologies by the shorthand *SAN*, *LAN*, and *WAN* (storage-area network, local-area network, wide-area network, respectively). The most familiar example of a WAN is the Internet, although it has enough unique characteristics that many people prefer to consider it a special case, distinct from a corporate WAN or a service provider backbone that might constitute one of its elements.

It is worth considering in a little more detail why these forms of separation are valuable. Networking delivers obvious value when it enables communication that is otherwise impossible, for example, when a person in location A must use a computer in location B, and it is not practical to move either the person or the computer to the other location. However, that kind of communication over distance is clearly not the motivation for storage networking, where typically all of the communicating entities are within a single data center. Instead, storage networking involves the decomposition of server/storage systems into aggregates of servers talking to aggregates of storage.

New efficiencies are possible with separation and consolidation. Here's an example: suppose that an organization has five servers and each uses only 20% of its disk. It turns out that it's typically not economical to buy smaller disks, but it is economical to buy only two or three disks instead of five, and share those among the five servers. In fact, the shared disks can be arranged into a redundant array of independent disks (RAID)[1] configuration that will allow the shared disks to handle a single disk failure without affecting data availability—all five servers can stay up despite a disk failure, something that was not possible with the disk-per-server configuration. Although the details vary, these kinds of cost savings and performance improvements are typical for what happens when resources can be aggregated and consolidated, which in turn typically requires some kind of separation from other kinds of resources.

Although these forms of networking (SAN, LAN, WAN) grew up more or less independently and evolved separately, all forms of networking are broadly equivalent in offering the ability to transport bit patterns from some origin point to some destination point. It is perhaps not surprising that over time they have borrowed ideas from each other and started to overlap or converge. Vendors offering "converged" or "unified" data center networking are effectively blurring the line between LAN and SAN, while vendors offering "WAN optimization" or "virtual private LAN services" are encouraging reconsideration of the separation between LAN and WAN.

Independently of the evolution of networking technologies, IT organizations have increasingly used virtualization technologies to create a different kind of separation. Virtualization creates the illusion that the entire computer is available to execute a progam while the physical hardware might actually be shared by multiple such programs. Virtualization allows the logical server (executing program) to be separated cleanly from the physical server (computer hardware). Virtualization dramatically increases the flexibility of an IT organization, by allowing multiple logical servers—possibly with radically incompatible operating systems—to share a single physical server, or to migrate among different servers as their loads change.

Partly as a consequence of the rise of the Internet, and partly as a consequence of the rise of virtualization, there is yet a third kind of technology that is relevant for our analysis. Cloud services offer computing and storage accessed over Internet protocols in a style that is separated not only from the end-users but also from the enterprise data center.

A cloud service must be both elastic and automatic in its provisioning—that is, an additional instance of the service can be simply arranged online without requiring manual intervention. Naturally, this also leads to requirements of automation with respect to both billing for and terminating service, or else those areas would become operational bottlenecks for the service. The need for elastic automatic provisioning, billing, and termination in turn demand the greatest possible agility and flexibility from the infrastructure.

If we want to build a cloud service—whether public or private, application focused or infrastructure focused—we have to combine the best available ideas about scaling, separation of concerns, and consolidating shared functions. Presenting those ideas and how they come together to support a working cloud is the subject of this book.

There are two styles of organization for the information presented in the rest of the book. The first is a layered organization and the other is a modular organization. The next two sections explain these two perspectives.

LAYERS OF FUNCTION: THE SERVICE-ORIENTED INFRASTRUCTURE FRAMEWORK

There are so many different problems to be solved in building a next-generation infrastructure that it's useful to organize the approach into layers. The top layer supplies various kinds of fantastically powerful, incredibly flexible services to end-users. The bottom layer is a collection of off-the-shelf hardware of various kinds—servers, storage, networking routers and switches, and long-distance telecom services. The intervening layers use the relatively crude facilities of the lower layers to build a new set of more sophisticated facilities.

This particular layered model is called a service-oriented infrastructure (SOI) framework and is illustrated in Figure 1.1. The layer immediately above the physical hardware is concerned with virtualization—reducing or eliminating the limitations associated with using particular models of computers, particular sizes of disks, and so on. The layer above that is concerned with management and provisioning—associating the idealized resources with the demands that are being placed. A layer above management and provisioning exports these automatic capabilities in useful combinations through a variety of network interfaces, allowing the resources to be used equally well for a high-level cloud software as a service (SaaS) and a lower-level cloud infrastructure as a service (IaaS).

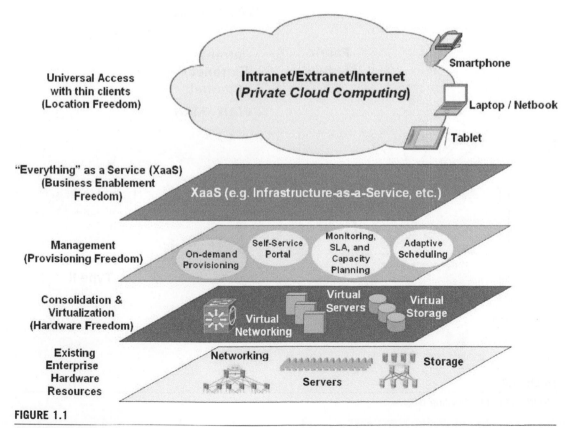

FIGURE 1.1

The SOI framework

In the course of discussing choices and trade-offs to be made, there will be references to these layers.

BLOCKS OF FUNCTION: THE CLOUD MODULES

Throughout the book, while keeping in mind the SOI structure, the chapters are organized around a different paradigm: consider a cloud computer to be made of various modules roughly similar to the central processing unit (CPU), RAM, bus, disk, and so on that are familiar elements of a conventional computer. As illustrated in Figure 1.2, there are several modules making up this functional layout:

- Server module
- Storage module
- Fabric module
- WAN module
- End-user type I—branch office
- End-user type II—mobile

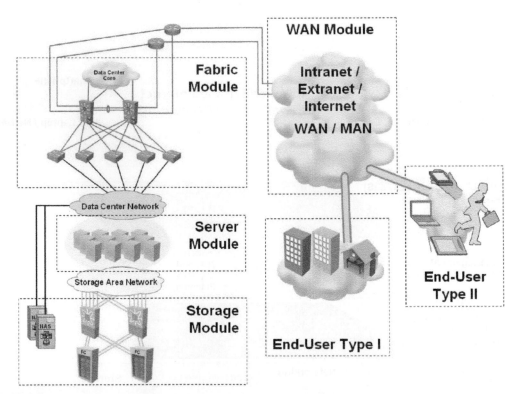

FIGURE 1.2

Cloud computing building blocks

Server module

The server module is analogous to the CPU of the cloud computer. The physical servers or server farm within this module form the core processors. It is "sandwiched" between a data center network and a storage area network.

As previously noted, server virtualization supports multiple logical servers or virtual machines (VMs) on a single physical server. A VM behaves exactly like a standalone server, but it shares the hardware resources (e.g., processors, disks, network interface cards, and memory) of the physical server with the other VMs. A virtual machine monitor (VMM), often referred to as a hypervisor, makes this possible. The hypervisor issues guest operating systems (OSs) with a VM and monitors the execution of these guest OSs. In this manner, different OSs, as well as multiple instances of the same OS, can share the same hardware resources on the physical server. Figure 1.3 illustrates the simplified architecture of VMs.

Server virtualization reduces and consolidates the number of physical server units required in the data center, while at the same time increasing the average utilization of these servers. For more details on server consolidation and virtualization, see Chapter 2, Next-Generation Data Center Architectures and Technologies.

Storage module

The storage module provides data storage for the cloud computer. It comprises the SAN and the storage subsystem that connects storage devices such as just a bunch of disks (JBOD), disk arrays, and RAID to the SAN. For more details on SAN-based virtualization, see Chapter 2.

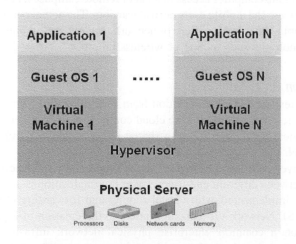

FIGURE 1.3

Simplified architecture of virtual machines

SAN extension

SAN extension is required when there is one or more storage modules (see Figure 1.2) across the "cloud" (WAN module) for remote data replication, backup, and migration purposes. SAN extension solutions include Wave-Division Multiplexing (WDM) networks, Time-Division Multiplexing (TDM) networks, and Fibre Channel over IP (FCIP). For more details on SAN extension solutions, see Chapter 7, SAN Extensions and IP Storage.

Fabric module

The fabric module functions somewhat like a cloud computer bus system that transfers data between the various cloud computing modules. In Figure 1.2, the server farm in the server module is sandwiched between a data center network (typically Ethernet) and an SAN, which is really a Fibre Channel (FC). The SAN is referred to as an isolated fabric topology. FC SANs are also known as SAN islands because FC uses a wholly different protocol stack from TCP/IP.

The main impetus of the fabric module is to transform this isolated fabric topology (IFT) to a unified fabric topology (UFT). How to achieve this UFT? The short answer is to extend or more precisely, to encapsulate the Fibre Channel over Ethernet (FCoE). The previous deterrent to using Ethernet as the basis for a unified fabric was its limited bandwidth. With the advent of 10-gigabit Ethernet, the available bandwidth now offers the feasibility to consolidate various traffic types over the same link. For more information on FCoE, see Chapter 2.

WAN module

The WAN module is the enterprise's intranet (internal access), extranet (business-to-business access), Internet (public access) over a WAN, and metropolitan-area network (MAN). From the cloud computing user's perspective, the WAN module provides access to the cloud. The main purpose of the WAN module is to extend the cloud computer access to local or remote campuses, branches or remote offices, teleworkers or home offices, and mobile users or road warriors. The actual connectivity provided by the WAN module is accomplished using a variety of network technologies, including long-haul fiber networks and mobile technologies such as 802.11 wireless Ethernet.

Network virtualization

As each end-user requires some level of isolation from each other and from each other's computing resources, one of the core requirements for the cloud computing environment is the creation of independent or isolated logical traffic paths over a shared physical network infrastructure and, for that matter, across the WAN.

Virtualization at Layer 3 (IP layer) provides the required end-to-end network segmentation and isolated connectivity between different end-users. Layer 3 virtualization is also known as network virtualization, and can be implemented with virtual routing and forwarding (VRF) and Multiprotocol Label Switching (MPLS). Network virtualization refers to the creation of logically isolated network partitions overlaid upon a common enterprise physical network infrastructure, as illustrated in Figure 1.4. To the end-users, these logical network partitions are no different from the original physical network. For more details on network virtualization, see Chapter 3.

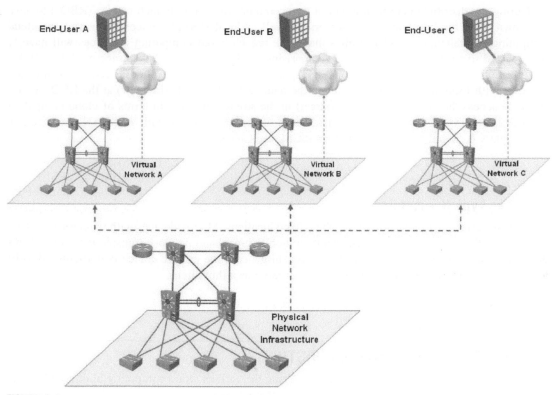

FIGURE 1.4

Network virtualization example

WAN optimization

Even as data and processing become more centralized with the advent of cloud computing, the new challenge is to provide LAN-like response times across the corporate "cloud" (WAN module) to the remote end-users. Moreover, given the resource limitations on the WAN, such as latency and constrained bandwidth, end-user quality of experience needs to be upheld. Remote access to a cloud computer should not result in lower productivity due to slower response time. This is why WAN optimization is a critical component of the architecture. Since WAN optimization "consolidates" data (using a more efficient data representation scheme and protocol) when it traverses the WAN, it can be used to extend constrained bandwidth resources and reduce round-trip delays. The WAN optimization function is typically implemented between the fabric and WAN modules, as well as between the end-user and WAN modules. For details on WAN optimization, see Chapters 4, 5, and 6.

End-user Type I—branch office

The locations for Type I end-users are usually fixed—local or remote campuses, branches or remote offices, and home offices. The network access can either be wired or wireless (or occasionally 3G/4G mobile).

During the distributed computing era, it was common for remote branch offices (RBOs) to have their own local file and application servers, as well as local storage devices. However, the cloud computing centralization model implies that these branch-based computing resources will have to be relocated to a centralized data center (comprising the fabric, server, and storage modules). WAN optimization can be used to maintain the same quality of user experience after the RBO consolidation process. With local storage also migrated to the data center, the hosts (initiator) at the RBO can use iSCSI to access the storage subsystem (target) in the storage module. In terms of cloud computing end-users, the Type I category is the main focus of this book. For details on WAN optimization, see Chapters 4, 5, and 6, and for details on iSCSI, see Chapter 7.

End-user Type II—mobile

Type II end-users are mobile workers with no fixed locations. Mobile devices with wireless access are the norm in this category. The next-generation mobile broadband network (outside the scope of this book) will play an important role in this aspect. In general, the mobile device is not required to be as high-powered as a traditional PC and may act more as a thin client.

CLOUD COMPUTING CHARACTERISTICS

The main objective of consolidating and virtualizing the various cloud computing building blocks in Figure 1.3[2] is to attain an SOI with the following characteristics:

- **On-demand self-service:** An end-user can unilaterally provision computing capabilities, such as server settings and network storage when needed, without any interaction from the provider's IT administrator.
- **Universal network access:** Capabilities are available over the network and accessed through standard mechanisms that promote use by heterogeneous thin or thick client platforms, such as mobile phones, laptops, netbooks, tablet computers, personal digital assistants (PDAs), and so on.
- **Resource pooling:** The provider's computing resources are pooled to serve multiple end-users using a multitenant model, with different physical and virtual resources dynamically assigned and reassigned according to the end-user needs. Examples of such resources include storage, processing, memory, network bandwidth, and virtual machines. There is a degree of location freedom (or independence) in that the end-user generally has no notion of the exact location of the provided resources but will be able to access these resources from an intranet if the end-user is an internal staff member or access from the extranet/Internet if the end-user is an external party.
- **Rapid elasticity:** Capabilities can be rapidly and elastically provisioned (in some cases automatically) to quickly scale out and rapidly released to quickly scale in. To the end-user, the capabilities available for provisioning often appear to be unlimited (or boundless) and acquirable.

With these essential characteristics defined, it is time to delve into the various cloud computing deployment and service models.

CLOUD COMPUTING TAXONOMY

Cloud computing is not a wholly new concept. It is worthwhile to mention that the first cloud evolved around TCP/IP abstraction, with the most significant being the Internet. With the entry of HyperText Transfer Protocol (HTTP), World Wide Web (WWW) data abstraction created the second cloud on top of the first one. The emerging cloud initiative abstracts infrastructure complexities of servers, applications, data, and heterogeneous platforms. It is established beneath the previous two.

Based on cloud computing taxonomy defined by the National Institute of Standards and Technology (NIST),[3] there are four deployment models and three service models that collectively encompass all of the various cloud approaches.

Deployment models

The four common deployment models are as follows:

- **Public cloud:** This cloud infrastructure is made available to the general public or a large industry group and is owned by an organization selling cloud services. Resources are typically provisioned on a dynamic and on-demand basis over the Internet. Small and medium enterprises (SMEs) benefit from using public clouds to minimize growth of data centers.
- **Community cloud:** This cloud infrastructure is shared by several organizations and supports a specific community that has shared concerns (e.g., mission, security requirements, policy, and compliance considerations). It can be managed by the organizations or a third party and can exist on premises or off premises.
- **Private cloud:** This cloud infrastructure is operated solely for an organization. It can be managed by the organization or a third party and can exist on premises or off premises. In short, the private cloud is an emulation of the public cloud, typically on a private network, and exists to support the goals of the organization, rather than to generically support resources for multiple organizations.
- **Hybrid cloud:** This cloud infrastructure is a composition of two or more clouds (private, community, or public) that remain unique entities but are bound together by standardized or proprietary technology that enables data and application portability (e.g., cloud bursting for load balancing between clouds).

There is a fine line between public and private clouds because this is determined by who controls the cloud and who the end-users are, not necessarily the technologies used in building the cloud. This book covers cloud computing that is operated solely for an organization, that is, private cloud computing. In this context, the organization is typically a large enterprise.

Organizations have more control over the security architecture of private clouds as compared to community and public clouds. In other words, private clouds can have less threat exposure than community and public clouds and better meet emerging regulatory requirements. Public clouds raise many more security concerns. This is an additional reason why this book focuses on private cloud computing.

The confidentiality, integrity, and availability (CIA) triad[4] is applicable to the cloud infrastructure except that it should be multitenant-based to provide secure separation and availability among computing resources and end-users alike. For more details on cloud security, see Chapter 8.

Service models

The three service models defined by NIST include:

- **Cloud software as a service (SaaS):** The consumer can use the provider's applications running on a cloud infrastructure. The applications are accessible from various client devices through a thin client interface such as a web browser. The consumer does not manage or control the underlying cloud infrastructure, including the network, servers, operating systems, storage, or even individual application capabilities. Possible exceptions are limited to user-specific application configuration settings. Web-based email is a good example of SaaS.
- **Cloud platform as a service (PaaS):** The consumer can deploy onto the cloud infrastructure consumer-created or -acquired applications created using programming languages and tools supported by the consumer. The consumer does not manage or control the underlying cloud infrastructure, including the network, servers, operating systems, or storage, but has control over the deployed applications and possibly application hosting environment configurations. A hosting provider that allows customers to purchase server space for web pages is an example of PaaS.
- **Cloud infrastructure as a service (IaaS):** The consumer can provision processing, storage, networks, and other fundamental computing resources.The consumer is able to deploy and run arbitrary software, which can include operating systems and applications. The consumer does not manage or control the underlying cloud infrastructure but has control over operating systems, storage, and deployed applications, and possibly limited control of selected networking components (e.g., firewalls and load-balancers). Providing organization-wide IaaS over the private cloud architecture is the main theme of this book.

Figure 1.5 illustrates the three different cloud computing services models. Each service model can be run directly and independently on top of the cloud infrastructure. They can also be overlaid on top of each other, acting as sandboxes.[5] For instance, SaaS overlays PaaS, which in turn overlays IaaS.

Of the three service models, IaaS is the most emergent because it is a natural transition point to evolve traditional enterprise data centers into a fully virtualized private cloud. The whole idea is to build an IaaS-ready infrastructure that consolidates and virtualizes existing computing and hardware resources, such as servers, storage, and networking with benefits already cited in previous sections. For more details on cloud IaaS, see Chapter 8.

Tying it all together

It is important not only to understand these concepts in the abstract, but also to see them put to use in practice. To that end, Chapter 9 is composed entirely of case studies. The design studies range over many of the topics explored in the earlier chapters. Also, recognizing that there are a lot of acronyms used in the text, there is a section at the end of the book that lists them for your reference. Finally, as cloud computing is such an active and developing area we have set up a small website for feedback and errata: see http://www.pcc-cvsoi.com/ for news.

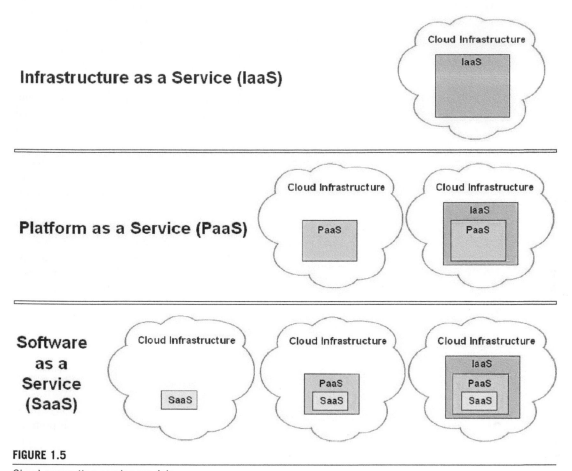

FIGURE 1.5

Cloud computing service models

SUMMARY

This book presents the technologies and techniques required for a next-generation infrastructure to support the implementation of a private cloud service. These technologies can be seen as the next evolution of networking and virtualization technologies that have already had a profound influence on the shape of modern IT implementations.

This book makes reference to both a layered SOI perspective and a modular block-diagram approach to the elements of a cloud service. The remaining chapters are organized primarily by reference to the modules making up a hypothetical cloud computer.

Next-Generation Data Center Architectures and Technologies

To know the road ahead, ask those coming back.
—Proverb

INFORMATION IN THIS CHAPTER:

* The Data Center Consolidation and Virtualization Modus Operandi
* Server Consolidation Drivers
* Server Virtualization
* Storage Virtualization
* Layer 2 Evolutions
* Unified Data Center Fabric
* Summary

INTRODUCTION

In Chapter 1, we introduced the following abstraction layers:

* Hardware
* Provisioning
* Business Enablement
* Location

To realize private cloud computing, we need to ensure the existing enterprise infrastructure has these abstraction layers (see Figure 1.1 in Chapter 1). In other words, large enterprise data centers must evolve to become private clouds. A journey of a thousand miles begins with a single step, and this pivotal step from the private cloud computing perspective is virtualization. The best approach to building a private cloud infrastructure starts with migration toward a fully virtualized next-generation data center (DC) over time, and continues to utilize existing enterprise IT resources.

This chapter discusses DC virtualization, particularly server and storage virtualization. It also covers loop free Layer 2 (L2) design, server I/O consolidation, and the unified DC fabric topology. The main focus of Chapter 2 is on building the service-oriented infrastructure (SOI) in the DC for cloud infrastructure-as-a-service (IaaS) offerings that can be realized through emerging next-generation DC architectures and technologies.

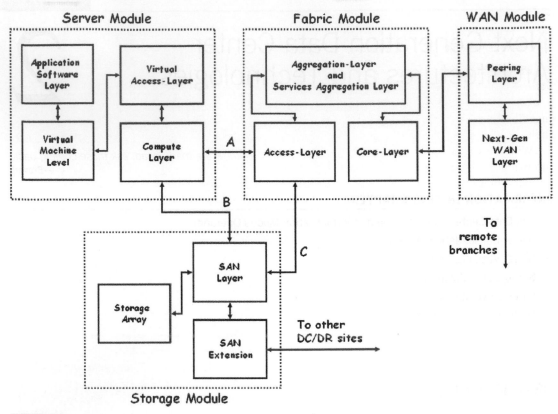

FIGURE 2.1

Building blocks within the private cloud

Figure 2.1 provides a preview on the various layers (or submodules) that make up the cloud computing building blocks:

- Server module:
  - Application software layer
  - Virtual machine level
  - Virtual access layer
  - Compute layer
- Storage module:
  - Storage array
  - SAN layer
  - SAN extension
- Fabric module:
  - Access layer
  - Aggregation layer and services aggregation layer
  - Core layer

- WAN module:
  - Peering layer
  - Next-generation WAN layer

Chapter 2 covers the server, storage, and fabric modules. For more details on the functionality of the various layers (or submodules), see the Cloud IaaS: The Big Picture section in Chapter 8.

Server virtualization helps to consolidate physical servers to virtual machines (VMs). These VMs must be interconnected to some form of L2 virtual access layer (see Figure 2.1). The first step is to build the virtual access layer. See the Server Virtualization section for more details on this process.

With the virtual access layer in place, the next step is to incorporate storage access to the VMs through a SAN (see Figure 2.1). You can take this opportunity to consolidate storage devices using various storage virtualization techniques. See the Storage Virtualization section for more details on these storage virtualization techniques.

Next is the consolidation of the DC LAN, particularly the aggregation and core layers (see Figure 2.1). Many techniques exist to achieve this. One way is to cluster multilayer switches at the aggregation/core layers to appear as a single virtual switch to the end devices. See the Layer 2 Evolutions section for more information on emerging L2 technologies and consolidation techniques.

Finally, the last step is the consolidation between the physical access layer of the DC LAN and the DC SAN (see Figure 2.1). This calls for a union between Ethernet and Fibre Channel, two very different transport media/protocols. You can achieve a unified DC fabric with a combination of "lossless" 10-gigabit Ethernet fabric and Fibre Channel over Ethernet (FCoE). See the Unified Data Center Fabric section for more details on some of these server I/O consolidation techniques.

THE DATA CENTER CONSOLIDATION AND VIRTUALIZATION MODUS OPERANDI

Our modus operandi for the DC consolidation and virtualization is illustrated in Figure 2.2. We will tackle one subject at a time for comprehensiveness, and one module at a time to reduce overall design complexity. Figure 2.2 is the high-level view of the server, storage, and fabric modules shown

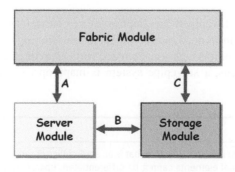

FIGURE 2.2

Data center consolidation and virtualization workflows

in Figure 2.1. The DC is generically divided into these three modules. The consolidation and virtualization of each module are discussed separately in this chapter.

In addition, the interface between the modules is as simple as "ABC," where A is the interface between the server and fabric modules, B is the interface between the server and storage modules, and C is the interface between the fabric and storage modules. These module interconnections or attachment points are covered in the subsequent sections.

SERVER CONSOLIDATION DRIVERS

Although there are many reasons for server consolidation, two causes are at the root. One is server sprawl and the other is application silos resulting in stovepiped data. The classic way for commissioning new applications—one-application-to-one-server model and stovepiped storage subsystem deployed in parallel—poses a scalability issue in the longer term, where the DC and its components will continue to grow without bounds as data size continues to soar.

The Classic Server Sprawl Syndrome

Server sprawl is a term used to describe a situation in DCs where a disproportionate quantity of physical server units are underutilizing internal system resources such as CPU cycles, memory, and storage, while at the same time overutilizing facilities such as power, cooling, and floor space.

In most classic cases, a one-application-to-one-server model is adopted. For instance, various servers for the purpose of development, testing, backup, and so on are required for each new application. The introduction of each new physical server into the existing DC setup creates complexity in terms of additional storage, networking, and security requirements.

Application silos and stovepiped data

As illustrated in Figure 2.3, DCs traditionally place applications into silos with their own servers and storage in an ad hoc manner. As a result of these application silos, data tends to become stovepiped.

The application silos and stovepiped data impose severe constraints on an organization's ability to adapt quickly to evolving business needs and on the rapid provisioning of new services to the emerging market because each instance of this highly customized vertical architecture is seldom adaptable to new applications. For these reasons, a stovepipe system is inappropriate in a private cloud computing environment.

NOTE:

In computing, a stovepipe system is a legacy system that is an assemblage of interrelated elements that are so tightly bound together that the individual elements cannot be differentiated, upgraded, or redeployed. The stovepipe system is typically maintained until it can be entirely replaced by a new system.

Application Based Silos

Stovepiped Databases

FIGURE 2.3

Application silos and stovepiped data

SERVER VIRTUALIZATION

Although there are various ways to alleviate server sprawl, the de facto standard is through server virtualization. A physical server can spawn multiple logical servers with the help of virtualization technologies. This means hordes of underutilized servers in the DC can be transformed into a seamless computing pool, while simultaneously decoupling applications from their silos, that in turn makes obsolete the need for stovepiped storage subsystems.

The most direct effect of server virtualization is the consolidation and reduction in the total number of physical servers in the DC as illustrated in Figure 2.4. The ongoing cost savings are compelling. The decrease in the number of physical servers as a result of server virtualization means lower power consumption, both from the servers and the corresponding cooling systems. This results in a reduction in operation expenditures (OPEX) and future DC hardware spendings or capital expenditures (CAPEX). Server virtualization frees up valuable rack space, giving an organization the room to expand at minimal cost. In addition, intertwined complexity between servers, storage, and networking are made simpler from the physical consolidation and administration standpoint.

Moving toward cloud computing does not need to be an entire overhaul, but a progressive migration or evolution toward a fully virtualized DC. There is no time like the present to start this process.

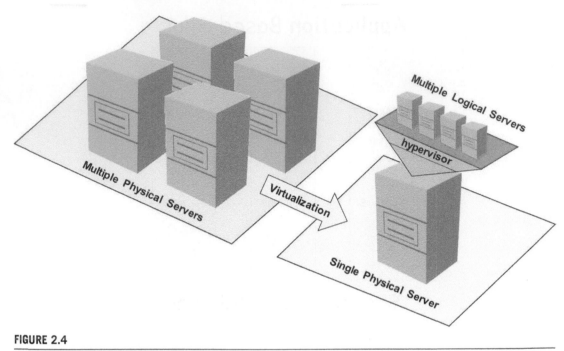

FIGURE 2.4

Server consolidation with virtualization

Virtual Machines and Hypervisor

Server virtualization adopts the one-to-many approach. In other words, a single physical server is partitioned to appear as multiple independent logical servers. The logical server corresponds to a VM providing a complete system platform that supports the execution of a complete operating system. Once the physical server is partitioned, each logical server can autonomously run an operating system and applications. Because the guest operating systems (OSs) do not have to be the same, it is possible to run several OSs and applications simultaneously on the same physical machine or server in a safe and controlled manner. The introduction of more powerful x86 platforms built to support a virtual environment, namely, the availability of multicore CPU, the use of AMD Virtualization (AMD-V),[1] and the Intel Virtualization Technology (Intel VT),[1] has made server virtualization more adoptable.

Virtualization software is available on the market for different system architectures. The most commonly known are VMware, XEN,[2] and Hyper-V.[3] Although they differ in architectures and features, all are based on the concept of a VM that shares the hardware resources (CPU, memory, disks, and I/O of the single physical server) with other VMs. The virtualization software typically achieves this by inserting a thin layer of software directly on the computer hardware or on a host OS. This software abstraction layer is commonly referred to as a hypervisor or a virtual machine monitor (VMM).

The hypervisor decouples the underlying physical hardware (such as CPU, memory, disks, and I/O) from the guest OS. It hides the actual hardware resources of the physical server from the partitioned VMs and projects the impression of a common pool of logical resources that can be shared among these VMs. The functions of the hypervisor include:

- Creating VMs
- Allocating "hardware resources" to VMs from the virtualized pool of hardware resources belonging to the physical server
- Monitoring the status of the VMs
- Taking part in the movement of VMs from one system to another

There are two types of hypervisors:

- **Type 1 (or native, bare-metal) hypervisor:** Type 1 hypervisor runs directly (at first level) on the server's hardware to control the hardware and to monitor guest OS. The guest OS runs at the second level above the hardware.
- **Type 2 (or hosted) hypervisor:** Type 2 hypervisor runs within a conventional OS environment with the hypervisor layer as a distinct second software level, and the guest OS runs at the third level above the hardware.

The server virtualization portion of this chapter covers the Type 1 or bare-metal hypervisor.

VMware Networking Primer

Understanding server virtualization begins with learning the networking basics of the hypervisor. This is essentially "interconnection point A" as shown in Figure 2.2. In this chapter, the VMware ESX Server is the example Type 1 hypervisor platform. The ESX server host interconnects local VMs to each other and to the network (fabric module) through a software virtual switch.

ESX Server networking components

The network interface card (NIC) in a VMware virtualized environment is a general term rather than a physical piece of hardware. Specifically, vmnic refers to a physical network adapter of the host server hardware, and vNIC refers to a virtual NIC that is a virtual hardware device presented to the VM by VMware's hardware abstraction layer (HAL). The vmnics are used as uplinks to the physical DC fabric module. The guest OS sees the vNICs as physical NICs. VMware can emulate several popular NIC types (vlance and Intel e1000), so the guest OS can use standard device drivers for these vNICs. Figure 2.5 shows the various interfaces in an ESX host. In Figure 2.5, four vmnics are available on the physical host (ESX Server) and four VMs are present, each configured with a single vNIC. The vmnics and vNICs are all interconnected together by a virtual switch.

Hosts running VMware ESX have a virtual management port called vswif, which is also known as the service console interface. This interface is used for communication with VMware vCenter Server to manage the host directly with the VMware vSphere client, or to use secure shell (SSH) to log in to the host's command-line interface (CLI). VMware ESXi hosts do not use vswif interfaces because they do not have a service console OS.

> **NOTE:**
>
> The service console OS is really a modified version of Red Hat Enterprise Linux OS that is installed and run in every ESX Server by default.

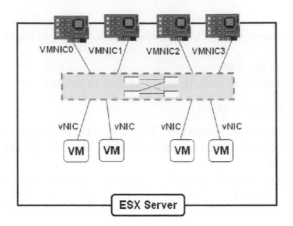

FIGURE 2.5

ESX server interfaces

Each host has one or more virtual ports called virtual machine kernel NICs (vmknics). These are used by VMware ESX for Internet SCSI (iSCSI), network file system (NFS) access, and VMware VMotion. The vmknic is also used on a VMware ESXi system for communication with the VMware vCenter Server.

> **NOTE:**
>
> ESXi is a "thinner" hypervisor as compared to the traditional (full) ESX since it has no service console. Because ESXi is relatively lightweight, installation and boot up time are much faster than ESX. As such, ESXi can be embedded within a physical server on a flash chip, on the motherboard, and so on.

VMware provides two types of software virtual switches: the vNetwork Standard Switch (vSS, formerly known as vSwitch) and the VMware vNetwork Distributed Switch (vDS). The vSS is individually created for each host. On the other hand, the vDS provides a consistent virtual switch across a set of physical hosts; this helps reduce network maintenance and allows VMs to be moved to any host using Network VMware VMotion without breaking network policies or disrupting basic connectivity.

Each vNIC is connected to a standard vSS or vDS through a port group. Each port group belongs to a specific vSS or vDS and defines a VLAN or a set of VLANs that a vNIC will use. In addition, the port group can specify other network attributes such as rate limiting and port security. VMs are assigned to port groups during the VM creation process or by editing the VM properties at a later stage.

The Cisco Nexus 1000V Series switch is implemented as a type of vDS. It is the example distributed virtual switch platform used in this chapter. For more details on the Nexus 1000V Series switch, see The Cisco Nexus 1000V Switch section.

vNIC MAC addresses and VM migration

VMs support up to four vNICs in ESX 3.x and up to 10 vNICs in ESX 4.x. In most cases, the vNIC media access control (MAC) address is automatically generated by the ESX Server. However, it can be statically defined by the administrator to facilitate a DHCP-based server addressing environment where a fixed IP address associated with the statically defined MAC address is always assigned to the same VM.

In the event that a MAC collision happens between VMs, the ESX Server host can detect the collision and resolve it accordingly. The range 00:50:56:00:00:00 to 00:50:56:3F:FF:FF is reserved for statically assigned VM MAC addresses. The administrator must assign static MAC addresses to VMs, within this range.

For each VM, a unique file with a .vmx extension contains the VM's configuration information, including the automatically generated MAC address. If this file is removed, the VM's MAC address might change because the address generation algorithm includes the location information of this file.

VMotion is a feature used by ESX Server to migrate VMs within an ESX Server farm from one physical ESX host to another. A VMotion migration does not result in the VM MAC being modified. If a VM moves with a VMotion migration from an ESX host to a different one, the MAC address of the VM will not change because the VMware virtual machine file system (VMFS) volume is on a SAN and is accessible to both the originating ESX host and target ESX host.

The limitations of vNetwork standard switch

VMware implements the vSS as part of the hypervisor. It is supported in ESX 3.5 (as vSwitch) and in ESX 4.0 and vSphere 4 (as vSS). A VM is connected to the vSS through a vNIC. The vSS allows the VM to send and receive traffic through the vNIC. If two VMs, each with a vNIC are attached to the same vSS and want to communicate with each other, the vSS performs the L2 switching function directly, without the need to forward traffic to the physical or external DC fabric module. The main benefit of the embedded vSS is its simplicity in which each hypervisor includes one or more independent instances of the vSS. However, the vSS limitations outweigh this advantage:

- **Lack of configuration scalability:** Because each embedded vSS represents an independent point of configuration (of local significance to each ESX server), this poses a scalability issue from the configuration perspective when deploying numerous ESX servers in the DC.
- **Poor operation manageability:** The vSS becomes a portion of the network that is not managed consistently like the rest of the DC network infrastructure. In most cases, network administrators do not have access to the vSS. This has also become a growing challenge to the server (or VM) administrators in terms of maintaining and securing the VMs on the unmanaged network created by the vSS (also considered as an unmanaged network device), especially when there is an increasing number of provisioned VMs. Thus, the vSS creates operation inconsistencies in a critical point of the DC infrastructure—the server farms.

> **NOTE:**
>
> While physical server sprawl is resolved with VMs, this also introduces another type of sprawl—VM sprawl. Therefore, ease of VM configuration, administration, and manageability is crucial in server virtualization.

The distributed virtual switch

The distributed virtual switch (DVS) is used to overcome the limitations of the embedded vSS. Switching properties for up to 64 ESX hosts at a time are defined with the DVS rather than configuring each ESX host individually when using the vSS. The DVS essentially decouples the control and data planes of the embedded virtual switch. It allows multiple, independent vSS (data planes) to be managed by a centralized management system (control plane). This approach effectively allows server administrators to move away from host-level network configuration and manage network connectivity at the ESX cluster level.

VMware implementation of the DVS is known as the vNetwork distributed switch (vDS). It is configured through the VMware vCenter server. Cisco leverages on the DVS framework with the Nexus 1000V Series switches. Both versions of DVS are supported in ESX/i 4.0 as well as vSphere 4 and above.

Overall, the Nexus 1000V Series DVS is preferred because it is more feature-rich[4] and robust as compared to vDS. The Nexus 1000V switch is the example DVS platform used in this chapter. For more details on the Nexus 1000V Series switch, see The Cisco Nexus 1000V Switch section.

The Cisco Nexus 1000V Switch

The Nexus 1000V (NX1KV) is a distributed software-based switch that extends across multiple hosts running VMware ESX/i 4.0. It addresses the limitations of vSS or vSwitch. The NX1KV has two main components:

- **Virtual Supervisor Module (VSM):** This module forms the control plane of the switch and is a VM that runs NX-OS.[5]
- **Virtual Ethernet Module (VEM):** This module forms the data plane of the switch. One or more VEMs are typically deployed. The VEM is essentially a virtual line card embedded in each ESX/i 4.0 host and provides the L2 forwarding capability. Each ESX Server host can have only a single VEM installed.

These two components provide the abstraction of a physical switch: the supervisor module is the VSM while the line cards are the VEMs that run within each ESX/i 4.0 host. All configurations are performed on the VSM and are propagated to all the VEMs that are part of the same domain (for more information, see the Domain ID section). Figure 2.6 shows the NX1KV components.

In a physical switch, the supervisor module and line cards have a shared internal fabric over which they communicate. The supervisor module and line cards in NX1KV are decoupled physically although they still function logically as a single switch. There is no internal fabric for communication but instead the external fabric (external DC network) is used. The physical NICs (vmnics) on the VEM are uplinks to the external fabric. The VEM switches data traffic between the local virtual Ethernet ports connected to the VM vNICs, but do not directly switch data traffic to other VEMs. Instead, a source VEM forwards packets to uplinks and relies on the external fabric to deliver these packets to the target VEM. The VSM is not in the data path and it does not take part in the actual forwarding of data packets.

The virtual access layer is the front end of server virtualization. It is built using the NX1KV switch. For details on virtual access–layer design examples using the NX1KV switch, see the Virtual Access-Layer Design Study section in Chapter 9.

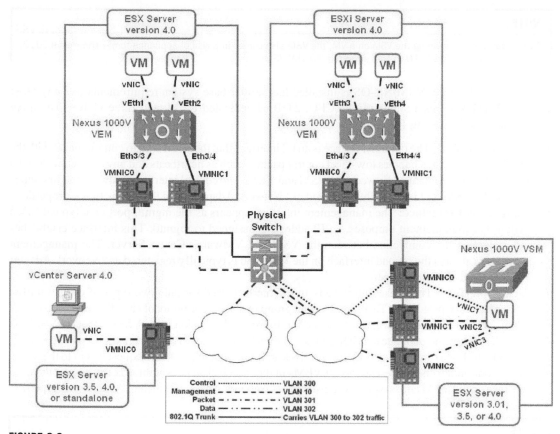

FIGURE 2.6

Nexus 1000V (NX1KV) components

NOTE:

To conform to the NX1KV VSM/VEM conventions and terminologies, the term packet is used interchangeably with frame in the section The Cisco Nexus 1000V Switch and its subsections.

Virtual Supervisor Module

The VSM forms the control (or management) plane of the NX1KV. It provides a single point of configuration management across various VEMs for the network administrator. Unlike a traditional switch where the management plane is integrated into the hardware, the VSM is deployed as a VM running the NX-OS as the OS. It is installed using either an ISO file[6] or an open virtualization format (OVF)[7] template.

> **NOTE:**
>
> As an alternative to running the VSM on a VM, the VSM also comes in physical appliance form—the Nexus 1010. You can use the Nexus 1010 to host up to four NX1KV VSMs.

The VM where the VSM/NX-OS is installed has similar base system requirements like any other OS. The VSM requires a single virtual CPU, 2 GB of dedicated RAM, and three vNICs. The three vNICs have the following functions:

- **Control interface:** The control interface is an L2 interface that the VSM uses to communicate with the VEMs. This interface handles low-level control packets such as heartbeats and any configuration data that needs to be exchanged between the VSM and VEM. The control interface is always the first interface on the VSM and is typically registered as "Network Adapter 1" in the VM network properties.
- **Management interface:** The management interface appears as the mgmt0 port on a typical Cisco switch. For management purposes, an IP address is assigned to mgmt0. This interface establishes and maintains the connection between the VSM and VMware vCenter Server. The management interface is always the second interface on the VSM and is typically registered as "Network Adapter 2" in the VM network properties.
- **Packet interface:** The packet interface is an L2 interface used for only two types of control traffic: Cisco discovery protocol (CDP)[8] and Internet group management protocol (IGMP)[9] control packets. When a VEM receives a CDP packet, the VEM retransmits that packet to the VSM so that the VSM can parse the packet and populate the CDP entries. The packet interface also coordinates IGMP across multiple VEMs. For example, when a VEM receives an IGMP join request, the request is sent to the VSM, which coordinates the request across all VEMs in the switch. The packet interface is always the third interface on the VSM and is typically registered as "Network Adapter 3" in the VM network properties.

> **NOTE:**
>
> The vNICs of the VSM VM require the Intel e1000 network driver. The e1000 network driver cannot be the default driver when the VM definition is built, and might not be an available option based on the OS selected when the VM is defined. However, you can manually change the driver in the VM configuration file. When you select "Other Linux 64-bit" as the OS, you enable the selection of the e1000 driver and set it as the default driver.

The NX1KV uses the concept of a virtual chassis to emulate a 66-slot modular Ethernet switch with redundant supervisor functions:

- Slot 1 is reserved for the active VSM.
- Slot 2 is reserved for the standby VSM in a dual supervisor system.
- Slots 3 to 66 are allocated to the VEMs in a sequential manner as their respective hosts are added to the NX1KV switch. In other words, a single VSM can manage up to 64 VEMs.

> **NOTE:**
>
> You can modify the VEM-to-slot-number mapping by changing the "host vmware id" configuration line. For details on this command, see the Managing Server Connections section in the Cisco Nexus 1000V System Management Configuration Guide.

High availability and VSM

A VSM can run in one of the following roles:

- **Active:** The active role controls the system and is reachable for configuration on the mgmt0 interface.
- **Standby:** The standby role continuously monitors the active VSM to take over in case of a switchover.
- **Standalone:** The stand-alone role is the default role for the VSM when there is no other VSM peer for active-standby configuration.

> **NOTE:**
>
> Use the command "system redundancy role {standalone | primary | secondary}" to control the VSM role and the command "show system redundancy status" to verify the system redundancy status of the VSM. Remember to perform "copy running-config startup-config" to save the configuration consistently through reboots and restarts. For details on these commands, see the Configuring System-Level High Availability section in the Cisco Nexus 1000V High Availability and Redundancy Configuration Guide.

The high availability (HA) deployment for the NX1KV switch works much like dual supervisors in a physical chassis. Two VSMs are deployed in an active-standby configuration in the virtual chassis. Slot 1 is for the active VSM while slot 2 is for the standby VSM. The first VSM takes up the active (or primary) role and the other VSM assumes the standby (or secondary) role. The two VSMs synchronize the state and configuration at regular interval to ensure a transparent and stateful switchover (SSO)[10] to the standby VSM if the active VSM fails.

VMware vCenter and Nexus 1000V

Each instance of the NX1KV switch is represented in the VMware vCenter Server as a vDS that enables a single virtual switch to span multiple ESX hosts. The NX1KV switch is created in the vCenter Server by establishing a link between the VSM and the vCenter Server using the VMware Virtual Infrastructure Methodology (VIM)[11] Application Programming Interface (API).

> **NOTE:**
>
> The management hierarchy of VMware is segregated into two main components: a DC and a cluster. A DC encompasses all components of a VMware deployment, including hosts, VMs, and network switches, including the NX1KV. Within a VMware DC, you can create one or more clusters. A cluster is a group of hosts and VMs that establish a pool of CPU and memory resources. You can create or migrate a VM within a cluster to any host in the cluster. Hosts and VMs do not need to be part of a cluster. They can also exist on their own within the DC.

Nexus 1000V vCenter Server extension

The vCenter Server allows third-party management plug-ins that enable external applications to extend the capabilities of the vCenter Server and its graphical user interface (GUI), the vSphere Client. The NX1KV switch uses a vCenter Server extension to display a representation of the NX1KV switch and its main components within the vSphere Client. The NX1KV extension is a small XML[12] file (cisco_nexus_1000v_ extension.xml) that is downloaded from the management IP address of the VSM using a web browser. This plug-in must be installed before the VSM can establish a link to the vCenter Server.

Opaque data

Opaque data comprises a collection of the NX1KV configuration parameters maintained by the VSM and are propagated to the vCenter Server when the link between the VSM and vCenter Server is established. The opaque data contains required configuration information for each VEM to establish connectivity to the VSM during VEM installation. The information includes:

- Switch domain ID
- Switch name
- Control and packet VLAN IDs
- System port profiles

When a new VEM comes online, either after initial installation or upon reboot of an ESX host, it acts as an unprogrammed line card. The vCenter Server automatically pushes the opaque data to the VEM. The VEM in turn uses this information to establish communication with the VSM and downloads the appropriate configuration data.

VSM-to-vCenter communication

The link between the VSM and vCenter Server maintains the definition of the NX1KV switch within the vCenter Server and propagates the port profiles (see the Port Profiles section). After the NX1KV vCenter Server plug-in is installed, a connection is defined for the link. The connection consists of the following parameters:

- vCenter Server IP address
- Communication protocol—VMware VIM over HTTPS
- Name of the VMware DC where the ESX hosts are located

After the connection is enabled, it establishes the link and creates the instance of the NX1KV switch within the vCenter Server. Each VSM is associated with the vCenter Server through a unique extension key. During the switch instance creation process, the VSM propagates any predefined port profiles and opaque data to the vCenter Server. The opaque data provides limited configuration information to the VEM so that it can communicate with the VSM after installation.

In the event the connection between the VSM and the vCenter Server is disrupted, the VSM ensures that any configuration changes made during the disruption are propagated to the vCenter Server once the connection is restored. After the connection between the VSM and the vCenter Server is established, the link propagates new port profiles and any changes to existing ones.

Virtual Ethernet Module

The VEM functions like a line card within a modular switching platform. Each VEM acts as an independent switch from a forwarding perspective. Unlike the VSM, the VEM is installed on each ESX host as a kernel component rather than a VM. The storage footprint of the VEM is fixed (approximately 6.4 MB of disk space) whereas its RAM utilization is variable.

In a typical configuration, each VEM requires 10 to 50 MB of RAM, with a hard upper limit of 150 MB for full scalability. Each instance of the NX1KV switch comprises 66 slots—two for the VSMs and the remaining 64 for the VEMs. The minimum configuration is one VSM (no VSM High Availability) and one VEM while the maximum configuration is two VSMs (one active and one standby) and 64 VEMs.

VEM switch port taxonomy

The VEM supports the following switch port types:

- **Virtual Ethernet (vEth):** This interface connects to the vNIC of a VM or to specialized interface types such as the vswif or vmknic interface. The vEth interfaces are virtual interfaces with no associated physical component. A vEth interface is denoted as vEthY where Y is the port number. This notation is designed to work transparently with VMotion by preserving the same interface name regardless of the location of the associated VM. The mapping of a VM's vNIC to a vEth interface is static. When a new VM is created, a vEth interface is also created for each of the vNICs associated with the VM. The vEth interfaces persist as long as the VM exists. If the VM is temporarily down (the guest OS is shut down), the vEth interfaces remain inactive but stay mapped to that particular VM. If the VM is deleted, the vEth interfaces are freed for connections to other newly provisioned VMs.
- **Ethernet (Eth):** This interface is the representation of a VMNIC (physical NIC). It is denoted as EthX/Y where X is the module number and Y is the port number on the module. These Eth interfaces are module specific.
- **PortChannel (Po):** A PortChannel is an aggregation of multiple Eth interfaces on the same VEM. It is not created by default and must be explicitly defined.

Port profiles

The NX1KV provides a feature called port profiles, that are network policies used to simplify network provisioning with VMware. A port profile is a collection of interface-level configuration commands that are congregated to create a complete network policy. Port profiles are created on the VSM and propagated (exported) to the vCenter Server through the VMware-VIM API. After propagation, the port profile configured on the NX1KV appears as VMware-distributed virtual port groups through the vSphere Client, similar to a standard vDS. A new or existing VM can have its vNICs assigned to the appropriate virtual port group, that will then inherit the port profile settings.

When a new VM is provisioned, the appropriate port profile is selected and the NX1KV creates a new switch port based on the policies defined by this port profile. The provisioning of similar VMs can be simplified by reusing the port profile. When the newly provisioned VM is powered on, a vEth interface is created on the NX1KV switch for each vNIC the VM contains. The vEth inherits the definitions in the selected port profile. Code Listing 2.1 illustrates a sample port profile configuration template at the vNIC end.

```
port-profile type vEthernet data302
  description "Data profile for VM traffic"
  switchport mode access
  switchport access vlan 302
  no shutdown
  vmware port-group data302
  state enabled
```

CODE LISTING 2.1

Data profile configuration template at vNIC end

Port profiles are dynamic policies that can be revised when network requirements change. Modifications to active port profiles are then applied to each switch port that is using the profile. Port profiles also manage the physical NICs (VMNICs) within an ESX host. These profiles are known as uplink port profiles that are assigned to physical NICs as part of the installation of the VEM on an ESX host. The uplink port profiles are also assigned to new physical NICs that are added to the VEM after the ESX host has been added to the switch. Code Listing 2.2 illustrates a sample port profile configuration template at the VMNIC end.

```
port-profile type Ethernet vm-uplink
  description "Uplink profile for VM traffic"
  capability uplink
  switchport mode trunk
  switchport trunk allowed vlan 300-302
  no shutdown
  vmware port-group vm-uplink
  state enabled
```

CODE LISTING 2.2

Uplink profile configuration template at VMNIC end

NOTE:

If a port profile is configured as an uplink (using the optional "capability uplink" command), it can only be applied to the physical ports (Eth) and cannot be used to configure the virtual ports (vEth).

Network policies enforced by a port profile follow the VM throughout its lifecycle, whether the VM is migrated from one server to another, suspended, hibernated, or restarted. During the VM migration, the NX1KV switch also moves the VM's network state, such as the port counters and flow statistics. VMs participating in traffic monitoring activities, such as NetFlow or Encapsulated Remote Switched Port Analyzer (ERSPAN),[13] continue these activities uninterrupted by VMotion operations. This is a crucial manageability factor required in cloud IaaS operations.

Whose turn: server or network administrator?

In a classic DC operation environment, the server administrator typically manages the OS and applications while the network administrator manages the switches and their associated policies. The NX1KV switch retains the different functional roles between the network administrator and the server administrator. It also creates distinct roles that are jointly managed by network and server administrators. This is achieved with the help of port profiles (for more details, see the Port Profiles section).

The network administrator defines port profiles and exports them to the vCenter Server. Within the vCenter Server, port profiles appear as the usual VMware port groups. When a new VM is provisioned, the server administrator selects the appropriate port profile and the NX1KV creates a new switch port based on the policies defined by this port profile. The server administrator can also simplify the provisioning of similar VMs by reusing the port profile.

VEM-to-VSM communication

Each VEM has a control and packet interface similar to the VSM. These interfaces are unmanaged and not directly configurable by the end-user. The VEM uses the opaque data provided by the vCenter Server to configure the control and packet interfaces with the correct VLANs. The VEM then applies the correct uplink port profile to the control and packet interfaces to establish communication with the VSM. After the VSM recognizes the VEM, a new module is virtually inserted into the virtual chassis of the NX1KV switch. The VEM will be assigned the lowest available module number between 3 and 66. When a VEM comes online for the first time, the VSM assigns the module number and tracks that module using the universally unique ID (UUID)[14] of the ESX server. The UUID ensures that the VEM retains its module number when the ESX host comes back online after a connectivity outage or a power cycle.

The VSM maintains a heartbeat with its associated VEMs. This heartbeat is transmitted at 2-second intervals. If the VSM does not receive a response within 8 seconds, the VSM considers the VEM removed from the virtual chassis. If the VEM is not responding due to a connectivity issue, the VEM continues to switch packets in its last known good state. When communication is restored between a running VEM and the VSM, the VEM does need to be reprogrammed.

System VLANs

The system VLAN is an optional parameter that can be included in a port profile. When used, this parameter transforms the port profile to a special system port profile that is included in the opaque data. Interfaces that use the system port profile and are members of one of the system VLANs, are automatically enabled, even if the VEM does not have communication with the VSM after ESX bootup. This behavior enables the use of critical VMNICs if the ESX host boots up but cannot communicate with the VSM. It is mandatory to define the control and packet VLANs as system VLANs. VLANs that are used for vswif and vmknic can be system VLANs as well. However, VLANs used for general VM data should not be defined as system VLANs. Code Listing 2.3 illustrates a sample port profile configuration template for critical ports.

```
port-profile type ethernet system-uplink
  description "System profile for critical ports"
  switchport mode trunk
  switchport trunk allowed vlan 300-302
  no shutdown
  system vlan 300-302
  vmware port group system-uplink
  state enabled
```

CODE LISTING 2.3

System profile configuration template for critical ports

Domain ID

Since multiple VSMs and VEMs can share the same control and packet VLANs, the system must be able to determine which VSM goes with which VEM. The concept of domain binds VSM to VEMs. A domain ID is a parameter used by the NX1KV switch to identify a VSM and its associating VEMs. The domain ID of the NX1KV switch is defined when the VSM is first installed and the domain ID becomes part of the

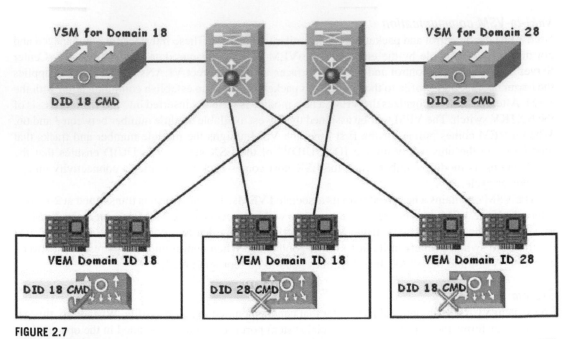

FIGURE 2.7

Domain ID example

opaque data that are transmitted to the vCenter Server. Each command sent by the VSM to any associated VEMs is tagged with this domain ID.

When a VSM and VEM share the same domain ID, the VEM accepts and responds to requests and commands from the VSM. If the VEM receives a command or configuration request that is not tagged with the correct domain ID, that request is ignored. Likewise, if the VSM receives a packet from a VEM that is tagged with an incorrect domain ID, it will be ignored. As illustrated in Figure 2.7, domain ID 18 "joins" the two VEMs that belong to the same VSM as part of the same DVS. The same applies to the VEM and VSM in domain 28.

Switch forwarding

Unlike physical switches with a centralized forwarding engine, each VEM maintains a separate forwarding table. There is no synchronization between forwarding tables on different VEMs. In addition, there is no concept of forwarding from a port on one VEM to a port on another VEM. Packets destined for a device not local to a VEM are forwarded to the external network switch, that in turn, forwards the packets to a different VEM.

MAC address learning

A MAC address is learned multiple times within a single NX1KV switch either statically or dynamically. Static entries are automatically generated for VMs running on the VEM. These entries do not time out. For devices not running on the VEM, the VEM can learn a MAC address dynamically, through the physical NICs in the ESX host. In other words, the entries related to locally attached VMs are statically learned while the MAC address entries associated with the uplinks are dynamically learned. Each VEM from the other ESX hosts maintains a separate MAC address table and thus, a single NX1KV switch might learn a given MAC address multiple times—once per VEM. For instance, one VEM is directly connecting a VM so the VM's MAC address will be statically learned on this VEM. Another VEM, in the same NX1KV switch, might also learn the VM's MAC address dynamically.

Loop prevention

The NX1KV switch does not run the spanning tree protocol (STP). It does not respond to bridge protocol data unit (BPDU)[15] packets, nor does it generate them. BPDU packets received by the NX1KV switch are dropped.

The NX1KV switch uses a simple technique that does not require STP to prevent loops. Every ingress packet on an Ethernet (Eth) interface is examined to ensure that the destination MAC address is internal to the VEM. If the destination MAC address is external, the NX1KV switch drops the packet to prevent a loop back to the physical network.

The NX1KV switch prevents loops between the VEMs and the first-hop access layer switches without the use of STP. Nevertheless, STP should still be enabled on the access layer switches to prevent loops elsewhere in the physical topology.

ESX Server storage networking overview

If you have read this far, you should give yourself a pat on the back before continuing. Now that you have made the first step with ESX Server networking, the next step is to tackle the storage networking fundamentals of the ESX Server. This is essentially about "interconnection points B and C" from Figure 2.2 that interconnect the server module to the storage module (directly or through the fabric module).

NOTE:

Interconnection point C is typically not fiber channel. It is used for NAS and FCoE access by the server module through interconnection point A.

ESX Server storage components

There are five main ESX Server components that perform the storage operations:

- **Virtual Machine Monitor (VMM):** The VMM (or hypervisor) contains a layer that emulates SCSI (Small Computer System Interface) devices within a VM. The VMM provides a layer of abstraction that hides and manages the differences between physical storage subsystems. To the applications and guest OS inside each VM, storage is simply presented as SCSI disks connected to either a virtual BusLogic or LSILogic SCSI host bus adapter (HBA).

NOTE:

VMs use either BusLogic or LSILogic SCSI drivers. BusLogic means Mylex BusLogic BT-958 emulation is used. BT-958 is a SCSI-3 protocol providing Ultra SCSI (Fast-40) transfer rates of 40 MB per second. The driver emulation supports the capability of "SCSI configured automatically," aka SCAM, that allows SCSI devices to be configured with an ID number automatically, so no manual ID assignment is required.

- **Virtual SCSI layer:** The primary role of the virtual SCSI layer is to manage SCSI commands and intercommunication between the VMM and the virtual storage system that is either the virtual machine file system (VMFS) or the network file system (NFS). All SCSI commands from VMs must go through the virtual SCSI layer. The I/O abort and reset operations are also managed at this layer. From here, the virtual SCSI layer passes I/O or SCSI commands from VMs to lower layers, through VMFS, NFS, or raw device mapping (RDM). RDM supports two modes: pass-through and nonpass-through. In the pass-through mode, all SCSI commands are allowed to pass through without traps. See the Raw Device Mapping section for details about RDM.
- **Virtual Machine File System (VMFS):** The VMFS is a clustered file system that leverages shared storage to allow multiple ESX hosts to read and write to the same storage simultaneously. VMFS provides on-disk distributed locking to ensure that the same VM is not powered on by multiple servers at the same time. In a simple configuration, the VMs' disks are stored as files within a VMFS. See the Virtual Machine File System section for details about VMFS.
- **SCSI mid-layer:** The main functions of the SCSI mid-layer are managing physical HBAs on ESX Server hosts, queuing requests, and handling SCSI errors. In addition, this layer contains automatic rescan logic that detects changes to the logical unit number (LUN) mapping assigned to an ESX Server host. It also handles path management functions, such as automatic path selection, path collapsing, failover, and failback to specific volumes.
- **Virtual SCSI HBAs:** In an ESX Server environment, each VM uses up to four virtual SCSI HBAs. A virtual SCSI HBA allows a VM access to logical SCSI devices. It functions just like a physical HBA to the VM.

The concept of virtual data store

The virtual SCSI disks inside the VMs are provisioned from virtual data stores derived from physical storage subsystems. A virtual data store is like a virtualized storage pool that provisions storage space for virtual disks within the VMs, and for storing the respective VM definitions.

A virtual disk (vmdk) is a file that resides in the virtual data store managed by ESX. The virtual data store is a VMFS volume for block-based storage (such as Fibre Channel SAN and iSCSI) or a mount-point for NAS storage (NFS-based volume). The VMFS volume typically consists of a single LUN although it can span across multiple LUNs. The virtual data store can be any of the following file system formats:

- **Virtual Machine File System (VMFS):** ESX Server deploys this type of file system on local SCSI disks (DAS), iSCSI volumes, or Fibre Channel (FC) volumes, creating one directory for each VM. VMFS is recommended for most virtual disk storage.
- **Raw Device Mapping (RDM):** RDM allows VMs to have direct access to raw devices using RDM as a proxy. An RDM can be perceived as providing a symbolic link from a VMFS volume to a raw volume.
- **Network File System (NFS):** ESX Server can use a designated NFS volume located on an NFS server (NAS appliance). The ESX Server mounts the NFS volume, creating one directory for each VM.

To summarize the virtual data store is just a VMFS volume or an NFS-mounted directory. A VMFS volume can span multiple physical storage subsystems to facilitate expansion. The virtual data store provides a simple model to allocate storage space for the VMs without exposing them to the various complex physical storage technologies. These technologies include:

- **FC SAN:** This is the most common deployment option because it supports VMFS, RDM, and HA clusters. FC SAN also supports VMotion and ESX boot.
- **iSCSI SAN:** Hardware-based iSCSI SAN supports functions similar to FC SAN. In the case of software-based iSCSI, booting from the iSCSI SAN is not supported.
- **NAS:** This deployment option utilizes the NFS protocol. NFS-based storage does not support RDM, HA clusters, and VMFS. It does allow VMotion migration and booting from NFS. Arguably, thin provisioning, dynamic expansion/contraction of storage, and cloning are easier to manage through NFS than with block-based storage, but the competition is close.

> **NOTE:**
>
> DAS is a valid deployment option but it is not commonly used because it is not shared.

Figure 2.8 illustrates the ESX Server storage architecture with a VMFS volume and a mounted NFS volume. Each VM is stored as a set of files in its own directory in the virtual data store. A single VMFS volume can contain one or more smaller volumes from an FC SAN disk farm or an iSCSI SAN disk farm. New volumes added to any of the physical storage, subsystems, or LUNs known to the ESX

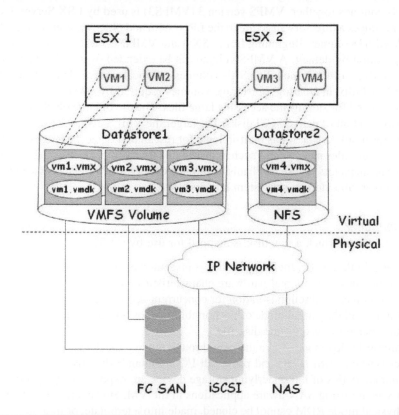

FIGURE 2.8

ESX Server storage architecture

Server that are expanded within the storage subsystem, are unveiled by the ESX Server through a rescan request issued by the vCenter Server.

> **NOTE:**
>
> To a certain extent, the ESX Server provisions host- (or server-) based storage virtualization because the VMFS volume supports block-level virtualization with FC and iSCSI SANs.

Virtual machine file system

VMFS stores VM files, which include disk images, snapshots, and so on. It is a clustered file system that uses shared storage to allow multiple physical servers to read and write to the same storage simultaneously, while individual VM files are locked to prevent conflicts. VMFS provides on-disk distributed locking to ensure that the same VM is not powered on by multiple servers at the same time. If a physical server fails, the on-disk lock for each VM is released so that VMs can be restarted on other physical servers.

VMFS volumes can be logically expanded (i.e., nondestructively increased in size) by spanning multiple VMFS volumes together. VMFS version 3 (VMFS3) is used by ESX Server 3.x and vSphere 4.x. VMFS3 introduces a directory structure in the file system and older versions of ESX Server cannot read or write VMFS3 volumes. Beginning from ESX 3 and VMFS3, VM configuration files are stored in the VMFS partition by default. A VMFS volume can be extended over 32 physical storage extents (32 extents per VMFS volume), including SAN volumes and local storage. This feature allows pooling of storage and flexibility in creating the storage volumes required by VMs.

VMFS is optimized for storing and accessing large files. The use of large block sizes keeps VM disk performance close to that of native SCSI disks. The larger the VMFS disk, the lower the percentage of space used for storing metadata. It has built-in logic for rescan that detects changes in LUNs automatically. VMFS also provides mechanisms such as distributed journaling, crash-consistent VM I/O paths, and machine-state snapshots. These mechanisms provide quick root-cause analysis and recovery from VM, physical server, and storage subsystem failures.

Raw device mapping

There are two modes in which a raw disk is mapped for use by a VM:

- **Virtual mode:** In this mode, the mapped disk is presented as if it is a logical volume, or a virtual disk file, to the guest OS. Its real hardware characteristics are hidden. In this mode, file locking provides data protection through isolation for concurrent updates, the copy on write operation enables snapshots, and the virtual mode offers portability across storage hardware because it presents the consistent behavior as a virtual disk file.
- **Physical mode:** In this mode—aka the pass-through mode—the VMM bypasses the I/O virtualization layer (virtual SCSI layer) and passes all I/O commands directly to the storage device. All physical characteristics of the underlying storage device are exposed to the guest OS. This mode is useful if you are using SAN-aware applications in the VM. However, the tradeoff is that a VM with the physical mode RDM cannot be cloned, made into a template, or migrated if the migration involves copying the disk. There is no file locking to provide data protection.

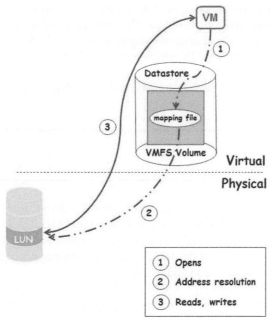

Note: The mapping file is also a type of vmdk file.

FIGURE 2.9

Raw device mapping

The RDM creates leeway for a VM to have direct access to a volume on the physical storage subsystem (with FC or iSCSI only). It provides a symbolic link from a VMFS volume to a raw volume. The mapping makes raw volumes appear as files in a VMFS volume. The RDM file (not the raw volume) is referenced in the VM configuration. It contains metadata that manages and redirects disk accesses to the physical storage device.

As illustrated in Figure 2.9, when a volume is opened for access, VMFS resolves the RDM file to the correct physical storage device and performs the necessary access checking and locking before accessing the volume. Subsequently, reads and writes go directly to the raw volume instead of going through the RDM file.

RDM provides the advantages of direct access to a physical storage device while retaining the benefits of a virtual disk in the VMFS. RDM is typically used for applications such as HA clusters running on the guest OS or SAN-based backups.

STORAGE VIRTUALIZATION

Storage virtualization, the main focus of the storage module (see Figure 2.2), facilitates location independence (an essential cloud computing attribute) by abstracting the physical location of the data from the logical representation that an application on a server uses to access data. The virtualization system presents logical entities known as volumes to the user and manages the process of mapping the volume to the actual physical location. The virtualization software or device is responsible for maintaining the mapping tables as metadata. The granularity of the mapping ranges from a portion of a physical disk up to the full capacity of a single physical disk. A single block of information in this environment is identified by its LUN which is the physical disk, and an offset within the LUN known as a logical block address (LBA).[16] The address space is mapped between the logical entity typically referred to as a virtual disk and the physical disks that are identified by their respective LUNs.

NOTE:

The physical disks can also be a portion of storage that is carved out of a RAID array in the underlying disk subsystem.

Put another way, traditional storage management is typically DAS to a host system in which the host system has sole control over the DAS. With the introduction of SANs, DAS is replaced by networks of storage. However, storage is still primarily created and maintained at the RAID system level. Virtualization is the next logical step beyond this traditional storage management model in that it provides a central point of control for disk creation and maintenance.

Before virtualization, individual host systems had its own stovepiped database or storage (see Figure 2.3) that wasted unused or over-provisioned storage capacity. Storage virtualization provides capacity on demand—storage is pooled (rather than dedicated as a stovepiped database) so that applications from any attached system that need large amounts of storage capacity use it as required. The pooled storage consists of mixed back-end storage from various vendors, thus allowing legacy and heterogeneous storage assets to be consolidated and fully utilized.

Virtualization helps to regulate the amount of available storage without having to power cycle storage devices in order to add or remove capacity. Host systems are no longer responsible for volume management and are insulated from storage changes, such as data migration or storage upgrades. Data protection techniques, such as snapshot and replication, are simplified and assigning different classes of storage for different applications has become easier. In addition, SAN-storage virtualization complements server virtualization because it simplifies the data linkage association when VMs are migrated among physical platforms. Last but not least, storage virtualization simplifies storage administration and reduces the costs for managing heterogeneous storage assets, a common sight in the modern day DC.

Block aggregation

So far this chapter has discussed block-level virtualization that consolidates several physical disks to present a single logical device. This is also commonly referred to as block aggregation, with reference to L2 of the Storage Networking Industry Association (SNIA) shared storage model. Why block-level virtualization? The main motivation is to overcome the physical limits of individual devices without requiring any additional intelligence in applications. The applications are presented with a larger disk, which in reality is a new virtual disk with a larger LBA range.

Block aggregation is realized within hosts (servers), in storage devices (intelligent device controller) or in the storage network (network-based appliance or FC switches). The following lists the pros and cons of these three common block-level virtualization solutions:

- **Host-based virtualization:**
  - **Pros:** A software solution that is independent of the storage platform or vendor and is independent of the underlying SAN technology, FC, iSCSI, and so on.
  - **Cons:** Host-based virtualization is typically licensed on a per host basis and can be expensive. The virtualization software can be complex and must intercept as well as redirect every frame before it reaches the storage target. Every host is managed individually and each requires a software driver to be installed. VMware VMFS resolves some of these issues because the actual hosts are VM based (for more details, see The Concept of Virtual Data Store section).
- **Device-based virtualization:**
  - **Pros:** The storage device or subsystem is independent of the host platform or OS. The virtualization function is implemented in the device controller with close proximity to the physical disk drives. This solution is responsive and provides better performance.
  - **Cons:** Usually it is vendor proprietary so it is difficult to manage in a SAN environment with heterogeneous storage assets. Data storage device vendors overcome this particular constraint by incorporating the support for widely diverse physical storage technologies such as NFS, CIFS, iSCSI, FC, and FCoE all in a single box based on a unified storage architecture. NetApp Data ONTAP 7G and 8.0, as well as EMC's Celerra/CLARiiON, are based on unified storage architectures.
- **Network-based virtualization:**
  - **Pros:** Network-based virtualization is achieved through a virtualization appliance or within the FC switch. This solution is completely independent of the storage platform, the host platform, and the OS. By being connected to the SAN, the network-based virtualization has access to all connected hosts as well as storage devices and provides high performance and scalability.
  - **Cons:** Network-based virtualization is usually proprietary. Virtualization appliances are often seen as a bottleneck if they are deployed inband in the data path. They can also have scalability issues and need to be clustered to prevent a single point of failure. Scalability is enhanced with switch-based virtualization by having access to a high performance backplane instead. This enhancement is limited to the specific switch type and hardware you select, that can lead to a forklift upgrade for any future changes. This calls for a vendor-independent standard, thus the Fabric Application Interface Standard (FAIS) was developed to overcome the objection to proprietary switch-based virtualization.

NOTE:

FAIS is an INCITS T11 standards-based effort to create a common API for fabric applications to run on an underlying hardware platform. The objective of FAIS is to help developers move storage and data management implementations off applications, hosts, and storage devices onto intelligent storage fabric-based platforms.

Symmetric and asymmetric storage virtualization

Symmetric virtualization is an inband network-based virtualization deployment where the data and control messages use the same path. A central virtualization storage manager routes all I/O and metadata. The virtualization engine is typically a separate network appliance although it can also be embedded in the FC switch as a specialized module or run on a server. The fact that all data I/O needs

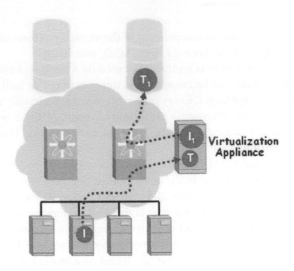

FIGURE 2.10

Symmetric virtualization

to pass through the virtualization appliance restricts the SAN topologies that can be used resulting in a bottleneck. The bottleneck is often addressed by caching to maximize the performance of the virtualization engine. The IBM SAN Volume Controller (SVC) is an example of a network-based inband appliance.

Figure 2.10 illustrates an example of symmetric virtualization. In this example, all server ports are zoned with the virtualization appliance's Virtual Target Port T and all storage ports are zoned with the virtualization appliance's Virtual Initiator Port I_1. All control and data frames from the host (initiator I) are sent to the virtual target T and are terminated at the virtual target. The SCSI CDB[17] (Command Descriptor Block) and LUN are remapped and the virtualization appliance proxying as the initiator (as I_1) sends a new frame to the physical target T_1.

The asymmetric approach is an out-of-band network-based virtualization deployment. The I/O operation can be separated into three phases:

1. The server intercepts the block I/O requests.
2. The server queries the metadata manager to determine the physical location of the data.
3. The server stores or retrieves the data directly across the SAN.

The metadata is transferred inband over the FC SAN or out-of-band over an Ethernet link. The out-of-band Ethernet link is preferred because it avoids congestion on the SAN due to IP metadata traffic. In this case, each server that uses the virtualized storage must have a special interface or agent installed to communicate with the metadata manager to translate the logical data access to physical access.

Figure 2.11 illustrates asymmetric virtualization where each server runs a virtualization host agent that intercepts block I/O requests and sends the metadata (CDB and LUN) to a virtualization (metadata) manager on an out-of-band LAN. The virtualization manager remaps the CDB as well as the LUN and returns it to the server. The server sends the modified control frame to the storage target port. All subsequent data and response frames flow directly between initiator (I) and target (T).

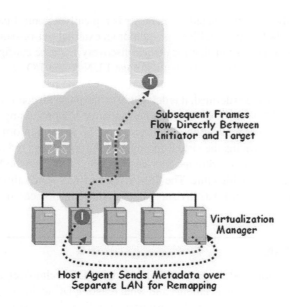

Subsequent Frames
Flow Directly Between
Initiator and Target

Virtualization
Manager

Host Agent Sends Metadata over
Separate LAN for Remapping

FIGURE 2.11

Asymmetric virtualization

Both deployment techniques have their pros and cons:

- **Symmetric virtualization:**
  - **Pros:** The inband deployment reduces complexity because it provides a single point of management. It is architecturally simpler and does not need host agents.
  - **Cons:** In symmetric virtualization, latency per frame increases because all frames are terminated, as well as remapped, by the appliance and then resent to their destination. Because all traffic passes through the appliance, the potential for single point of failure and performance bottleneck arises. These issues are typically alleviated using a clustered solution and a huge cache. However, this leads to issues of consistency between the synchronization of metadata databases on the clustered virtualization appliances that are used to perform the virtualization.
- **Asymmetric virtualization:**
  - **Pros:** Low latency is the main advantage of this particular deployment.
  - **Cons:** As asymmetric virtualization is out-of-band, host agents are required to intercept the control frames. Furthermore, the virtualization (metadata) manager could pose a single point of failure.

For network-based virtualization, which deployment technique is preferred: inband or out-of-band? Is there an architecture that combines the best of both worlds without the potential bottlenecks with symmetric virtualization or the required host agents in asymmetric virtualization? The optimal architecture would be a split-path architecture based on intelligent switches. In other words, use a switch-based implementation with a hybrid (split-path) approach where the control path is effectively out-of-band while the data path is inband. Inherently, switch-based virtualization will not require agents on the host nor will it pose a performance bottleneck.

In the split-path architecture, the metadata manager is typically a control path processor (CPP) embedded on a specialized blade in the intelligent switch or an external out-of-band controller (appliance). The CPP supports FAIS and is responsible for device discovery, volume configuration (such as administering the LBA metadata and mapping hosts to storage LUNs), and I/O error or exception handling. These operations do not require the CPP to be inband or in the data path. After the volume information (host-to-storage mapping) has been defined, it is delegated to the data path controller (DPC). The DPC also resides on the specialized blade and contains high performance I/O processing ASICs.[18] The DPC performs inband operations such as replication. After receiving the volume information from the CPP, the DPC works independently, providing the virtual-to-physical I/O translation and forwarding the data to the correct targets. For example, the Cisco Storage Services Module (SSM)[19] on the MDS 9000 Series storage switches supports the split-path architecture. The SSM supports FAIS which allows integration with third-party virtualization engines (such as EMC Invista[20]) to pass virtualization control data to the MDS switch.

LAYER 2 EVOLUTION

Before delving into the fabric module, let's think about what DC technological constraints in the past have been overcome by present enhancements and what existing DC technologies in the present can be improved. The latter is more crucial than the former as it will lead to a better future in terms of technological effectiveness and efficiency. One question to keep in mind is the side effects of the Spanning Tree Protocol (STP) in redundant L2 designs. Although enhancements have been made to STP (which date back to 1985), these enhancements still do not address two essential L2 design issues:

- STP does not support L2 multipathing for a particular VLAN. Also, the per-VLAN load-balancing that allows using both uplinks of an access-layer switch, requires user configuration. There is no good workaround because this behavior is required by the STP in the data plane to prevent loops.
- Reliance on STP for the creation of a spanning tree topology (or loop-free topology) in the data plane introduces delay in convergence, as well as potential risks such as networkwide flooding, and link saturation.

NOTE:

Some of the STP enhancements include Rapid Spanning Tree Protocol (RSTP), Per-VLAN Spanning Tree (PVST), Rapid Per-VLAN Spanning Tree Plus (Rapid PVST+), and Multiple Spanning Tree Protocol (MSTP).

One way around these issues is to deploy L2 loop-free access topologies that have no spanning tree blocking ports as compared to the classic L2 looped topology that has one forwarding link per access-layer switch and the redundant link or links in blocking mode. Figure 2.12 illustrates the L2 loop-free access design, namely, the loop-free U and loop-free inverted U topologies. There are some subtle differences in terms of L2/L3 line of demarcation in each design.

The loop-free U topology design offers a L2 access solution with active uplinks and redundancy through an inter-switch link between the access-layer switches. The VLANs are configured on each access-layer switch, and on the 802.1Q inter-switch link between the access-layer switches and its corresponding 802.1Q uplink, but are not extended between the aggregation-layer switches to avoid a looped topology. Because a loop does not exist, there are no blocked paths by the spanning tree. The main disadvantage of the loop-free U design is the inability to extend VLANs outside of an access

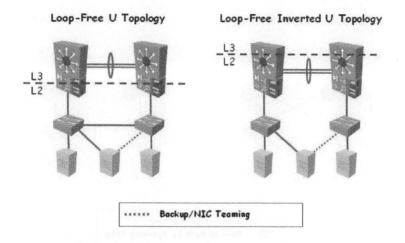

Loop-Free U Topology   **Loop-Free Inverted U Topology**

$\frac{L3}{L2}$ $\frac{L3}{L2}$

•••••• **Backup/NIC Teaming**

FIGURE 2.12

U and inverted-U loop-free access topologies

pair, and failure conditions can result in black holes. Workarounds such as extending VLANs outside of a single access pair, will cause a loop through the aggregation layer, going back to a four-node looped topology with blocked links if STP is enabled.

In the loop-free inverted U topology, the VLANs are configured on each access-layer switch as well as its corresponding 802.1Q uplink. They are also extended between the aggregation-layer switches. In this case, the VLANs are not extended between the access-layer switches to prevent a looped topology. This topology allows both uplinks to be active for all VLANs to the aggregation layer switches and allows VLAN extension across the access layer. The main disadvantage of the loop-free inverted U design is the lack of an alternate path during an aggregation-layer switch failure or an access-layer switch uplink failure that can result in black holes or inaccessible servers.

Although no loop is present in either design topology, it is still necessary to run STP as a safety precaution to prevent loop creation due to a cabling or configuration error that could bring down the network.

The "U" implementations sound novel; however, the consequences or constraints lead you to reconsider the classic way of doing things—L2 looped access topologies. Looped access topologies consist of a triangle (that is, V-shaped) and square design as shown in Figure 2.13.

L2 looped access topologies have the same L2 design constraints as STP—longer convergence time in a larger network and the lack of L2 multipathing support. One way of retaining a logical spanning tree in the data plane with redundancy and load-balancing intact is through the use of port channels. Although port channels can overcome STP limitations, link aggregation alone cannot be used to create a fully redundant DC because it does not allow for the failure of a single switch. The virtual switching systems (VSS) and virtual port channels (vPCs) from Cisco address this limitation by allowing the creation of an L2 port channel interface to be distributed across two different physical switches. This enhanced capability in port channeling is sufficient to take away the reliance of STP from the entire DC. This book only covers vPC because VSS and vPC are similar technologies. For further details on vPC, see the section Virtual Port Channels: The STP Makeover.

Transparent Interconnection of Lots of Links (TRILL) is one leading technology that completely breaks away from the classic spanning tree–based frame forwarding by routing frames at L2. TRILL[21] is an IETF initiative that replaces STP with a network routing protocol, Intermediate System to Intermediate System (IS-IS),[22] to provide a more flexible and scalable next-generation DC design from the

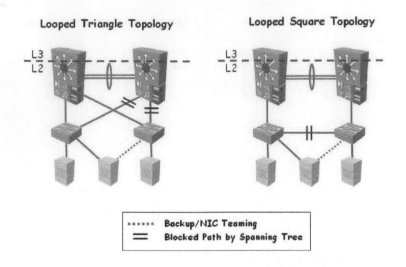

FIGURE 2.13

Triangle- and square-looped access topologies

L2 perspective. With TRILL, all the links are in the forwarding state as IS-IS is computing the forwarding tables. Without STP there will no longer be any blocked ports. This facilitates L2 multipath (L2MP) forwarding and bisectional bandwidth[23] increase, thus a less loaded path can forward delay-sensitive frames.

Because IS-IS is a link-state routing protocol, convergence time is much faster than STP. The chances of networkwide flooding are significantly reduced with the concept of intra-area (level 1) and inter-area (level 2) routing variants. Moreover, the best path with the lowest cost is always selected to forward frames, traversing fewer hops to the destination, thus reducing latency. TRILL interoperates with existing the spanning tree implementation to facilitate progressive transition. TRILL provides a way to achieve an "STP-less" DC and vPC provides a transition path to TRILL. TRILL is still evolving making further discussion of TRILL beyond the scope of this book.

Virtual port channels: the STP makeover

vPCs allow links that are physically connected to two different switches to appear to a third downstream device as coming from a single device and as part of a single port channel. The third device can be a switch, a server, or any other networking device that supports IEEE 802.3ad port channels. However, the concept is slightly different from VSS in the way that the two switches are still independent switches, with different control and forwarding planes. This section looks at vPCs that are implemented on the Cisco Nexus 7000 (NX7K) and Cisco Nexus 5000 (NX5K) Series switches.

Succinctly, vPC helps to consolidate/virtualize the aggregation/core layer switches as a single logical entity. For a configuration example on vPC, see the Basic vPC Design Study section in Chapter 9.

vPC nuts and bolts

A vPC setup comprises of the following components:

- **vPC domain:** A vPC domain groups together the two vPC peer switches running vPC with a unique domain ID.

- **vPC peer switches:** vPC peer switches are the two switches that are connected as peers through the peer link. They form the single logical endpoint for a vPC. Although only two switches can be part of this peer association, this simple feature is adequate to overcome the limitations of classic STP.
- **vPC peer link:** This is the link between the vPC peer switches and is also commonly referred to as a Multichassis EtherChannel (MEC) trunk. This link is a standard IEEE 802.3ad port channel with a modified STP weight. Some functions of the peer link include synchronizing MAC addresses between the peer switches, providing the necessary transport for multicast traffic, and for the communication of orphaned ports.
- **vPC member port:** A vPC member port is a physical port on one of the vPC peer switches that is a member of a vPC. A running vPC instance requires at least one port channel with a vPC member port on each peer switch.
- **Orphaned ports:** The ports connecting devices in a non-vPC mode to a vPC topology are referred to as orphaned ports.
- **vPC peer keepalive link:** The peer keepalive link is a logical link that runs over an out-of-band management network (without using the peer link). It provides an L3 communications path that is used as a secondary test to determine whether the remote peer is operating properly. A frame (heartbeat message) is sent over the vPC peer keepalive link, that indicates that the originating switch is up and running vPC. Data or synchronization traffic is not sent. The peer keepalive link is used to resolves dual-active failures (failures where the peer link between vPC peers is lost).
- **Cisco Fabric Services (CFS) protocol:** The CFS protocol is a reliable messaging protocol designed to support rapid stateful configuration message passing and synchronization. The vPC uses CFS to transfer a copy of the system configuration for a comparison process and to synchronize MAC and Internet group management protocol (IGMP) state information between the two vPC peer switches. The CFS protocol also validates the compatibility of vPC member ports to form the port channel and to monitor the status of the vPC member ports.

As illustrated in Figure 2.14, SW01 and SW02 are two vPC peer switches (which can be NX7K or NX5K switches) that form a vPC domain. Access-layer switches SW03 and SW04, as well as server H2, are connected to the vPC peer switches with a normal port channel configuration. Servers H1 and H3 are single-homed to the vPC topology. The ports that connect devices in a non-vPC mode to a vPC topology are referred to as orphaned ports. Servers H1 and H3 are connected to such ports. H2, SW03 and SW04 are connected to vPC member ports.

NOTE:

It is recommended to dual-attach all the access-layer switches to the vPC peers. If not, a switch or host that only connects to one vPC peer consumes precious bandwidth on the peer link. It also risks being isolated from the network in the event the peer link or a vPC peer fails.

STP farewell not
Although vPC implementations overcome the limitations of STP, it does not remove STP altogether. vPC modifies the spanning tree running on the peer switches in two ways:

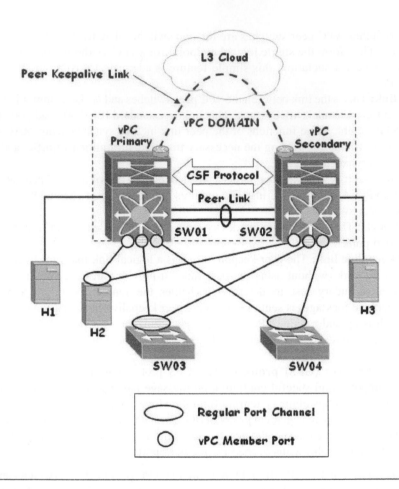

FIGURE 2.14

vPC at work

- It ensures that the peer link is always forwarding and the secondary vPC peer switch always treats the peer link as the root port towards the primary vPC peer switch.
- It ensures that only the primary vPC peer switch forwards bridge protocol data units (BPDUs) on vPCs so that the other access-layer switches connected to the vPC system or topology see the two peer switches as a single entity from a spanning tree perspective. This modification is only applicable to vPC member ports. When BPDUs are received by the secondary vPC peer switch on a vPC member port, they are forwarded to the primary vPC peer through the peer link for processing.

During a port channel member link failure, the vPC approach uses the port channel recovery mechanism instead of STP. This significantly reduces the overall convergence time.

> **NOTE:**
>
> Non-vPC ports or orphaned ports (normally single-homed rather than dual-homed) operate like regular ports with standard STP options such as MSTP and Rapid PVST+. The vPC special behavior applies uniquely to vPC member ports.

vPC design brief

This section briefly discusses the following vPC concepts and components from the design perspective:

- vPC role and priority
- vPC peer link
- vPC peer keepalive
- vPC initiation
- vPC and HSRP

vPC role and priority

The vPC feature must first be globally enabled using the "feature vpc" command. A domain must be defined as indicated by the domain ID (in the range of 1 to 1000) along with priorities to define primary and secondary roles in the vPC configuration. The role priority is a 16-bit integer with a default value of 32767. In a vPC system, one vPC peer switch is defined as primary and the other is defined as secondary, based on defined priorities. The primary peer switch is defined with a lower value than the secondary peer switch because the lower value has higher priority. Code Listing 2.4 illustrates the configuration template for vPC domain and priority.

```
feature vpc
vpc domain 3
  role priority 300
```

CODE LISTING 2.4

Configuration template for vPC domain and priority

> **NOTE:**
>
> For two vPC peer switches to establish a vPC system, the domain ID of these switches must match.

vPC peer link

The peer link is a port channel that interconnects the peer switches and carries all user-defined access VLANs. This link also carries control traffic such as BPDUs, Hot Standby Router Protocol (HSRP[24]) hellos, and MAC address synchronization between the vPC peers. For HA purposes, the peer link must be configured in a redundant fashion. On the NX7K, this port channel must be configured on dedicated mode 10-Gb Ethernet interfaces across two separate 10-Gb Ethernet line cards. Code Listing 2.5 illustrates the configuration template for vPC peer link.

```
interface port-channel30
  switchport
  switchport mode trunk
  switchport trunk allowed vlan 201,205,252-258, 301-302
  vpc peer-link
  spanning-tree port type network
```

CODE LISTING 2.5

Configuration template for vPC peer link

> **NOTE:**
>
> The port channel (peer link) connecting the vPC peers carry only the VLANs used by the vPC member ports. If VLANs used by orphaned ports are carried across this same link and a peer link outage occurs, communication between the orphaned ports are disrupted. To avoid this issue, it is recommended that servers are dual-connected with a port channel to vPC member ports, one on each peer switch.

vPC peer keepalive

The vPC management system uses peer keepalive messages to determine if the failure is related to the peer link or the remote peer switch. If the remote peer is still alive (a dual-active situation where the peer link is down but peer keepalive messages are still received through the out-of-band peer keepalive link), the vPC secondary peer switch will disable its vPC member ports. The remote peer switch is considered down if the peer-keepalive messages are not being received. In this case, the peer that originates the keepalive messages - assumes that it is the only remaining peer switch and continues to forward traffic. When the peer link or remote peer switch recovers from failure, the system resynchronizes any MAC addresses learned during the disruption and continues forwarding as per normal.

The keepalive message should not be carried on a VLAN associated with the peer link. It is recommended to carry the keepalive message over a routed infrastructure (L3 cloud). The peer-keepalive is identified by a destination IP address (remote), a source IP address (local), and a VRF[25] that will carry the peer-keepalive traffic. Code Listing 2.6 illustrates the configuration template for vPC peer-keepalive link.

```
vrf context vpc-pklink

interface Ethernet8/13
  vrf member vpc-pklink
  ip address 172.16.3.1/24
  no shutdown

vpc domain 3
  peer-keepalive destination 172.16.3.2 source 172.16.3.1 vrf vpc-pklink
```

CODE LISTING 2.6

Configuration template for vPC peer keepalive link

> **NOTE:**
>
> On NX7K switches, when using redundant supervisors, only one management interface is active at a time on a given vPC peer. Therefore, do not use a direct back-to-back connection between the management interfaces of two NX7K peer switches because it is difficult to tell which supervisor is active at any given time. For an out-of-band connection, it is recommended to connect each NX7K peer switch to a management network (L3 cloud) through the mgmt0 interfaces of supervisor slot 5 and supervisor slot 6.

vPC initiation

On each vPC peer switch, a vPC is a regular port channel configuration with the addition of the "vpc <vpc_number>" command. Member ports (switch ports) on each peer switch are then associated with the vPC. The vpc number is exchanged between the vPC peer switches and it binds the two separate local port channel configurations into a distributed vPC virtual port.

It is recommended to use the Link Aggregation Control Protocol (LACP) over static link aggregation, when possible on vPCs and the peer link, to prevent erroneous configurations and to provide more refined failover handling. With LACP, ports that are mismatched due to configuration errors will not form a port channel. In this case, the port channel ports are categorized as Individual (I) state and conventional spanning tree is run instead.

LACP is a standards-based mechanism introduced by IEEE 802.3ad for two switches to negotiate the establishment of port channels. LACP is configured using the "channel-group" command with the "active" or "passive" keyword in the interface configuration. For channel negotiation to take place, at least one end of the port channel connection must be placed in active mode. Code Listing 2.7 illustrates the configuration template for vPC and vPC member port.

```
interface port-channel33
  switchport
  switchport mode trunk
  switchport trunk allowed vlan 320-329
  vpc 33
  spanning-tree port type network
interface Ethernet2/13
  switchport
  switchport mode trunk
  switchport trunk allowed vlan 320-329
  no shutdown
  channel-group 33 mode active
```

CODE LISTING 2.7

Configuration template for vPC member port

> **NOTE:**
>
> The vpc number does not have to be the same as the port channel number. However, for better manageability, it is recommended to configure these values the same.

vPC and HSRP

HSRP has a unique behavior with the NX7K switches worth highlighting. The assumption here is both peer switches are NX7K switches: one configured as the active HSRP peer and the other as the standby HSRP peer. The enhancement was made to the forwarding engine to allow local L3 forwarding at both the active HSRP peer and at the standby HSRP peer. This, in effect, provides an active/active HSRP configuration without any changes to the existing HSRP configuration. The HSRP control protocol still behaves like an active/standby pair where only the active HSRP peer responds to Address Resolution

Protocol (ARP) requests. If an ARP request coming from a server (dual-connected with a port channel to vPC member ports, one on each peer switch) arrives on the standby HSRP peer, it is forwarded to the active HSRP peer through the peer link. When it comes to forwarding routable traffic, both HSRP interfaces (active and standby) on the respective peer switches can forward the traffic. If the traffic originating from the same server arrives on the standby HSRP peer, it is forwarded directly by the standby peer to the next-hop (assuming the next-hop is valid). There is no requirement to send this traffic through the peer link to the active HSRP peer for forwarding.

NOTE:

Keeping the default gateway collocated on the vPC primary peer is recommended. To do so, configure the same vPC primary peer as an active HSRP peer for all the VLANs.

---

vPC and Nexus 1000V

In most NX1KV designs, port channels are required to span multiple access-layer switches. To facilitate this spanning of switches, the NX1KV switch provides two main configurations that do not require configuration of a port channel at the upstream switches:

- vPC host mode (vPC HM)
- MAC pinning

vPC host mode

In vPC-HM mode, the port channel configured on the NX1KV switch is divided into subgroups (logical, smaller port channels). Each subgroup represents one or more uplinks (Eth interfaces) to one upstream physical switch. A round-robin mechanism maps each vEth interface (for more details, see the VEM Switch Port Taxonomy section) on the VEM to one of the two subgroups. Subsequently, all traffic from the vEth interface uses the assigned subgroup. In the event the assigned subgroup is unavailable, the vEth interface will fail over to the remaining subgroup but traffic will shift back to the originally assigned subgroup when it becomes available again.

Two vPC-HM examples are shown in Figure 2.15. The left side of the diagram shows two NICs with a single port channel using vPC-HM. In this example, the two NICs are part of port channel 1 configured in vPC-HM and are connected to two upstream switches. A single uplink profile is applied to both NICs. The load-balancing algorithm with source MAC address hashing distributes the load of the VMs across both uplinks.

NOTE:

The NX1KV switch offers 17 hashing algorithms to load-balance traffic across physical interfaces in a port channel. These algorithms are divided into two categories: source-based hashing and flow-based hashing. Source-based hashing algorithms ensure that a MAC address is transmitted down only a single link in the port channel, regardless of the number of links in a port channel.

The right side of the diagram shows four NICs with two port channels using vPC-HM. Each port channel consists of one link to each upstream switch. In this case, each vPC-HM subgroup consists of a single link so there is no need to configure port channel on the upstream switches. Load-balancing, with source MAC address hashing, is still applied in this example.

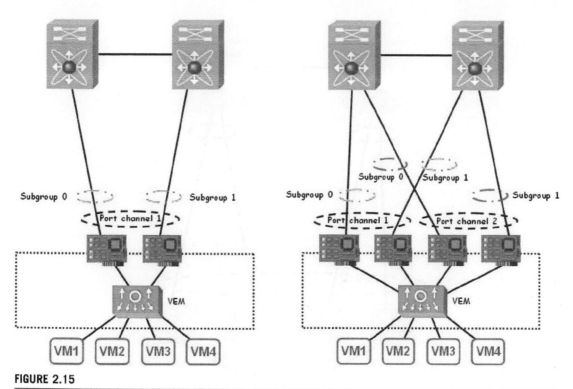

FIGURE 2.15

vPC-HM examples

Eth interfaces within the port channel that are connected to the same upstream physical switch are bundled in the same subgroup automatically through the use of the CDP messages received from the upstream switch if CDP is supported on the upstream switch. These interfaces can also be manually assigned to a specific subgroup through interface-level configuration if the upstream switch does not support CDP or there is a need to override CDP.

When multiple uplinks are attached to the same subgroup in the NX1KV switch, the upstream switch needs a port channel configured to bundle these links together. This port channel has to be configured with the "mode on" command option. Figure 2.16 illustrates another vPC-HM example, this time with four NICs and one port channel. A single vPC-HM–based port channel is deployed to distribute the VM's load over as many NICs as possible. The main benefit of this design is that the VM data traffic can utilize all four NICs, with the flexibility to support flow-based hashing. If flow-based hashing is used, each upstream switch must be configured with a port channel; however, this is not required if source-based hashing is used.

NOTE:

Flow-based hashing enables traffic from a single MAC address to be distributed down multiple links in a port channel simultaneously, providing a more granular load-balancing approach. This increases the bandwidth available to a VM and offers better utilization of the uplinks in a port channel.

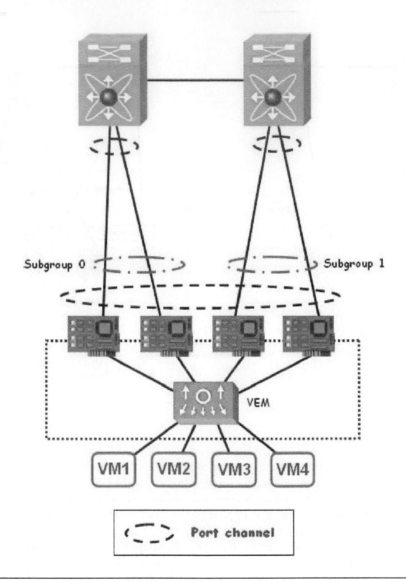

FIGURE 2.16

vPC-HM with four NICs and one port channel

MAC pinning

MAC pinning treats all the uplinks (Eth interfaces) coming out of the server as separate links and pins unique MAC addresses from different vEth interfaces to these links in a round-robin fashion. This is illustrated in Figure 2.17 on the left side of the diagram. The MAC pinning approach ensures that the MAC address of a VM will never be seen on multiple interfaces on the upstream switches. If an uplink failure occurs, the NX1KV switch sends a gratuitous ARP[26] message to inform the upstream switch that the MAC address of the vEth interface learned on the previous Eth interface will now

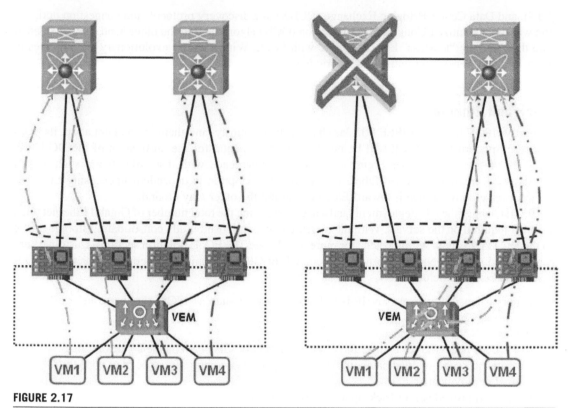

FIGURE 2.17

MAC pinning example

be repinned on a different Eth interface. This is illustrated in Figure 2.17, on the right side of the diagram. With MAC pinning, no upstream configuration is required to connect the VEM (or Eth interfaces) to the upstream switches.

UNIFIED DATA CENTER FABRIC

While digesting the nitty-gritty of the emerging L2 technologies, it is time to advance to the next course—the fabric module. What we want to achieve in this module, from the standpoint of private cloud computing and SOI, is the unification of the DC fabric. In other words, Ethernet and FC must become a single unified fabric rather than two different isolated fabrics. To achieve this, some enhancements or extensions must be in place for both interconnection technologies.

With the availability of 10-Gb Ethernet (10GE) since 2008, the increase in bandwidth enables more data traffic to be carried over fewer links in DC setups, providing better throughput than before. Nevertheless, a 10GE fat pipe alone is not enough to emulate FC. Ethernet overall has to be "lossless" to be on par with FC. What emerges is an Ethernet remake whose features include Priority-based Flow Control (PFC), bandwidth management with Enhanced Transmission Selection

(ETS), and Data Center Bridging Exchange (DCBX) as a discovery protocol, and congestion notification with the Quantized Congestion Notification (QCN) algorithm. On the other hand, FC is extended onto this new-age "lossless" Ethernet fabric with FCoE. With all these evolutionary technologies in place, the next-generation unified DC fabric is born.

10-gigabit Ethernet

Currently, 10GE (based on IEEE 802.3ae) has reached maturity, and there is no doubt about its practicality in modern DCs. 10GE will be pivotal and instrumental for the unification of the DC fabric within the fabric module (see Figure 2.2), or the convergence with dissimilar fabric such as FC. Any hope of creating a unified fabric with ubiquitous adoption is dependent upon using Ethernet. Therefore, the convergence is toward Ethernet and not the other way around.

10GE changes the DC deployment landscape by reducing the total number of Gigabit Ethernet (GE) adapters required on the servers. With the increase in network bandwidth, consolidating storage traffic on the DC LAN is now within reach (for more details, see The FCoE Solution section). Customers are beginning to see the benefit of moving beyond GE or GE port channel implementations to 10GE instead. The benefits include:

- Increased feasibility to deploy IP-based storage access such as iSCSI (for more information on iSCSI, see Chapter 7).
- Enhanced NAS performance.
- With 10GE access-layer uplink, the implementation of GE port channels can be foregone. This alleviates the need of load-balancing hashing algorithms commonly associated with the GE port channel deployments.
- Provides improved server back up and recovery times.

The additional bandwidth provided by 10GE also goes well with multicore CPUs and server virtualization. Multi-core processor architectures allow bigger and multiple workloads on the same machine while server virtualization drives the need for more bandwidth per server. Although applications are often throttled by the socket size, with virtualized servers, the individual VM traffic often is aggregated onto the same NIC and 10GE comes in handy, in this case. Moreover, VMotion migration (live VM migration) can take advantage of the additional bandwidth for simultaneous VMotion migration of multiple VMs. Nevertheless, 10GE is most applicable to FCoE as it closes the gap between Ethernet and FC in terms of high bandwidth support.

> **NOTE:**
>
> Ethernet evolution does not stop at 10GE. IEEE 802.3ba has been ratified for 40GE and 100GE.

Ethernet reloaded

To be on par with FC, 10GE alone is not enough because in the FC world, losing frames is not an option. Therefore, in conjunction with high bandwidth support, Ethernet has to be lossless as well. But can Ethernet be really lossless? The answer is a big yes, with the following mechanisms built-in:

- Priority-based Flow Control (PFC)
- Delayed drop
- Enhanced Transmission Selection (ETS)
- Data Center Bridging Exchange (DCBX)
- Congestion notification

Priority-based Flow Control

Losing frames is not permitted for FC. FC uses the concept of credits to implement lossless behavior. During FC link initialization, the number of buffers is predefined on each link and the endpoint of each link then keeps track of the available or unused buffers. Link level flow control is known as buffer-to-buffer (B2B) flow control in FC. B2B flow control paces the transmission of FC frames so as to prevent a transmitter from overrunning the receiver's buffers. Buffer-to-buffer credit (BB_Credit) is the unit used by B2B flow control to pace frame transmissions. Each sent frame decrements the corresponding available BB_Credit by one. On the other hand, each receiver-ready (R_RDY)[27] response received will increment the BB_Credit by 1, allowing additional frames to be sent. When BB_Credit becomes zero, frames are no longer transmitted until an R_RDY is returned. Ethernet uses the PAUSE frame (based on IEEE 802.3x) to match this capability. The receiving port (the receiver) issues a PAUSE frame to stop the transmission from the remote peer (the transmitter) when its buffer is about to be depleted. This is illustrated in the top diagram of Figure 2.18. However, the PAUSE mechanism provides no granularity. It is essentially a PAUSE for the entire link. When a PAUSE frame is received, the sender stops all transmission on the port and this does not fit well with the objectives of the unified DC fabric.

PFC based on IEEE 802.1Qbb is an enhancement to the PAUSE mechanism. An additional field within the PAUSE frame specifies which priorities (up to eight values based on IEEE 802.1p) are to be paused. In other words, PFC creates eight separate "virtual links" on the physical Ethernet link and allows any of these "virtual links" to be paused and restarted autonomously. The additional priority granularity allows us to create different classes of services (CoS) for different protocol traffic on the link. For instance, protocols such as FCoE (for more details, see The FCoE Solution section), which assumes reliability at the media level and cannot tolerate any frame loss, are mapped to a no-drop (with PAUSE) class, while protocols such as IP that will suffice with best-effort frame delivery are mapped to a drop (no PAUSE) class.

The bottom diagram of Figure 2.18 illustrates a simplified PFC example showing only two classes: CoS 0 for IP traffic and CoS 3 for FCoE traffic. A PAUSE frame is applicable only to the CoS (with priority 3) to which FCoE is mapped. IP traffic belonging to a different CoS (with priority 0) is not affected. During congestion, the overflowing frames belonging to CoS 0 are simply dropped without generating a PAUSE. IP does not require a lossless Ethernet since TCP or the upper layer protocols (if UDP is used) will take care of any IP packet losses.

NOTE:

The PFC frame has an Ethertype value of 0x8808 (same as PAUSE frame) and an Opcode value of 0x0101 (PAUSE frame has an Opcode value of 0x0001).

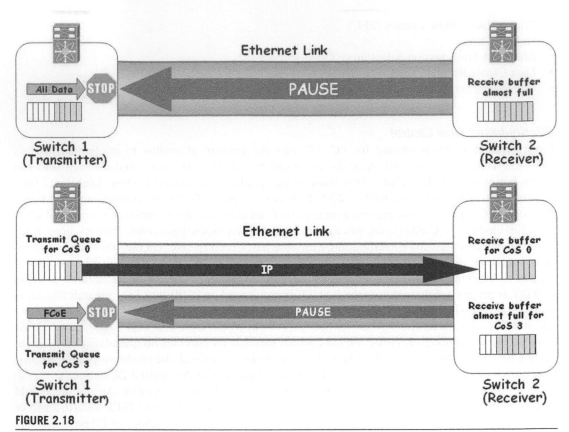

FIGURE 2.18

PAUSE frame and PFC comparison

Delayed drop

PFC does not differentiate short-lived traffic bursts from persistent congestion because it pushes the buffering requirements back to the source. Delayed drop comes in between the traditional Ethernet and PFC behavior. It is another Ethernet enhancement that uses the PAUSE or PFC mechanism to reduce frame drop on short-lived traffic bursts, while triggering upper-layer congestion control through frame drops to handle long-term congestion. This feature allows congestion to persist only for short-term bursts but not for the long-term.

Delayed drop can be enabled with per-user priority. It uses a proxy queue to measure the duration of traffic bursts. During normal operation, the proxy queue emulates the actual queue in which frames are added or removed. When a burst of traffic causes the actual queue to reach a specific threshold, a PAUSE or PFC frame is sent to the source. The proxy queue, which is significantly bigger than the actual queue, continues to receive frames. When the proxy queue is filled, the PAUSE or PFC is released from the transmitter, in turn causing frames to drop if the congestion persists. This condition is required to trigger the TCP flow control mechanism for long-lived streams.

During short-term bursts, both queues should drain fast enough so that the actual queue itself will release the PAUSE. In the case of long-term congestion, the proxy queue will fill to its maximum limit, and release the PAUSE. When this happens, the actual queue starts to drop frames, and the congestion is handled through the upper layer protocols. With delayed drop, a particular CoS can be flow controlled for a fixed amount of time so that the traditional drop behavior follows if the congestion still persists after this period of time. Delayed drop offers the capability to tune "short-lived congestion" with PFC, removing the need to increase physical buffers on the interfaces.

Enhanced Transmission Selection

PFC can create eight distinct virtual link types on a physical link and ETS based on IEEE 802.1Qaz complements PFC by enabling optimal bandwidth management of these virtual links. ETS provides prioritized processing based on bandwidth allocation and latency. ETS defines priority groups where different frames can be assigned based on their priority. The allocation of bandwidth to the priority groups is based on a percentage of the maximum bandwidth available on the physical link. The objective of ETS is to implement a hardware efficient two-level Deficit Weighted Round Robin (DWRR)[28] scheduling with strict priority support.

Figure 2.19 shows three different types of application traffic: Inter-Processor Communication (IPC), LAN, and SAN (i.e., FCoE). These application traffic types have a mixed variety of priority or CoS. For example, IPC has CoS 7, LAN traffic comprises of CoS 0, 1, 4–6, and SAN traffic contains CoS 2 and 3. Regardless of how many traffic classes are available, in ETS, they will be grouped into different priority groups (PGs) each identified by a priority group ID (PGID). In our example, SAN traffic classes (CoS 2, 3) are mapped to PGID 0, LAN traffic classes (CoS 0, 1, 4–6) are mapped to PGID 1, and IPC (CoS 7) goes to PGID 15.

The first level of scheduling occurs within each PG while the second level is based on the bandwidth (BW) allocated to each PG. In this example, 50% of the available bandwidth on the physical link is

CoS to Priority Group Mapping

Priority (CoS)	Priority Group ID (PGID)	Application
7	15	IPC
6	1	LAN
5	1	LAN
4	1	LAN
3	0	SAN
2	0	SAN
1	1	LAN
0	1	LAN

Bandwidth Allocation to Priority Groups

PGID	Priority Group (PG) %	Application
15	-	IPC
1	50	LAN
0	50	SAN

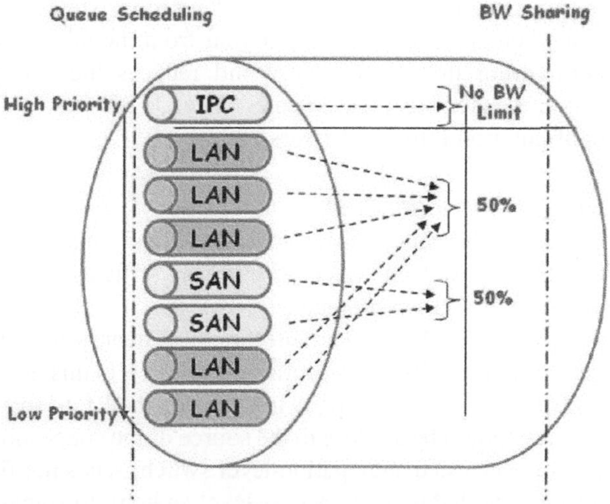

FIGURE 2.19

ETS example

allocated to PGID 0 and the remaining 50% to PGID 1. A PGID of 15 has a special meaning in which priorities mapped to this PGID will not be subjected to bandwidth limit. Any priority that is mapped to PGID 15 uses strict priority scheduling (not scheduled by ETS) and this applies to the IPC (CoS 7) traffic.

> **NOTE:**
>
> PGID has a range of 0–15. The Priority Group with PGID 15 must not be allocated any PG%. Priorities belonging to this group are not subjected to bandwidth limit. PGID values 8–14 are reserved. PGID values between 0 and 7 (inclusive) must be used for configuring bandwidth allocation (or limit).

Data Center Bridging eXchange

DCBX based on IEEE 802.1Qaz is the management protocol of the IEEE 802.1 Data Center Bridging (DCB). It is an extension of the link layer discovery protocol (IEEE 802.1AB) that allows auto-exchange of Ethernet parameters and discovery functions between switches and endpoints. Parameters pertaining to the following Ethernet extensions and features can be exchanged:

- PFC
- Priority groups in ETS
- Congestion notification
- Applications (e.g., FCoE)
- Logical link down
- Network interface virtualization

DCBX discovers the capabilities of the two peers at the two ends of a link and can detect peer configuration mismatches. It can provide base configuration if one of the two peers is not configured and is supported on point-to-point configuration. The two peers involved can choose supported features and whether to accept configuration from the other peer. In a nutshell, the DCBX protocol helps in configuring links consistently and reduces the configuration overhead associated with the new Ethernet extensions and features. The DCBX protocol provides Ethernet enhancements with fewer configuration effort and errors.

Congestion notification

Lossless Ethernet can result in "contagious" congestion spreading across the network and cause detrimental head-of-line (HOL)[29] blocking. This can be alleviated by some form of L2 end-to-end congestion notification protocol.

The IEEE 802.1Qau architecture uses quantized congestion notification (QCN) that defines a congestion point (CP) and a reaction point (RP). In this model, congestion is measured at the CP, and rate-limiting, or back pressure, is imposed on the RP to shape traffic and reduce the effects of congestion. The RP should be as close to the source of the congestion as possible. When congestion occurs, the CP (e.g., a congested aggregation-level switch) sends notification messages toward the source of the congestion, the RP (e.g., an access-level switch), to signal its congestion state. Upon receiving the congestion notification messages, the rate-limiter or traffic-shaper at the RP comes into play and traffic transmission is slowed down. The idea is to shift the congestion from the network core to the network

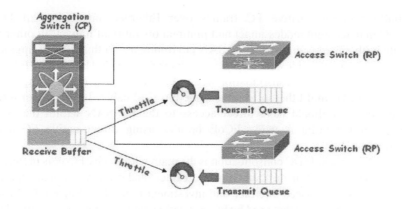

FIGURE 2.20

QCN signaling

edge to avoid congestion spreading to the rest of the network. Congestion is easier to deal with at the network edge since the number of flows is much smaller than at the network core. This also means the flows that cause the upstream congestion are easier to identify and rate-limit at the network edge.

> **NOTE:**
> The congestion notification message contains a feedback quantity that is quantized to a 6-bit value. This is how "quantized" congestion notification is derived.

In Figure 2.20, an aggregation-level switch, acting as the CP, sends congestion notification messages to two access-level switches, acting as the RPs, requesting them to slow down their traffic transmission rate. This eases off the congestion in the network core preventing the congestion from becoming networkwide and affects only the portions of the network close to the source of the congestion.

> **NOTE:**
> The difference between QCN signaling and PAUSE is that PAUSE is hop by hop, whereas QCN congestion notification messages are end to end. These notification messages are propagated to the source of the congestion. A similar scheme called the Fibre Channel Congestion Control (FCC) is implemented on the MDS switches for FC.

The FCoE solution

With 10GE as well as the lossless Ethernet extensions and features, it is now possible for Ethernet to be on par with FC. The next question is: how to create a unified DC fabric incorporating both FC and the new lossless Ethernet? The answer is FCoE.

FCoE is based on the INCITS T11 Fibre Channel Backbone (FC-BB-5) specifications that map native Fibre Channel over Ethernet, independent of the indigenous Ethernet forwarding scheme.

FCoE essentially transports native FC frames over Ethernet, preserving all FC constructs, with existing FC management modes intact and minimal operational impact. In other words, FCoE can interoperate with any existing native FC SAN environments so that forklift upgrade is not necessary. FCoE depends on a reliable underlying network fabric provided by lossless Ethernet. It allows an evolutionary approach to I/O consolidation and I/O unification by transporting diverse types of application data (e.g., FC and Ethernet) on the same physical cable. In the longer term, the server module (see Figure 2.2) should have direct access to the FC SAN within the storage module through interconnection point A using FCoE besides using direct native FC access through interconnection point B.

Why not use iSCSI instead? DC consolidation is the main reason why FCoE is preferred. While in a greenfield approach iSCSI is ideal, most enterprises are interested in an evolutionary approach, because native FC is already an established interface and investment in the DC. Since iSCSI uses a different mapping of SCSI commands than that used by FC, a stateful gateway function is required to consolidate native FC with iSCSI. This poses issues such as single point of failure, and limited scalability. In addition, the existing FC management model must be replaced by a different management model. It is unlikely that an existing DC will go for a full iSCSI revamp to achieve consolidation. An incremental approach is more common and in this aspect, FCoE will be the better bet. That said, iSCSI is still a formidable alternative when it comes to new DC designs in the small to medium business (SMB) market segment. It is also a good candidate for pure IP SAN. For more details on iSCSI, see Chapter 7.

FCoE data plane

FCoE actually comprises two different protocols: FCoE itself and the FCoE Initialization Protocol (FIP). FCoE takes care of the data plane functionalities while FIP belongs to the control plane. This section looks at the FCoE data plane. See the FCoE Control Plane section for more information on FIP.

Figure 2.21 illustrates a simplified version of the FCoE components and architecture:

- **FC entity:** The interface between an FC switching element (of the FCF) or an FC stack (of the ENode) and the FCoE Entity. Each FC Entity contains a single instance of a VE_Port, a VF_Port, or a VN_Port.
- **FCoE entity:** The interface between the FC Entity and a lossless Ethernet MAC. Each FCoE Entity contains one or more FCoE_LEPs.
- **FC switching element (not shown in diagram):** This is the architectural entity for forwarding FC frames among VF_Ports and VE_Ports.
- **Lossless Ethernet bridging element (not shown in diagram):** An Ethernet bridging function supporting the base capabilities of lossless Ethernet MACs.
- **Lossless Ethernet MAC:** A full duplex Ethernet MAC supporting at least 2.5-KB jumbo frames and implementing extensions to avoid Ethernet frame loss due to congestion (for more details, see the Ethernet Reloaded section).
- **Lossless Ethernet network:** An Ethernet network composed only of full duplex links, lossless Ethernet MACs, and lossless Ethernet Bridging elements.
- **Virtual F_Port (VF_Port):** The data forwarding component of a FC Entity that emulates an F_Port and is dynamically instantiated upon successful completion of a FLOGI Exchange. Each VF_Port is paired with one or more FCoE_LEPs.

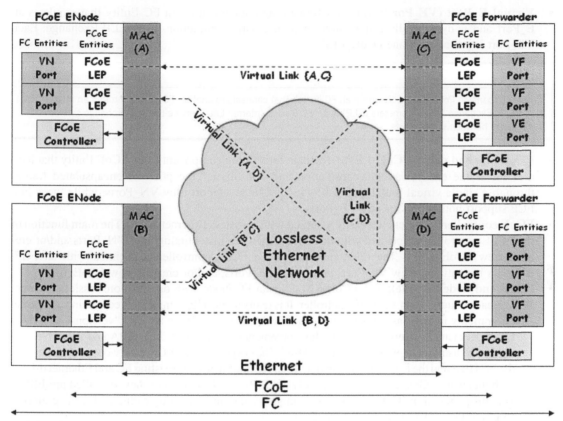

FIGURE 2.21

FCoE components and simplified architecture

NOTE:

The F_Port (Fabric Port) is the port within a FC fabric that provided an attachment for an N_Port (Node Port). Fabric Login (FLOGI) is used by a N_Port to establish a session with the fabric. FLOGI is required before the fabric will accept frames from the N_Port.

- **Virtual N_Port (VN_Port):** The data forwarding component of an FC Entity that emulates an N_Port and is dynamically instantiated upon successful completion of a FLOGI or FDISC Exchange. Each VN_Port is paired with one FCoE_LEP.

NOTE:

The N_Port is the port with an FC Node that provides FC attachment. Discover Fabric Service Parameters (FDISC) is used in N_Port ID Virtualization (NPIV), which sends a request to fabric login address 0xFFFFFE to obtain an additional N_Port ID.

- **Virtual E_Port (VE_Port):** The data forwarding component of an FC Entity that emulates an E_Port and is dynamically instantiated upon successful completion of an ELP Exchange. Each VE_Port is paired with one FCoE_LEP.

> **NOTE:**
>
> E_Port (Expansion Port) is the port within an FC switch that connects to another FC switch through an inter-switch link (ISL). Exchange Link Parameters (ELP) is an FC Switch Internal Link Service used to exchange service parameters between switch ports.

- **FCoE link end point (FCoE_LEP):** The data forwarding component of an FCoE Entity that handles FC frame encapsulation/decapsulation and transmission/reception of encapsulated frames through a single virtual link. FCoE_LEPs in an ENode support only VN_Ports, while those in a FCF support both VF_Ports and VE_Ports.
- **FCoE controller:** A functional entity, coupled with a lossless Ethernet MAC. The main function of the FCoE controller, associated with an ENode, includes instantiating new VN_Ports and/or creating new FCoE_LEPs. The main function of the FCoE controller, associated with an FCF-MAC, is instantiating new VF_Ports as well as VE_Ports, and/or creating new FCoE_LEPs.
- **FCoE end node (ENode):** The FCoE ENode is an FC Node with one or more lossless Ethernet MACs, each coupled with an FCoE controller. It is really an FC HBA implemented within an Ethernet NIC commonly referred as CNA (converged network adapter). There are two "versions" of CNAs:
  - **First-generation (Gen-1) CNA:** In this implementation, a standard FC HBA and 10GE NIC are connected using an intermediary "glue" ASIC. The OS perceives the CNA as two separate adapters, the FC HBA and the Ethernet NIC, so that it can continue to use the existing FC and Ethernet drivers without change. Gen-1 CNAs are typically not FIP-capable and hence they are called pre-FIP.
  - **Second-generation (Gen-2) CNA:** This implementation uses a single chip and is the preferred solution. Gen-2 CNAs are FIP-compliant.

> **NOTE:**
>
> You can also implement FCoE through the use of a software driver (for details, see http://www.open-fcoe.org/). This might be useful for servers that do not have intensive I/O loads but need to frequently access the FC storage arrays.

- **FCoE forwarder (FCF):** The FCF is an FC switching element, with one or more lossless Ethernet MACs, each coupled with an FCoE controller. Each Ethernet MAC has a MAC address known as the FCF-MAC address. Each FCF-MAC can be coupled with a lossless Ethernet bridging element. The FC switching element can be coupled with an FC Fabric interface, providing native E_Port and F_Port connectivity. If the Ethernet destination address is an FCF, the FCoE frame is forwarded to the corresponding FCF-MAC address where the encapsulated FC frame is decapsulated by the FCoE_LEP. The decapsulated FC frame is then forwarded by the FC switching element based on its FC destination address or FC destination ID (D_ID). If the FC frame is forwarded out of an Ethernet port, the FC frame is encapsulated within an Ethernet frame with the Ethernet source address set to the associated FCF-MAC and the Ethernet destination address set to the appropriate destination MAC. The FCF function is basically an FC switch with one or more Ethernet ports. Native FC ports are optional for the FCF.

> **NOTE:**
>
> If FCF is coupled with a native FC fabric interface, a frame bound for a native FC destination is forwarded out a native FC port, and the frame is transmitted as a native FC frame on the associated FC link. If FCF-MAC is coupled with an Ethernet bridge (or Ethernet switch), a received Ethernet frame that is not addressed to an FCF-MAC address is forwarded by the Ethernet bridge in the usual way based on the destination address of the Ethernet frame.

- **Virtual link:** The virtual link is the logical link connecting two FCoE_LEPs over a lossless Ethernet network. It is identified by the pair of MAC addresses of the two link end-points as shown in Figure 2.21. It can also be perceived as a tunnel through the lossless Ethernet network that transports encapsulated FC frames from the source MAC to the destination MAC.

FC is a layered architecture defined by five different functional levels denoted as FC-0 through FC-4. In FCoE, the FC-2 level is further divided into three sublevels to better facilitate virtualization as illustrated in the top left diagram of Figure 2.22:

- FC-4 defines how various upper-level protocols (ULPs), such as SCSI, IPv4, or IPv6 are mapped to FC.
- FC-3 defines optional common services or functions across multiple node ports.
- FC-2V (FC-2—Virtual) defines the handling of FC frames to support upper levels.
- FC-2M (FC-2—Multiplexer) defines the multiplexing of FC frames from instances of the FC-2P sublevel to instances of the FC-2V sublevel.
- FC-2P (FC-2—Physical) defines the functions associated with the actual transmission and reception of frames on the underlying physical media. The functions include frame transmission and reception, CRC[30] generation and validation and link-level (buffer-to-buffer) flow control.
- FC-1 defines the transmission protocol that includes serial encoding, decoding, and error control.
- FC-0 defines the characteristics of the specific physical media used.

The FC-2P, FC-1, and FC-0 levels specify the functions and behaviors of an FC physical port, such as Physical N_Port (PN_Port), Physical F_Port (PF_Port), and Physical E_Port (PE_Port). In an FCoE environment, these functions are replaced by FCoE_LEP and lossless Ethernet as illustrated in the top right diagram of Figure 2.22. Keeping the FC-2V sublevel and the upper levels intact implies that FCoE is transparent to the OS. For this reason, the same operational and management models of FC can be maintained.

The FCoE encapsulation is shown in the bottom diagram of Figure 2.22. The FCoE Ethertype is 8906h. FCoE encapsulations and decapsulations are stateless. The actual FC frame remains intact. This capability enables FCoE to integrate with existing FC SANs without the need of a gateway. The maximum size of an FCoE frame is 2180 bytes inclusive of Frame Check Sequence (FCS) or 2176 bytes excluding FCS. To accommodate a maximum-size FC frame, FCoE requires the use of baby jumbo Ethernet frames of at least 2.5-KB. The FCoE frame also meets the minimum Ethernet payload of 46 bytes: 14 bytes (FCoE header) + 24 bytes (FC header) + 0 bytes (FC payload) + 4 bytes (CRC) + 4 bytes (FCoE trailer). The fixed FCoE header and trailer ensure that a minimum size FC frame always results in a valid minimum size Ethernet frame.

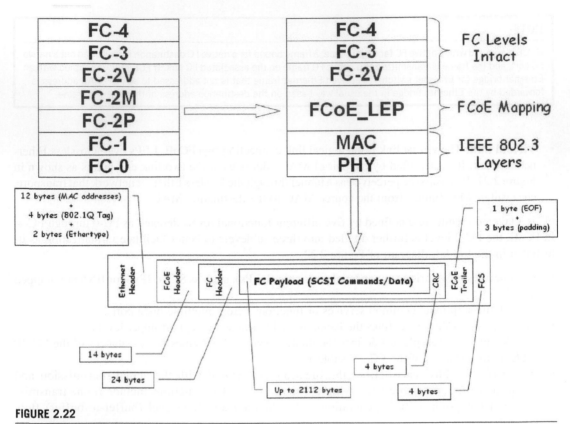

FIGURE 2.22

FCoE stack and encapsulation

> **NOTE:**
>
> The FC start-of-frame (SOF) delimiter is represented as an encoded value in the FCoE header. Likewise, the FC end-of-frame (EOF) delimiter is represented as an encoded value in the FCoE trailer.

FCoE control plane

In a native FC environment, an N_Port simply sends FLOGI on the point-to-point physical link connected to the FC fabric. In FCoE, an ENode needs to know the MAC address of the FCF to perform the FLOGI. Since Ethernet is a multiaccess media, point-to-point virtual links between the VN_Ports and VF_Ports are used to emulate the native FC environment. However, the setup of the FCoE virtual links between the VN_Ports and VF_Ports would require considerable effort if they were manually configured. It would be great if a protocol could perform this task instead. This is where FIP fits in. The content of an FIP frame is different from an FCoE frame, but it is still encapsulated within an Ethernet frame with an Ethertype value of 8914h. FIP belongs to the FCoE control plane so frames with the FIP

Ethertype are directed to the control plane of an Ethernet switch (with FCoE capability) for processing or inspection, whereas frames with the FCoE Ethertype are immediately forwarded by the data plane. FIP specifically performs the following control phase duties before the data forwarding phase commences with the data plane FCoE:

- FCoE VLAN discovery
- FCoE entities discovery
- Virtual link instantiation
- Virtual link maintenance

FCoE VLAN discovery

The FIP VLAN discovery protocol uses the FIP VLAN Request and FIP VLAN Notification operations. The protocol is initiated by the ENode MAC or FCF-MAC in which an FIP VLAN Request is transmitted using any available (or a default) VLAN. The destination MAC address is the "ALL-FCF-MACs" multicast address and the source MAC address is the sender's ENode MAC or FCF-MAC address. FCFs that support the FIP VLAN discovery protocol listen for the FIP VLAN Request on all VLANs. The FIP VLAN Notification returns a list of VLANs available to the requestor for FCoE operations.

> **NOTE:**
>
> A different VLAN should be used for the FCoE traffic of each Virtual SAN (VSAN) so that the administrator can identify the FCoE traffic for that VSAN and control the span of this traffic over Ethernet. The FCoE VLAN should also be dedicated solely to FCoE traffic, that is, it should not carry any other traffic such as IP.

FCoE entities discovery

After FIP has discovered the FCoE VLANs, it is time for ENodes and FCFs to discover each other over the FCoE VLANs using the FIP discovery protocol. The FIP discovery protocol allows ENodes to discover FCFs so as to establish VN_Port to VF_Port virtual links, and FCFs to discover other FCFs so as to establish VE_Port to VE_Port virtual links. To create these, the protocol uses discovery advertisement messages sent by FCFs and discovery solicitation messages sent by ENodes and FCFs.

> **NOTE:**
>
> The FCF can send and receive discovery solicitation and discovery advertisement messages. The ENode can only send discovery solicitation messages and receive discovery advertisement messages.

Virtual link instantiation

Once an ENode has discovered reachable FCF-MACs, it performs FIP FLOGI to establish a virtual link with the FCF-MAC and to acquire an FC address (aka N_Port_ID or FC_ID). With successful completion of FLOGI, the FCoE controller associated with the FCF-MAC instantiates a VF_Port and an FCoE_LEP for this virtual link and the FCoE controller of the corresponding ENode instantiates a VN_Port and an FCoE_LEP. Subsequent data operations use the FCoE protocol and normal encapsulated FC frames.

NOTE:

In NPIV applications, an ENode can issue an FIP NPIV FDISC (similar to an FIP FLOGI) to acquire an additional N_Port_ID. Upon successful completion of an FIP NPIV DISC exchange initiated by an already logged in ENode, the FCoE controller associated with the FCF-MAC instantiates an additional FCoE_LEP.

On the other hand, in FCF-to-FCF discovery, the FCF-MAC sends an FIP ELP to the other FCF-MAC. The FCoE controller of each FCF-MAC instantiates a VE_Port and an FCoE_LEP for the virtual link upon successful completion of the ELP exchange.

The MAC addresses associated to VE_Ports and VF_Ports are derived from the FCF pool. These are universal MAC addresses assigned from IEEE and are unique worldwide. There are two types of MAC addresses that the VN_Port can choose from: server-provided MAC addresses (SPMAs) or fabric-provided MAC addresses (FPMAs). In the SPMA method, the end device (server or storage) provides the MAC address to be used for each VN_Port. FPMAs are MAC addresses assigned by the FCF during the FIP login process (FIP FLOGI or FIP NPIV FDISC). FPMA is the preferred method. It is constructed by concatenating a 24-bit FCoE MAC address prefix (FC-MAP) and the 24-bit FC_ID of the VN_Port together. For instance, an FC-MAP of 0EFC00h and an FC_ID of 040506h results in an FPMA of 0EFC00040506h.

The FC-MAP is an organization unique identifier (OUI) with the U/L bit set to 1 to indicate that it is a local address, and not unique worldwide. The recommended range is from 0EFC00h to 0EFCFFh (default is 0EFC00h). The FC-MAP range was introduced so that different values can be assigned to different SANs. This ensures the uniqueness of the constructed FPMA, which can prevent addressing conflicts if two separate SAN fabrics are merged together accidentally or intentionally. Since FC_IDs are uniquely assigned within a SAN, the resulting FPMA will also be unique within the SAN.

Virtual link maintenance

In FCoE, the virtual link between a VF_Port and a VN_Port or between two VE_Ports can span a series of Ethernet links and switches. When an intermediate Ethernet link or switch fails, the FCoE ports might not be directly aware of the failed link or switch. A physical link failure status is not be sufficient to indicate whether the remote entity is still reachable through the virtual link. Some enhanced failure detection mechanism needs to be in place. The FCoE controller assumes this maintenance role and maintains the state of the virtual link using timer-based messages.

NOTE:

For an ENode, the associated FCoE controller maintains the state of the VN_Port to VF_Port virtual links by monitoring the received FIP discovery advertisement messages and by generating the appropriate FIP keepalive messages. For a VF_Port-capable FCF-MAC, the associated FCoE controller maintains the state of the VN_Port to VF_Port virtual links by monitoring the received FIP keepalive messages and by generating the appropriate FIP discovery advertisement messages. For a VE_Port-capable FCF-MAC, the associated FCoE controller maintains the state of the VE_Port to VE_Port virtual links by monitoring the received FIP discovery advertisement messages and by generating them.

On an ENode, a VF_Port is considered reachable if the FCoE controller continues to receive periodic multicast advertisements from the FCF. The VF_Port is considered unreachable and the associated VN_Port/FCoE_LEP pairs are deinstantiated after two missed advertisements. On an FCF, a VN_Port or an ENode is considered reachable if the FCoE controller continues to receive the periodic unicast FIP keepalive messages from the VN_Port or ENode. The VN_Port or ENode is considered unreachable and the associated FCoE_LEPs are deinstantiated after two missed FIP keepalive messages.

> **NOTE:**
>
> For an ENode, a VN_Port/FCoE_LEP pair is deinstantiated when that VN_Port is logged out. In the case of a VF_Port-capable FCF-MAC, when a VN_Port is logged out, the VF_Port/FCoE_LEP pair associated to that VN_Port is deinstantiated if that FCoE_LEP is the only one associated with that VF_Port.

In the case of a virtual link between VE_Port to VE_Port, the periodic unsolicited multicast advertisement is used instead to verify the state of this virtual link. In addition, the FIP clear virtual link message is used by an FCF to explicitly deinstantiate remote VN_Ports or VE_Ports.

I/O Consolidation with FCoE

If you find the previous FCoE inner workings too heavy, hopefully this section will be easier to digest as it discusses the various I/O consolidation phases and scenarios with FCoE. The DC today looks like the left diagram of Figure 2.23 and comes with the following constraints:

- Parallel Ethernet LAN and FC SAN infrastructure, since they are based on different interconnection media and protocols. Ethernet is more "network-wide" than FC, but FC is more strategic because it involves server I/O and storage access.
- Multiple connections per server that have numerous implications, such as:
  - Higher adapter and cabling costs.
  - Each connection incurs additional points of failure in the fabric.
  - More power consumption and higher cost of cooling.
  - Server provisioning takes a longer lead time.
- Management complexity, including:
  - Separate Ethernet and FC access-layer or top-of-rack (ToR) switch requirements.
  - Ethernet and FC result in multiple fault management domains that make troubleshooting and diagnostics complex.
  - The use of disparate Ethernet and FC devices makes configuration management, such as firmware upgrading, driver-patching, and versioning a challenge.

The first phase (also the most pragmatic) toward the unified DC fabric goal starts at the server farms and the access-layer consolidation as shown in the right diagram of Figure 2.23. We have covered most of server consolidation using server virtualization techniques (for more details, see the Server Virtualization section). The remaining items concern the consolidation of multiple adapters, which is discussed in this section. You can compare the "before and after effects" between the two diagrams in Figure 2.23. Before phase 1, each server has two Ethernet NICs and two FC HBAs. After phase 1, the four server adapters have been reduced to two CNAs. The number of cables has also been reduced

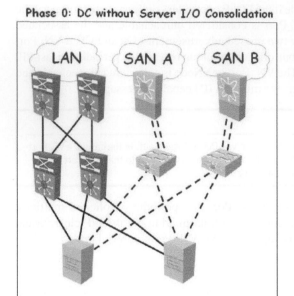
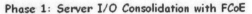
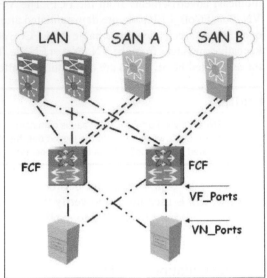

Phase 0: DC without Server I/O Consolidation   Phase 1: Server I/O Consolidation with FCoE

—————— Gigabit Ethernet

— — — — · FC

— · — · 10 Gigabit Ethernet

— · · — Lossless Ethernet with FCoE

FIGURE 2.23

FCoE phase 1 deployment

from eight to four. DC LAN and SAN traffic are both transported within the same 10GE cable rather than using different cables (one for Ethernet and another for native FC). This also enables the effective sharing of the high-bandwidth (10GE) link.

On the access-layer side, the two ToR Ethernet switches and the two ToR FC switches have been reduced to only one set of ToR switches—a pair of FCFs (FCoE switches). For this reason, the access layer and cabling are simplified, resulting in lower total cost of ownership (TCO). Investment protection is also assured since the installed base of existing LAN and SAN infrastructures remains intact from the aggregation layer onwards (or upwards). The operational model is now consistent at the access layer and server farms since all the servers' I/O is consolidated to FCoE and is directly connected to FCoE access-layer switches. The uplinks from the access-layer FCFs to the aggregation-layer Ethernet switches have also been upgraded to 10GE links. Phase 1 is anticipated to be the most common initial FCoE deployment although it might still be lacking in terms of a fast provisioning infrastructure (unified DC fabric) that is required for cloud IaaS.

Figure 2.24 illustrates phase 2. The focus is now shifted to the distribution or aggregation layer of the DC LAN. The existing aggregation-layer switches are moved to a services aggregation layer, acting as external services chassis that provide the DC services (e.g., firewalls and server load-balancers). In its place are two aggregation-layer FCFs that transform the legacy DC Ethernet

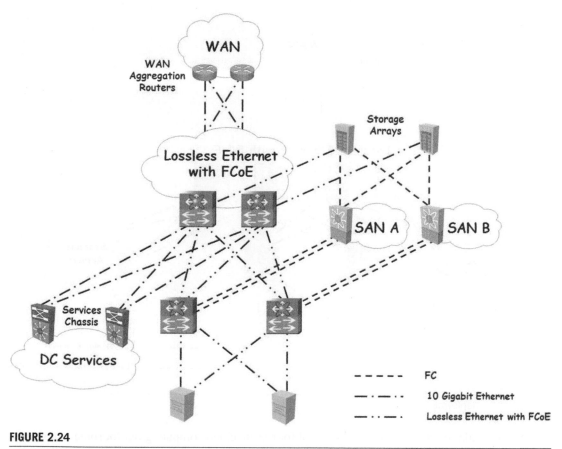

FIGURE 2.24

FCoE phase 2 deployment

LAN into a lossless Ethernet LAN with FCoE capability. Phase 2 provides the leeway or redundancy to access the storage arrays either through native FC or through lossless Ethernet, leading us a step closer for the elimination of parallel network infrastructure in phase 3. Since the DC fabric has been unified to a certain extent in phase 2, infrastructure provisioning becomes much faster and TCO gets lower. This is exactly what is required in a successful private cloud computing setup. Rapid provisioning in an on-demand basis is core to an adaptive SOI that is responsive to evolving business needs. For this reason, phase 2 is the recommended step to take with the fabric module (see Figure 2.2) for cloud IaaS. To complete the big picture, the services chassis and WAN aggregation routers are connected to this "semi-unified" DC fabric using 10GE links. For more details on DC service integration and the next-generation WAN, see Chapter 3.

Figure 2.25 illustrates phase 3 of the FCoE deployment where networkwide unified fabric is achieved for the DC LAN and SAN. The native FC switches and FC storage arrays are converted to FCoE I/O access. With a full unified fabric, consistent network policies can be set across the DC, which further reduces TCO.

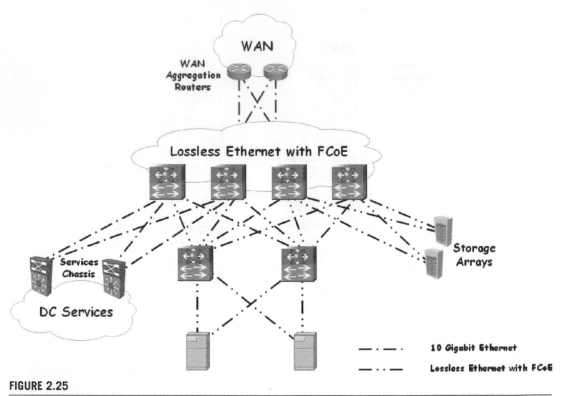

FIGURE 2.25

FCoE phase 3 deployment

This particular phase is considered the ideal for private cloud computing but for some will remain hypothetical. This phase is ideal but not pragmatic because it can be difficult to do away with the existing native FC infrastructure in the short or middle term whether for sentimental reasons or investment protection. It is hypothetical because this particular setup can remain a future objective. We first do things incrementally in phase 1 followed by phase 2 and finally phase 3 as the ultimate goal. Since we are talking about DC evolution, phase 3 could take quite a while to realize.

In the long term, cloud IaaS providers are expected to move from phase 2 to phase 3 at their own pace. The unified DC fabric initiative will probably end up with a blend of phase 1 and phase 2 setups, depending on how urgently the SOI needs to be available for the cloud IaaS offerings. On the other hand, new enterprise DC setups could jump straightaway to phase 3 to attain network-wide unified fabric as the base to quickly propel private cloud computing services into play. For more FCoE design considerations, see the Unified Fabric Design Study section in Chapter 9.

Cable considerations

What does I/O consolidation imply for the DC at the rack level? Dramatic reduction in adapters, switch ports, and cabling requirements that in turn reduces power consumption, cost of cooling, and even floor space, coincides with the Green IT initiatives. With regard to cabling interfaces, the technology has evolved from SFP (small form-factor pluggable) to SFP+ transceivers to support data rates up to 10 Gbps. SFP+ has a comparable panel density as SFP but with a lower power consumption. Most importantly, SFP+ is backward compatible with SFP optical modules.

To wire up the DC rack for FCoE solutions, SFP+ with copper (CX-1) Twinax cable is recommended. The cable is small (approximately 6 mm in diameter) and flexible so that it can be contained within the rack making cabling deployment easier and less time consuming. In addition, it has low power consumption, a negligible error rate (10^{-15}), and most notably, a low cable cost. Although its distance limitation is 10 meters (33 feet), this should be sufficient to connect a few (approximately one to five) racks of servers to a common ToR switch.

> **NOTE:**
>
> Although the SFP+ CU Twinax cable specification allows for 10 meters, the available cable length options are typically 1, 3, or 5 meters.

Rack topologies

The DC access layer can be partitioned into pods for a modular build up. A pod represents an access-layer building block that defines the number of servers connected to a network aggregation block. Within the pod, server connectivity is handled at the rack level by ToR access switches that in turn are connected to the network aggregation layer. The idea is to facilitate the *rack-and-roll* approach for rapid server provisioning in the DC. A pod is comprised of racks of servers that are dependent on the following rack topologies (that are often used together):

- **End-of-the-row topology:** This topology uses large, director-class switching devices at the end of each row of server racks that require significant cabling bulk to be carried from all server racks to the network rack. The main benefit of this topology is that fewer configuration points (switches) control a large number of server ports.
- **Top-of-the-rack topology:** This topology consists of one rack-unit (1RU) or two rack-unit (2RU) access-layer switching devices at the top of each server rack, providing the server connectivity within each rack. This topology is more efficient in terms of cabling because fewer cables are required from each rack to the end-of-the-row switch. Nevertheless, the top-of-the-rack topology requires more ToR switches as compared to the end-of-the-row topology for the same number of switch ports, which increases the management burden.

I/O consolidation with FCoE reduces the number of adapters required on servers. This reduces the total number of cables required to link up the servers and thus eases the cabling bulk in end-of-the-row topologies. Because FCoE extends native FC access to Ethernet, there is no need for separate ToR FC switches. In other words, one homogeneous set of ToR FCoE switches will suffice and this alleviates the requirement to have more ToR switches in top-of-the-rack topologies.

Figure 2.26 illustrates a simple top-of-the-rack topology based on FCoE phase 1 deployment (see Figure 2.23) but this time from the rack level perspective with 12 servers instead. The server I/O consolidation effort with FCoE reduced the overall cables from 56 to 32 (approximately 43% reduction). The number of single-port adapters was reduced from 48 to 24 (50% reduction) and the number of ToR switches was reduced from 4 to 2 (50% reduction)–not bad from the DC consolidation standpoint and certainly a plus in private cloud computing environments.

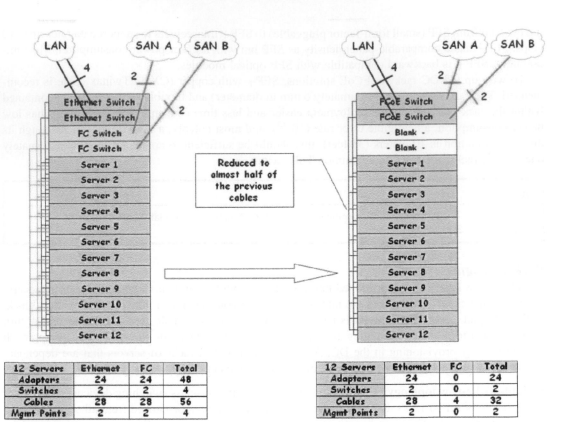

FIGURE 2.26

Cabling reduction with FCoE

In short, the ToR architecture helps to modularize and mobilize server racks into a rack-and-roll deployment model. For more details on the ToR architecture and design, see the Top-of-Rack Architecture Design Study section in Chapter 9.

> **NOTE:**
>
> If dual-port adapters are used, a total of 24 units are required before the FCoE phase 1 deployment. This total is cut in half to just 12 units after the consolidation.

SUMMARY

Enterprise DCs are experiencing a paradigm shift. Private cloud computing requires a more flexible, efficient, and available infrastructure that can dynamically adapt to the needs of the business. To realize this trend, existing DCs have to adopt the virtualization model with new DCs going for a modular approach. In general, virtualization plays a major role in the consolidation of DC since it essentially decouples the underlying physical devices from their logical representation. Specifically, virtualization in the enterprise encompasses server, storage, and network virtualizations. These three main areas of virtualization form a triad foundation for a SOI that in turn provides the dynamic service-platform for cloud IaaS offerings. In addition, the benefits that can be reaped from virtualization are unprecedented. They include a significant decrease in power consumption, reduced cooling, smaller floor space for the DC, enhanced reliability, serviceability, and manageability and, most importantly, a lower TCO, CAPEX, and OPEX.

10GE infrastructure is rolling into the mainstream. This is a boon for faster server and inter-switch connectivity. However, 10GE alone is not enough to mandate a unified DC fabric due to the best-effort nature of classical Ethernet. Ethernet must be lossless in a differentiated manner to be on par with native FC, and this calls for implementing a series of Ethernet extensions such as PFC, ETS, DCBX, and so on. With all these in place, native FC can be extended to Ethernet with FCoE and a unified DC fabric begins to see the light. There are three phases in creating unified DC fabric with phase 1 being the most conservative, phase 3 the most ideal, and phase 2 anticipated as the mainstream stopping point for now. As part of the DC evolution, cabling infrastructure and rack topologies must also be considered. The top-of-the-rack topology and cabling architecture not only enable a rack-and-roll deployment model for modularity at the rack level, but also provide a smooth transition from 1GE to 10GE attached servers.

Next-Generation WAN and Service Integration

Computer science is no more about computers than astronomy is about telescopes.
—**E.W. Dijkstra**

INFORMATION IN THIS CHAPTER:

- Service Integration in the Data Center
- Infrastructure Segmentation
- The Next-Generation Enterprise WAN
- Summary

INTRODUCTION

In Chapter 2, a new services aggregation layer is created to make way for the FCoE consolidation at the existing distribution or aggregation layer of the enterprise data center (DC) LAN. Chapter 3 discusses the virtualization and integration of intelligent service elements such as firewalls and server load balancers (SLBs) in the services aggregation layer before moving on to tackle the various next-generation WAN technologies for the WAN Module (see Figure 1.2) of the enterprise.

SERVICE INTEGRATION IN THE DATA CENTER

The SOI of the enterprise DC cannot do without important network services such as firewall capabilities and server load balancing. The services aggregation layer is a good place to integrate firewalls and SLBs because it is typically the demarcation between L2 and L3 in the DC, and it allows these intelligent service devices to be shared across multiple switches in the access layer. There are two ways to integrate firewalls and SLBs:

- The use of separate services aggregation–layer switches as external services chassis to house firewall and SLB service modules.
- The use of standalone appliance devices.

This book covers only the services chassis approach for housing firewalls and SLBs.

One way to deploy the services chassis method is to use the active/standby approach as illustrated in Figure 3.1 where one of the services chassis is active while the other is in standby. The active services chassis provides the primary path for all serviced data flows while the standby services chassis provides the backup path when the primary path is unavailable. Aggregation 1 and Aggregation 2 in Figure 3.1

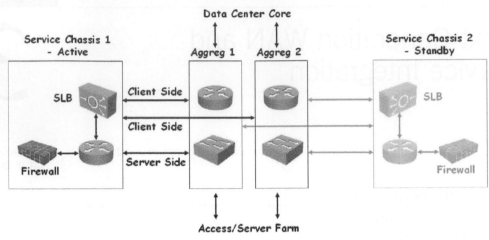

FIGURE 3.1

Traffic flow for active/standby services chassis approach

have enhanced Ethernet extensions that tie the services chassis back to the unified DC fabric discussed in Chapter 2 (see Figures 2.24 and 2.25).

> **NOTE:**
>
> An example of a services chassis is a dedicated Cisco Catalyst 6500 Series switch chassis, housing the firewall services module (FWSM) as the firewall and the application control engine service module (ACESM) as the SLB. The Cisco Nexus 7000 Series switches are examples of Aggregation 1 and Aggregation 2.

In terms of device virtualization, the services chassis and the stand-alone appliance approaches are similar except that the services chassis method adopts slot-in service modules, whereas the stand-alone appliance method uses physical external service devices in appliance form factor. Why is virtualization important for firewalls and SLBs? A single physical firewall or SLB provides no isolation for resources, configurations, and applications. The workaround is to deploy several of these physical devices to alleviate the mentioned constraints. However, this gives rise to another set of constraints such as physical device sprawl and the underutilization of these devices and their resources. This is where virtualization found its value by addressing and mitigating both sets of constraints. The capability to provide virtual partitions or virtual contexts on these service devices helps to:

- Isolate resources, configurations, and applications
- Prevent physical device sprawl
- Enhance resource management by better utilizing the resources on the devices
- Provide multitenant-based network services for cloud IaaS offerings

The specific inner workings of firewalls and SLBs are beyond the scope of this book. The focus of this chapter is on how these service devices can become multitenant ready for cloud IaaS offerings with the help of virtual contexts (or virtual device contexts).

Firewall virtualization

In line with server virtualization, a physical firewall should have the capability to be virtualized, or partitioned into separate (device) contexts to increase with the number of VMs. From the cloud security standpoint, VMs are just like physical servers. A firewall must provide the same level of protection to VMs that it does to an ordinary IP host. The virtual firewall contexts work like separate physical firewall devices. These virtual firewalls share the same set of physical resources on the actual physical firewall, so proper resource management is essential. Resource management limits the use of resources per context. This is achieved by assigning contexts to resource classes. Each context then uses the resource limits set for the resource class.

Figure 3.2 shows a virtual server farm (physically an ESX Server host) that is connected to a firewall where the firewall contexts are used to provide various virtual firewalls to the different VMs. The firewall contexts are not only fully isolated from each other, but they also retain the secure separation of rules and other customer features, essentially what a multitenant environment would require.

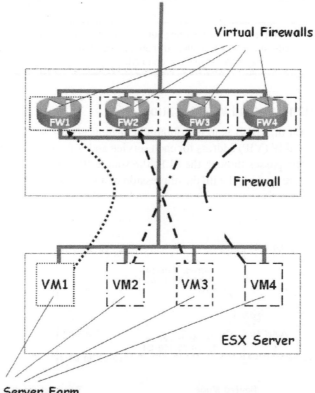

FIGURE 3.2

Firewall virtualization with virtual firewall contexts

Firewall modes

From the deployment perspective, a firewall can run in either routed or transparent mode. These firewall modes are illustrated in Figure 3.3. In routed mode, the firewall is considered to be an L3 device in the network. It supports multiple interfaces with each interface on a different subnet and can perform network address translation (NAT) between connected networks.

In transparent mode, the firewall is an L2 device and not an L3 or routed hop. Since the transparent mode firewall is not a routed hop, it can be easily introduced into an existing network without IP readdressing. Maintenance is simpler because there are no complicated routing patterns to troubleshoot.

Per context, the firewall connects the same network on its inside and outside interface in transparent mode. It can support multiple pairs of inside and outside interfaces as a bridge group with each bridge group connecting to a different network. Each bridge group requires a management IP address and the transparent firewall uses this IP address as the source address for packets originating from the bridge group. The management IP address must be on the same subnet as the connected network. Transparent mode is sometimes called bump-in-the-wire mode.

NOTE:

A FWSM context supports either bridging or routing but not both. The number of bridged interface pairs is limited to eight. In transparent mode, an interface cannot be shared across contexts. For this reason, each context must use different interfaces when transparent mode is enabled.

Server load balancing and virtualization

The primary function of a SLB is to distribute client requests for services across active servers. An SLB provides a virtual IP (VIP) address for each service and is the destination of client requests. When the return reply traffic passes through the SLB, the source IP of the real server is changed to the VIP address. The clients are presented with the impression of a single server to which they can send all their requests.

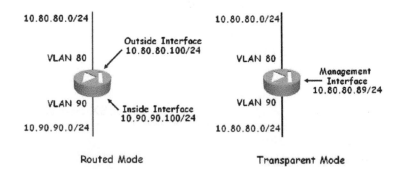

FIGURE 3.3

Firewall modes

Based on load and configured rules, the SLB intelligently passes through traffic to a pool of real servers (which can also be VMs). The SLB allows a heavy workload to be distributed across multiple real servers. The SLB also monitors the health and performance of the real servers so that when a particular server needs to go offline for maintenance, it can be removed straightaway from the server pool while the SLB continues to provide the services using the remaining active servers. Likewise, additional server capacity can be added to the pool if the requirement mandates. These features enhance availability and provide better scalability for DC services and applications. For this reason, SLBs have become important integrating components in the DC.

However, as the number of new enterprise applications grows, continuous requests for additional SLBs become inevitable. A "SLB sprawl" scenario with tens of load balancer pairs, each running a few large applications but up to hundreds of small applications, could surface. In the case of hundreds of small applications on a single physical device, the SLB configurations will be very large and challenging to maintain. This is where the benefits of implementing virtual (device) contexts on SLBs can be quickly realized. Figure 3.4 illustrates that rather than having five physical SLBs (i.e., SLBs 1 to 5) taking care of five different applications (i.e., applications 1 to 5) in the enterprise DC, two SLBs (i.e., SLBs 11 and 12) with virtual context support is sufficient to handle all five applications using five virtual contexts (two on SLB 11 and three on SLB 12). As a result, this consolidation effort helps to significantly reduce the overall amount of required boxes and expenditure.

The introduction of virtual contexts on the SLB allows applications managed by different groups (or tenants) or business units to be handled on the same physical SLB, without requiring dedicated devices. This virtualization effect makes SLB deployment more flexible and scalable, while at the same time reducing the size of single configurations. This, in turn, simplifies troubleshooting and maintenance. In general, SLBs can load balance all sorts of IP-based devices beyond servers which include firewalls, caches, WAN optimizers, and so on. Virtual SLBs make such implementations much easier.

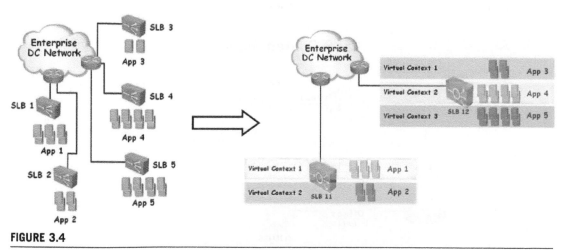

FIGURE 3.4

Consolidating physical SLBs with virtual SLB contexts

SLB bridged and routed modes

The SLB in-line bridged mode works similar to the firewall transparent bridging mode. It functions as a "bump in the wire" or as a transparent bridge between the upstream L3 device (e.g., a router, a L3 switch, a firewall, and so on) and the server farm. The top diagram of Figure 3.5 illustrates the SLB bridged mode. In this mode, the upstream VLAN and the server farm VLAN are part of the same IP subnet. The real servers in the server farm are in a routable IP subnet and the VIP addresses of services are in the same or a different subnet. One IP subnet is required for each server farm. The SLB uses its address resolution protocol (ARP) table to track the actual MAC addresses of the real servers. The MAC address of the common VIP is changed to the specific MAC address of a real server to direct traffic to the appropriate real server. In addition, the default gateway of the real servers in a bridged mode deployment is configured to use the IP address of the upstream router interface.

The bottom diagram of Figure 3.5 illustrates the routed mode. The SLB routes between the outside and inside subnets. The upstream (outside) VLAN 80 and server farm (inside) VLAN 90 belong to

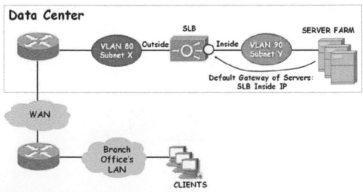

FIGURE 3.5

SLB bridged and routed modes

different IP subnets. The VIP addresses of services are typically in a routable public subnet while the real servers are in a private IP subnet. This mode supports multiple IP subnets for each server farm. The SLB routes a packet from the outside subnet to the inside subnet when it sees its MAC address as the destination. The default gateway of the real servers in a routed mode deployment is configured to use the SLB inside-interface address.

NOTE:

There are no practical limits on the number of bridged or routed interfaces on an individual ACESM context. An ACESM context can bridge two interfaces together and route between others.

SLB one-arm mode

Figure 3.6 illustrates the SLB one-arm mode. The SLB one-arm mode is not directly in line with the traffic path. This out-of-band approach supports scaling. Inbound client requests reach the VIP address of the SLB through routing. The SLB then figures out which real server IP address to forward the request packets.

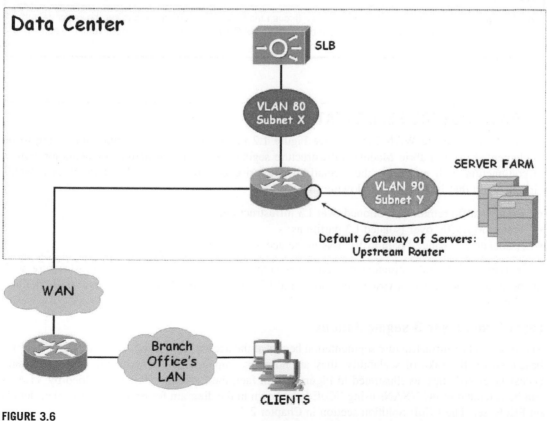

FIGURE 3.6

SLB one-arm mode

The main concern when using one-arm mode is that return traffic needs to go back to the "off line" SLB. The following are a few approaches to ensure the return traffic goes back through the SLB:

- **Source (or client) NAT:** In this approach, the client source address is replaced with the SLB address. The server then sends its reply back to the SLB in turn changing the destination address back to the real client address and then forwarding the packet.
- **Policy-based routing (PBR):** PBR redirects the appropriate outbound server traffic over to the SLB as the next-hop.

Source NAT is not suitable in situations where the original client IP is required for client usage pattern tracking, security audit, and so on. PBR avoids this problem but has other issues such as routing complexity and asymmetric routing for non–load-balanced flows. In addition, PBR is not directly supported on virtual routing and forwarding (VRF)-based interfaces. In VRF implementations that involve the one-arm mode, source NAT is the only way to return traffic back to the SLB. On the other hand, one-arm mode improves performance by offloading non–load-balanced traffic from the SLB because this traffic does not have to go through the "offline" SLB and is implicitly bypassed.

> **NOTE:**
>
> Another way to ensure the return traffic goes back through the SLB in one-arm mode is to set the server default gateway to the SLB rather than to the router. In this case, the SLB VIP and the real servers (server farm) addresses have to be in the same VLAN or subnet.

INFRASTRUCTURE SEGMENTATION

Before diving into the WAN Module (see Figure 1.2 in Chapter 1), there is one more thing to be implemented in the Fabric Module: infrastructure segmentation. Infrastructure segmentation comes in conjunction with extending the virtualized enterprise DC over the WAN. It involves network virtualization that includes the following functions:

- Ensure traffic remains partitioned over L3 infrastructure.
- Transport traffic over isolated L3 partitions.
- Associate L3 isolated path to VLANs in the access and services edge.

In other words, infrastructure segmentation helps to achieve a multitenant infrastructure with the desired isolation over a virtualized and shared L3 infrastructure. It forms an important ingredient for cloud IaaS.

Layer 2 and layer 3 segmentations

The first level of infrastructure segmentation begins at the access layer using VLANs. VLANs are L2 based, so for the sake of scalability, they are normally implemented between the aggregation-and access-layer switches, as illustrated in Figure 3.7. In fact, the L2 segmentation provided by VLANs can be extended to FC VSANs using FCoE (not shown in the diagram for brevity). For further details on FCoE, see The FCoE Solution section in Chapter 2.

End-to-end VLANs are generally not desirable as they are equivalent to end-to-end broadcast domains. L3 segmentation is used instead between the core-and aggregation-layer switches. This is where

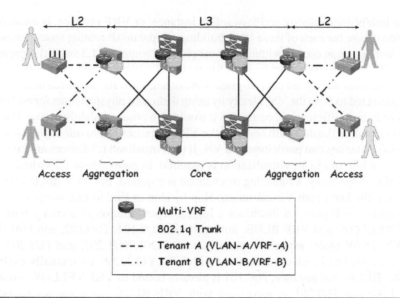

FIGURE 3.7

L2 and L3 segmentations

virtual routing and forwarding (VRF) comes into play. VRFs are analogous to VLANs from the L3 perspective. They "partition" a router by creating multiple routing and forwarding instances. Dedicated interfaces (physical and/or logical ones) are bound to each VRF. An interface cannot be in multiple VRFs at the same time. Put another way, each interface can only be associated with a single VRF.

Figure 3.7 depicts a multitenant environment where Tenant A and Tenant B are L2 segmented between the aggregation- and access-layer switches on VLAN-A and VLAN-B respectively. VLAN-A and VLAN-B traffic are then routed over 802.1q trunks between the core and aggregation-layer switches. The routed interfaces, that are typically switch virtual interfaces (SVIs) on the core and aggregation-layer switches, are assigned to VRF-A and VRF-B accordingly for L3 segmentation. The ability to support multiple VRFs is known as multi-VRF or VRF-lite. Throughout the L2/L3 segmentation process, Tenant A and Tenant B are completely isolated from each other. L2 and L3 segmentations can also be "mapped" to virtual device contexts to support multitenancy for intelligent network services such as firewalls and SLBs (for more details, see the Service Integration in the Data Center section).

NOTE:

L3 segmentation is also commonly known as network virtualization.

L3 control-plane virtualization: the VRF approach

What exactly are VRFs? The short answer is L3 control-plane virtualization. The main idea of L3 control-plane virtualization is to implement the concept of Closed User Group (CUG[1]) from the L3 perspective. In other words, virtual private networks (VPNs[2]) or virtual networks (VNs) are constructed as part of the control-plane virtualization process and these VNs are totally isolated or segmented from each other. An independent control and forwarding instance, or VRF instance, is created to propagate the routing information for each of these VNs, building a separate IP routing space for each VN. Since multiple VRF instances can coexist within the same physical router (or L3 switch) separately, the same or overlapping IP address spaces can be used for each VN without conflicting with each other.

After the L3 devices have been control-plane virtualized, the VRF instances in the various devices must be interconnected to form the VN, ideally by using dedicated physical links for each VN. In reality, this would not only be inefficient and costly, but it would also pose a scalability issue. For this reason, it is necessary to virtualize the data path between the VRF instances to provide logical interconnectivity between the VRF instances that participate in a VN. If the virtualized L3 devices are directly connected to each other, then link or circuit virtualization is required. In cases where L3 virtualized devices are connected multiple hops away, a tunneling mechanism is required. For more discussions on data-path virtualization, see the Data-Path Virtualization: Hop by Hop or End to End section.

The left diagram in Figure 3.8 illustrates a logical representation of a router with two VRF instances: VRF YELLOW and VRF BLUE. Subinterfaces f1/0.101, f1/0.102, and f1/0.103 are bound to the VRF YELLOW table, whereas subinterfaces f1/1.201, f1/1.202, and f1/1.203 are bound to the VRF BLUE table. The interfaces associated with VRF YELLOW are mutually exclusive to those mapped to VRF BLUE. For instance, f1/0.101 is already bound to VRF YELLOW, so it cannot be in VRF BLUE. Likewise f1/1.201 is associated with VRF BLUE, so it cannot be bound to VRF YELLOW.

The right diagram in Figure 3.8 zooms into one of the multi-VRF-enabled core switches previously illustrated in Figure 3.7. As 802.1q trunking is implemented in this example, an SVI is used for each VRF. Code Listing 3.1 illustrates a sample multi-VRF configuration template for an L3 switch.

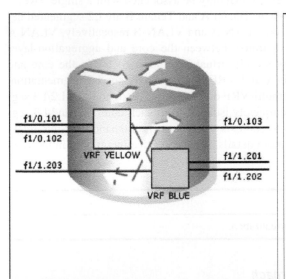
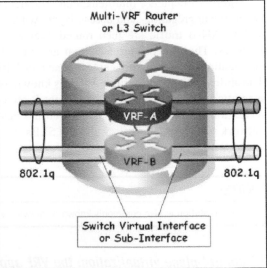

FIGURE 3.8

Multi-VRF examples

The core-layer switch has both upstream and downstream 802.1q trunks while the aggregation-layer switch has upstream 802.1q trunks and downstream access links. The multi-VRF configuration is similar on both switches except that on the aggregation-layer switch, the multi-VRF configuration also completes the VLAN-to-VRF mapping. Based on Code Listing 3.1, access ports on the aggregation-layer switch that are assigned to VLAN 100 will be mapped to VRF-A and those that are assigned to VLAN 200 will be mapped to VRF-B.

```
ip vrf VRF-A
  rd 100:100
!
ip vrf VRF-B
  rd 200:200
!
interface vlan 100
  description SVI for VRF-A
  ip vrf forwarding VRF-A
  ip address 10.100.100.9
!
interface vlan 200
  description SVI for VRF-B
  ip vrf forwarding VRF-B
  ip address 10.200.200.9
!
```

CODE LISTING 3.1

Multi-VRF configuration template for L3 switch

For L3 devices to support multiple control and forwarding instances, they must be VRF-aware and this involves an assortment of L3 protocols and IP services. The most essential are the routing protocols because they are required to move packets across the VNs. To support per-VRF routing, extensions are incorporated into routing protocols such as the Routing Information Protocol version 2 (RIPv2[3]), Open Shortest Path First (OSPF[4]), Border Gateway Protocol (BGP[5]), and so on. The details of these VRF-aware routing protocols are not elaborated further in this book.

Data-path virtualization: hop by hop or end to end

L3 control-plane virtualization is just one part of network virtualization. The segmentation provided by L3 control-plane virtualization has to be extended to the data-path level. Data-path virtualization basically creates independent logical paths (or provides path isolation) for multiple VNs over a single shared physical topology. It is generally implemented in one of two ways: hop by hop (HBH) or end-to-end (E2E).

The simplest L3 HBH data-path virtualization is through the use of 802.1q trunking as illustrated in Figure 3.7. This particular approach mandates the implementation of multi-VRF at every L3 hop, which includes all the core- and aggregation-layer switches. The appropriate SVIs on these switches must be assigned to the respective VRFs to achieve the desired data-path isolation. Although this solution has certain design constraints on scalability and high provisioning complexity, it is still commonly adopted in most enterprise DC networks.

> **NOTE:**
>
> The 802.1q trunks can also be L2 port channels with trunk mode enabled. If L3 port channels are used, the port channel interface rather than the SVI becomes the VRF interface.

The data-path virtualization design for the setup shown in Figure 3.7 can be further improvised with L3 tunnels as illustrated in Figure 3.9. In Figure 3.9, the multi-VRF configurations are dropped from the core-layer switches to remove some configuration burden from these switches. The setup in Figure 3.9 implements L3 E2E data-path virtualization using point-to-point (P2P), generic routing encapsulation (GRE[6]) tunnels between the aggregation-layer switches that are multiple hops apart. The multi-VRF configurations are deployed only at the aggregation-layer switches but remain transparent to the core-layer switches.

Since the GRE tunnels are E2E between the aggregation-layer switches, the actual multi-VRF configurations are "pushed" to these aggregation-layer switches and are no longer required on the core-layer switches. However, the configuration simplification on the core-layer switches results in a different set of scalability issues on the aggregation-layer switches with the addition of the GRE tunnels. Figure 3.9 illustrates two tunnel overlays: one for VRF-A, and the other for VRF-B. This means that as new VRFs are created, the number of tunnel overlays will also increase in proportion. GRE tunnels are by nature P2P and thus have inherent scalability issues, especially when it comes to resiliency designs and the emulation of a LAN. These scalability issues are addressed in the next section, The Next-Generation Enterprise WAN.

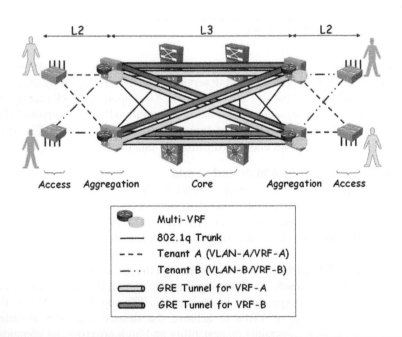

FIGURE 3.9

End-to-end data-path virtualization example

THE NEXT-GENERATION ENTERPRISE WAN

This section discusses the WAN Module (see Figure 1.2). The modern-day WAN services offered by providers are typically in the form of IP services or L2 circuits. IP services include L3 VPN or the Internet. L2 circuits include Time-Division Multiplexing (TDM[7]), Frame Relay, Asynchronous Transfer Mode (ATM[8]), or Synchronous Optical Networking (SONET[9]). To maintain end-to-end multi-VRF tenancy to the remote sites, it is necessary to extend L3 segmentation from the enterprise DC (fabric module) over these WAN services to the end-user module (see Figure 1.2). This brings up a list of next-generation WAN refurbishment techniques, such as:

- Multi-VPN service from a service provider (SP)
- Multiprotocol Label Switching (MPLS[10]) over L2 circuits
- Dynamic Multipoint Virtual Private Network (DMVPN[11]) per VRF
- MPLS VPN over DMVPN (hub and spoke only)
- Carrier supporting Carrier (CsC[12])
- MPLS VPN over IP using Layer 2 Tunneling Protocol version 3 (L2TPv3[13])

There are some limitations for CsC and MPLS VPN over L2TPv3 deployments. The main barrier against adopting CsC is its scarce offering by providers. It is hardly ever offered to enterprises. For MPLS VPN over L2TPv3, it is supported only in a limited subset of most enterprise product lines making it a less generalized solution. These two particular solutions are not discussed further in the later subsections. The techniques discussed in this section only pertain to the deployment between the enterprise DC and the remote branches across a WAN. The deployment between enterprise DCs across an MAN is covered in Chapter 7.

MPLS VPN prelude

Since the various next-generation WAN deployment options involve MPLS and MPLS VPN, before covering these techniques further, it is worthwhile to include a brief MPLS VPN prelude. As MPLS is a huge topic, only its bare necessities are reviewed in this section.

MPLS goes under the umbrella of data-path virtualization. One quick way to understand MPLS is through an analogy: MPLS to ATM. An MPLS cloud is comparable to an ATM cloud. ATM cells are forwarded within the ATM cloud based on Virtual Path Identifiers/Virtual Circuit Identifiers (VPIs/VCIs), whereas MPLS tagged IP packets are forwarded within the MPLS cloud based on MPLS labels. An MPLS label is a 20-bit value found in the 32-bit MPLS shim header that is wedged between the L2 header and the IP packet. In other words, MPLS encapsulations are performed on IP packets entering the MPLS cloud. The MPLS label switching idea basically transmutes the hop-by-hop IP forwarding paradigm into an end-to-end one. This MPLS label switched path (LSP) is analogous to an ATM virtual circuit (VC) or it can be likened to a tunnel.

The MPLS cloud is commonly referred to the MPLS domain. MPLS-aware L3 devices within the MPLS domain are generically termed as label switch routers (LSRs). MPLS is enabled on the interfaces of all LSRs. At the edge of the MPLS domains are the label edge routers (LERs) or edge LSRs. LERs have at least one MPLS-enabled interface. They either act as the ingress to an MPLS domain or the egress to a non-MPLS domain.

At the control plane of the LERs/LSRs, a signaling protocol such as Label Distribution Protocol (LDP[14]), Multiprotocol BGP (MP-BGP[15]), and so on is required for distributing labels. An LSR uses an IP routing protocol to construct routing tables just like non–MPLS-based routers. However, the LSR also performs label assignment using a signaling protocol for each destination in the routing table and it advertises the label-to-forwarding-equivalence-class (label/FEC) mapping to adjacent LSRs.

NOTE:

A label mapping or binding is a label that is bound to a forwarding equivalence class (FEC). The FEC is a group of packets that receive the same forwarding treatment throughout the MPLS domain.

MPLS also supports label stacking where LSPs are nested within each other. This label stacking functionality is required in MPLS VPN deployments. In MPLS VPN terminologies, the LERs are the provider edge (PE) routers and the LSRs are the provider (P) routers. The customer edge (CE) router on the customer (C) network or VPN connects to the PE router.

Figure 3.10 illustrates a simple MPLS VPN example. Two different labels are typically used in MPLS VPNs:

- The VPN route label is used for the route that best matches the packet's destination address in the remote VPN. The VPN route label forms the bottom label.

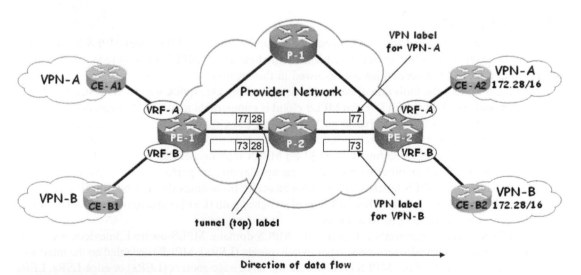

FIGURE 3.10

MPLS VPN example

> **NOTE:**
>
> The VPN routes in the first place are propagated to the respective VPN sites through mutual route redistribution in the PE router between the PE-CE routing protocol and Multiprotocol internal BGP (MP-iBGP). These VPN routes are in the VPNv4 address space and are propagated by MP-iBGP in the provider (P) network. The VPNv4 address is a 12-byte value formed by an 8-byte route distinguisher (RD) prefixed to the customer's 4-byte IPv4 address. An overlapping IPv4 address space is still considered unique in the VPNv4 address space if the RD is unique.

- The tunnel label is used for the route that best matches the address of the multiprotocol internal BGP next-hop. The tunnel label is pushed on as the packet's top label. This means the VPN route LSP is "nested" within the tunnel LSP.

> **NOTE:**
>
> Multiprotocol external BGP (MP-eBGP) replaces MP-iBGP when the PE devices are in different BGP autonomous systems.

The VPN route label is distributed by MP-iBGP, which is only configured between the PEs (i.e., PE-1 and PE-2). The tunnel label is distributed by LDP, which is enabled on all the MPLS-aware devices (i.e., P-1, P-2, PE-1, and PE-2) within the MPLS domain or provider (P) network. An IPv4-based interior gateway protocol (IGP) such as OSPF, or IS-IS is configured between the P and PE routers for global IPv4 routing.

The fact that packets with VPN route labels are tunneled through the P network between the PE routers is what makes it possible to keep all the VPN routes out of the P routers. A VRF is configured at the PE router for each corresponding VPN. Based on the VRF information configured on the PE router, the VRF-aware PE-CE routing protocols such as OSPF or BGP, running between the corresponding PE and CE routers, selects the appropriate VRF, does an IP lookup, and routes the packets at the last leg to the final destination.

> **NOTE:**
>
> MPLS VPNs are sometimes referred to as 2457 VPNs. This is derived from RFC2547, the original RFC that describes MPLS VPN functionality. RFC2547bis, now published as RFC4364, was the name of the RFC draft that documented the actual implementation of MPLS VPN technology.

Multi-VPN service from a service provider

To extend segmentation from the enterprise DC to the remote branches over the WAN, the simplest way is to subscribe multiple L3 VPN services from an SP and perform a one-to-one mapping from each internal VN to each subscribed L3 VPN. In this deployment, the branch routers become multi-VRF CEs. The head-end (or DC) router might be a multi-VRF enterprise customer edge (E-CE) router or an enterprise provider edge (E-PE) router depending on the setup at the head-end site.

Figure 3.11 shows three different VRFs or tenants extended to three separate remote branch offices (RBOs). Each tenant is mapped to a separate IP VPN service in the provider cloud. Different subinterfaces connect the different enterprise VRFs in the E-CE/E-PE to the multiple subscribed VRFs in the

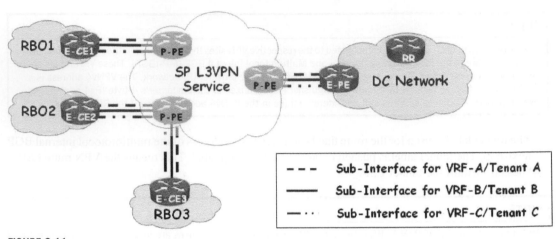

FIGURE 3.11

Multi-VPN service from SP example

P-PE devices. These connections provide the one-to-one mapping between the enterprise VRFs and the SP VPNs. In other words, the enterprise and provider VRFs are connected back-to-back at the enterprise-provider edge with the subinterfaces. Multi-VRFs are implemented on E-CE1, E-CE2, E-CE3, and E-PE. Each of these devices runs a routing protocol such as OSPF, BGP, and so on, with the P-PE on a per-VRF basis.

NOTE:

In the multi-VPN service from an SP approach, the E-PE has the additional functionality as a MP-iBGP speaker and it peers to other MP-iBGP speakers (i.e., other E-PE routers) in the DC network. For better scalability, the MP-iBGP speakers are peered to a route-reflector (RR) instead, as this does away with the full-mesh peering requirement between the MP-iBGP speakers.

Simplicity is the main advantage of this design. However, the cost becomes prohibitive as the number of VRFs and branch sites increases. From the private cloud computing perspective, the over-reliance on the SP to provide the L3 VPN services makes this option less attractive in terms of full autonomous control and service provisioning.

MPLS over L2 circuits

In this particular approach, the enterprise DC network has existing L2 services, such as Frame Relay, ATM, and so on, which interconnect the remote branches. The L2 connectivity is typically a hub and spoke or partial mesh topology. Spoke-to-spoke communication is handled through the hub.

As shown in Figure 3.12, the head-end (or branch aggregation) router in the enterprise DC is converted into a P router (i.e., E-P1) with MPLS enabled over its interfaces, that include the L2 WAN links or virtual circuits provisioned from the SP L2 service. The remote branch routers become PE routers (i.e., E-PE1, E-PE2, E-PE3, and E-PE4) with VRF interfaces facing the branch LAN

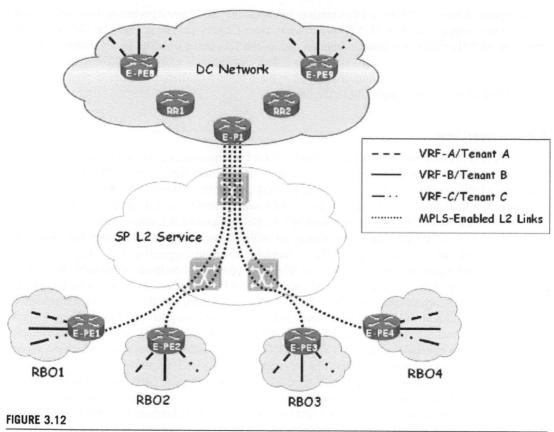

FIGURE 3.12

MPLS over L2 circuits example

and MPLS-enabled interfaces (i.e., L2 WAN links) facing the WAN toward the head-end router. E-PE1, E-PE2, E-PE3, and E-PE4 establish LDP and IGP sessions with E-P1. They also establish MP-iBGP sessions with the route-reflectors (i.e., RR1 and RR2) residing behind E-P1. E-PE8 and E-PE9 are PE devices in the enterprise DC.

There will be instances where segmentation is not required at some of the remote branches. In this case, the branch routers at these sites do not need to enable MPLS on their L2 WAN connection. This will be a breeze for the head-end router at the enterprise DC, especially if it is using P2P connections for each remote branch since each P2P subinterface can be configured independently. If multipoint, rather than P2P connections, are used at the head-end router, the multipoint connections for the MPLS-enabled remote branches must be different from those of the non-MPLS remote branches. In cases where non-MPLS remote branches are present, the head-end router must double up as a PE device to terminate the VPNs (VRFs) to which the non-MPLS remote branches will be connected.

The main advantage of this design is that the enterprise has full autonomous control over the IP infrastructure. There is no reliance on the SP for the extension of enterprise VNs or the requirement of what technology to use. However, a full mesh is required if true any-to-any connectivity needs to be incorporated into the design and this tends to be expensive. SPs these days are moving toward more cost-effective services such as IP VPNs, and away from L2 services, so it might be difficult for the enterprise to fully realize the benefit from an end-to-end L2 circuit over the WAN. Even though L2 circuits are generally considered private in nature, data encryption is often mandated as part of the enterprise security policy between remote sites. Encryption poses a challenge because it requires a tunnel overlay that adds further complexity to the design.

DMVPN overview

Before the DMVPN discussion, it is a good idea to revisit GRE tunnels as discussed in the Data-Path Virtualization: hop-by-hop or end-to-end section. Recall that the inherent P2P property of GRE tunnels poses scalability challenges from the design and deployment perspective. Multipoint GRE (mGRE) tunnels overcome this limitation. For instance, in a hub-and-spoke scenario, the configuration of multiple P2P GRE tunnel interfaces at the hub are replaced by a single multipoint GRE tunnel interface.

Unlike with the P2P GRE tunnel, when using an mGRE tunnel at the hub, the router has a single interface where all spoke sites are mapped. The routing table at the hub maps all spoke route prefixes to the mGRE tunnel interface. Because there are multiple spokes (or tunnel endpoints) reachable through the single mGRE tunnel interface, a mechanism is required at the hub to forward packets out the mGRE tunnel interface to the correct spoke. The Next Hop Resolution Protocol (NHRP) is one such mechanism.

NHRP is an L2 address resolution protocol and cache, similar to ARP and Frame Relay inverse-ARP. When a tunnel interface is in mGRE mode, NHRP instructs the mGRE process where to tunnel a packet to reach a particular address (or spoke). NHRP is a client/server protocol in which the spokes are the clients and the hub is the server. The hub maintains an NHRP database where it registers, for each spoke, the association between the physical address (that is used as GRE tunnel destination) and the logical address assigned to the spoke tunnel interface. Each spoke sends this information to the hub using a NHRP registration message when it first connects. The NHRP database is queried by the spokes to resolve the actual addresses of destination spokes to construct dynamic direct tunnels between spokes.

Figure 3.13 illustrates an example of a DMVPN overlay across an IP WAN. Permanent mGRE tunnels are built from the hub to the spokes, whereas direct tunnels from spokes to spokes are dynamically constructed. NHRP resolution requests and responses are used to dynamically discover spoke-to-spoke mapping information, which allows spokes to bypass the hub and contact each other directly. This capability effectively creates a full-mesh–capable network without having to discover all possible connections in advance. This type of network is called a dynamic-mesh network. In a dynamic-mesh network, a spoke is required to support only a limited number of tunnels to its hubs plus any currently active tunnels to other spokes. In the event a spoke cannot construct any more spoke-to-spoke tunnels, it still sends its data traffic via the spoke-hub-spoke path. As such, connectivity is always preserved even when the preferred single hop path is no longer available.

The use of an mGRE hub and NHRP is only a subset of DMVPN. A full DMVPN implementation also includes an encryption component involving Internet Protocol Security (IPSec[16]). Code Listing 3.2 illustrates a sample DMVPN IPSec configuration template. With DMVPN, it is not possible to know beforehand which router will create a tunnel to a particular spoke or hub. Therefore, the wildcard addressing (0.0.0.0 0.0.0.0) in the Internet Key Exchange (IKE[17]) security association allows any IP address to initiate an incoming IPSec session.

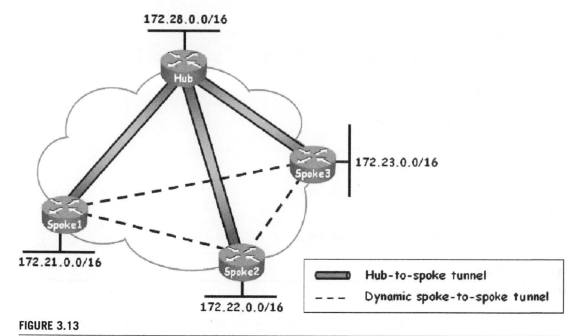

FIGURE 3.13

DMVPN example

```
!
crypto isakmp policy 10
  authentication pre-share
!
crypto isakmp key IaaS address 0.0.0.0 0.0.0.0
!
crypto ipsec transform-set CLOUD_SEC esp-3des esp-md5-hmac
!
!
crypto ipsec profile DMVPN
  set transform-set CLOUD_SEC
!
```

CODE LISTING 3.2

DMVPN IPSec configuration template

Code Listing 3.3 illustrates a sample DMVPN hub configuration template (unrelated to Figure 3.13). The command "ip nhrp network-id <*value*>" enables NHRP on the mGRE interface. The value specified must match the one specified on the spokes. The command "ip nhrp map multicast dynamic" ensures dynamic routing works properly over the mGRE tunnel with IGPs that use multicast packets.

```
!
interface Tunnel0
  bandwidth 1000
  ip address 10.10.1.1 255.255.255.0
  no ip redirects
  ip mtu 1440
  ip nhrp authentication abc123
  ip nhrp map multicast dynamic
  ip nhrp network-id 77
  tunnel source FastEthernet0/0
  tunnel mode gre multipoint
  tunnel key 100
  tunnel protection ipsec profile DMVPN
!
interface FastEthernet0/0
  ip address 192.168.100.19 255.255.255.0
!
```

CODE LISTING 3.3

DMVPN hub configuration template

Code Listing 3.4 illustrates a sample DMVPN spoke configuration template (unrelated to Figure 3.13). The spoke-to-spoke tunnel is built over the mGRE interface and is established on demand whenever there is traffic between the spokes. Subsequently, packets are able to bypass the hub and use the direct spoke-to-spoke tunnel. For the spoke, the "ip nhrp nhs" command is added to define the

```
!
interface Tunnel0
  bandwidth 1000
  ip address 10.10.1.2 255.255.255.0
  no ip redirects
  ip mtu 1440
  ip nhrp authentication abc123
  ip nhrp map multicast dynamic
  ip nhrp registration timeout 60
  ip nhrp map 10.10.1.1 192.168.100.19
  ip nhrp map multicast 192.168.100.19
  ip nhrp network-id 77
  ip nhrp nhs 10.10.1.1
  tunnel source FastEthernet0/0
  tunnel mode gre multipoint
  tunnel key 100
  tunnel protection ipsec profile DMVPN
!
interface FastEthernet0/0
  ip address 192.168.100.21 255.255.255.0
!
```

CODE LISTING 3.4

DMVPN spoke configuration template

address of the NHRP server (i.e., the hub). The frequency (in seconds) at which the spoke sends the NHRP registration message is changed to a lower value of 60 sec (from a default of 2400 sec) with the "ip nhrp registration timeout" command. This ensures a faster re-registration time when the connectivity with the hub is disrupted and restored.

Other considerations include:

- **GRE tunnel bandwidth:** The default bandwidth of a GRE tunnel is 9 kbps. Hence, configuring the bandwidth of the GRE tunnel interface to the actual bandwidth available on the link is recommended.
- **IP maximum transmission unit (MTU):** The recommended MTU value is 1400 bytes. This value suffices for GRE and IPSec overheads and avoids packet fragmentation.

To sum up, DMVPN:

- Overcomes the overall complexity at the hub through the use of mGRE mode, which only requires a single multipoint tunnel interface to be configured. With mGRE, only a single subnet is required to connect the hub to all the spokes.
- Alleviates the requirement of a preconfigured fully meshed network with NHRP.
- Provides data integrity and confidentiality over IP WANs with IPSec.

DMVPN per VRF

The main idea behind this approach is to use a mesh of GRE tunnels to create dedicated back-to-back connections between VRFs at the enterprise DC and the remote branches. In this approach, VRFs belonging to different tenants are interconnected to different logical tunnel overlays. Each tenant's VN has a dedicated tunnel overlay and dedicated VRFs that are completely separated from each other. This approach can be deployed over an L2 or L3 service from a provider. The enterprise must purchase a single L3 VPN or a single set of L2 circuits from the provider and it must use a mix of multi-VRF and GRE tunnels to overlay the VNs over the purchased L3 or L2 service.

Figure 3.14 illustrates a deployment example using the DMVPN per VRF approach. The head-end or hub router (i.e., E-PE) at the enterprise DC has an mGRE tunnel per VRF and the remote branches can have either an mGRE or a GRE tunnel per VRF. mGRE is necessary when spoke-to-spoke communication between the remote branches is required. GRE is used if spoke-to-spoke communication is not involved. DMVPN caters to spoke-to-spoke communication (or dynamic tunnel building) and bulk encryption (for more details, see the DMVPN Overview section). The mGRE tunnel interface gives the spokes the ability to create dynamic tunnels to other spokes (which should also be configured with mGRE) on a per-VRF basis. In addition, the hub router is configured as the NHRP server while the spoke routers are configured with NHRP client capabilities.

In most enterprises, the larger sites need to be meshed together, whereas the smaller sites are typically connected to the head-end router in a hub-and-spoke topology. In this solution, the general deployment is expected to be a combination of GRE and mGRE at the spokes. In Figure 3.14, spokes E-CE1 and E-CE2 use mGRE while spoke E-CE3 uses GRE. The hub router E-PE hosts all the VRFs (i.e., VRF-A, VRF-B, and VRF-C). It can be a plain multi-VRF hop or it can have the added functionality of a PE device if MPLS VPN is enabled at the DC site. In the PE role, the hub router establishes the MP-iBGP session with the route-reflector (RR) in the enterprise DC network.

Built-in encryption is one of the advantages of this design as well as simpler hardware capabilities and requirements. Besides, enterprise operations personnel are often familiar with DMVPN as a branch

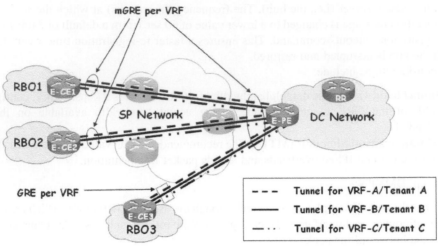

FIGURE 3.14

DMVPN per VRF example

aggregation strategy. Nevertheless, the scalability factor is a major stumbling block for this solution. The proliferation of DMVPN or mGRE tunnel mesh instances eventually lead to a capacity limit on the hub device. Manageability is the other deterring factor when the number of tenants and remote sites increases. This solution is be ideal for enterprises with a small number of remote branches and a small number of tenants or segments.

MPLS VPN over DMVPN (hub and spoke only)

In the DMVPN per VRF approach, a separate DMVPN overlay needs to be created for each VRF.

The MPLS VPN over DMVPN approach addresses this scale limitation by using a single DMVPN overlay instead. In this approach, the GRE tunnels are created outside the VRFs. A single DMVPN overlay can carry multiple VRFs.

Figure 3.15 illustrates a deployment example using the MPLS VPN over DMVPN approach. The hub is configured with a single mGRE tunnel while the spokes have a single GRE tunnel. The hub router (i.e., E-P) acts as a P router while the branch routers (i.e., E-PE1, E-PE2, and E-PE3) act as PE routers. E-PE1, E-PE2, and E-PE3 establish LDP and IGP sessions with E-P, as well as MP-iBGP sessions with the route-reflector (RR) in the enterprise DC network.

NOTE:

The spoke can use a P2P GRE tunnel only if spoke-to-spoke communication is not necessary. Otherwise, it needs to use mGRE.

Direct spoke-to-spoke communication is not possible in MPLS VPN over DMVPN, because the MPLS network requires packets to be label-switched all the way to the PE routers. The remote branch

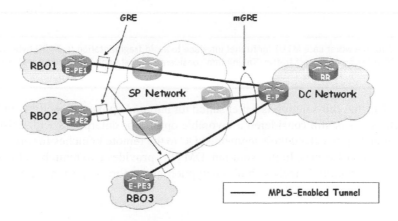

FIGURE 3.15

MPLS VPN over DMVPN (hub and spoke only) example

routers (i.e., the spokes) in this solution are PE routers, and they perform label imposition and label switching. If a dynamic tunnel is set up directly between spokes, label imposition for this tunnel will not be available. Hence, all spoke-to-spoke label switching is implemented through the hub router. Although this design nullifies the benefit of dynamically building spoke-to-spoke tunnels, it provides a more straightforward and deterministic spoke-hub-spoke label switched path (LSP) for spoke-to-spoke communication. At the same time, it meets the segmentation requirement. This design is recommended mainly for branch aggregation where most of the communication take place between the hub and the remote branches but not directly between the remote branches. Code Listing 3.5 illustrates a sample MPLS VPN over DMVPN hub configuration template.

```
!
interface Tunnel1
  bandwidth 1500
  ip address 172.16.1.1 255.255.255.0
  no ip redirects
  ip mtu 1368
  ip nhrp authentication cloud9
  ip nhrp map multicast dynamic
  ip nhrp network-id 88
  mpls ip
  tunnel source 192.168.200.21
  tunnel mode gre multipoint
  tunnel key 200
  tunnel protection ipsec profile 2547oDMVPN
!
```

CODE LISTING 3.5

MPLS VPN over DMVPN hub configuration template

> **NOTE:**
>
> The safest MTU (or the worst case MTU) for tunnel interface to avoid fragmentation is 1400 bytes for unicast traffic and 1376 bytes for multicast traffic. Taking into consideration that each MPLS label is 4 bytes, the safest MTU on a 2547oDVMPN tunnel is 1392 bytes for unicast traffic and 1368 bytes for multicast traffic.

Despite the fact that this solution is better suited for hub-and-spoke connectivity rather than any-to-any connectivity, it is still considered a favorable option for enterprises with existing DMVPN deployments, intending to extend their segmented DC to the remote branches for private cloud computing and cloud IaaS offerings. In this solution, DMVPN provides two main benefits for extending MPLS VPNs to the remote branches: bulk encryption and, more importantly, a single DMVPN overlay.

Redundancy design

Redundancy can be incorporated into the MPLS VPN over DMVPN deployment in two ways:

- Using multiple hub routers at the head-end site. This will typically be a pair of DMVPN hub routers acting as P routers.
- Using multiple branch routers and a first hop redundancy protocol such as the Hot Standby Router Protocol (HSRP), Virtual Router Redundancy Protocol (VRRP[18]), or Gateway Load Balancing Protocol (GLBP[19]), with Enhanced Object Tracking (EOT[20]) at the remote branches.

Due to cost issues, it might not be practical to have two routers at every remote branch. The pragmatic solution is to implement this only at larger remote branches when high availability (HA) requirements mandate. In a hub-and-spoke topology, the hub router is a single point of failure. So the loss of the hub router might imply the loss of multiple remote branch sites at the same time. In a design with redundancy, each spoke must be connected to multiple hubs through GRE tunnels. These GRE tunnels are maintained in active/standby state by controlling the route metrics. Although retaining both (or all) the hubs as active/active allows the traffic to be load balanced, keeping the tunnels as active/standby reduces the load on the spoke routers, allows the hubs to be better engineered for steady state performance, and provides more deterministic traffic path characteristics.

Figure 3.16 illustrates two remote branch (or spoke) sites that are connected to two hubs (i.e., DC-P1 and DC-P2). DC-P1 is the primary hub and DC-P2 is the backup. RBO1 is considered as a dual-tier branch, representing a large branch with two WAN routers (i.e., PE1A and PE1B) with the two DMVPN tunnels that provide the required redundancy. HSRP with EOT provides the network resiliency for the clients in this branch. RBO2 is considered as a single-tier branch, where it has only one WAN router (i.e., PE2) with two DMVPN tunnels terminating at DC-P1 and DC-P2. In the event the primary tunnel fails, traffic goes through the backup tunnel after the routing protocol convergence. Two VRFs are implemented: VRF-A (for tenant A) and VRF-B (for tenant B). The route-reflectors (i.e., RR1 and RR2) establish MP-iBGP adjacency with all PE devices in the enterprise network. RR1 and RR2 are responsible for distributing VPN routes between the PE devices (i.e., PE1A, PE1B, PE2, and DC-PE).

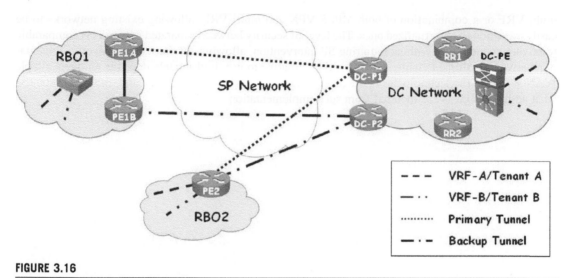

FIGURE 3.16

MPLS VPN over DMVPN redundancy design

SUMMARY

Intelligent network services such as firewall capabilities and server load balancing are essential in private cloud computing and cloud IaaS. For this purpose, a services chassis layer is incorporated with the SOI of the enterprise DC. As such, the virtualization and consolidation efforts must be extended to firewall devices and SLBs through the support of virtual device contexts or virtual partitions on the physical firewall or server load-balancing devices.

Cloud IaaS offerings mandate infrastructure segmentation to support secure separation between multiple tenants. L2 segmentation is easily achieved using VLANs but L3 segmentation has advantages for many environments. There are two components to L3 segmentation: control-plane virtualization and data-path virtualization. Control-plane virtualization is addressed by VRF instances while data-path virtualization extends the VRF instances either by hop-by-hop or end to end. Hop-by-hop data-path virtualization typically uses L2 interconnection types such as 802.1q trunks, port channels, and so on, whereas end-to-end data-path virtualization adopts L3 tunnels.

L3 segmentation and virtualization have to be extended from the enterprise DC over the WAN to the remote branches (or end-users). To achieve this, we need a new-age path-based forwarding technology rather than the legacy HBH-oriented method. MPLS and MPLS VPNs, thus come into play for next-generation enterprise WANs. For simplicity, enterprises can choose to subscribe multi-VPN service from the SP to extend the L3 segmentation from the DC across the WAN to the remote branches.

However, enterprise autonomy and control are required in private cloud computing. The enterprise might want to consider a self-managed MPLS-based network instead. With a self-managed MPLS-based network, L3 segmentation across the WAN to the remote branches is achieved with MPLS VPN over L2 services, DMVPN per VRF, or MPLS VPN over DMVPN. These approaches use either multi-VRF or a combination of both MPLS VPN and multi-VRF, allowing existing networks to be easily transitioned to virtualized ones. The level of security between separated networks is comparable to private connectivity without requiring SP intervention, allowing for consistent network segmentation between multiple tenants. As for which alternative to use, it ultimately depends on the available WAN services, the technologies that existing enterprise devices can support, and, most importantly, what additional costs are incurred from such implementation.

Branch Consolidation and WAN Optimization

4

Hope is not a strategy.
—**Unknown**

INFORMATION IN THIS CHAPTER:

- What Is the WAN Performance Challenge?
- WAN Optimization Benefits
- Requirements for WAN Optimization Deployment
- Remote Office Virtualization Designs
- Summary

INTRODUCTION

Having considered the virtualization and integration of services in the services aggregation-layer in Chapter 3, let us take a step back and consider the purpose of the data center. The data center not only provides a set of interesting local networking and virtualization problems, but serves as an engine to the rest of the enterprise. The driver for a private cloud is to provide applications for the employees of the business. For the cloud to be most effective, the performance of these applications running in the enterprise's cloud (or data center) when *used from outside the data center* is critical. Enabling high performance applications over a WAN can be difficult due to the bandwidth and latency constraints of the links involved. The cloud makes this more challenging, as even the end-users in headquarters might be remote from their applications.

Because this chapter moves away from the familiar ground of the DC design, it begins by examining the WAN performance problem from a theoretical viewpoint to derive the required elements of a solution. WAN optimization, the broad area for these solutions, helps to resolve WAN performance problems. Implementing WAN optimization devices into the network imposes engineering constraints. These constraints will be discussed to examine the implications on other systems in the network. Finally, the chapter will explore how an optimized WAN enables remote office server consolidation, virtual desktops, and other cost-saving architectures. The investigation of WAN optimization will continue in Chapters 5 and 6 as well looking at the network integration challenge within the DC.

WHAT IS THE WAN PERFORMANCE CHALLENGE?

It would be delightful to build a rich private cloud of applications that can be used effortlessly from Ulan Bator to Tierra del Fuego. Unfortunately, the real world is often disappointing. Over the last decade many efforts at developing centralized services for a far-flung working population have been attempted—it is common to hear discussions of data center reduction, consolidation, and increased use of WAN-friendly application structures (e.g., web-based services). These discussions are driven by IT savings in simplified backups, management, reduction in numbers of servers, and so on, in addition to increases in the quality of applications created due to economies of scale. The problem with realizing these savings is the ensuing user complaints. In fact, the term WAN-friendly presages the problem—many of the existing applications and protocols were developed for the LAN and experience problems when naively moved into a WAN context. There are two fundamental performance challenges that limit WAN application performance: bandwidth and latency. This section begins by exploring the most basic and obvious, bandwidth. Next, the three aspects of latency's impact on performance are examined. Together these four bottlenecks describe what must be attacked to resolve the WAN performance problem, a task accomplished by WAN optimization.

First challenge: limited bandwidth

The bandwidth of an end-to-end connection is governed by the lowest bandwidth link in the chain. While the data center typically has high bandwidth links, a user at a branch office or at an airport lounge will not likely see the same Gigabits per second of bandwidth that would be seen in most data center networks. It is difficult to provide high bandwidth everywhere due to the costs involved when considering the number of locations, sites where high bandwidth is unavailable for purchase, or to handle users who are traveling, working from home, or stationed at temporary locations. Of course, the application usually must share the link, further reducing the bandwidth it sees out of the network. Congested links cause loss and TCP backoff, which has enormous performance penalties. Any connection from a remote location to a server in the cloud will be bottlenecked by this slowest connection if it is not limited by congestion or the latency considerations discussed below.

Second challenge: high latency in WAN connections

Network latency (the "round-trip time" of a packet of data) has a direct effect on the performance or throughput of a window-based protocol like TCP or any request–response protocol such as Common Internet File System (CIFS), used by Microsoft Windows for file sharing) or Messaging Application Programming Interface (MAPI), used by Microsoft Outlook/Exchange. High round-trip times particularly slow down "chatty" applications, even if the actual amounts of data transmitted in each transaction are not large.

Adding bandwidth (or reducing data sent) does not improve throughput when the round-trip time exceeds the critical point where throughput is bounded, or when the problem is primarily latency and not bandwidth related. Figure 4.1 illustrates that connection performance is initially bounded by inline bandwidth, but after latency exceeds a critical point, it declines exponentially. This effect is easy to understand intuitively: the rate of work that can be performed by a client–server application that executes serialized steps to accomplish its tasks is inversely proportional to the round-trip time between the client and the server. If the client–server application is bottlenecked in a serialized computation (i.e., it is chatty), then increasing the round-trip time by a factor of 2 causes the throughput to decrease by a factor of 2—it takes twice as long to perform each step (while the client waits for the server and vice versa).

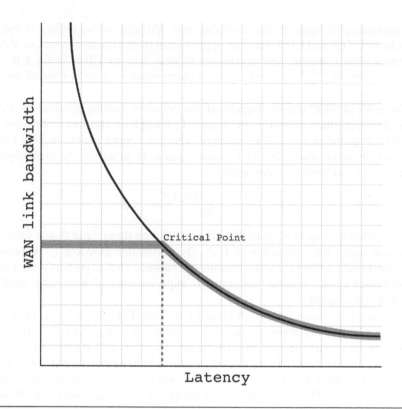

FIGURE 4.1

Impact on connection performance with increasing latency

The throughput of client–server applications that are not chatty but run over a window-based protocol (like TCP) can also suffer a similar fate. This can be modeled with a simple equation that accounts for the round-trip time (RTT) and the protocol window (W). The protocol window is how much the sender can transmit before receiving acknowledgment from the receiver. Once a protocol window's worth of data is sent, the sender must wait until it hears from the receiver. Since it takes a round-trip time to receive the acknowledgment from the receiver, the rate at which data can be sent is the window size divided by the round-trip time:

$$T = \frac{W}{RTT}$$

The TCP protocol must determine how to set its window. The optimal choice depends on a number of factors. To perform well across a range of network conditions, TCP attempts to adapt its window to the underlying capacity of the network. If the underlying bottleneck bandwidth (or the TCP sender's share of the bandwidth) is roughly B bits per second, then TCP will set the sender's window to $B \times RTT$, as follows:

$$T = \frac{B \times RTT}{RTT} = B$$

That is, the throughput is equal to the available rate. Unfortunately, reality is not this simple. Many protocols, like TCP and CIFS, have an upper bound on the protocol window size that is built into the protocol. For example, the maximum request size in CIFS is 64 KB on Windows XP. And, in the original TCP protocol, the maximum window size is limited by the fact that the advertised window field in the protocol header is 16 bits, limiting the window also to 64 KB. While modern TCP stacks implement the window scaling method in RFC 1323[1] to overcome this problem, there are still many legacy TCP implementations that do not allow scaled windows in their negotiated connection settings. There are more protocols like CIFS that have application-level limits on top of the TCP window limit. In practice, the throughput is actually limited by the maximum window size (*MWS*):

$$T = \frac{\min(B \times RTT, MWS)}{RTT} \leq B$$

Even more problematic, there is an additional constraint on throughput that is fundamental to the congestion control algorithm designed into TCP. This constraint turns out to be non-negligible in WANs where bandwidth is above a few megabits per second. This is probably the key reason why enterprises often fail to see marked performance improvements of nonchatty applications after substantial bandwidth upgrades.

This performance limit stems from conflicting goals of the TCP congestion control algorithm that are exacerbated in a high-delay environment. Namely, upon detecting packet loss TCP reacts quickly and significantly to err on the side of safety (i.e., to prevent a set of TCP connections from overloading and congesting the network). To probe for available bandwidth, TCP dynamically adjusts its sending rate and continually pushes the network into momentary periods of congestion that cause packet loss. In other words, TCP continually sends the network into congestion, and then aggressively backs off. In a high-latency environment, the slow reaction time results in throughput limitations. Only in recent years have network researchers begun to understand this problem. The following equation was derived in the late 1990s that models the behavior as a function of the packet loss rate that TCP induces[2]:

$$CWS = \frac{1.2 \times S}{\sqrt{\rho}}$$

This equation says the average congestion window size (*CWS*) is roughly determined by the packet size (*S*) and the loss rate (ρ). Taking this equation into account, the actual throughput of a client–server application running over TCP is as follows:

$$T = \frac{W}{RTT} = \frac{\min(MWS, CWS, B \times RTT)}{RTT}$$

This analysis shows that WAN latencies will have more impact on performance than LAN latencies. Often the chatty nature of applications will cause the bottleneck, but even efficient applications can end up bottlenecked on the TCP window size. Additionally when there are high bandwidth links, the congestion control mechanism will limit the ability of a single connection to fill the pipe. These three latency-driven bottlenecks will choke down your application performance. Figure 4.2 illustrates that application performance is limited by four key areas when it takes place over a wide-area

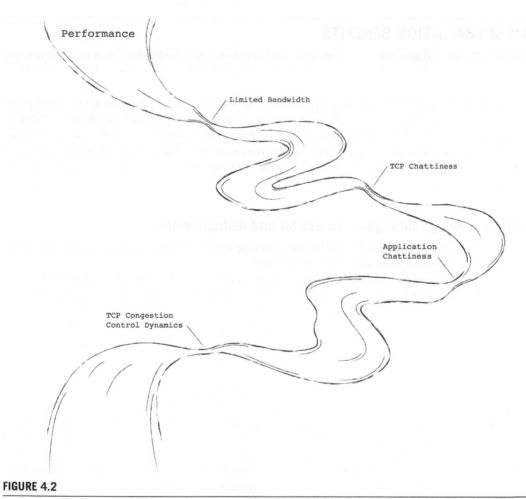

FIGURE 4.2

The four bottlenecks to cloud application performance

connection. Once these barriers are removed, application performance can flow freely and enable users to be more productive.

Solution: WAN optimization

In the mid-2000s, the Steelhead appliance from Riverbed was the first product to enable dramatic reduction of all four bottlenecks at once, not just the bandwidth reduction piece, but also the latency alleviation. It was followed by solutions from other vendors, and the technical area became known as WAN optimization. The following sections will explore how this kind of product can resolve the bottlenecks and how they can be deployed in your network to increase application performance. The move to the cloud puts more distance and more variable bandwidth between end-users and servers, making WAN optimization almost a prerequisite.

WAN OPTIMIZATION BENEFITS

It is more difficult to figure out how to integrate and maintain a new technology than to do something trivial like "buy more bandwidth." What does WAN optimization do to be worth the hassle? How does it resolve the bottlenecks discussed above? This section will explore WAN optimization techniques and how they unleash high performing cloud applications. The section begins by looking at the easiest problem to tackle—saving bandwidth. Then the discussion moves to removing latency at the application layer, which usually provides the greatest gains in performance. Additionally, there is a combination effect—the techniques for latency reduction can also remove bytes from the network because they prevent redundant data from being sent. The last section examines techniques that can be applied to the TCP layer in isolation.

Bandwidth savings through compression and deduplication

With limited bandwidth, there are two techniques leveraged by WAN optimizers at the pure data sending level: lossless compression and data deduplication.

Lossless compression, most commonly Lempel Ziv,[3] or LZ, typically reduces the data transmitted by two to three times (e.g., 100 KB transferred by the client is only 33 to 50 KB on the WAN). LZ compression is popular because it can be run with low memory and CPU impact and it is suitable for low level implementation or for running on thousands of connections simultaneously. LZ compression is typically used alone in devices whose primary task is not optimization, such as QoS-focused devices or storage elements that try to save a few bytes.

Data deduplication is a more sophisticated technique where specific byte patterns are recognized as having been sent "before" and the previous element is referenced instead of sending the original raw data again. Deduplication can be applied at different granularities. For example, trivial deduplication might recognize that two files within a transfer are byte for byte identical (such as in a backup) or a block based deduplication algorithm might reference identical blocks. Fine-grained deduplication that recognizes patterns as short as a few bytes, and not be limited by arbitrary limits like block boundaries, enables much higher data reduction ratios. WAN optimization devices use deduplication first, and compression on what remains after the stream is reduced to unique data.

An example of deduplication

The deduplication algorithm from the Riverbed Steelhead appliance-scalable data referencing (SDR)-provides a detailed example of how deduplication can work. It is the algorithm with which we are the most familiar, and while it isn't reasonable to cover it in its entirety in less than a chapter, a brief and simplified look will help explain how different it is from compression, and why more sophisticated deduplication provides benefits on enterprise traffic.

Reflecting on the traffic that traverses enterprise WANs, you realize it has a high degree of redundancy—emails read by multiple recipients, documents saved repeatedly to remote file shares after small edits, web applications used by hundreds or tens of thousands of employees, and so on. Compression can help somewhat to reduce this traffic, but compression is limited to individual transactions, and it will fail to realize savings across multiple agents executing transactions and multiple transactions over time. Greater reduction will come through recognizing the parts of the data that are redundant and transferring them much more compactly than LZ can. To achieve the most efficiency, the algorithm will need to identify small parts of streams of data, not just entire messages otherwise, redundancy in operations like repeated edits will be missed. These must be matched over time so that today's savings continues tomorrow, and are not limited to a single packet or single network connection's lifetime. In addition, there will be cross-protocol savings, not simply redundancy within protocols, such as a file that is edited is later emailed or posted to Microsoft SharePoint and downloaded by another user.

Picture the packet flow of some simple operation, for example, downloading a document from Microsoft SharePoint. When examining the packets as they flow across the wire, it is possible to see redundant sections from one user's download to another, but these will be interrupted by nonredundant bits, such as the TCP/IP protocol headers. The view can be restricted to only look at the content—the data payloads and not the noisy headers (the sequence numbers, for example). These payloads can still have some vexing noise like the HTTP headers. For the sake of discussion, let's wave a magic wand, and just look at the pure data being transferred in one direction, ignoring these application headers. In some sense this is the file itself, that is, what has been reconstructed from the packets is what one would see when reading the file directly on the server. We could think about saving this file like a cache and checking for it later; however, the goal is to be able to match changes *within* this content, when it is edited, and resent later, so we will need to look deeper into its content.

Suppose that the file could be broken up into small segments in some deterministic way (i.e., an algorithm that will divide it the same way next time if the content is unchanged) by a *segmentation* algorithm. The segments could be taken and checked if they have been sent before. If segments are made small, then they are more likely to remain unchanged through edits, and even when areas of the byte stream have been modified, the segmentation will quickly switch back to matching the segments of the last transmission.

Several techniques could accomplish this. A simple technique would be to divide the content into fixed-size regions or blocks and generate segments for each block. However, this scheme often results in poor compression because of how small changes can cascade. For example, inserting a character at position 2 of a 1000-block stream would mean that all 1000 blocks would change, and thus will need to be retransmitted for a one character change!

A better technique involves moving a window of visibility over the data that is a fraction of the desired segment size, and computing a function deterministically based on that window's contents alone. Unchanged data will always have the same function results, and thus will generate the same "cut points" and-the same segments. Changed data will alter one or more segments, but soon the window will again move over data whose window's contents are unchanged, and the segmenter will start to divide the data in the same locations as the previous segmentation. With a window-based scheme like SDR, there will not be segments of a fixed size, and therefore the segmentation will be much more resilient to insertions, deletions, and edits.

Given a segmentation of the data, how do we use this to deduplicate? These segments can be numbered or labeled in a space that is very large but still much smaller than the size of the segments themselves (i.e., one can represent ~128 bytes with a ~16-byte label). When these same segments are seen, only the label can be transmitted to save on bytes. Given that, what size should the segments and the labels be? There is an inherent trade-off on the segment size. If the segments are very large, there is impressive compression. For example, if 8000 bytes are labeled with 16-byte names, then sending the label results in a 512:1 compression! However, the odds of a match will go down substantially with larger segments, because it is more likely that changes will occur within the segments. If the segments are small, odds will be high they do not contain edits, but it will dramatically reduce the compression ratio. Also note that the number of segments representable by the labels must be large enough that no WAN optimizer will ever run out—there should always be a way to create new ones and never worry about conflicts in which segment a label decodes to. Furthermore, a 1:1 mapping from data segments seen to labels will guarantee that this deduplication never corrupts the data being sent, and if the labels are globally unique, determining the correct one will not be a problem.

So, what should be done to resolve the sizing dilemma? The segments should be both small and large, which is impossible. The solution comes from leveraging locality. Consider that the two versions of the file are not only likely to contain many of the same segments, but where they do, the segments will usually be in the same order! The locality enables us to increase the effective segment size by using small base segments that are combined into large effective segments. One way to do this is to repeat the same encoding trick take the sequence of labels generated from the segmentation, cut that sequence of labels into new segments, if pre-existing, replace with definitions, otherwise generate new labels for the new segments and replace with the new definitions. After applying this encoding trick several times, a staggering amount of data can be referred to with a single label, even if the initial segments are very small.

Figure 4.3 illustrates an extremely simplified example of scalable data referencing. Alyssa's message is segmented into seven basic segments and three hierarchical segments. The hierarchical segments are sent to the file server. When she edits it, the transmission reuses segments 8 and 4 from the previous transmission and creates new segments as needed. Her final edit creates a few new segments. When Ben reads the message, it is represented by a single segment and transmitted in just one label.

Original bytes can be converted into a combination of references to previous data and definitions of new labels using SDR (when the base-level raw data is sent, standard compression (LZ) can reduce transmission size even further). To keep the data reduction levels high, information about segments needs to be available, so the label to segment mappings are stored to disk. When the same data is seen later, it is deduplicated using the same reference. Similarly, the other Riverbed Steelhead appliances that see this data save the definitions provided, so that the same labels will be used if the data is sent on or sent back. The peak in deduplication can be approached by using SDR universally—across different connections from the same user, across different protocols used, across multiple sites communicated with, and across time from hours to months.

What impact does all this have on the network? One key thing is that the deduplicated data no longer resembles the original data at all. This has some light data-protection benefits, and of course the data reduction benefits, but it has an architectural impact. For example, it is not recommended to run virus detection or an intrusion detection system on deduplicated streams, as no patterns will match. Similarly it does not make sense to do deep packet inspection (DPI) with Cisco NBAR (Network Based Application Recognition) to classify the streams after deduplication. The same can be said for devices in the network that monitor and record traffic for network management purposes. Additional services, such as these, must be deployed in the network where they can inspect the original data, so either they are deployed outside the optimized parts of the network or their functionality must be within the WAN optimizer.

Speeding up the application layer

Even if the bandwidth reduction has eliminated every repetitive byte of data that traverses the network, there will still be a performance bottleneck tied to the inherent latency imposed by the speed of light. A WAN optimizer must address the latency challenges as well. As described in earlier

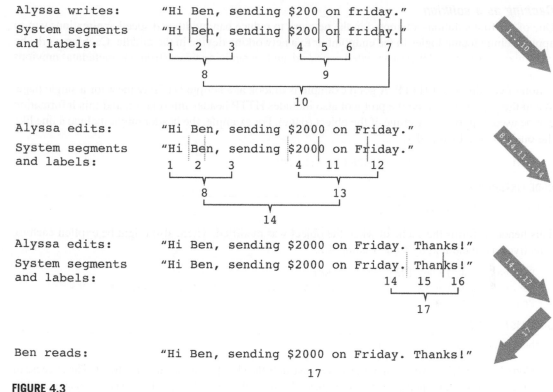

Alyssa writes: "Hi Ben, sending $200 on friday."

System segments
and labels: "Hi Ben, sending $200 on friday."
                  1   2   3   4   5   6   7
                         8   9
                              10

Alyssa edits: "Hi Ben, sending $2000 on Friday."

System segments
and labels: "Hi Ben, sending $2000 on Friday."
                  1   2   3   4   11   12
                         8   13
                              14

Alyssa edits: "Hi Ben, sending $2000 on Friday. Thanks!"

System segments
and labels: "Hi Ben, sending $2000 on Friday. Thanks!"
                                            14   15   16
                                                 17

Ben reads: "Hi Ben, sending $2000 on Friday. Thanks!"
                                    17

FIGURE 4.3

Simplified example of scalable data reduction

sections, this latency bottleneck will have a dramatic impact on overall client–server performance. Many client–server applications and protocols were designed for use on local networks, where round trips are not costly in terms of performance. Because low latency was assumed, client–server applications and protocols were not optimized for high-delay environments. The original implementers did not consider the effects of many successive round trips on throughput and application performance; the round trips on a LAN simply do not cost much in terms of time or performance. Chatty protocols suffer extreme performance degradation when the users are distant from their servers.

On the WAN, each round trip can take 30 ms to over a second, depending on the distance involved, the hops required, and the processing delays encountered throughout the path. This level of delay, as much as 1000 times higher than typical LANs, wreaks havoc with the performance of file systems and protocols such as CIFS, MAPI, and NFS, rendering them either very slow or in some cases, unusable. To solve this network performance problem, WAN optimizers dynamically change the protocol requests to mask the effects of WAN latency, providing application acceleration.

Caching as a solution

One of the first solutions attempted in the network to reduce bandwidth and speed applications was to apply caching technologies to the endpoint or to a networking device in the middle. Caching works by recognizing *objects* and their associated *metadata*, and recognizing when (from the metadata) previous versions of the object can be delivered instead of requesting a new copy. The most successful application of caching is for HTTP. A good example is to look at a simple HTTP request for a single page. When the page is delivered the protocol also includes HTTP header information and this information can be used to judge the lifetime of the object (page). For example, the header might include a line like the one in Code Listing 4.1.

```
Last-Modified: Sun, 27 Jul 2008 03:15:27 GMT
```

CODE LISTING 4.1

Example HTTP header segment

This header informs the cache of when the object was modified. There also might be explicit caching directives as illustrated by Code Listing 4.2:

```
Expires: Thu, 19 Nov 1981 08:52:00 GMT
Cache-Control: no-store, no-cache, must-revalidate, post-check=0, pre-check=0
Pragma: no-cache
```

CODE LISTING 4.2

Caching directives from HTTP header

Code Listing 4.2 illustrates that the server instructs the client to not cache the object. The success of HTTP caching is that when objects are requested a second time (PNGs, JPEGs, HTML pages, and so on), the local cache can check for copies that are valid (i.e., where the expiration date has not been hit and where caching was allowed). However, the Code Listings 4.1 and 4.2, from a web page downloaded in March 2011, illustrate one hazard of caching as a solution—this page has not changed since 2008, yet the headers ban caching explicitly (cache control) and implicitly (already past the expiration date). Even so, caches are built into nearly every web browser to aid in performance.

What about caches outside of HTTP? They are harder to write and use effectively. The virtue of HTTP is that it was designed for wide-area communication and has explicit information for cache control, expiration times, and so on. For most other protocols, such as those used by a file server, this information is lacking. For example, when a CIFS server delivers a file over a Windows file share, what would it set as an expiration time? Some files are never modified, some yearly, others might be changed multiple times within an hour. CIFS makes no promise (outside of the locking protocol). In order to cache the file, a file cache needs to make its own assumptions, or else check on every access. Even with explicit metadata checks, it is unclear—the file server will typically only provide information such as the timestamp and size. While these might be sufficient to verify user accesses (i.e., What are the odds that two people changed the file at the same time but did not change the length?), they might not be for machine accesses (consider multiple programs accessing the file, all triggered by the same external event—they might all complete within a timestamp and not alter the length). For good reason, administrators often feel queasy about relying on the consistency provided in a caching environment. The vast majority of administrators prefer slow accurate files over fast potentially inaccurate files. The next section discusses a newer option for fast accurate files.

Another challenge caching architectures have is whether the cache acts as the server for everything, or not. This difference might seem subtle, but it has profound engineering implications. To take the simplest example, the users can be required to mount the local cache instead of mounting the file server directly. This has operational issues (how to configure it differently in each office, how to handle users who move offices, what to do about users who try to mount directly to the server, how to handle cache failure, and so on), but the engineering issues are even more challenging. When the cache acts as an authoritative server, it must completely implement every aspect of the protocol. A device that is not acting as the server can pass through protocol elements where it adds no value, greatly simplifying the implementation (and maintenance) task. This might seem like a small distinction, but consider the number of protocols that can be in use across the network. For each protocol to accelerate, nearly the entire server must be implemented within the cache for it to work properly (and updated as the protocols evolve). It is also possible that server-like parameters will need to be configured for each of these caches (e.g., the Squid cache has more than 350 configuration parameters[4]), which is an operational issue for the administrators, and can additionally be complicated by network team versus server team organizational boundaries.

The use case of end-users communicating over multiple protocols exposes an additional efficiency issue with caching. Caching saves bandwidth by not resending data. However, it does this on a per-protocol basis by recognizing the object metadata. Consider a user receiving a file over email, saving and editing it over a Windows file share, posting it to a Microsoft SharePoint server—this will leverage three different caches (email, CIFS, and HTTP). Because caches identify duplication separately at the object level, this means the caching device will store the same object three times, in three different caches. Additionally if the caching device performs cross-protocol bandwidth savings on top of caching, it will store the object a fourth time for that. This inefficiency places a large burden on the caching device's specifications.

Application acceleration

Surely there is a better way to attack application latency in a WAN optimizer than caching. *Application acceleration* is a technique that anticipates client and server behaviors before they occur, executes predicted transactions ahead of client activity, and removes unneeded actions. For predicted actions, once the client issues the predicted transaction, the answer can be immediately produced locally without incurring a wide-area round-trip delay. To do this, the WAN optimizer must have a deep understanding of the protocol to know which elements can be safely changed. Unlike many caches, a WAN optimizer does not need to implement the whole protocol, as the server is always the authoritative source of data. To be efficient, the application acceleration must run on top of a high quality deduplication and compression platform like SDR; this platform is responsible for much of the efficient transmission, rather than relying on local delivery of cached objects.

This approach is quite different from how the conventional caching systems discussed above function, although caching can play some part within a well-designed application acceleration system. Simple caching requires maintaining a store of data that represents the objects to be served locally (e.g., files, file blocks, HTTP objects, email messages, and so on). While building a store of such objects is straightforward, keeping the store coherent with the original copies in the midst of multiple clients accessing and modifying the objects, with security protocols, locking mechanisms, and so on, can create a complex, difficult to manage architecture. An example of where caching can take place within an application acceleration environment is for an exclusively locked file; when a file is in use by a client, if the WAN optimization device has retrieved a certain block, it does not need to recheck freshness with the server.

Performing application acceleration on multiple protocols does require protocol-specific code for each protocol. This task is simplified by having an architecture that can off-load obscure protocol elements to the server, and by relying on a common (unified) data store for the data being transmitted instead of implementing multiple object storage systems within the device. An additional benefit of the unified data store is that cross-protocol bandwidth savings is much simpler to implement and requires less storage and RAM to achieve the same or greater protocol speedup and data reduction. One of the inherent WAN optimization challenges is supporting the breadth of protocols to match the broad suite of protocols used within the enterprise.

NOTE:

Application-level changes can result in speed improvements so dramatic as to make centralization into the cloud possible. Consider encrypted MAPI (Microsoft Exchange/Outlook protocol): with a local server users can send and receive mail to their neighbors with little delay. However, once the server is centralized to a cloud on the other side of a 100-ms RTT T1 link (1.5 Mbps) an email send to a neighboring desk can take over 2 min (with 6.3-MB attachment). Leveraging application acceleration (and initial data reduction of 64%), this drops to approximately 40 seconds. For a second send (to another user, for example), SDR can bring it down to 6 seconds (23 times faster).[5]

Another challenge is how applications perform over generic protocols. While some protocols are uniquely associated with their applications (e.g., FTP or MAPI), other protocols are a platform on which application structures is built (e.g., CIFS or HTTP). An application acceleration device that looks only at pure HTTP will do little to accelerate HTTP applications. It is essential to understand how the application uses HTTP—a particular optimization can greatly speed one application, yet slow another. Similarly, more optimized traffic can be achieved for Microsoft Office applications, by studying how they use CIFS, than a generic CIFS module would be able to achieve. Thus, it is essential to look not only for the breadth of application protocol support, but also the depth within the key protocols in your cloud.

Read-ahead application acceleration example

The sequential read of a file provides a simple but illustrative example of how application acceleration can work. Consider an application that reads a file, computes something, and appends it to the file. A simplified view of the activities in the wide-area file protocol will go something like this:

1. Verify user has permissions on the file
2. Lock file
3. Read file size
4. Open file
5. Update read time attributes
6. Read block 0
7. Read block 1
8. . . .
1000. Read final block
1001. Write a block
1002. Close file

The commands in the preamble represent two different opportunities for optimization. Figure 4.4 illustrates that when the file is locked, the server-side of the network could check the file size and return it as it returns the lock status. This is an example of a speculative prediction. Checking the file size does no harm, and it can avoid a round trip, like it would in this example. Another potential optimization is the open file and update attributes sequence; it can be the case that in this protocol these commands are always linked. This happens when the protocol is written more generally than the implementations of it. The WAN optimizer can know that it is always the case that doing one implies the other, and it can go ahead and do both at once.

The most important optimizations occur in the read sequence. Here the file is read a block at a time, synchronously. This sequence of dependent requests has much the same slow-down effect as the window size, as discussed in section High Latency in WAN Connections and it will have the same exponentially declining effect on performance as the latency increases. By monitoring the lock granted, the WAN optimizer recognizes the client has exclusive access to the file, and it will be free to read ahead of the client (because no other clients can change the file). The WAN optimizer on the server-side of the network reads multiple blocks at once and sends them together. If this technique effectively increases the window size to one large enough to cover the WAN latency, then the performance moves back into LAN levels. In the extreme case, the WAN optimizer might read the entire file once the lock is granted, send it across the network, and answer all local read operations using that file image on the client-side of the network.

Figure 4.4 illustrates that sequence of transactions over the network with application acceleration in place as described above. While the endpoint and server see a normal sequence of operations over the WAN, the operations are sent in advance and interleaved. This reduces the effective wait time for the user.

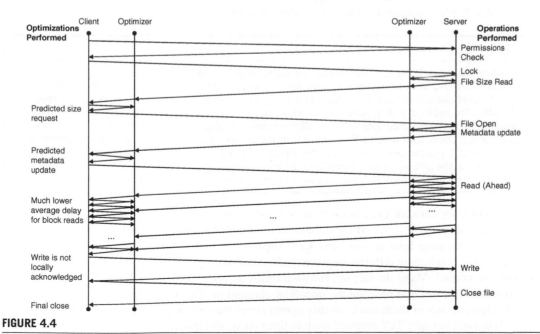

FIGURE 4.4

Example sequence diagram for an optimized file read

Architectural implications of application acceleration

In order to affect the acceleration techniques, the WAN optimizer needs to change what is communicated over the WAN at the protocol layer. This enables the client- and server-side WAN optimizers to communicate their understanding of the optimized protocol. This communication between the client and server of the optimized protocol is sometimes referred to as translating the protocol. By understanding the application layer protocols, the WAN optimizer can separate data from headers, as described in the section above on deduplication. Like deduplication, the change in the protocol in the optimized traffic stream will prevent devices that interpret the protocol from doing so on optimized traffic. For example, a firewall that inspects connection content would no longer recognize optimized HTTP as valid HTTP streams. Additionally, this tight coordination can impose operational handcuffs. For example, the software versions might need to be kept within the optimization fabric at the same or similar levels, so that they properly understand the modified protocol.

TCP acceleration

While the vast majority of enterprise application protocols use TCP, some do not have chatty behavior, or have large data transfer segments which are not chatty. In these cases protocol chattiness at the TCP layer will be exposed under the majority of WAN network conditions. As is well understood, TCP operates with a windowing algorithm to know how much data can be safely sent at once. This is required for congestion avoidance, for fairness, and for handling a large variety of different machine capabilities and implementations on the Internet. This chattiness causes exponentially declining performance as latency increases, just like application layer chattiness. There are several different techniques that a WAN optimizer uses to resolve this challenge.

> **NOTE:**
>
> This chapter focuses on TCP-based protocols and the applications that use them because they make up the vast majority of enterprise traffic. Nearly any application an end-user will name (file sharing, email, FTP, remote desktop, and web, for example) is based on TCP. The two notable exceptions on enterprise networks are VOIP and live-streaming media traffic. The nature of VOIP prevents deduplication and it is already compressed; the only bandwidth savings opportunity is in the headers. Because VOIP uses UDP, it is also not subject to the TCP bottlenecks discussed in this chapter, nor is it chatty. Live video traffic is similar in all these respects except that it is also usually a much larger consumer of traffic and can overwhelm links. Some approaches to video are possible, such as *splitting* a stream to multiple users on the LAN, and could be considered a form of deduplication. Prerecorded video is amenable to deduplication (consider multiple users watching the same training video) as described in this chapter.

In any complex network there is likely to be a variety of operating systems, versions, and device types. There will be very different capabilities in a tuned NAS server and a 10-year-old workgroup printer, not to mention how memory and CPU capabilities have changed on client machines over the past decade, resulting in different implementations and settings on various Microsoft Windows flavors (among others). Many devices use software based on older implementations of TCP that do not support newer features that mitigate the impact of congestion. The WAN optimizer offers an opportunity to clean up any of these stacks as they operate over the wide area to the private cloud services.

WAN optimizers split TCP connections into three parts, and manage the WAN connection in their stack with modern TCP options. Figure 4.5 illustrates how the connection between the application

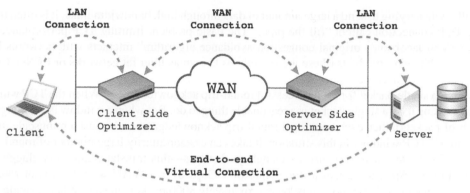

FIGURE 4.5

WAN optimization effectively divides an end-to-end connection into three

running on the user's computer and the application running in the cloud are broken up into three parts through WAN optimization. This enables the WAN optimizers to be tuned for, and focused on, the WAN aspects of the connection to reduce bandwidth required and effective latency. There is no need to detail the effects of these RFCs here, but in aggregate, they improve wide-area throughput significantly on their own, without specialized optimization improvements.

The splitting of the TCP connection not only provides a way to leverage modern TCP innovations, but also enables a surprising speed-up opportunity. This opportunity results from the combination of the TCP connection split and the data reduction on the WAN connection. The sliding window enables a sender to send multiple packets, but the data sent cannot exceed the current window size until it hears back from the other side of the network. As the latency increases, the window fails to slide in time, and the sender essentially sends one window's worth of data per round-trip time. However, with the connection split at a WAN optimizer, there will be various effective windows on the different connections. The LAN side connection can run at a very high rate, keeping the WAN optimizer supplied with data to send. The WAN connection will still be constrained by the window, but recall that the data in this connection has gone through data reduction already. The perceived throughput is higher (e.g., with four times the data reduction a 64-KB WAN window represents 256 KB of data to the client and server, thus the connection will effectively have a 4x speedup).

NOTE:

Let's look briefly at a customer use case where TCP acceleration comes into play. A manufacturing company wanted to migrate all engineering designs into a cloud environment. The workflow was simple: at the start of the day engineers would FTP the designs from the cloud to their local workstations (locking them in a PLM system), work locally, and upload at the end of the day (and unlock). Performance, however, was a problem. In the offices, physically proximate to the cloud, performance was annoying as the 200+-MB files would take 5 to 25 min to FTP, but do-able. However, from India, the system was essentially unusable (3.5+ hr for just one engineer and worse with congestion). Deploying Riverbed Steelhead appliances on the E1 (2 Mbps) resulted in a performance change to less than 5 min for the transfer (87% data reduction) for the users in India. And for local users, access fell to under a minute. These changes were due to deduplication and TCP acceleration alone, as FTP has no appreciable application-layer delay.

Finally, when trying to send a large amount of data through high bandwidth links, it is often the case that the TCP connection cannot "fill the pipe." The basic problem limiting TCP performance arises from how Van Jacobson's original congestion avoidance algorithm[6] interacts with networks having large bandwidth-delay products (these are sometimes known as long fat networks or LFNs). Congestion avoidance increases the sender's TCP window (equivalently the sending computer's transmission rate) by only a single packet for each successful round-trip acknowledgment. When the TCP window is small, increasing it by a single packet is a reasonable thing to do. But when a window is very large (say, hundreds of packets), then each additional round-trip acknowledgment adds just a minuscule increase to the sender's TCP window. In this situation, it takes an extraordinarily large number of round trips to rebuild the TCP window in response to a single packet loss—this translates into very sluggish TCP behavior. For example, to sustain a throughput of 1 Gbps over a WAN with 100 ms of round-trip latency, the sender's TCP window must be approximately 8000 packets in size. When a single packet is lost with a TCP window this large, the window will be cut in half to about 4000 packets. It then takes 4000 successful round trips between the sender and receiver for the window to grow back to its original 8000 packets. At 100 ms per round trip, this adds up!

Once again, the WAN optimizer provides an ideal platform to resolve this problem. Supporting a "high-speed" mode for the wide-area link will reduce or eliminate this problem. This is useful for large transfers into the data center, or replication tasks between data centers. There are various implementations, such as high-speed TCP (RFC 3649[7]/3742[8]) on the Riverbed Steelhead appliance,[9] hard boost on Citrix's Branch Repeater VPX,[10] or Transport Flow Optimization (TFO) on Cisco WAAS.[11]

QoS as TCP acceleration

Devices that only implement quality-of-service (QoS) or QoS with LZ compression are often discussed as WAN optimization devices. Treating them as WAN optimizers is odd, as without solutions at the application level or for LFNs, these devices can optimize only a small subset of enterprise network situations: congested low to medium bandwidth-delay product links with only nonchatty protocols in use. Indeed, QoS itself does not perform optimization it merely prioritizes—for any packets that are advanced in the queue, there must be another protocol that is slowed. Instead, QoS is better viewed as an element of a WAN optimization device required as a consequence of optimization itself. This will be discussed at the end of the next section in "Implications of optimized traffic on Monitoring and prioritization."

REQUIREMENTS FOR WAN OPTIMIZATION DEPLOYMENT

While WAN optimization delivers a clear and compelling performance improvement in most WAN networking environments, deploying it often does not merit the description "plug and play." To properly architect an optimized network you must understand the requirements that adding optimization to your network will impose. These vary from vendor to vendor but there exist wide similarities to form an understanding of potential constraints and benefits (e.g., any optimization solution must have some way to see the traffic; they all change the traffic in some way, and so on).

In this section we will examine the most important and universal areas of concern to account for in your network designs. First, we will examine how a WAN optimizer intercepts, or gets hold of, traffic in order to optimize it. The second section examines how the WAN optimizer identifies which optimizer to connect to on the other side of the network. The third section explores how optimized traffic can look different at the network layer and the network visibility options for it. Finally, we examine the implications of optimization on other services running on WAN traffic.

Getting hold of traffic

To materially improve the TCP performance, the packets must be changed as they flow across the wire. This raises a question about how and where a device can be inserted in the network to accomplish this improvement. There are many different ways for a WAN optimizer to capture traffic in order to optimize it. Figure 4.6 illustrates four different WAN optimizer deployment options. Being physically in the path to the server is the simplest and most common deployment, however policy based routing (PBR) or WCCP enable logical in-path deployment designs as well. A virtual appliance can be logically in-path and it can leverage virtualization mechanisms or other tricks to capture the traffic. In some cases, the device is

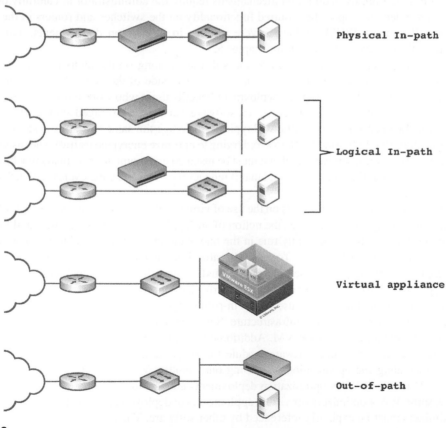

FIGURE 4.6

Some simple WAN optimizer deployment options

configured like a proxy that is explicitly addressed. Where there is no device to insert, such as for software-based optimization, there is no similar network integration to accomplish, but there are still important deployment concerns to be addressed. Throughout the rest of this section we will introduce these deployment options. Several of these deployment options will be investigated in detail in Chapters 5 and 6.

Typically, administrators want to find a location that aggregates a variety of user traffic on its way to the WAN. Often, such a link is between the local switch and the routing infrastructure (e.g., between WAN aggregation and core layers). This style of deployment is called physical in-path or inline. Devices typically sport pairs of interfaces, a *LAN side* and *WAN side*, so that traffic can be received and either processed and sent on or forwarded unchanged. These interface pairs will often be on *fail-to-wire* hardware so that if the appliance crashes, basic connectivity will be maintained. The use of an appliance simplifies the install and the in-path design is suitable for most deployments.

Logical in-path deployments redirect the packet flow from the normal path to the WAN optimization device. Such redirection mechanisms (WCCPv2, PBR load balancers, and so on) enable topology changes through configuration commands but can impose a maintenance burden on the organization going forward. Additionally, redirection mechanisms require the administrator to carefully determine which software releases support the required functionality on the switches and routers in the network because not all support WCCP or have severe caveats in production deployments. This type of deployment will be examined in depth in Chapter 5.

The third deployment method is optimization software running on the endpoints (not pictured in Figure 4.6). Most commonly the software is run on the client side of the network, leveraging a WAN optimizer at the server side. This type of deployment benefits users who work outside the office—they can bring their optimization with them! However, software can also be leveraged at the core, co-resident with the server. Interception of the traffic will typically leverage the same operating system hooks that VPN software does (but before the VPN, to avoid trying to optimize encrypted traffic). The disadvantages of this type of optimization software are that it must be installed and maintained on many machines, that it removes cross-user benefits (client-side) and that it reduces the available CPU cycles/ram/disk available on the endpoints.

A growing deployment model centers on the use of virtualized appliances. As architects leverage virtualization more widely in their designs, the notion of an "appliance" seems antiquated, and virtualized versions are preferred. This is especially true in the public cloud where a provider is providing the infrastructure for the services to run on. To date, virtualized optimization devices closely resemble their hardware appliance counterparts in their capabilities and features. Virtualized appliances add more flexibility to upgrade, the ability to leverage more powerful base hardware, and a split-termination mode. Most virtualized optimization services use logical in-path integration techniques but these can be difficult where you do not control the routing infrastructure. Some vendors split the optimization into an in-path interception VM and an optimization VM. Additionally, a split-termination mode has been developed that leverages a small server-side software module for integration, putting the packet intercept on the server, while isolating the optimization processing onto another VM (e.g., Riverbed Cloud Steelhead appliance[12]). Virtualized WAN optimization deployments are considered further in Chapter 6.

Finally, some WAN optimizers (or virtual appliances) are deployed out-of-path. In this deployment WAN optimizers must be explicitly referenced by other software. The most basic form of out-of-path deployment is a client-side proxy setting, where browsers (or other applications) leverage configuration hooks to talk to nodes in the network other than the servers. Another form leverages normal interception on the client side, but uses configuration on the client-side WAN optimizer to locate and communicate with the server-side WAN optimization appliance. This appliance then communicates with the server like a proxy (e.g., using its own IP address rather than a transparent one (for details, see The LAN Traffic section).

Identifying an optimization partner

Now that traffic has been intercepted, how does a WAN optimizer decide what to do with it? For example, what if only some remote sites need optimization? How can the data center's outgoing traffic be processed properly? There are two different technologies applied to this problem: tunneling and auto-discovery.

Tunneling does exactly what you would expect: the local configuration defines remote subnets or services and identifies which tunnel should be used for the communication. This configuration can be static and manually defined or it can be pulled from a centralized manager that monitors and identifies the required tunnels. The disadvantages of tunneling are that it can greatly obscure WAN traffic, preventing integration with wide-area QoS or reporting, as well as requiring more network management as sites and subnets are added and deleted.

Auto-discovery was invented to dynamically discover optimization opportunities. Leveraging TCP's ability to carry a set of option bits, auto-discovery works by adding optimization-identifying TCP options to connection requests. If the packets reach these servers directly, the servers will ignore the unknown options. However, optimization devices in the path will see the options and form end-to-end optimized connections. This enables sites without optimization to automatically be passed through and the most remote WAN optimizer to be located for sites with optimization. Auto-discovery does not have the ongoing maintenance issues that tunneling has, but installation can require changes on firewalls to permit the new options to pass, and it cannot be used in the rare case that the TCP options field does not have room for additional options.

What does optimized traffic look like?

As implied in the description of how WAN optimization works, the WAN optimizer's traffic must look different from the preoptimization traffic, certainly in the data payload, but what about in the packet headers? As discussed above in the section Identifying an Optimization Partner, some WAN optimizers will use tunnels, while others maintain TCP connections to match the pre-optimization headers. Tunnels enable one to freely mix multiple streams within a single channel. In contrast, TCP proxying architectures maintain a WAN-based TCP connection for each LAN connection. Each has benefits and disadvantages in both encapsulation and in how packets are addressed on the network, an aspect we'll call network visibility. Let's briefly explore this area, considering the various addressing schemes that network-based WAN optimizers can employ. One warning: many WAN optimizers support multiple visibility modes and different terminology, making this a confusing area. Figure 4.7 provides a quick guide to the network visibility options discussed in the following sections. The first three techniques discussed are for the prevalent TCP proxy architecture, followed by a subsection on tunneling. LAN traffic is unchanged in most environments, and the exceptions are discussed. Finally, addressing where software is installed on the client or in virtualized server environments is examined. There is no one answer in this area; each option has different trade-offs so we will describe the visibility mode and briefly examine the pluses and minuses for it.

```
+- - - - - - - -+- - - - - - - -+
| Client IP    | Server IP     |
+- - - - - - - -+- - - - - - - -+    Transparent
| Client Port  | Server Port   |
+- - - - - - - -+- - - - - - - -+


+- - - - - - - -+- - - - - - - -+
| C-Opt IP     | S-Opt IP      |
+- - - - - - - -+- - - - - - - -+    Port Transparent
| C-Opt Port   | Server Port   |
+- - - - - - - -+- - - - - - - -+


+- - - - - - - -+- - - - - - - -+
| Client IP    | Server IP     |
+- - - - - - - -+- - - - - - - -+    Transparent Tunnels
| New Port     | Server Port   |
+- - - - - - - -+- - - - - - - -+


+- - - - - - - -+- - - - - - - -+
| C-Opt IP     | S-Opt IP      |
+- - - - - - - -+- - - - - - - -+    Optimizer Addressing
| New Port     | S-Opt Port    |
+- - - - - - - -+- - - - - - - -+


+- - - - - - - -+- - - - - - - -+
| C-Opt IP     | S-Opt IP      |
+- - - - - - - -+- - - - - - - -+    Tunnel(example)
|        Session ID            |
+- - - - - - - -+- - - - - - - -+
```

FIGURE 4.7

Different packet headers for different network visibility modes

Network addressing transparency

One network visibility technique is to leave the headers unchanged, most commonly called *transparency*. In this form, the quadruple (source IP, Source port, destination IP, destination port) matches that of the original connection. The great advantage of this technique is that it maintains the most similarity for inspection or control devices on the WAN side of the optimization. For example, a QoS implementation on the router that uses IP addresses and ports to distinguish traffic will not need modification for transparent connections. Similarly, reporting metrics, such as top talkers or tracking for departmental chargebacks, will be unchanged. The great danger of this mode is that the packet headers contain misinformation. The fundamental goal of the IP network is to deliver packets according to these addresses, yet given that the optimized payloads will be meaningless to the end hosts; this delivery *must not happen* in a transparent deployment. Usually the end connection's integrity is protected by the sequence number verification, which acts as a backstop. However, any mistake, such as unrealized asymmetrical routing, can cause end-users' sessions to be mysteriously reset leading to complaints to the help desk that are difficult to track down. It is possible in most cases for the WAN optimizer to realize the asymmetry exists and report on it, but this style of deployment is like a very sharp knife—useful but potentially dangerous.

Port transparency and transparent tunnels

Because of the risks of transparent deployment, some vendors have developed halfway points in an attempt to keep some benefits of having the endpoint quadruple, without keeping it exactly the same.

The first is to have the IP addresses match the WAN optimizers, but the ports match the endpoints. This *port transparency* enables the packets to match QoS rules, most firewall rules, and some accounting systems (though not most), but retains the property that packets should be delivered to the IPs with which they are marked. This prevents asymmetry or other delivery mishap from causing reset connections, reducing the risk of the deployment. However, it does not completely solve the management issue—top talkers reports, IP-specific internal firewalls, and so on—will all have issues with packets in this form.

The other approach to this technique is to change the port numbers (or just one) while retaining the endpoint IP addresses in the header. This also reduces the hazard of misdelivery (although one could accidentally hit another valid port pair, with low probability). If the server port is retained, then many WAN systems will function correctly: IP/port-based QoS, network usage reporting, and firewalls will likely not need changes to handle optimized environment. This approach is (somewhat confusingly) called *transparent tunnels* by one vendor. The disadvantage remains that the packets must not be delivered according to the IP header, as they will be meaningless to the destination client/server.

> **NOTE:**
> ___
> Terminology for WAN optimization has not settled down. Terms such as in-path, inpath, and inline are used interchangeably; different vendors will use terms like correct addressing and tunneling to mean the same thing, and so on. *Caveat emptor.*

Optimizer addressing

The most honest design is for the WAN traffic's headers to reflect the addressing information of the devices which generate it. In this case, the identifying quadruple will be defined by the WAN optimizers. There are a couple advantages of this technique, first and foremost, is that the routing infrastructure will always be doing the right thing by delivering packets properly. Additionally, this gives the opportunity for intermediate processing systems (reporting, QoS, and so on) to treat optimized traffic differently from unoptimized traffic. The disadvantage is that existing intermediate systems might have to be changed or moved to handle the traffic. For example, server-specific QoS settings need to be moved to the WAN optimizer or Netflow information collected by an intermediate router must move to the LAN side because the original connection information is no longer evident in the TCP headers.

Tunneling solutions

Tunneling solutions, as the name implies, encapsulate the original packets into new packets, and the impact is similar to that of optimizer addressing discussed previously. However, tunneling goes further by comingling multiple flows into a single opaque tunnel that results in obfuscation of the original connections. One property of all the above network visibility modes has been that for every origin session (LAN), there was similarly one session on the WAN. This enables a host of useful network properties to be properly executed—QoS can distinguish the sessions, sessions compete with each other fairly (or at least as fairly as in the unoptimized case), firewalls can block single sessions, and so on. With a tunnel, this session delineation is lost, and all of the sessions are comingled. This forces all the WAN-side intelligence to be moved into the WAN optimizer or LAN. The advantage of tunneling is that it permits further optimization of traffic. For example, the TCP/IP header can typically be encoded into fewer bytes once it has been established within the tunnel. In addition, a tunnel simplifies the implementation of forward-error correction techniques that can assist in very lossy environments like microwave links or tactical satellite connections. Tunnels also make it simpler to optimize non-TCP sessions. Finally, the delivery issues of transparency will not apply to a tunnel.

Tunneling introduces a new set of potential problems not seen in the above solutions. First, it introduces static IP information into a dynamic network—typically the optimizers must be configured to know which subnets are in which locations, thus adding a new maintenance burden on the network administrators. Second, in a mesh network, there are tunnels between every pair of sites; thus the configuration overhead grows at $O(n^2)$ in the number of locations. Overlaying tunnels on a dynamic infrastructure of even moderate complexity can cause a bewildering puzzle in how to properly configuring the send rates for the tunnels. Centralized configuration assists greatly, but it is no panacea. For a quick glimpse of the configuration complexity, consider a simple network where a regional office has a single router with two uplinks—one toward the hub and one to a handful of satellite sites. The bandwidth constraints of the downstream sites must be aggregated as well as imposed individually, and kept separate from constraints to the upstream site. The problem is worse if both links end up serving all the sites, with the upstream/downstream distinction merely preferred. Additionally, failure scenarios can take elegantly constructed designs and force multiple tunnels onto the same links, where they fight each other for bandwidth because they both believe they have links entirely to themselves. And finally, there is the question of pass-through traffic and how it should fairly compete with the tunnel—should each unoptimized session be equal in weight with the tunnel? Should the tunnel be weighted by its number of connections? How can any device know? All of these questions must be considered in designing a network with a tunneling overlay for optimization.

The LAN traffic

There has been no discussion yet around the question of the LAN traffic. Between the client and the WAN optimizer, nearly all network-based WAN optimizers will maintain *LAN transparency*, where the packet headers are identical to the pre-optimization state. (The only exception that comes to mind is considering an explicit HTTP proxy to be a WAN optimizer.) On the server side, it is similarly possible to act as a proxy, communicating with the server using the WAN optimizers' IP address. This is unusual, but can be greatly advantageous where it is difficult or impossible to place the WAN optimizer in a position suitable to intercept all of the WAN-related traffic due to the complexities of the data center network. The disadvantage is that servers will see optimized traffic as coming from the WAN optimizer, potentially disrupting logging systems or authentication. These must be investigated before deploying in such a configuration.

Network visibility in software WAN optimization environments

When software is added to the client itself, the network visibility options are not quite as diverse as when appliances are integrated into the network. In such cases the IP addressing of the optimization software will reflect the client, removing concerns about "What happens if packets do not route to the WAN optimizer?" at least on the client side. This sort of split-optimizer addressing mode is most common. The other addressing mode in use is tunneling from the client to the remote WAN optimizer(s).

The challenge for most end-user optimization software is not addressing or port remapping; it is configuration. The majority of client optimization solutions require an inordinate amount of configuration to be pushed out to the edge. For example, administrators might need to identify every server-side WAN optimizer, every potential server subnet and (incredibly) every server to be optimized in the configuration on the end-user device. Some lack any way to distinguish different groups of configuration, forcing all clients to share the same configuration regardless of their location, role, or hardware platform. Many of the software-based solutions seem to be afterthoughts sourced from different codebases compared to the vendors' appliance-based solutions. This is especially troublesome, because managing far-flung and numerous clients is a more difficult task than managing fixed networking infrastructure such as WAN optimization appliances or VMs.

Client software-based optimization solutions seem a better match for the cloud vision than optimization appliances—providing access from anywhere, all the time. However, we've focused more on WAN optimization appliances in this chapter for two reasons. The first is that optimization appliances in general provide better performance—appliances can leverage one user's actions to speed up access for the next. To take a trivial example, the bandwidth savings alone are tremendous for email attachments sent to multiple people. The second reason is that to-date sales of optimization appliances have vastly outpaced end-user or virtual machine sales. It will be interesting to see how the deployment choice changes as cloud paradigms become more deeply ingrained in enterprise IT thinking and as End-User Type II's increase within enterprises.

Given that both optimization appliances and software can be present at the same time, this exposes a design question—how to handle users with optimization software who move on to and off of LANs with optimization hardware. Foremost you must ensure there is only one optimized connection. Either the endpoint software should optimize to the server or it should leverage the appliance. Optimization from client to a local WAN optimizer and again from local to a remote WAN optimizer is inefficient and likely to run into performance issues. More importantly, it prevents optimization from being solely between the endpoint and the local optimizer, leaving the actual WAN link unoptimized.

Forcing the correct optimization to happen is the reason for some of the WAN optimization vendors' heavyweight configuration requirements, but a more elegant solution can be found. First, auto-discovery removes the need to specify tunnel endpoints on each end-user's PC. Second, auto-discovery requires a detection algorithm so that the optimization software can detect the local WAN optimizer and give way to it automatically. While this solution neatly prevents double optimization, it can result in odd performance profiles because when the user leaves the office, the laptop WAN optimization software will not have seen the data patterns that the in-network device created. To prevent a performance decline outside the office, an enhancement to detection is available—at present only from Riverbed Technology—where the software actively communicates with the optimization device to learn the segment patterns used on the WAN. When the user next goes on the road, they have no performance hit from not having used the software while on premises.

> **NOTE:**
>
> Let's tie this all together with an example. Before coming into the office, Ben downloads a project and works on it over coffee (accelerated over software, entering its data store). Once in the office, he posts it to a file share and three coworkers hack on it during the day (accelerated with local WAN optimizer). Ben goes home and continues working on it that night. When he first opens it from home, this operation is still fast as his software optimizer has been "watching" his optimized connection while in the office. Finishing it over lunch the next day at work, he mails it to the whole group. The upload to the mail server is fast due to the work over the file share, and the mail downloads to all 30 recipients are lightning fast due to the commonality recognized by the WAN optimizer (across both protocols and users).

Addressing in virtualized environments

Until very recently there was little reason to run software on the servers themselves, favoring hardware WAN optimization in the data center. Dedicated hardware seems desirable for the high scale performance requirements of a DC and also removes concerns about load from the minds of the server administrator. However, the increased presence of fully virtualized environments has altered the landscape and a new mode has been created to handle integration into virtualized environments. Split termination uses a small program called a *discovery agent* running within the VMs. This agent detects incoming new optimization requests and currently optimized connections and redirects the packets to a WAN optimizer in another VM. On the WAN, the connection looks normal (per the options described above) but there is now an additional LAN hop between the WAN optimizer and its agent. The traffic there will not look transparent, but it will have the server IP and optimizer IP in its address fields to ensure proper delivery. The agent can rewire the packet addressing before the server software sees it. This enables integration where it is difficult or impossible to affect routing directly such as in hybrid private cloud deployments.

Implications of optimized traffic on monitoring and prioritization

The changes in packet contents and potentially of their network addressing have dramatic implications on architectures and products for network management and packet prioritization. Because optimization changes packets so severely in contents and perhaps in addressing, many architects view the network between WAN optimizers as a black box from the perspective of high level monitoring and prioritization services. They consider the WAN optimizer to be the last step where they can acquire information that it is richer than simple packet counts and interface information. There is great pressure on WAN optimization vendors to integrate all of the higher level services: Netflow record collection, firewalls, QoS, route optimization, antivirus, intrusion prevention, IP address management, web filtering, web proxy service, and even stream splitting for rich media delivery. While it is possible to optimize some of this traffic, it is impossible to do others, and might not be worth the hassle (e.g., you can usually do a simple port blocking firewall but you cannot implement a payload inspecting firewall). Consequently, you must pay careful attention in designing your WAN architecture to make sure the services you need are taken into account. Some of these services (e.g., QoS) are now viewed as an essential feature of a WAN optimizer, and over time the set of such services seems likely only to grow.

REMOTE OFFICE VIRTUALIZATION DESIGNS

This chapter has focused on one particular SOI implementation—workers in offices running applications that access the cloud over the enterprise network. In fact, this form is just one of several application delivery possibilities. The remainder of the chapter will briefly examine three WAN optimizer deployment architectures for advantages and disadvantages. The first type we will call *consolidation* because this reflects how services that might have previously been offered through servers out in the network (mail servers, databases, and so on) have been consolidated into the cloud infrastructure. The second type is Virtual Desktop Infrastructure (VDI), where again the computation and storage are centralized, but the access method is changed to leverage Citrix ICA, VMware View, or Microsoft RDP. Finally, we will examine a nascent structure that tackles services that cannot be centralized while still providing some of the benefits of consolidation.

Figure 4.8 illustrates the technical differences of each design. Notice how the location of the application (APP) changes, and the consequent changes in what protocols go over the WAN to be optimized. The disks overlaid on the remote WAN optimizer in the VSI illustration reflect that it has is authoritative storage unlike the other designs.

Consolidation

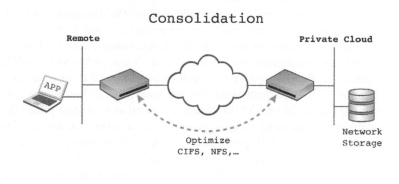

VDI

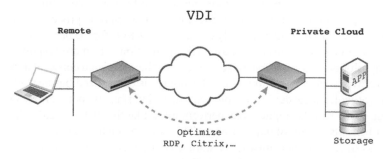

VSI

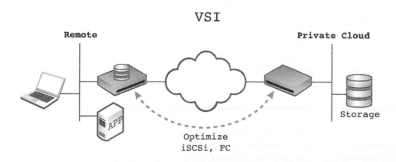

FIGURE 4.8

Remote services architecture options

When using consolidation designs, protocols like CIFS, MAPI, FTP, HTTP, and so on act over the WAN connection—the protocols WAN optimization has focused on. This optimization architecture has enabled consolidation to be a successful strategy. Consolidation offers tremendous benefits to most organizations, in cost savings, in simplified management, in higher quality backups, improved resilience, improved compliance—the list goes on and on. One serious disadvantage is that it depends on the network being up. Secondly the WAN protocols in use by the application must be optimizable—some are not—and without that WAN optimization will fail to provide its usual benefits. Barring these two objections, most organizations can realize the benefits of a private cloud and leverage WAN optimization to remove the performance concern.

VDI enables IT to reap similar benefits to consolidation on the data center side of the network. Further, it hopes to reduce the management costs of remote desktops and increase security. For most architects, the main benefits come from locking down the desktop image with its improved security and manageability. For VDI implementations like Citrix, VMware View, or Microsoft's RDP, remote performance is a potential killer. Because so little computation is performed at the edge, latency and bandwidth limits can hamper VDI implementations that are more than a few hundred miles away. In practice, WAN optimization can assist with this distance, as well as in at least three other areas. First, many enterprises want to pack as many users as possible over a given link and the deduplication in WAN optimization outperforms the VDI compression (especially by taking advantage of cross-user optimized traffic). It will reduce the bandwidth of native application traffic by 60% to 80% as well. Second, some WAN optimizers can perform QoS within VDI streams, to advance keyboard and mouse events over other traffic, making the image more responsive for users. And finally, traditional WAN optimization techniques apply to the printing, file upload, and upgrade processes that travel over the protocols. Together these VDI designs not only enable a better ROI for the project (i.e., more users) but also they create more productive users because their applications are more responsive.

The emerging solution for the troublemaker servers that have resisted consolidation is VSI. VSI is a new concept (so new its name is in flux) where the storage is centralized but instead of using a wide-area file system protocol, a local device will present a drive interface to local servers (VMs) over iSCSI or Fibre Channel. With VSI the applications perform more like the disk is local, while still providing the management benefits of consolidated storage. This solution enables cost savings and eased management for a class of services not suitable for storage centralization, such as graphics-heavy applications and services that must remain up through WAN disconnection. Key to this solution is using storage at the edge authoritatively and replicating changes to the core storage efficiently. The block-based protocol is subject to application acceleration and bandwidth reduction just as the consolidation-focused protocols are. The authoritative disk enables fast cold writes and disconnected operations. The synchronization with the core enables DC-run backup schemas and local maintenance (e.g., bring down remote server, bring up in DC, maintain, down it, restore at edge, and then the blocks are updated as needed).

NOTE:

The application (labeled APP in the VSI section of Figure 4.8) can run on local servers as depicted. This is common where existing hardware is to be leveraged. An additional option is to move the services to a virtualization platform on the WAN optimizer. This creates a *branch office in a box* deployment where a single device or a redundant pair provides all local services for users and accelerates all remote ones. Finally, a remote VDI deployment has the desktop images running on the WAN optimizer but their storage and applications are optimized through the WAN link from the cloud.

SUMMARY

This chapter has shown that the private cloud will be challenged by both bandwidth and latency constraints. The solution is WAN optimization. WAN optimization uses deduplication, compression, TCP acceleration, and application acceleration to break through these network bottlenecks. Implementing WAN optimization results in several integration challenges stemming from changes in payload, packet headers, and integration with other network services. However, WAN optimization enables cloud services to be designed and implemented with a choice of different designs to suit enterprise business needs. These designs not only impact the branch office network design, but also the DC, which will be discussed in the next two chapters.

Session Interception Design and Deployment

He that will not sail till all dangers are over must never put to sea.
—Thomas Fuller

INFORMATION IN THIS CHAPTER:

- Selecting an Interception Mechanism
- The WCCP Deep Dive
- In-Path Deployment in Brief
- PBR Deployment Overview
- Summary

INTRODUCTION

Chapter 4 discussed how useful WAN optimization is to enable private cloud success. WAN optimization permits greater service consolidation by keeping performance high. The centralized architecture is possible because WAN optimization nips the long-standing issue of WAN latency in the bud.

However, to realize the WAN optimization technology benefits, WAN optimizers must intercept the TCP sessions between end hosts that require WAN optimizations and servers in the DC. This chapter focuses on the design and deployment of the various WAN optimization interception and redirection mechanisms in the DC. This will form the cornerstone for cloud interception discussed in Chapter 6.

SELECTING AN INTERCEPTION MECHANISM

Is there an ultimate interception mechanism that we can use? The answer is: it depends. The selection of an appropriate interception mechanism for DC deployment is based on platforms, normal operations, planned operational changes, and failure considerations. These can be categorized into three main areas of concern:

- Placement decision
- Operational impact
- Manageability

Placement decision

Interestingly, the placement decision or the location of the WAN optimizer is more important than what interception mechanism to use. The various locations where the WAN optimizer can be deployed include:

- WAN edge/peering layer
- Core/aggregation layer
- Access layer
- Server distribution layer

The placement decision in turn determines which particular platform (depending on its interception capabilities) to use for the interception deployment. For instance, at the aggregation layer, the platform could be a Catalyst 6500 (Cat6K) switch, whereas over at the WAN edge, the platform could be an ASR 1000 (ASR1K) router, and so on.

Operational impact

The top concern for enterprise DCs is the operational repercussion as a result of the interception deployment. Some of the typical operational concerns are as follows:

- Will the interception deployment cause any operational disruption? What level of disruption is considered acceptable?
- Is a maintenance window required? If so, how long will it be?
- How resilient is the interception mechanism?
- What are the recovery procedures if the interception deployment goes haywire?
- What are the failover/fallback behaviors?

IT management usually makes the decisions regarding the above concerns.

Manageability

The manageability attributes for the interception deployment include:

- Scalability
- High availability (HA)
- Support for infrastructure virtualization (e.g., VRFs, virtual device contexts, and so on)

Because the design of the interception deployment is from the context of enterprise DCs and private clouds, scalability and HA are two important attributes that cannot be overlooked.

As the nature of cloud-based service delivery (e.g., cloud IaaS) involves multitenancy, the support for infrastructure virtualization technologies such as VRFs and virtual device contexts (VDCs) is required to ensure that the various tenants can be securely isolated from each other.

THE WCCP DEEP DIVE

There is one interception mechanism that can fulfill most of the criteria mentioned in the preceding subsections. This mechanism is known as the Web-Cache Communication Protocol version 2 (WCCPv2). WCCPv2-enabled router or L3 switch platforms can transparently intercept and redirect

TCP sessions that require WAN optimizations to the appropriate WAN optimizers. In this case, the intercepting devices (routers or L3 switches) are physically in-path and the WAN optimizers are physically out-of-path. This is one of the logical in-path designs from Chapter 4. In most cases, these intercepting devices already exist so no operational disruption is incurred.

> **NOTE:**
> Throughout this chapter the term "WCCP" refers to WCCPv2.

WCCP definitions

To learn more about WCCP, it is worthwhile to become familiarized with some of the commonly used WCCP terms:

- **WCCP client:** The WCCP client refers to cache, web-cache, cache-engine, WAN optimizer, appliance, proxy, and so on.

> **NOTE:**
> The WCCP client in this chapter refers to the WAN optimizer.

- **WCCP server:** A WCCP server is a WCCP-enabled router or L3 switch. It is commonly referred to as a WCCP router. The WCCP router redirects "interesting" traffic to the WCCP client for optimization. The WCCP routers in this chapter are either Cisco routers or L3 switches.

> **NOTE:**
> "Interesting" traffic refers to traffic that requires WAN optimization.

- **Service Group (SG):** An SG is a group of one or more routers and one or more WAN optimizers working together in the redirection of traffic whose characteristics are part of the SG definition. An SG is a unique arbitrary number from 0 to 255. Web-cache (HTTP) is the only well-known SG denoted by SG 0. The rest of the SGs are considered as dynamic SGs.
- **Farm or cluster:** A cache farm or cluster refers to a grouping of up to 32 caches (or WCCP clients) associated with up to 32 WCCP routers using a single SG.
- **Designated cache:** Where there is more than one cache or a cache farm, the designated cache or lead cache is elected based on the lowest IP address. The designated cache instructs the WCCP router(s) on how redirected traffic is distributed between members of the cache farm.
- **Priority:** The WCCP priority is a value from 0 to 255. It controls the evaluation order of the SGs defined on an interface of the WCCP router. Only one SG is processed on the interface although more than one can be evaluated. The higher priority SG is typically evaluated before the lower priority SG.
- **Weight:** The assignment weight indicates to the designated web-cache how new assignments are made among the web-caches in the same SG.

WCCP control plane messages

A successful registration must take place between the WCCP-enabled WAN optimizer and the WCCP router before traffic interception and redirection can proceed. WCCP achieves this using the Here_I_AM (HIA) and I_See_You (ISU) control-plane messages.

> **NOTE:**
> WCCP control plane messages are exchanged over UDP port 2048.

A WCCP client joins and maintains its membership in an SG by transmitting an HIA message to each WCCP router in the same SG at 10-second intervals. The web-cache info component in the HIA message identifies the WAN optimizer by its IP address. The service info component of the HIA message identifies the SG in which the WAN optimizer wishes to participate.

Each WAN optimizer advertises its view of the SG through the web-cache view info component in the HIA message, which it sends to WCCP routers in the same SG. This component includes the list of WCCP routers that have sent the WAN optimizer an ISU message and a list of WAN optimizers learned from the ISU messages. The web-cache view info component also includes the change number (CN), which is incremented by the WCCP client (WAN optimizer) each time that there is a change in the WCCP client's view.

> **NOTE:**
> WCCP clients publish the information about the WCCP routers that they are communicating with through the web-cache view info component.

A WCCP router responds to an HIA message with an ISU message. The router identity component in an ISU message contains the WCCP router ID (highest IP address on the WCCP router or highest loopback if enabled) and includes a list of the WAN optimizers that are part of the SG. A WAN optimizer that is not in the list discards the ISU message.

Each WCCP router advertises its view of an SG through the router view info component in the ISU message it sends to WAN optimizers. This component includes a list of the useable WAN optimizers in the SG as seen by the WCCP router and a list of the WCCP routers in the SG as reported in HIA messages from WAN optimizers. A membership change number (MCN) in the component is incremented by the WCCP router each time there is a change in the SG membership.

> **NOTE:**
> The router view info component in the ISU message reflects the latest WCCP client information when the MCN is incremented.

> **NOTE:**
> WCCP control plane messages have different "components" encoded in TLV (type-length-value) format. Each component serves a particular purpose. Not all components are presented in all the messages and some are optional. Nevertheless, the service info component and security info component are contained in all the messages.

The WAN optimizer and the WCCP router may negotiate the following:

- Redirection (or forwarding) method
- Assignment method
- Return method

The negotiation is per WAN optimizer, per SG. Thus WAN optimizers participating in the same SG can negotiate different redirection, assignment, and return methods with the SG routers.

A WCCP router advertises the supported redirection, assignment, and return methods for an SG using the optional "capabilities info" component of the ISU message. The absence of an advertisement for the redirection, assignment, and return methods means the router supports the default GRE redirection method, the default hash assignment method, and the default GRE return method.

A WAN optimizer inspects the advertisement for the redirection, assignment, and return methods in the first ISU message received from a WCCP router for a specific SG. If the WCCP router does not advertise the redirection, assignment, and return methods supported by the WAN optimizer, the WAN optimizer aborts its attempt to join the SG. Otherwise the WAN optimizer selects one method each for redirection, assignment, and return from those advertised by the WCCP router, and specifies them in the optional capabilities info component of its next HIA message. Absence of the method advertisement for redirection, assignment, and return in an HIA message means the WAN optimizer is requesting the default GRE redirection method, the default hash assignment method, and the default GRE return method.

A WCCP router inspects the redirection, assignment, and return methods selected by a WAN optimizer in the HIA message received in response to an ISU message. If the selected methods are not supported by the WCCP router, the WCCP router ignores the HIA message. If the selected methods are supported, the WCCP router accepts the WAN optimizer as usable and adds it to the SG.

In WCCPv2, a "receive ID" verifies two-way connectivity between a WCCP router and a WAN optimizer. The router identity info component of an ISU message contains the "receive ID" field. This field is maintained separately for each SG and its value is incremented each time the WCCP router sends an ISU message to the SG.

The "receive ID" sent by a WCCP router is reflected back by a WAN optimizer in the web-cache view info component of an HIA message. A WCCP router checks the value of the receive ID in each HIA message received from an SG member. If the value does not match the receive ID in the last ISU message sent to that member, the HIA message is discarded.

A router considers a WAN optimizer to be a usable member of an SG only after it has sent that WAN optimizer an ISU message and received a corresponding HIA message with a valid receive ID in response.

The Redirect_Assign (RA) message assigns the hash/mask assignment tables to the WCCP router for distributing redirected traffic across all of the WAN optimizers in the SG. The RA message is sent from a designated or lead WAN optimizer (selected based on lowest IP address in the SG) to all WCCP routers in the SG. It is identified by an assignment key and an assignment change number (ACN).

The left diagram of Figure 5.1 shows the WCCP initial handshake sequence:

- The first HIA message from the WCCP client to the WCCP router defines the SG properties.
- The first ISU message from the WCCP router to the WCCP client acknowledges the previous HIA message, accepts the SG properties, and initializes the receive ID to 1.
- The second HIA message reflects receive ID 1 and sets assignment weight and status.

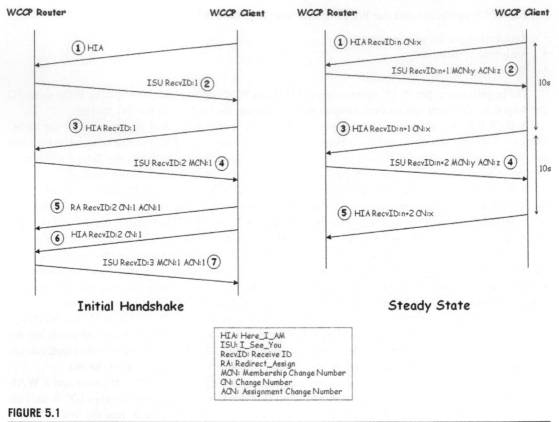

FIGURE 5.1

WCCP initial handshake and steady state communication

- The second ISU message includes the WCCP client in router view, increments the receive ID to 2, and initializes the membership change number (MCN) to 1.
- The first RA message reflects receive ID 2, sets the hash/mask tables (depending on whether the hash or mask assignment method is used), and initializes both the CN and ACN to 1.
- The third HIA reflects receive ID 2. CN remains unchanged at 1.
- The third ISU increments the receive ID to 3 and reflects ACN 1. MCN remains unchanged at 1.

The right diagram of Figure 5.1 shows the WCCP steady-state sequence:

- The HIA message reflects receive ID n. CN x remains unchanged.
- The next ISU message increments receive ID to n+1. MCN y and ACN z remain unchanged.
- The next HIA message reflects receive ID n+1. CN x remains unchanged.
- The next ISU message increments receive ID to n+2. MCN y and ACN z remain unchanged.
- The next HIA message reflects receive ID n+2. CN x remains unchanged.

If a WCCP router does not receive an HIA message from an SG member (WAN optimizer) for 25 sec, it queries the member by sending a Removal_Query (RQ) message to it.

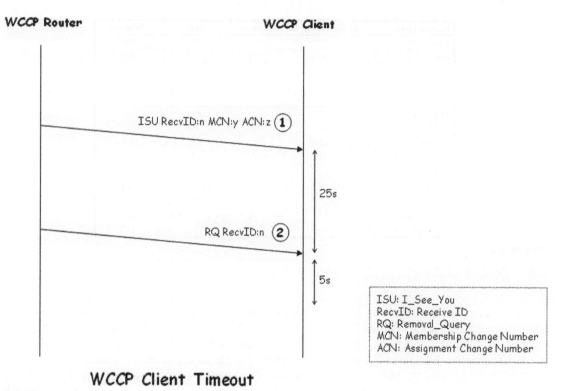

WCCP Client Timeout

FIGURE 5.2

WCCP client timeout

If the WCCP router does not receive an HIA message from the SG member for 30 sec, it considers the WAN optimizer to be unusable and removes it from the SG. The WAN optimizer no longer appears in the router view info component of the ISU message.

Figure 5.2 shows the WCCP client time-out sequence:

- WCCP router sends ISU message to WCCP client.
- WCCP client fails to send HIA message back to WCCP router within 25 sec.
- WCCP router sends RQ (removal_query) message to WCCP client directly.
- WCCP client fails to respond to RQ message within 5 sec.
- WCCP router removes WCCP client from its hash/mask assignment table, updates the router view, and increments MCN.

WCCP service groups

As discussed in the earlier subsection, the service info component of an HIA message specifies the SG in which a WAN optimizer wishes to participate. An SG is identified by a service type and an SG ID. There are two types of SGs:

- Well-known services
- Dynamic services

Service Name	Service Group ID	Protocol	Port	Priority
web-cache	0	tcp	80	240
dns	53	udp	53	202
ftp-native	60	tcp	21	200
tcp-promiscuous	61	tcp	*	34
tcp-promiscuous	62	tcp	*	34
https-cache	70	tcp	443	231
rtsp	80	tcp	554	200
wmt-mmst	81	tcp	1755	201
wmt-mmsu	82	udp	1755	201
rtspu	83	udp	554	201
cifs-cache	89	tcp	139, 445	224
custom	90-97	tcp	User Defined	220-227
custom-web-cache	98	tcp	User Defined	230
reverse-proxy	99	tcp	80	235

FIGURE 5.3

Cisco WCCP service groups

Well-known services are known by both WCCP routers and WCCP clients and do not require a description other than an SG ID. SG IDs range from 0 to 255. Currently, web-cache (HTTP) is the only defined well-known service. On the other hand, dynamic services are fully described to a WCCP router. The traffic description is communicated to the WCCP router in the HIA message of the first WCCP client that joins the SG. A WCCP client describes a dynamic service using the protocol, service flags, and port fields of the service info component. Once a dynamic service has been defined, the WCCP router discards any subsequent HIA message that contains a conflicting description. The WCCP router also discards an HIA message that describes an SG for which the router has not been configured.

Figure 5.3 lists the various WCCP SGs defined by Cisco.

In a WAN optimizer farm or cluster deployment, two SGs with opposing assignment methods (e.g., source-ip-hash in one direction and destination-ip-hash in the other) are recommended on the WCCP routers to ensure that the response packet is redirected to the same WAN optimizer that handled the request packet, regardless of which intercepting interface or on which WCCP router is participating in the SG where the packets are intercepted.

WCCP packet redirection can be processed on any interface in the ingress, the egress direction, or both. While multiple SGs can be defined on an interface in either direction, only one SG in each direction is selected for redirection based on the defined SG priority (see Figure 5.3 for the assigned SG priorities pertaining to Cisco WCCP service groups).

NOTE:

IOS and NX-OS provide optional support to evaluate all SGs configured on an interface in order of highest WCCP priority (using the "ip wccp check service all" command).

NOTE:

Cat6K evaluates all SGs regardless of WCCP SG priority in order of lower SG value (web-cache SG 0 is always first).

WCCP interception operation

WCCP interception is performed by the intercepting device or WCCP server that is physically in-path. The intercepting device monitors traffic traversing its interfaces based on interception configuration criteria to identify interesting traffic to be redirected to a WCCP service group client for WAN optimization. In this case, the WCCP client is the WAN optimizer.

WCCP interception takes place in two directions:

- **Ingress redirection (or inbound interception):** When ingress redirection ("ip wccp <SG> redirect in") is applied to an interface, the WCCP router monitors traffic entering an interface to determine whether it matches the intercept policies for any of the running SGs. The left diagram of Figure 5.4 illustrates an example of a WCCP ingress redirection.
- **Egress redirection (or outbound interception):** When egress redirection ("ip wccp <SG> redirect out") is applied to an interface, the WCCP router monitors traffic exiting an interface to determine whether it matches the intercept policies for any of the running SGs. The right diagram of Figure 5.4 shows an example of a WCCP egress redirection. For egress redirection, the exclude-in feature ("ip wccp exclude redirect in" command) is required on the WCCP router interface to which the WAN optimizer is connected. This is because packets returning from a WAN optimizer are routed normally and if redirection were not specifically excluded for these packets coming in from the router interface connecting the WAN optimizer, they are reintercepted and redirected again on egress from the router, resulting in a redirection loop (i.e., WCCP black hole).

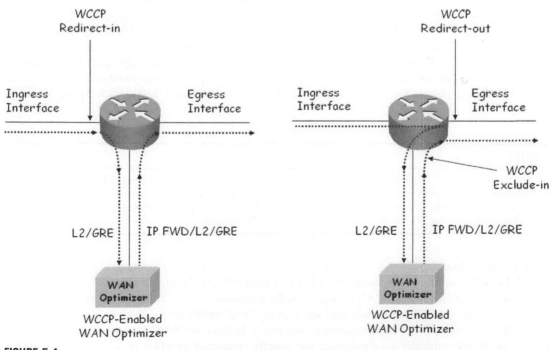

FIGURE 5.4

WCCP interception illustrations

> **NOTE:**
>
> Ingress redirection does not perform a routing table lookup before redirection, whereas egress redirection needs to perform a routing table lookup to reach the outbound interface for the egress redirection. Therefore, ingress redirection is more efficient and is generally preferred as it limits the CPU utilization impact of WCCP on the intercepting device as compared to egress redirection.

WCCP redirection schemes

The WCCP redirection scheme or forwarding method determines how intercepted traffic is sent to a specific WAN optimizer. There are two different redirection schemes:

- **GRE redirection:**
  - In the GRE redirection scheme, the entire intercepted packet is GRE encapsulated with the GRE header containing the routing information to the selected WAN optimizer. The WAN optimizer then decapsulates the packet for optimization.
  - When using GRE encapsulation for WCCP redirection, the WCCP router uses the WCCP router ID as its source IP address. The WCCP router ID is the highest loopback address on the WCCP router, or if the loopback interface is not configured, the highest address of the physical interfaces.
  - Since the WCCP router ID is used as the source address for packets redirected from the router to the WAN optimizer, it is also the corresponding destination address for traffic from the WAN optimizer to the router during GRE return (for more details, see the WCCP Return Schemes section).
  - The GRE redirection scheme allows the intercepted packets to reach the WAN optimizer even if there are multiple hops in the path between the WCCP router and the WAN optimizer. This allows the flexible placement of the WAN optimizer in cases where only L3 adjacency is provisioned.
  - In GRE redirection, the packet redirection is handled entirely by the router software. Therefore, the GRE redirection scheme is by default used by software routers (C7200 and Integrated Services Router) and the ASR1K.

> **NOTE:**
>
> In WCCPv2, the WCCP router ID is selected based on the highest IP address on the router or highest loopback (if configured). The WCCP process will automatically perform this task and you cannot override it with another user-defined value. Currently, the user-configurable WCCP router ID is only supported on the ASR1K router running IOS-XE Release 3.1S, using the "ip wccp source-interface" global command.

- **L2 redirection:**
  - In the L2 redirection scheme, the original Ethernet frame header is rewritten with the MAC address of the selected WAN optimizer as the destination MAC. The Ethernet frame containing the intercepted packet is then forwarded to the WAN optimizer.
  - The L2 redirection scheme requires L2 adjacency. In this case, WCCP router ID configuration of the WAN optimizer must reference the directly connected interface IP address of the WCCP router and not a loopback IP address or any other IP address configured on the WCCP router.

- The L2 redirection is performed in hardware and is typically available on L3 switches such as the Cat6K and C7600 platforms as well as the Nexus 7000 switch.
- Because L2 redirection is hardware assisted, it incurs a lower CPU utilization on the WCCP router. For this reason, L2 redirection is generally preferred over GRE redirection.

NOTE:

In L2 redirection, unless multicast IP addresses are used and multicast routing is enabled, the WCCP configuration of the WAN optimizer must reference the directly connected interface IP address of each WCCP router.

NOTE:

L2 redirection requires ingress redirection.

WCCP assignment methods

The assignment method is the mechanism that determines how intercepted traffic is distributed across the WCCP clients that are registered in the same SG. The assignment method is negotiated between a WCCP router and all WCCP clients on a per-SG basis. WCCP clients participating in multiple SGs can have different assignment methods for each SG, but all WCCP clients within a single SG will use the same assignment method. There are two available assignment methods: hash assignment and mask assignment.

A WCCP router advertises the supported assignment methods for an SG using the optional capabilities info component of the ISU message. The absence of such an advertisement means that the WCCP router only supports the default hash assignment method.

Hash assignment

The default assignment method, hash assignment, uses a 256-bucket redirection hash table to distribute traffic across the WCCP clients in an SG. The source/destination IP address or source/destination port (depending on the SG configuration) of the intercepted packet is run through a hash function to produce an index value. The index value maps into one of the 256 buckets in the hash table. Each bucket in the hash table is assigned to a WCCP client in the SG. Hash assignment is typically the default assignment method on software IOS routers.

Figure 5.5 illustrates the hashing and bucket assignment concept.

When a WAN optimizer joins a WCCP SG, it is allocated a portion of the address buckets. If there is only one WAN optimizer, then all buckets are assigned to that single WAN optimizer. When multiple WAN optimizers join the SG, the address buckets are divided among them. By default, each WAN optimizer is allocated an equal proportion of address buckets. An unequal division can be accomplished specifying an assignment weight.

NOTE:

The "show ip wccp <service-group-ID> hash <dst-ip> <src-ip> <dst-port> <src-port>" IOS exec command (hidden) can be used to verify the target WAN optimizer for a particular src/dst IP address and port combination that is used for the hash assignment. For instance, "show ip wccp 90 hash 0.0.0.0 10.1.2.3 0 0" reveals the target WAN optimizer for the source IP address 10.1.2.3.

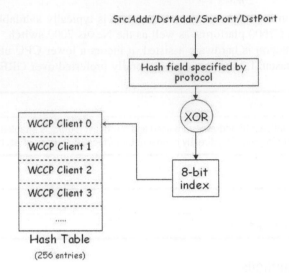

FIGURE 5.5

WCCP hashing assignment illustration

Mask assignment

The mask assignment method uses configurable mask values (up to 7 bits) to distribute traffic across the WAN optimizers in an SG. It allows WCCP interception to be performed completely in hardware on the WCCP server platforms. As the WCCP router intercepts traffic, a bitwise AND operation is performed between each mask value and the contents of the packet (specifically the source/destination IP addresses and ports). The result is then compared to a list of values for each mask. The value that matches the result corresponds to a specific WAN optimizer in the SG. The redirected traffic is forwarded to this WAN optimizer.

Figure 5.6 illustrates the masking and value assignment concept.

The mask value can be specified up to a maximum of 7 bits (128 address buckets). The number of bits that is specified determines the number of address buckets created for the assignment pool.

For example, an src-ip-mask value of 0x7 creates 8 address buckets (or a bucket size of 8). An assignment weight is used to manipulate the assignment of these buckets to a WAN optimizer.

The following mathematical terms are used for bucket calculation:

- Unit size is the bucket size divided by the total weight
- Buckets to assign is the WAN optimizer weight multiplied by the unit size, rounded to the nearest whole number

As an illustration, assuming there is only one WAN optimizer in the SG, using a weight of 25 results in:

- Unit size $= 8/100 = 0.08$
- Buckets to assign $= \text{round} (25 \times 0.08) = 2$

In this example, only two of the available eight address buckets are assigned to the WAN optimizer. Any source IP address whose mask result falls into one of the other (unassigned) six buckets will not be redirected and will be routed normally.

SrcAddr+DstAddr+SrcPort+DstPort

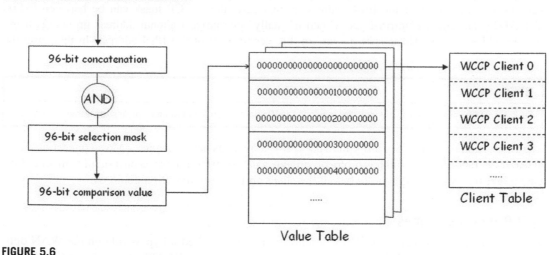

FIGURE 5.6

WCCP mask assignment illustration

Selecting a mask

What mask value to use? There are no simple answers to this question. This subsection will attempt to describe some of the basic fundamentals when constructing a mask. However, the mask to be derived really depends on the actual deployment environment and scale.

First, the number of bits used in the mask must provide enough address buckets to be allocated to each WAN optimizer assigned to the SG, taking into consideration the weight assigned to each WAN optimizer. For example, a 1-bit mask can support only two WAN optimizers ($2^1 = 2$). To support the maximum number of WAN optimizers in an SG, a 5-bit (or more) mask is required. A 5-bit mask is sufficient to support 32 WAN optimizers ($2^5 = 32$).

An IPv4 address in dotted decimal notation consists of four octets. When written in hexadecimal notation, each octet becomes two hexadecimal digits in the range of 0 to F. The WCCP mask is normally denoted in hexadecimal with leading zeros omitted. For example, assume the IP address is 10.1.2.3, which is equivalent to 0x0A010203 in hexadecimal notation, and the WCCP mask is 0x7 (eight address buckets). The result after the bitwise AND between these values is 0x3 (0x0A010203 AND 0x00000007 = 0x00000003).

The default source IP address mask is 0x1741 (the default destination IP address mask is 0x0). Although this is the default, it is not a recommended mask assignment because this mask value is inadequate to provide proper load balancing in most cases. However, if there is only one WAN optimizer in the SG, the mask used is irrelevant and the default mask can be used.

In a remote branch office (RBO), source IP addresses are usually assigned sequentially by DHCP. This results in addresses that vary only in the last octet of the IP address. In this scenario, mask distribution can be fully utilized by defining a WCCP mask in the range of 0x1 to 0x7F depending on the number of WAN optimizers deployed at the RBO.

A regional enterprise DC would typically have IP subnets with the /24 address mask. These subnets vary in the third octet of the IPv4 address. In this case, the WCCP mask can be between 0xF00 to 0x7F00. The main enterprise DC would normally summarize regional address groupings using the /16 address mask. These subnets vary in the second octet of the IPv4 address. In this case, the WCCP mask can be in the range of 0xF0000 to 0x7F0000.

> **NOTE:**
> For large-scale environments, higher-order octets in the IP address can load balance entire sites rather than hosts.

The connection ports are very difficult to use constructively as part of a mask. Most connections have at least one 'random' port and few protocols provide a nice distribution based on a small number of bits. One might try using the low order bits of the client port as a source of randomness.

WCCP return schemes

Packets that are not selected for WAN optimization (e.g., matched a bypass rule on the WAN optimizer) are returned to the WCCP router for normal forwarding. The WCCP return scheme (i.e., bypass return scheme) defines how this is done. There are two different return schemes:

- **GRE return (or L3 GRE return):** In the GRE return scheme, returning packets on the WAN optimizer are encapsulated with a GRE header specifying the WCCP router ID as the destination. Upon receipt, the WCCP router decapsulates the GRE-encapsulated packet and performs normal forwarding on the GRE-decapsulated packet. Since GRE decapsulation is processed on the router typically at the software level, the GRE return potentially increases the CPU load on the WCCP router.
- **L2 return (or L2 rewrite return):** The L2 return scheme rewrites the destination MAC address of the original Ethernet frame header with the MAC address of the WCCP service group router. Upon receiving the frame containing the return packet, the router proceeds to route the packet normally. The L2 return scheme requires the WAN optimizers to be L2 adjacent to the WCCP router.

> **NOTE:**
> The WCCP return scheme does not have to correspond to the redirection scheme. The return method is negotiated between a WCCP router and the WAN optimizer on a per–service group basis. A WCCP-enabled Cisco router advertises the supported packet return methods for a service group using the optional capabilities info component of the WCCP ISU message. The absence of such an advertisement implies the router supports the default GRE packet return method only.

WAN optimizer egress methods

Egress methods determine how the WAN optimizer sends traffic back to the WCCP router. The egress method includes both optimized packets and packets specified by policy action as pass-through. This is different from the return scheme, which is applicable only for pass-through packets.

The three options for egress traffic from the WAN optimizer to the WCCP router are as follows:

- IP forwarding
- Negotiated return
- Generic GRE return

IP forwarding

IP forwarding sends optimized packets to the configured default gateway of the WAN optimizer. With the IP forwarding egress method, the WAN optimizer cannot be placed on the same VLAN or subnet as the clients and servers that it optimizes. Otherwise, the egress traffic is reintercepted by the WCCP router creating a redirection loop. In addition, the IP forwarding egress method does not guarantee that the optimized packets are returned to the original intercepting WCCP router.

The IP forwarding is generally the default egress method for most WAN optimizers. However, this poses challenges in WAN optimizer deployments with multiple routers or redundant paths or in cases where the default gateway of each WAN optimizer points to a virtual IP address implemented by first-hop redundancy protocols such as GLBP, VRRP, and HSRP.

In such deployments, there might be a tendency for the WAN optimizer to send packets to a router other than the one that was used for interception and redirection. Negotiated return and generic GRE return are two other egress methods that ensure network path affinity. These methods ensure packets leaving the WAN optimizer return through the same forwarding path back to the intercepting WCCP router.

> **NOTE:**
> The Riverbed Steelhead appliance uses a "sticky-MAC" approach to ensure network path affinity.

Negotiated return

The negotiated return egress method determines what WCCP has negotiated for bypass return and uses that on the egress of the WAN optimizer for optimized packets. The behaviors of the negotiated return egress methods are similar to the bypass return schemes (for more details, see the WCCP Return Schemes section).

Generic GRE return

The generic GRE return egress method returns packets to the intercepting router by using a GRE tunnel manually configured on the WCCP router. Unlike the negotiated GRE return method, generic GRE return was designed to allow packets to be processed in hardware (hardware acceleration processing) on platforms like the C7600 router and the Cat6K switch (with Supervisor 32/720). Hence, generic GRE return overcomes the limitation of negotiated GRE return where packets are processed in software resulting in high CPU utilization.

Besides ensuring network path affinity, the GRE return egress method also removes requirement for a separate subnet dedicated to the WAN optimizer. By using the GRE return egress method, the WAN optimizer can now be placed on the same VLAN or subnet as the clients and servers that it optimizes.

> **NOTE:**
> The Cisco WAAS (wide-area application services) appliance supports negotiated return and generic GRE return.

WCCP server platform considerations

The WCCP server is the main focus of this chapter. It plays a pivotal role in WCCP-based WAN optimization deployments. Therefore, the correct selection of the various WCCP server platforms for WCCP implementation in different scenarios is instrumental. There are two main types of WCCP server platforms: hardware based and software based.

Hardware-based WCCP server platforms generally provide better performance and scalability as well as the support for the mask assignment method. Some of the WCCP hardware-based platforms include:

- Nexus 7000 switch
- ASR 1000 router
- C7600 router
- Cat6K Sup32/720 switch

Software-based WCCP server platforms are generally not suitable for large-scale environments or in cases where the WCCP router is already handling large traffic volume. The minimum IOS version for support per platform must be determined on a case by case basis. Software-based WCCP server platforms typically support only the hash assignment method where the hashing algorithm is hard-coded. Some of the software-based WCCP server platforms include:

- C7200 router
- Integrated services router (ISR)

NOTE:

The WCCP Server Platform Considerations section in this chapter was written in relation to cloud interception and private cloud computing. This is an ad hoc discussion session and not an authoritative guide. The reader is reminded to refer to appropriate official documents when evaluating products, designing solutions, or conducting business.

Nexus 7000 WCCP compatibility

The WCCP compatibility attributes for Nexus 7000 (NX7K) include:

- **Assignment method:** The NX7K supports only mask assignment.
- **Redirection method:** The NX7K supports L2 redirection in hardware. This requires that the WAN optimizers be directly connected to the Nexus switch. At the time of writing, GRE redirection is not supported.
- **Bypass packet return:** The NX7K supports WCCP L2 return in hardware. WCCP GRE return is not supported.
- **Packet egress:** IP forwarding and negotiated L2 return are the available egress return methods. The NX7K does not support GRE return (negotiated or generic).
- **Interface assignment:** Both ingress and egress redirections are supported. In most cases, ingress redirection is recommended for optimum performance.
- **Redirect list:** Redirect access control lists (ACLs) are supported.
- **VRF support:** The NX7K provide support for VRF-aware WCCP.

Since the NX7K switch supports VRF-aware WCCP and is hardware based, it is an ideal WCCP server platform for cloud interception implementations. The NX7K switches are normally located at the core/aggregation layers in the enterprise DC. In this case, cloud interception will take place at the core/aggregation layer. For more details, see the Cloud Interception with VRF-Aware WCCP section in Chapter 6.

> **NOTE:**
>
> The use of redirect ACLs (if supported) is recommended because they provide an explicit fan-in control mechanism that minimizes unnecessary routing, redirection, and packet processing.

C7600/Cat6K Sup32/720 WCCP compatibility

The WCCP compatibility attributes for C7600/Cat6K Sup32/720 include:

- **Assignment methods:** The C7600/Cat6K Sup32/720 supports both hash and mask assignments. For optimum performance, mask assignment should be used whenever possible.
- **Redirection methods:** The C7600/Cat6K Sup32/720 supports L2 redirection in hardware and GRE redirection in software. L2 redirection in hardware is recommended.
- **Bypass packet return:** The C7600/Cat6K Sup32/720 supports WCCP L2 return in hardware and WCCP GRE return in software. WCCP L2 return in hardware is recommended.
- **Packet egress:** The C7600/Cat6K Sup32/720 supports IP forwarding, negotiated return, and generic GRE return. IP Forwarding is typically not recommended, because there is no guarantee of network path affinity in a redundant WCCP deployment. Negotiated L2 return is recommended if the selected bypass packet return scheme is also L2. Otherwise, generic GRE return is recommended.
- **Interface assignment:** Both ingress and egress redirections are supported.
- **Redirect list:** Redirect ACLs are supported.

At the time of this writing, C7600 running IOS 12.2(33)SRE supports VRF-aware WCCP. The C7600 routers are normally located at the WAN edge/peering layer in the enterprise DC and the cloud interception takes place at the WAN edge/peering layer. The Cat6K platforms are generally deployed as aggregation/services aggregation-layer switches. In this case, cloud interception takes place either at the aggregation or services aggregation layer.

In terms of cloud interception, the main deterrent is the lack of support for VRF-aware WCCP in the existing IOS versions running on these platforms. Nevertheless, this deficiency can be overcome using the not-so-VRF (NSV) solution. For more details, see The Not-So-VRF Solution section in Chapter 6.

> **NOTE:**
>
> GRE redirection in hardware is supported on the Cat6K with the Sup720 Policy Feature Card 3 (PFC3).

> **NOTE:**
>
> For generic GRE return, the packets are processed in hardware on the C7600 router and the Cat6K switch with Sup32/720.

> **NOTE:**
>
> You can include the "accelerated" keyword in the "ip wccp <SG>" global command to enforce the use of L2 redirection and mask assignment on the C7600/Cat6K Sup 32/720 platforms.

> **NOTE:**
>
> The redirect-list on the C7600/Cat6K should be straightforward extended ACL with no permit port ranges, DSCP matches, and so on.

ISR and C7200 WCCP compatibility

The WCCP compatibility attributes for ISR and C7200 include:

- **Assignment methods:** The ISR and C7200 support only hash assignment prior to IOS 12.4(20)T. Mask assignment is available as of IOS 12.4(20)T.
- **Redirection methods:** The ISR and C7200 support only GRE redirection prior to IOS 12.4(20)T. L2 redirection is available as of IOS 12.4(20)T.
- **Bypass packet return:** The ISR and C7200 support only GRE packet return prior to IOS 12.4(20)T. L2 return is available as of IOS 12.4(20)T.
- **Packet egress:** The ISR and C7200 support IP forwarding and negotiated GRE return. Negotiated L2 return is available as of IOS 12.4(20)T.
- **Interface assignment:** Both ingress and egress redirections are supported.
- **Redirect list:** Redirect ACLs are supported.

Currently, ISR and C7200 running IOS 15.x support VRF-aware WCCP. For better performance of WCCP redirection and return, Cisco Express Forwarding (CEF) must be enabled. The ISRs are normally deployed at the remote branch offices (RBOs) as WAN branch routers.

ASR 1000 WCCP compatibility

The WCCP compatibility attributes for ASR 1000 (ASR1K) include:

- **Assignment method:** The ASR1K supports only mask assignment currently.
- **Redirection methods:** The ASR1K supports both the L2 and GRE redirection methods.
- **Bypass packet return:** The ASR1K supports both the L2 and GRE return methods.
- **Packet egress:** The ASR1K supports IP forwarding and negotiated return.
- **Interface assignment:** The ASR1K supports only ingress redirection.
- **Redirect list:** Redirect ACLs are supported.

At the time of this writing, ASR1K running IOS-XE 3.1.0S supports VRF-aware WCCP. The ASR1K routers are normally located at the WAN edge/peering layer in the enterprise DC. In this case, cloud interception takes place at the WAN edge/peering layer.

> **NOTE:**
>
> The ASR1K router incorporates WCCP variable timers in its IOS-XE WCCP feature set. The WCCP variable timers feature is a WCCPv2 enhancement not identified in the draft RFC. The variable timers are meant to improve (shorten) the current failover time (of 3 × 10 sec). Currently the WCCP variable timers are enabled by default and can pose WCCP registration issues with WAN optimizers (WCCP clients) that do not support this nacent feature. The workaround is to turn off the WCCP variable timers on the ASR1K router using the "no ip wccp variable-timers" (hidden) command.

WCCP design examples

It is time to explore some WCCP DC designs at the following locations:

- Core layer
- WAN edge/peering layer
- Aggregation/server distribution layer

Core layer: example 1

The DC core layer is typically the ideal placement for WCCP deployment because it sits in between the aggregation layer and the WAN edge/peering layer. The DC core layer is often where L3 design begins and L2 terminates. As shown in Figure 5.7, WAN optimizers (1 to 4) establish L2 adjacency with both SW1 and SW2 and are physically connected to both switches on a common subnet/VLAN.

In this scenario, the links from WAN optimizers 1 and 2 to SW1 are active while the links from WAN optimizers 1 and 2 to SW2 are standby. On the other hand, the links from WAN optimizers 3 and 4 to SW1 are standby, while the links from WAN optimizers 3 and 4 to SW2 are active. Thus to-be-optimized traffic from links 1, 3, 5, and 7 is redirected to WAN optimizers 1 and 2, whereas to-be-optimized traffic from links 2, 4, 6, and 8 is redirected to WAN optimizers 3 and 4, achieving N+1 redundancy. WCCP should not be implemented on the inter-core link (link 9) between SW1 and SW2.

> **NOTE:**
>
> In Example 1, N+1 redundancy implies that a WAN optimizer failure is only covered by another WAN optimizer. For instance, when WAN Optimizer 1 fails, it is backed up by WAN Optimizer 2. However, there is no redundancy (or backup) when both WAN optimizers 1 and 2 fail.

> **NOTE:**
>
> You can implement multi-interface WCCP using Riverbed Steelhead appliances. In this case, both links on the WAN optimizer (e.g., the Steelhead appliance) are considered active, achieving N+N redundancy.

Assuming SW1 and SW2 are hardware-based platforms (e.g., C7600/Cat6K), the WCCP attributes that are adopted in this example include:

- **Registration:** Since the WAN optimizers are L2 adjacent to SW1 and SW2, the corresponding WCCP router IDs must be the IP address of the directly connected interfaces in SW1 and SW2.

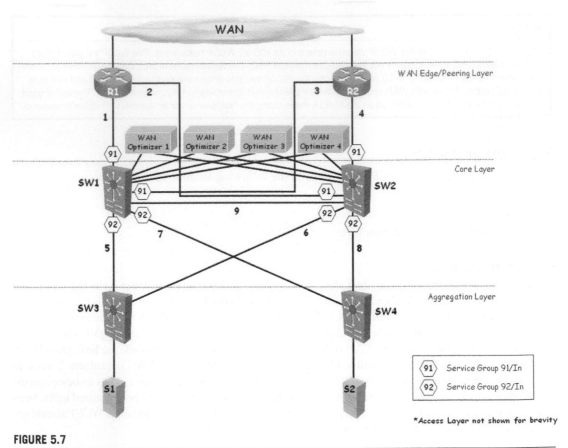

FIGURE 5.7

L2 WCCP deployment at the core layer

- **Assignment:** Mask assignment is recommended for optimum performance.
- **Redirection:** L2 redirection scheme is implemented.
  - WCCP SG 91 redirect-in, based on source IP address, is applied on links 1 and 3 of SW1 as well as links 2 and 4 of SW2 for traffic in the WAN-to-LAN direction.
  - WCCP SG 92 redirect-in, based on destination IP address, is applied on links 5 and 7 of SW1 as well as links 6 and 8 of SW2 for traffic in the LAN-to-WAN direction.
  - In other words, to cover all the traffic paths at the core layer in the topology shown in Figure 5.7, four point-of-interceptions (POIs) are required in each direction (i.e., WAN to LAN and LAN to WAN).
  - Since SG 91 load balances on the source IP and SG 92 load balances on the destination IP, the same TCP session in WAN-to-LAN and LAN-to-WAN directions goes back to the same WAN optimizer for optimization.
- **Return:** L2 return scheme is implemented.
- **Egress:** IP forwarding, negotiated L2 return, or generic GRE return.

> **NOTE:**
>
> The placement and direction of WCCP SG definitions is a key design requirement.

> **NOTE:**
>
> Although hardware-based platforms such as C7600/Cat6K support the negotiated return and generic GRE return, in order for these egress methods to work, the WAN optimizers involved must also support these methods.

Core layer: example 2

Example 2 shares the same network topology as Example 1. The difference is the WAN optimizers (1 to 4) now establish L3 adjacency with both SW1 and SW2. As shown in Figure 5.8, WAN optimizers 1 and 2 are each connected to a dedicated subnet/VLAN local to SW1. Likewise, WAN optimizers 3 and 4 are each connected to a dedicated subnet/VLAN local to SW2.

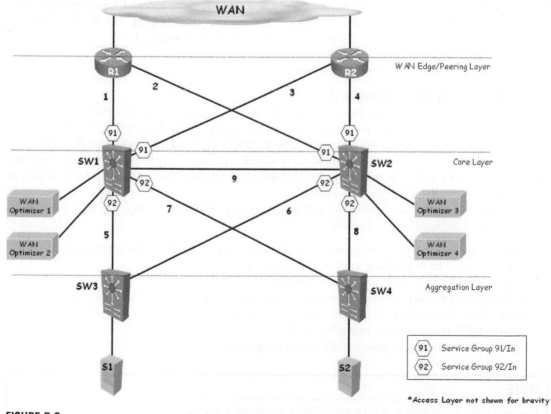

FIGURE 5.8

L3 WCCP deployment at the core layer

There are no standby WAN optimizer links in this example. In other words, the link from each WAN optimizer is active. Thus WAN optimizers 1 to 4 form a logical WCCP cluster, achieving N+N redundancy, even though they are each at a different subnet. Hence, to-be-optimized traffic from links 1 to 8 are redirected to WAN optimizers 1 to 4 accordingly based on the WCCP assignment scheme. WCCP must not implemented on the intercore routed link (link 9) between SW1 and SW2.

> **NOTE:**
>
> In Example 2, N+N redundancy means that a WAN optimizer failure is fully covered by the other WAN optimizers in the same SG. For instance, when WAN Optimizer 1 fails, it is backed up by WAN Optimizer 2. When both WAN optimizers 1 and 2 fail, they are backed up by WAN Optimizer 3 and/or WAN Optimizer 4.

Assuming that SW1 and SW2 are again hardware-based platforms (e.g., C7600/Cat6K), the WCCP attributes that are adopted in this example include:

- **Registration:** Since the WAN optimizers are L3 adjacent to SW1 and SW2, the corresponding WCCP router IDs must be the highest loopback IP address in each switch.
- **Assignment:** Mask assignment is recommended for optimum performance.
- **Redirection:** The GRE redirection scheme is implemented as there is only L3 adjacency between the WAN optimizers (1 to 4) and the WCCP servers (SW1 and SW2). The WCCP point-of-interceptions (POIs) and SG configurations are the same as in Example 1.
- **Return:** GRE return scheme is implemented.
- **Egress:** IP forwarding or generic GRE return.

WAN edge/peering layer: example 3

Example 3 is adapted directly from Example 2. As illustrated in Figure 5.9, the WCCP POIs and SG configurations are the only modifications. They are now implemented at R1 and R2 in the DC WAN edge/peering layer. In this example, the WAN optimizers (1 to 4) establish L3 adjacency with both R1 and R2.

Because the WCCP implementation is at the WAN edge/peering layer to cover all the traffic paths in the topology, only two POIs are required in each direction (i.e., WAN to LAN and LAN to WAN) as compared to four POIs in the previous examples.

Assuming R1 and R2 are hardware-based platforms (e.g., C7600/ASR1K), the WCCP attributes that are adopted in this example include:

- **Registration:** Since the WAN optimizers are L3 adjacent to R1 and R2, the corresponding WCCP router IDs must be the highest loopback IP address in each router.
- **Assignment:** Mask assignment is implemented.
- **Redirection:** The GRE redirection scheme is implemented as there is only L3 adjacency between the WAN optimizers (1 to 4) and the WCCP servers (R1 and R2).
- **Return:** GRE return scheme is implemented.
- **Egress:** IP forwarding or generic GRE return (negotiated return if ASR1K is used).

> **NOTE:**
>
> Hardware-based platforms (e.g., ASR1K and C7600) are preferred over software routers (e.g., C7200) at the WAN edge/peering layer. If software routers are used, the WCCP performance impact on these routers must be taken into consideration.

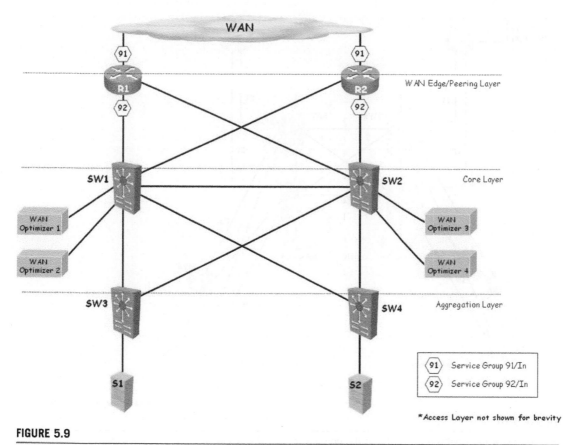

FIGURE 5.9

L3 WCCP deployment at the WAN edge/peering layer

WCCP deployment between two data centers: example 4

Instead of just a single DC, Example 4 goes one step further by examining the WCCP deployment between two DCs. As shown in Figure 5.10, there are two DCs: DC #1 and DC #2. Each DC has a single WAN edge/peering-layer router, two core-layer switches and two aggregation/server distribution-layer switches.

At DC #1, SW1 and SW3 are the core-layer switches and are interconnected by links 11 and 12 to the WAN edge/peering layer router, R1. WAN Optimizer 1 is connected to a dedicated subnet/VLAN local to SW1. Likewise, WAN Optimizer 3 is connected to a dedicated subnet/VLAN local to SW3. SW5 and SW7 are the aggregation/server distribution-layer switches. SW5 connects SW1 and SW2 with links 13 and 14 while SW7 connects SW1 and SW2 with links 15 and 16. Server S1 connects to SW5 while server S3 connects to SW7. S1 and S3 form the server farm in DC #1.

At DC #2, SW2 and SW4 are the core-layer switches and are interconnected by links 21 and 22 to the WAN edge/peering layer router, R2. WAN Optimizer 2 is connected to a dedicated subnet/VLAN local to SW2. Likewise, WAN Optimizer 4 is connected to a dedicated subnet/VLAN local to SW4. SW6 and SW8 are the aggregation/server-distribution-layer switches. SW6 connects SW2 and SW4

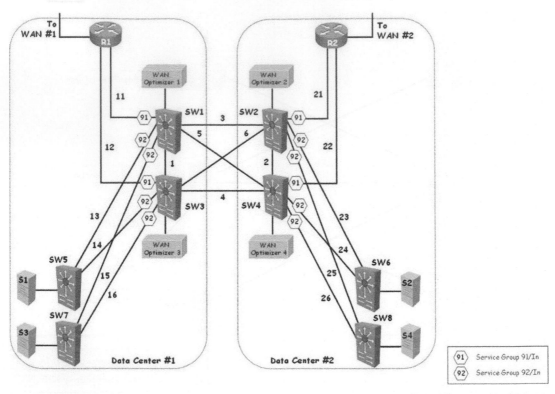

FIGURE 5.10

WCCP deployment between two DCs at the core layer

with links 23 and 24 while SW8 connects SW2 and SW4 with links 25 and 26. Server S2 connects to SW6 while server S4 connects to SW8. S2 and S4 form the server farm in DC #2.

The WCCP point-of-interceptions (POIs) and SG configurations are implemented on SW1 to SW4. The WAN optimizers (1 to 4) establish L3 adjacency with SW1 to SW4. Thus WAN optimizers 1 to 4 are a logical WCCP cluster, achieving N+N redundancy even though WAN optimizers 1 and 3 are in a different DC site from WAN optimizers 2 and 4. Hence, to-be-optimized traffic from links 11 to 16 and links 21 to 26 are redirected to WAN optimizers 1 to 4 accordingly based on the WCCP assignment scheme. WCCP must not be implemented on the fully meshed connection (links 1 to 6) between the four core-layer switches (SW1 to SW4).

> **NOTE:**
>
> The WCCP cross-registration between the WAN optimizers and the core-layer switches in both DCs helps to prevent issues that might arise from asymmetric routing.

> **NOTE:**
>
> Asymmetric routing can also be avoided by advertising only a summary route for each DC to the remote branch offices.

Assuming SW1 to SW4 are hardware-based platforms (e.g., C7600/Cat6K), the WCCP attributes that are adopted in this example include:

- **Registration:** Since L3 adjacency is established between the WAN optimizers (1 to 4) and the core-layer switches (SW1 to SW4), the corresponding WCCP router IDs must be the highest loopback IP address in each switch.
- **Assignment:** Mask assignment is implemented.
- **Redirection:** The GRE redirection scheme is implemented as there is only L3 adjacency between the WAN optimizers (1 to 4) and the WCCP servers (SW1 to SW4).
  - WCCP SG 91 redirect-in, based on source IP address, is applied on link 11 of SW1, link 12 of SW3, link 21 of SW2, and link 22 of SW4 for traffic in the WAN-to-LAN direction.
  - WCCP SG 92 redirect-in, based on destination IP address, is applied on links 13 and 15 of SW1, links 14 and 16 of SW3, links 23 and 25 of SW2, as well as links 24 and 26 of SW4 for traffic in the LAN-to-WAN direction.
  - To cover all the traffic paths at the core layer in the topology shown in Figure 5.10, four POIs are required in the WAN-to-LAN direction and eight POIs are required in the LAN-to-WAN direction.
- **Return:** GRE return scheme is implemented.
- **Egress:** IP forwarding or generic GRE return.

> **NOTE:**
>
> Since Example 4 involves WAN optimizers and WCCP servers at different physical locations, the WCCP peering between the WAN optimizers and WCCP servers with GRE return could be either over the metro area network (MAN) or the WAN. As the MAN typically has a lower latency than the WAN, the preferred WCCP peering path should ideally be over the MAN.

> **NOTE:**
>
> For optimal WCCP GRE return, explicitly specify a /32 (host) static route to the WCCP router ID or the GRE loopback.

WCCP deployment between two data centers: example 5

The network topology in Example 5 is adapted directly from Example 4. As illustrated in Figure 5.11, the WCCP POIs are shifted further down to the server-farm edge. The WCCP SG configurations are now implemented from SW5 to SW8 in the aggregation/server distribution layer for all the WAN-facing and server-facing links.

At DC #1, WAN Optimizer 1 is connected to a dedicated subnet/VLAN local to SW5. Likewise, WAN Optimizer 3 is connected to a dedicated subnet/VLAN local to SW7. At DC #2, WAN Optimizer 2 is connected to a dedicated subnet/VLAN local to SW6. Likewise, WAN Optimizer 4 is connected to a dedicated subnet/VLAN local to SW8.

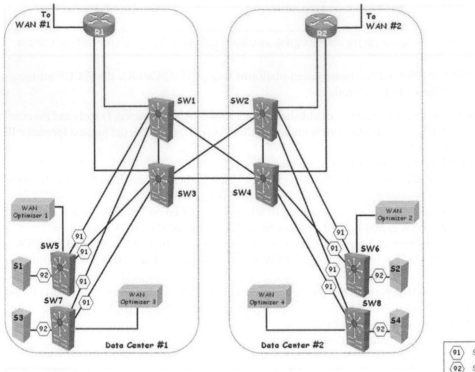

FIGURE 5.11

WCCP deployment at the server distribution layer

The WAN optimizers (1 to 4) establish L3 adjacency with SW5 to SW8. Thus WAN optimizers 1 to 4 are a logical WCCP cluster, achieving N+N redundancy. To cover all the traffic paths at the aggregation/server distribution layer, eight POIs are required in the WAN-to-LAN direction and four POIs are required in the LAN-to-WAN direction.

> **NOTE:**
> Implementing WAN optimizers and WCCP POIs at the aggregation/server distribution layer is another way to alleviate the asymmetric routing issue.

> **NOTE:**
> The connection forwarding feature in Riverbed Steelhead appliances can also be used to mitigate the impact of asymmetric routing.

Assuming SW5 to SW8 are hardware-based platforms (e.g., C7600/Cat6K), the WCCP attributes that are adopted in this example include:

- **Registration:** Since L3 adjacency is established between the WAN optimizers (1 to 4) and the aggregation/server distribution layer switches (SW5 to SW8), the corresponding WCCP router IDs should be the highest loopback IP address in each switch.
- **Assignment:** Mask assignment is implemented.
- **Redirection:** The GRE redirection scheme is implemented as there is only L3 adjacency between the WAN optimizers (1 to 4) and the WCCP servers (SW5 to SW8).
- **Return:** GRE return scheme is implemented.
- **Egress:** IP forwarding or generic GRE return.

WCCP configuration example

Figure 5.12 illustrates the simplified and scaled-down WCCP deployment between two DCs: DC-30 and DC-31. R30 and R31 are acting as both WAN and MAN routers. Branch office-to-DC (BO-to-DC) and DC-branch-office (DC-to-BO) traffic are through the WAN, whereas inter-DC traffic is through the MAN link. The only time the MAN link should be utilized for BO-to-DC and DC-to-BO traffic flows is when either one of the DC WAN links goes down.

Each DC is running a different application: File backup (FTP) in DC-31 and web applications (HTTP) in DC-30. FTP traffic from remote branch office RBO-32 goes to SERVER-31 (10.3.38.31) while HTTP traffic from RBO-32 goes to SERVER-30 (10.3.39.30). These application traffic flows between RBO-32 and the respective DCs are to be optimized by the corresponding WAN optimizers. WAN Optimizer 30 is connected to a dedicated subnet/VLAN local to R30, whereas WAN Optimizer 31 is connected to a dedicated subnet/VLAN local to R31.

The WAN optimization is based on the nearest WAN optimizer servicing the nearest application server, in this case, WAN Optimizer 30 for SERVER-30 and WAN Optimizer 31 for SERVER-31. The HA (backup redundancy) scheme is achieved via the far end WAN optimizer across the MAN link. In other words, WAN Optimizer 30 is the backup of WAN Optimizer 31 for SERVER-31 (FTP) and WAN Optimizer 31 is the backup of WAN Optimizer 30 for SERVER-30 (web services).

In this example, R30 and R31 are software routers running on IOS version 12.4(15)T9. The WCCP attributes to be implemented include:

- **Registration:** L3 adjacency is established between the WAN optimizers (30 and 31) and the WAN edge routers (R30 and R31). Therefore, the corresponding WCCP router ID is the highest loopback IP address in each router.
- **Assignment:** Hash assignment is implemented because the IOS version 12.4(15)T9 running on the software routers only supports this particular assignment method.
- **Redirection:** The GRE redirection scheme is implemented because there is only L3 adjacency between the WAN optimizers (30 and 31) and the WCCP servers (R30 and R31).
  - WCCP HA redundancy can be implemented through the use of two SGs, each with a different assignment weight.
  - The hash assignment in this example is based on both the source and destination IP addresses so the same WCCP SG can be utilized in both the WAN-to-LAN and LAN-to-WAN directions.

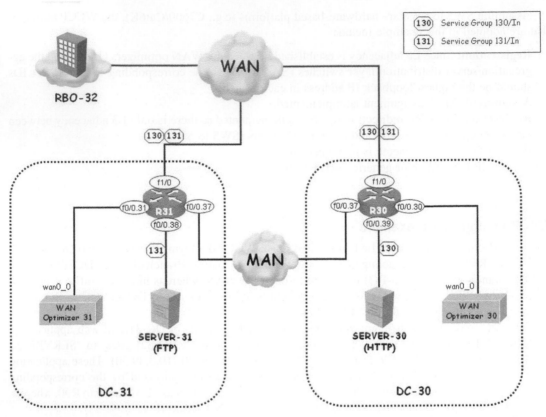

FIGURE 5.12

WCCP deployment between two DCs at the WAN edge

SG 130 and SG 131 are defined in both the WAN optimizers (30 and 31). WCCP SG 130 is created for redirecting traffic (HTTP) pertaining to DC-30 and WCCP SG 131 is created for redirecting traffic (FTP) pertaining to DC-31.

- WAN Optimizer 30 is the active WAN optimizer for DC-30 and the standby WAN optimizer for DC-31. Different assignment weights can be allocated to SG 130 and SG 131 on WAN Optimizer 30 to achieve this HA configuration. In the example, SG 130 is configured with an assignment weight of 100 (active) and SG 131 is configured with an assignment weight of 0 (standby).
- WAN Optimizer 31 is the active WAN optimizer for DC-31 and the standby WAN optimizer for DC-30. Different assignment weights are allocated to SG 130 and SG 131 on WAN Optimizer 31 to achieve this HA configuration. In the example, SG 130 is configured with an assignment weight of 0 (standby) and SG 131 is configured with an assignment weight of 100 (active).

- At R30 in DC-30, WCCP SG 130 redirect-in is applied on interface f1/0 for redirecting WAN-to-LAN HTTP traffic flows and on interface f0/0.39 for redirecting LAN-to-WAN HTTP traffic flows to WAN Optimizer 30. In addition, WCCP SG 131 redirect-in is applied on interface f1/0 for redirecting WAN-to-LAN FTP traffic flows to WAN Optimizer 31 when the WAN link of DC-31 is out of service.
- At R31 in DC-31, WCCP SG 131 redirect-in is applied on interface f1/0 for redirecting WAN-to-LAN FTP traffic flows and on interface f0/0.38 for redirecting LAN-to-WAN FTP traffic flows to WAN Optimizer 31. In addition, WCCP SG 130 redirect-in is applied on interface f1/0 for redirecting WAN-to-LAN HTTP traffic flows to WAN Optimizer 30 when the WAN link of DC-30 is out of service.
- To cover all the traffic paths at the WAN edge as shown in Figure 5.12, one POI (not considering the standby POI) is required in each direction (i.e., WAN-to-LAN and LAN-to-WAN) per DC.
- Since both SG 130 and SG 131 load-balance based on the source and destination IP hash, the same TCP session in the WAN-to-LAN and LAN-to-WAN directions will go back to the same WAN optimizer for optimization.
- The MAN link must be the best path for inter-DC traffic. WCCP redirection must not be implemented on the MAN link between R30 and R31.
- **Return:** GRE return scheme is implemented.
- **Egress:** IP forwarding is implemented.

> **NOTE:**
> In this example, the WCCP priority value of 250 is set for both SG 130 and SG 131.

> **NOTE:**
> The WAN optimizers that are deployed in this example are Riverbed Steelhead appliances running RiOS 5.x.

WCCP client configurations

Code Listing 5.1 shows the WCCP configurations for WAN Optimizer 30 (i.e., a Riverbed Steelhead appliance). To facilitate WAN Optimizer 30 as the active WAN optimizer for DC-30 and the standby WAN optimizer for DC-31, WCCP SG 130 is configured with an assignment weight of 100 and WCCP SG 131 is configured with an assignment weight of 0.

The priority for both SGs is 250. The encap-scheme (redirection) is set to "either," which means that WAN Optimizer 30 can support both the GRE and L2 redirection schemes. Likewise, the assign scheme is set to "either," which means WAN Optimizer 30 can support both the hash and mask assignment methods. Since the WCCP servers are software-based platforms, GRE redirection and hash assignment will eventually be negotiated and selected.

The hash assignment is based on source and destination IP hash so a single SG can be utilized in both WAN-to-LAN and LAN-to-WAN directions. In terms of WCCP registration, L3 adjacency is established between WAN Optimizer 30 and the highest loopback IP address (WCCP router ID) of the WAN edge routers (R30 and R31). In this case, the loopback IP addresses are 10.3.0.3 and 10.3.0.1 for R30 and R31, respectively.

```
## Network interface configuration
##
    interface inpath0_0 ip address 10.3.30.101 /24


##
## Routing configuration
##
    ip in-path-gateway inpath0_0 "10.3.30.3"


##
## Other IP configuration
##
    hostname "WANOPTIMIZER30"


##
## WCCP Service Groups
##
    wccp service-group 130 protocol tcp weight 100 encap-scheme either priority 250
flags dst-ip-hash,src-ip-hash routers 10.3.0.1,10.3.0.3 assign-scheme either
    wccp service-group 131 protocol tcp weight 0 encap-scheme either priority 250 flags
dst-ip-hash,src-ip-hash routers 10.3.0.1,10.3.0.3 assign-scheme either


##
## General Service
##
    in-path enable
    in-path module wccp-adjust-mss enable
    in-path oop enable
    wccp enable
```

CODE LISTING 5.1

WCCP configuration for WAN Optimizer 30

NOTE:

Do not use a virtual gateway address (derived from HSRP, VRRP, or GLBP) as the WCCP router ID.

NOTE:

The "in-path module wccp-adjust-mss enable" command adjusts the appropriate MSS size for the Riverbed Steelhead appliance during WCCP operation to avoid unnecessary packet fragmentation or drops due to outsize packets when WCCP GRE redirection and return are selected.

> **NOTE:**
>
> The Riverbed Steelhead appliance allows the WCCP redirection of ICMP messages to support Path MTU Discovery (PMTUD).

> **NOTE:**
>
> PMTUD uses ICMP type 3, subtype 4 (Fragmentation needed and DF set) for notification. This is equivalent to the "packet-too-big" ICMP message defined on ICMP extended ACLs.

Code Listing 5.2 shows the WCCP configuration for WAN Optimizer 31 (i.e., a Riverbed Steelhead appliance). To keep WAN Optimizer 31 as the standby WAN optimizer for DC-30 and the active WAN optimizer for DC-31, WCCP SG 130 is configured with an assignment weight of 0 and WCCP SG 131 is configured with an assignment weight of 100. The rest of the WCCP configuration is similar to those in Code Listing 5.1.

```
## Network interface configuration
##
    interface inpath0_0 ip address 10.3.31.101 /24


##
## Routing configuration
##
    ip in-path-gateway inpath0_0 "10.3.31.1"


##
## Other IP configuration
##
    hostname "WANOPTIMIZER31"


##
## WCCP Service Groups
##
    wccp service-group 130 protocol tcp weight 0 encap-scheme either 250 flags dst-ip-
hash,src-ip-hash routers 10.3.0.1,10.3.0.3 assign-scheme either
    wccp service-group 131 protocol tcp weight 100 encap-scheme either priority 250
flags dst-ip-hash,src-ip-hash routers 10.3.0.1,10.3.0.3 assign-scheme either
    ##
## General Service
##
    in-path enable
    in-path module wccp-adjust-mss enable
    in-path oop enable
    wccp enable
```

CODE LISTING 5.2

WCCP configuration for WAN Optimizer 31

WCCP server configurations

Code Listing 5.3 illustrates the WCCP server configurations for R30. The WCCP router ID is 10.3.0.3, which is based on Loopback0. WCCP SG 130 is configured to redirect TCP traffic from CLIENT-32 (10.3.32.99) from remote branch office RBO-32 to SERVER-30 (10.3.39.30) at DC-30 and from SERVER-30 back to CLIENT-32. The WCCP POIs for SG 130 are at FastEthernet0/0.39 and FastEthernet1/0. WCCP SG 131 is configured to redirect TCP traffic from CLIENT-32 to SERVER-31 when the WAN link at DC-31 is out of service. The WCCP POI for SG 131 is at FastEthernet1/0.

```
!
hostname R30
!
!
ip wccp check services all
ip wccp 130 redirect-list 130
ip wccp 131 redirect-list 131
!
!
interface Loopback0
  ip address 10.3.0.3 255.255.255.255
!
!
interface FastEthernet0/0.30
  encapsulation dot1Q 30
  ip address 10.3.30.3 255.255.255.0
!
!
interface FastEthernet0/0.37
  encapsulation dot1Q 37
  ip address 10.3.37.3 255.255.255.0
!
interface FastEthernet0/0.39
  encapsulation dot1Q 39
  ip address 10.3.39.3 255.255.255.0
  ip wccp 130 redirect in
!
interface FastEthernet1/0
  ip address 10.254.3.3 255.255.255.0
  ip wccp 130 redirect in
  ip wccp 131 redirect in
!
!
access-list 130 permit tcp host 10.3.32.99 host 10.3.39.30
access-list 130 permit tcp host 10.3.39.30 host 10.3.32.99
access-list 131 permit tcp host 10.3.32.99 host 10.3.38.31
!
```

CODE LISTING 5.3

WCCP configuration for R30

NOTE:

When there are multiple WCCP SGs configured on an interface, the SGs are considered in priority order (not applicable to Cat6K) until an SG is found that matches the IP packet. If an SG matches the packet and has a redirect ACL configured, the IP packet is checked against the redirect ACL. If the packet is rejected by the ACL, the packet is not be passed down to lower priority SGs for further matching unless the "ip wccp check services all" command is configured. When the "ip wccp check services all" command is configured, WCCP continues to match the packet against any remaining lower priority SGs configured on the interface.

Code Listing 5.4 illustrates the WCCP server configuration for R31. The WCCP router ID is 10.3.0.1, which is based on Loopback0. WCCP SG 131 is configured to redirect TCP traffic from CLIENT-32 (10.3.32.99) to SERVER-31 (10.3.38.31) at DC-31 and from SERVER-31 back to CLIENT-32. The WCCP POIs for SG 131 are at FastEthernet0/0.38 and FastEthernet1/0. WCCP SG 130 is configured to redirect TCP traffic from CLIENT-32 to SERVER-30 when the WAN link at DC-30 is out of service. The WCCP POI for SG 130 is at FastEthernet1/0.

```
!
hostname R31
!
!
ip wccp check services all
ip wccp 130 redirect-list 130
ip wccp 131 redirect-list 131
!
!
interface Loopback0
  ip address 10.3.0.1 255.255.255.255
!
!
interface FastEthernet0/0.31
  encapsulation dot1Q 31
  ip address 10.3.31.1 255.255.255.0
!
interface FastEthernet0/0.37
  encapsulation dot1Q 37
  ip address 10.3.37.1 255.255.255.0
!
interface FastEthernet0/0.38
  encapsulation dot1Q 38
  ip address 10.3.38.1 255.255.255.0
  ip wccp 131 redirect in
!
interface FastEthernet1/0
  ip address 10.254.3.1 255.255.255.0
  ip wccp 130 redirect in
  ip wccp 131 redirect in
!
```

```
!
access-list 130 permit tcp host 10.3.32.99 host 10.3.39.30
access-list 131 permit tcp host 10.3.32.99 host 10.3.38.31
access-list 131 permit tcp host 10.3.38.31 host 10.3.32.99
!
```

CODE LISTING 5.4

WCCP configuration for R31

IN-PATH DEPLOYMENT IN BRIEF

Deploying WAN optimizers in-line to cover the enterprise DC is a challenging task suitable for some, but not most, DC designs. In terms of POIs, physical in-path or in-line deployment has to be properly aligned with the actual physical links to cover all the traffic paths in a particular network topology in the DC. The in-path deployment can pose scalability challenges as the number of links (for HA purposes) increases in a large redundant DC network topology. It is likely that multiple WAN optimizers will be required and that they will need to communicate with each other. This cross-communication (like active–active firewalls) is necessary because a single connection can only be sensibly optimized at the application layer from one device. The in-path deployment might be considered disruptive as well since the placement of the WAN optimizer appliance would have to come in between the two endpoints of an existing physical link. Therefore, an in-path deployment is not a common practice for WAN optimization interception in the DC.

Figure 5.13 illustrates a very simple in-path deployment between two sites, A and B. The WAN optimizer is connected physically between network elements such as the switch and the router (or firewall) with an LAN-facing and a WAN-facing interface, respectively. It inspects all traffic and determines which traffic to optimize with the help of optimization rules. In this case, interception takes place in both directions (i.e., WAN-to-LAN and LAN-to-WAN). Non-TCP traffic is automatically bypassed, whereas TCP traffic that does not require optimization is passed through with a bypass rule.

NOTE:

In physical in-path deployment, all traffic traverses the respective WAN optimizers and there is no traffic fan-in control.

Since a physically in-path WAN optimizer constitutes a single point of failure during a hardware, software, or power failure, it typically is equipped with a mechanical fail-to-wire mechanism to form a link between the LAN-facing and WAN-facing interfaces when these events occur. It is a best practice to match the number of parallel routing paths with the number of WAN optimizers (i.e., redundant WAN routers imply redundant WAN optimizers). A single layer of WAN optimizers can be supported using fail-to-block (where, upon failure, they take the link down) if cross-connects enable traffic to flow through the other path. Two layers of WAN optimizers enable the use of fail-to-wire where the second layer picks up optimized connections. These levels of redundancy also require that the WAN optimizers communicate with each other to maintain an optimized connection state (e.g., connection forwarding on Riverbed Steelhead appliances).

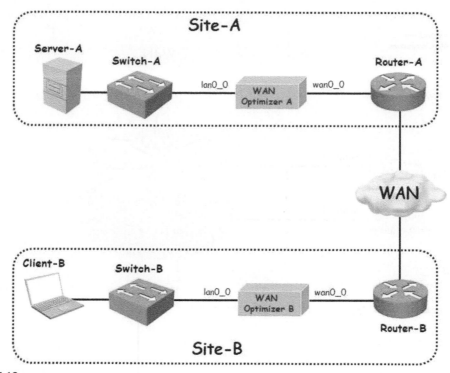

FIGURE 5.13

Simple physical in-path deployment illustration

Physical in-path deployment is extremely common for smaller sites such as remote branch offices (RBOs). This leads to the temptation to use it for regional DCs as well. One advantage of a physical in-path deployment is that it might not require any configuration changes on the in-line network elements (e.g., switches, routers, firewalls, etc.) and it is not dependent on the interception capabilities of other platforms. A physical in-path deployment is an alternative interception method for WAN optimization in DCs when WCCP is not available.

PBR DEPLOYMENT OVERVIEW

In policy-based routing (PBR) deployments, the WAN optimizer is placed physically out-of-path just like in WCCP implementations. The POIs are implemented on the in-line network elements such as the routers (or L3 switches). These in-line devices also have to support PBR. PBR that is configured on the intercepting router performs traffic inspection to match interesting traffic with an ACL and redirects the traffic to the WAN optimizer for optimization. In this case, the WAN optimizer is the L3 next-hop.

Figure 5.14 illustrates a simple PBR deployment for WAN optimization in the DC. WAN Optimizer 101 is the primary and WAN Optimizer 102 is the secondary. Each WAN optimizer is connected to a dedicated subnet local to R1. PBR interception is implemented at POI A, the WAN-facing interface of R1, as well as at POI B and POI C, the LAN-facing interfaces of R1.

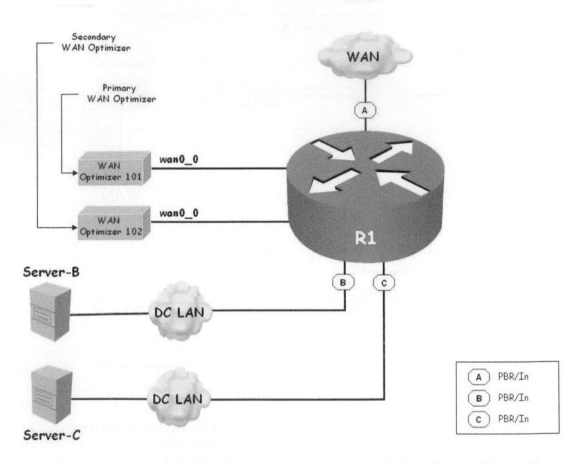

FIGURE 5.14

Simple PBR deployment for WAN optimization

NOTE:

The implicit direction of PBR "interception" is ingress. Put another way, PBR is only applicable to inbound traffic going through an interface.

PBR is not considered a leading practice for WAN optimization interception in the DC because it does not scale well and cannot easily load balance across multiple WAN optimizers. PBR is also more tedious to configure as compared to WCCP because it is not really a protocol, but rather an administratively configured static mechanism ("route-map"). PBR deployment is an alternative interception method for WAN optimization in DCs when WCCP is not available.

PBR failover

A PBR deployment for WAN optimization can support failover if multiple next-hop addresses are defined. The multiple next-hop addresses correspond to the IP addresses of the WAN optimizers. This requires the implementation of PBR with CDP support on the WAN optimizer or with object tracking. The object tracking is performed with the help of an IP service-level agreement (SLA) monitoring agent or probe. The IP SLA probe ensures the liveliness of the primary WAN optimizer by performing active health monitoring. A track object is then defined to track the corresponding IP SLA probe operation. If the operation fails, the primary WAN optimizer (i.e., the next-hop) is considered to be "down" (i.e., out of service). To-be-optimized traffic is then redirected to a secondary WAN optimizer.

Code Listing 5.5 depicts a sample IP SLA and objection tracking configuration template. The IP addresses of WAN Optimizer 101 and WAN Optimizer 102 are 10.10.10.101 and 10.20.20.102, respectively. IP SLA 101 is created to monitor the L3 connectivity status of WAN Optimizer 101. Likewise, IP SLA 102 is created for WAN Optimizer 102. An ICMP probe is sent to each WAN optimizer every 5 sec ("frequency 5"). For continuous monitoring, each IP SLA monitoring agent is scheduled to run permanently ("forever") with immediate effect ("now"). Track object 1 ("track 1") is defined to track the operational status (up/down) of IP SLA 101 ("rtr 101") while track object 2 ("track 2") is defined to track the operational status (up/down) of IP SLA 102 ("rtr 102")

NOTE:

The default frequency for IP SLA probes is 60 seconds.

```
!
ip sla 101
  icmp-echo 10.10.10.101
  frequency 5
ip sla schedule 101 life forever start-time now
!
!
ip sla 102
  icmp-echo 10.20.20.102
  frequency 5
ip sla schedule 102 life forever start-time now
!
!
track 1 rtr 101 reachability
track 2 rtr 102 reachability
!
```

CODE LISTING 5.5

IP SLA and object-tracking configurations

> **NOTE:**
>
> Some IOS versions support IP SLA operations with slightly different navigation or methods of creation although the overall methods for creating IP SLA operations are the same. The question mark (?) command can assist to find the correct commands for that IOS. The IP SLA and object-tracking configuration examples in this section are based on IOS version 12.4(15)T9.

> **NOTE:**
>
> Although the example uses ICMP probes for simplicity reasons, TCP probes are preferred when it comes to monitoring the WAN optimizers. TCP probes are able to detect both L3 and L4 connectivity issues, whereas ICMP probes can only detect L3 connectivity issues.

Code Listing 5.6 depicts a sample PBR object-tracking route-map. The route-map "PBR" matches traffic permitted by ACL 100 (actual ACL is not shown in the code listing for purposes of brevity). The route-map redirects the traffic matched by ACL 100 only to the first available next-hop (with sequence number "10"), in this case, the IP address (10.10.10.101) of WAN Optimizer 101. If the L3 connectivity to WAN Optimizer 101 becomes unavailable, the traffic matched by ACL 100 is redirected to the succeeding next-hop (with sequence number "20"), i.e., WAN Optimizer 102 (10.20.20.102). In the event when both WAN optimizers are unavailable, traffic matched by ACL 100 is not redirected by PBR; instead the router reverts to normal destination-based forwarding.

```
!
route-map PBR permit 10
  match ip address 100
  set ip next-hop verify-availability 10.10.10.101 10 track 1
  set ip next-hop verify-availability 10.20.20.102 20 track 2
!
```

CODE LISTING 5.6

PBR object-tracking route-map configurations

> **NOTE:**
>
> A large number of IP SLA monitoring sessions can result in CPU spikes because the CPU generates ICMP or trace-route packets for the ICMP probes. The workaround is to set the track interval (frequency) to a longer value. Instead of using a frequency of 5 seconds in Code Listing 5.5, you might want to revert to the default frequency of 60 seconds. In this case, the trade-off is a slower detection time during a next-hop outage.

SUMMARY

When designing and deploying session interception for WAN optimization in the DC, consideration must be taken in terms of hardware platform, placement, scalability requirements, load balancing, high availability, operational impact, and manageability.

WCCP is one of the most comprehensive interception solutions available and is widely deployed in most enterprise DCs. WCCP can be implemented on a wide range of platforms. It also provides good load balancing, failover, and scalability. WCCP can be deployed at most of the hierarchical network layers in the DC, provided the available network elements (e.g., L3 switch, router, and so on) at these locations support WCCP. The placement locations include:

- WAN edge/peering layer
- Core/aggregation layer
- Access layer
- Server distribution layer

Physical in-path is the least complex interception mechanism from a router configuration point of view. However, great care must be taken in the configuration of redundancy and scaling mechanisms in order to meet DC resiliency and uptime goals. Because of in-path's dominance outside the DC there are diverse configurations available to engineer an in-path deployment for a small DC. A direct in-path WAN optimizer deployment is not well suited to clustering for load scaling, although it has been deployed in practice.

PBR is another interception option. It can be used with many platforms, thus it provides the flexibility of placement in the DC. However, PBR lacks the scalability options for load balancing without incurring considerable configuration complexity. Therefore, the recommendation is to use WCCP whenever possible and revert to physical in-path or PBR when WCCP is not available.

The next chapter (Chapter 6) covers WCCP further from the cloud interception and L3 VRF perspective. The Application Control Engine Service Module (ACESM), a more scalable alternative to WCCP, is also discussed extensively with respect to cloud interception and network virtualization.

WAN Optimization in the Private Cloud

6

If everything seems under control, you're just not going fast enough.
—**Mario Andretti**

INFORMATION IN THIS CHAPTER:

- WAN Optimization Requirements in the Cloud
- Interception at the VM Level
- Cloud Interception with VRF-Aware WCCP
- Cloud Interception with Non–VRF-Aware WCCP
- Interception at the Services Aggregation Layer
- Summary

INTRODUCTION

Chapter 4 discussed the need for WAN optimization and its benefits. Chapter 5 looked at standard appliance-based integration options for WAN optimization within the DC. However, cloud deployment has rapidly evolved to virtual private clouds moving away from the appliance model. Private clouds are typically co-located on the enterprise DC premises while virtual private clouds are built by cloud service providers to allow enterprises a way to extend their resources in an on-demand and adaptive manner. This can further increase latency and the need for WAN optimization.

> **NOTE:**
> A virtual private cloud is a private cloud existing within a shared or public cloud (i.e., the intercloud). The term is derived from the familiar concept of a virtual private network (VPN), but applicable to cloud computing.

WAN optimization defuses the adverse effects of latency on application performance over the WAN, clearly useful where you run your own cloud. By incorporating WAN optimization as part of the cloud infrastructure, private and virtual private cloud service providers can now offer value-added cloud-optimized application services (e.g., cloud IaaS). This can improve their value proposition by removing the WAN bottleneck they would otherwise force on their customers. In cloud computing, WAN optimization is strategically more important than before because it expedites cloud adoption. WAN optimization has become an indispensable component in cloud-based service delivery architectures or the service-oriented infrastructure (SOI).

Chapter 6 extends Chapter 5 further by elaborating on the session interception techniques that can be deployed in private cloud computing building blocks (see Figure 2.1).

WAN OPTIMIZATION REQUIREMENTS IN THE CLOUD

There are more requirements to consider for WAN optimization in the cloud as compared to WAN optimization for conventional remote branch consolidation. Some of these requirements include:

- **Adaptive deployment model:** Use the WAN optimization service to construct cloud service offerings (e.g., cloud IaaS) in a modular fashion on top of the SOI so that these offerings can be repurposed adaptively in response to changing user requirements. WAN optimization is a clear service differentiator as the cloud provider can now offer an optimized application service in contrast to a basic computing service.
- **Minimal network configuration and disruption:** There should be minimal network configuration needed to optimize newly commissioned VM instances and ideally no network disruption throughout the WAN optimization deployment process.
- **Support for multitenant environments:** Multitenant environments should be supported, especially in cloud IaaS offerings. The idea is to reduce the CAPEX and OPEX for the cloud service provider.
- **VMotion aware:** The WAN optimization service deployed for a set of application servers must be constantly available regardless of the physical location of the application server VMs.
- **Elastic scale-out:** The WAN optimization service requires an elastic scale-out deployment approach to dynamically adapt to growth fluctuations as the number of tenants/subscribers increases or decreases. Elastic scale-out involves adding more WAN optimizers to match the server increase. The best approach is to have these WAN optimizers in a virtual form-factor.
- **Virtualized deployment:** The WAN optimization service should be based on virtual appliances rather than physical ones. The virtual form-factor can be deployed on demand (i.e., in a precabled and preracked server), whereas physical appliances need to be racked, stacked, and cabled. Virtual appliances reduce hardware costs in multitenant environments because a dedicated physical device is no longer required for each tenant. Cloud providers can also scale up the performance of virtual appliances when user demand increases by moving to more powerful platforms or by adding more resources to existing platforms.

> **NOTE:**
>
> A virtual appliance is considered as a logical entity or virtual device context (VDC) partitioned out of a physical appliance. The virtual appliance is basically software. Unlike a physical appliance, it does not come with a hardware platform. The user has to provide this.

INTERCEPTION AT THE VM LEVEL

The WAN optimizer in virtual form-factor alone is not sufficient to meet all the requirements mentioned in the previous section. It has to work in conjunction with the various interception methods adopted. This section briefly describes a "deep in the DC" interception approach at the VM level (see Figure 2.1).

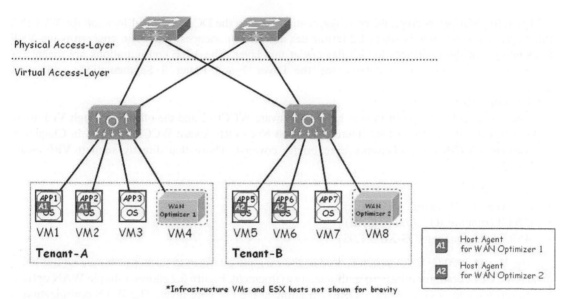

FIGURE 6.1

Interception with host agents

In the application host level or VM level interception approach, each tenant VM that needs to be optimized has a special interface driver or agent installed for intercepting and redirecting the "interesting" traffic to and from the tenant VM to the virtual WAN optimizer for optimization. Although the concept of a host agent per tenant VM might seem tedious, this particular method actually fulfills most of the requirements discussed in the WAN Optimization Requirements in the Cloud section without requiring sophisticated network integration. Figure 6.1 illustrates the VM level interception.

NOTE:

The Riverbed Cloud Steelhead appliance supports interception at the VM level. The tenant VM that needs to be optimized requires a discovery agent for intercepting and redirecting traffic to the Cloud Steelhead appliance. Cloud Steelhead appliance clustering is supported using either a priority (default) or a round-robin load-balancing scheme.

CLOUD INTERCEPTION WITH VRF-AWARE WCCP

Other than the deep-in-DC interception tactic at the VM level, traditional out-of-path interception mechanisms can also be deployed in the private cloud farther away from the server farms (or VMs) but closer to the WAN edge. In this section, the focus is on the more conventional ways of intercepting and redirecting traffic for private cloud deployments using VRF-aware WCCPv2 at the core/aggregation layer (see Figure 2.1).

From the SOI perspective, the core/aggregation layer in the DC is the ideal location for WCCPv2 interception because this is where L2 terminates and L3 commences. The main concern is the VRF associations on the interfaces for L3 devices at this layer. The VRF configurations are meant for L3 path isolation (for more details, see the Layer 2 and Layer 3 Segmentations section in Chapter 3) but this creates issues for a standard WCCPv2 deployment, which requires the global IPv4 routing table.

One way to solve the problem is to have VRF-aware WCCPv2 and the other is through VRF route leaking (for details, see the Cloud Interception with Non–VRF-Aware WCCP section). In Chapter 5, the various WCCP server platforms were briefly covered. Those that directly support VRF-aware WCCPv2 include:

- Nexus 7000
- C7200 and ISR (running IOS 15.x)
- C7600 (running IOS 12.2(33)SRE)
- ASR 1000 (running IOS-XE 3.1.0S)

The Nexus 7000 (NX7K) switch is used as the example platform to further elaborate on the VRF-aware WCCPv2 configurations in a multitenant environment. Figure 6.2 shows a simple WAN optimization setup on an NX7K switch, CORE-1 residing at the DC core layer. The WAN optimization is provisioned for both Tenant-B and Tenant-C. CORE-1 is functioning as a multi-VRF L3 switch, with VRF Tenant-B and VRF Tenant-C created for the corresponding tenants. Because there are now two different VRFs in CORE-1, VRF-aware WCCPv2 (or two separate instances of WCCPv2) will have to be implemented on CORE-1 for proper interception and redirection to the correct WAN optimizers. TCP traffic to and from server S1 will be intercepted by the WCCPv2 instance for VRF Tenant-B and redirected to WAN optimizer "B" for optimization. TCP traffic to and from server S2 will be intercepted by the WCCPv2 instance for VRF Tenant-C and redirected to WAN optimizer "C" for optimization. The WAN optimizers in this example can be physical or virtual appliances.

NOTE:

In the example shown in Figure 6.2, the remote branch traffic must traverse from the WAN edge/peering layer through the core/aggregation/access layers to reach servers S1 and S2. The DC WAN optimizers deployed are the Riverbed VSH-2050-H Virtual Steelhead appliances with WCCPv2 enabled. The branch WAN optimizers (not shown in diagram for brevity) are the Riverbed SH-1050-H Steelhead appliances deployed physically in-path at the remote branches.

NOTE:

Although VRF-aware WCCPv2 is supported on the NX7K switch, it is not required if the virtual device context (VDC) is configured on the switch instead of VRF. In this case, the WCCPv2 configurations use the usual global IPv4 routing table. Nevertheless, currently the Nexus 7000 switch supports only a maximum of four VDCs including the default VDC, so VRF would still be required when the number of tenants exceeds four. Put another way, VDC and VRF can be used together, with VRF being the subset of the VDC. Each VDC can be further virtualized to support VRFs.

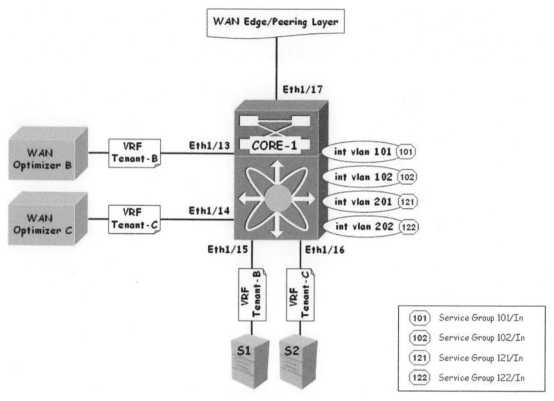

FIGURE 6.2

WAN optimization with VRF-aware WCCPv2

Code Listing 6.1 depicts the L2 baseline configurations for CORE-1 (see Figure 6.2). Five ports are utilized; four as access ports and the remaining one as an 802.1Q trunk port. Out of the four access ports, two (Eth1/13 and Eth1/15) are for Tenant-B connecting WAN optimizer "B" and server S1. The other two access ports (Eth1/14 and Eth1/16) are for Tenant-C connecting WAN optimizer "C" and server S2. The trunk port (Eth1/17) connects to a WAN edge/peering-layer router (not shown in the diagram for brevity).

```
vlan 10,20,101-102,201-202

interface Ethernet1/13
  description "Connects WAN Optimizer B"
  switchport
  switchport access vlan 10
  no shutdown
```

```
interface Ethernet1/14
  description "Connects WAN Optimizer C"
  switchport
  switchport access vlan 20
  no shutdown

interface Ethernet1/15
  description "Connects Server S1"
  switchport
  switchport access vlan 102
  no shutdown

interface Ethernet1/16
  description "Connects Server S2"
  switchport
  switchport access vlan 202
  no shutdown

interface Ethernet1/17
  description "802.1Q Trunk from Peering Layer"
  switchport
  switchport mode trunk
  switchport trunk allowed vlan 101,201
  no shutdown
```

CODE LISTING 6.1
___

NX7K L2 baseline configurations

> **NOTE:**
> ___
> Module 1 on the NX7K switch, CORE-1 (as shown in Figure 6.2), is a 48-port 10/100/1000 Mbps Ethernet Module (N7K-M148GT-11).

Code Listing 6.2 depicts the L3 baseline configurations for CORE-1 (see Figure 6.2). Based on the six VLANs created in Code Listing 6.1, six corresponding L3-switch virtual interfaces (SVIs) are also created. The default VDC is used for VRF Tenant-B and VRF Tenant-C. SVIs Vlan10, Vlan101, and Vlan102 are associated with VRF Tenant-B. SVIs Vlan20, Vlan201, and Vlan202 are associated with VRF Tenant-C. Two OSPFv2 processes are instantiated, one (router ospf 100) for VRF Tenant-B and the other (router ospf 200) for VRF Tenant-C.

```
feature ospf
feature interface-vlan

vrf context Tenant-B
vrf context Tenant-C
```

```
interface Vlan10
  no shutdown
  vrf member Tenant-B
  ip address 10.1.10.1/24
  ip router ospf 100 area 0.0.0.0

interface Vlan101
  no shutdown
  vrf member Tenant-B
  ip address 10.1.101.1/24
  ip router ospf 100 area 0.0.0.0

interface Vlan102
  no shutdown
  vrf member Tenant-B
  ip address 10.1.102.1/24
  ip router ospf 100 area 0.0.0.0

interface Vlan20
  no shutdown
  vrf member Tenant-C
  ip address 10.2.20.1/24
  ip router ospf 200 area 0.0.0.0

interface Vlan201
  no shutdown
  vrf member Tenant-C
  ip address 10.2.201.1/24
  ip router ospf 200 area 0.0.0.0

interface Vlan202
  no shutdown
  vrf member Tenant-C
  ip address 10.2.202.1/24
  ip router ospf 200 area 0.0.0.0

router ospf 100
  vrf Tenant-B

router ospf 200
  vrf Tenant-C
```

CODE LISTING 6.2

NX7K L3 baseline configuration

Code Listing 6.3 depicts the VRF-aware WCCPv2 configuration for CORE-1 (see Figure 6.2). To facilitate the WCCP mask assignment scheme on the NX7K switch, two WCCP service groups are created for each tenant. The WCCP interception is based on the inbound direction for each service group. For more details on the WCCP functionality supported on the NX7K switch, see the Nexus 7000 WCCP Compatibility section in Chapter 5.

```
feature wccp

vrf context Tenant-B
  ip wccp 101 redirect-list 101
  ip wccp 102 redirect-list 102

vrf context Tenant-C
  ip wccp 121 redirect-list 121
  ip wccp 122 redirect-list 122

interface Vlan101
  no shutdown
  vrf member Tenant-B
  ip address 10.1.101.1/24
  ip router ospf 100 area 0.0.0.0
  ip wccp 101 redirect in

interface Vlan102
  no shutdown
  vrf member Tenant-B
  ip address 10.1.102.1/24
  ip router ospf 100 area 0.0.0.0
  ip wccp 102 redirect in

interface Vlan201
  no shutdown
  vrf member Tenant-C
  ip address 10.2.201.1/24
  ip router ospf 200 area 0.0.0.0
  ip wccp 121 redirect in

interface Vlan202
  no shutdown
  vrf member Tenant-C
  ip address 10.2.202.1/24
  ip router ospf 200 area 0.0.0.0
  ip wccp 122 redirect in

ip access-list 101
  10 permit tcp 192.168.100.0/24 10.1.102.100/32
```

```
ip access-list 102
    10 permit tcp 10.1.102.100/32 192.168.100.0/24

ip access-list 121
    10 permit tcp 192.168.200.0/24 10.2.202.100/32

ip access-list 122
    10 permit tcp 10.2.202.100/32 192.168.200.0/24
```

CODE LISTING 6.3

NX7K VRF-aware WCCPv2 configuration

> **NOTE:**
>
> HA and other more complex WCCPv2 configurations are omitted in Code Listing 6.3 for brevity.

In Tenant-B's case, inbound TCP traffic from remote branch "B" (192.168.100.0/24) to server S1 (10.1.102.100/32) is intercepted by service group 101 and redirected to WAN optimizer "B" for optimization. Inbound TCP traffic from server S1 (10.1.102.100/32) to remote branch "B" (192.168.100.0/24), is intercepted by service group 102 and redirected to WAN optimizer "B" for optimization. Service groups 101 and 102 are local to VRF Tenant-B.

In Tenant-C's case, inbound TCP traffic from remote branch "C" (192.168.200.0/24) to server S2 (10.2.202.100/32) is intercepted by service group 121 and redirected to WAN optimizer "C" for optimization. Inbound TCP traffic from server S2 (10.2.202.100/32) to remote branch "C" (192.168.200.0/24), is intercepted by service group 122 and redirected to WAN optimizer "C" for optimization. Service groups 121 and 122 are local to VRF Tenant-C.

> **NOTE:**
>
> In VRF-aware WCCPv2, a service group definition is local to the VRF where it is defined. In other words, the service groups defined within a VRF are logically separated from each other, implying that the service group IDs can be reused across VRF (not illustrated in Code Listing 6.3). This will be particularly useful in scenarios where the cloud service providers adopt the same addressing scheme for different tenants. In this case, the same WCCPv2 configurations (including redirect ACLs) can be implemented for the various tenants.

> **NOTE:**
>
> Redirect access-control lists (ACLs) are supported in the NX7K switch. The redirect ACLs in Code Listing 6.3 assume there is only a single TCP application running in the respective server that requires optimization. In most cases, it is recommended to refine the ACLs according to the number of TCP applications that requires optimization for better fan-in control.

CLOUD INTERCEPTION WITH NON–VRF-AWARE WCCP

VRF-aware WCCPv2 can be implemented using the C7200, C7600, or ASR 1000 (ASR1K) routers provided they are running a version of IOS (IOS-XE for ASR1K) that directly supports VRF-aware WCCP. What about cases where router platforms other than these routers are deployed at the WAN edge/peering layer, or the IOS (or IOS-XE) version does not support VRF-aware WCCP at all?

In cases where the VRF-aware WCCPv2 feature is not directly supported, WCCPv2 and VRF can still interoperate. This section examines some of the VRF integration mechanisms that can enable WCCPv2 and VRF to interoperate seamlessly (without the VRF-aware WCCP feature) at the core/aggregation and WAN edge/peering layers (see Figure 2.1).

The topics to be covered in the subsequent subsections include:

- VRF select
- The WCCP two-way connectivity challenge
- The Not-So-VRF (NSV) solution
- The NSV illustration

VRF Select

The WCCPv2 and VRF integration technique relies on a mechanism known as VRF Select. The VRF Select mechanism basically decouples the association between the VRF routing table and an interface. Applying VRF Select to an interface opens up a "crack" between the global IPv4 routing table and the VRF routing table for that particular interface. Hence, the interface with VRF select configured, is "Not-So-VRF" anymore.

The VRF Select mechanism is summarized as follows:

1. Instead of associating an interface to a VRF, the VRF Select configuration defines policy-based routing (PBR) and the "ip vrf receive" interface command at the ingress interface of the multi-VRF/WCCPv2 router.
2. VRF Select matches an interesting packet against the access control list (ACL) defined in the PBR route map and select (or set to) a corresponding VRF routing table if a match is found.
3. VRF Select looks up the destination IP address of the packet on the selected VRF routing table to determine the corresponding next-hop, output interface, and adjacency.

NOTE:

VRF Select is applicable only for the inbound direction.

NOTE:

The VRF Select feature is typically referenced as MPLS VPN VRF Selection using Policy Based Routing (PBR). The supported IOS versions are IOS 12.3(7)T onward for the C7200 router platforms, IOS 12.2(33)SRB1 and above for the C7600 router platforms, and IOS XE 2.1.0 and above for the ASR1K platforms.

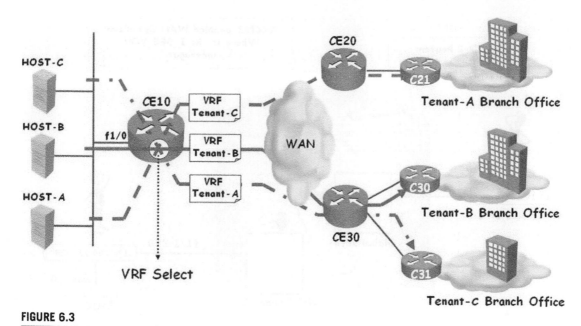

FIGURE 6.3

VRF Select example

Figure 6.3 illustrates how VRF Select decouples interface f1/0 of router CE10 from VRFs Tenant-A, Tenant-B, and Tenant-C. Even though interface f1/0 is disassociated with these VRFs, packets from HOST-A, HOST-B, and HOST-C can still be effectively forwarded to their respective remote branches through the PBR route map defined at the ingress of CE10f1/0.

The WCCPv2 two-way connectivity challenge

The two main criteria for establishing a successful WCCPv2 two-way connectivity are as follows:

- The WCCPv2 router ID must be a valid IPv4 address reachable by the WCCPv2-enabled WAN optimizer.
- The WCCPv2 router must know how to reach the WCCPv2-enabled WAN optimizer through its global IPv4 routing table.

These conditions pose a certain challenge for WCCPv2 and VRF integration. The WCCPv2-enabled WAN optimizer deployed in a particular VRF address space is only reachable through the corresponding VRF routing table. The WCCPv2 router ID is only reachable through the global IPv4 routing table. Figure 6.4 illustrates the problem. Since the global IPv4 routing table and the VRF routing table are disparate, WCCP two-way connectivity will never be established unless there is a workaround mechanism to address these two connectivity establishment factors.

In Figure 6.4, the HIA message sent from the WCCP-enabled WAN optimizer, SH10 (a Riverbed Steelhead appliance) will never reach WCCP router ID 10.10.10.10 using the VRF Tenant-D routing table because loopback10 is only reachable via the global IPv4 routing table. Therefore, if SH10 is in a

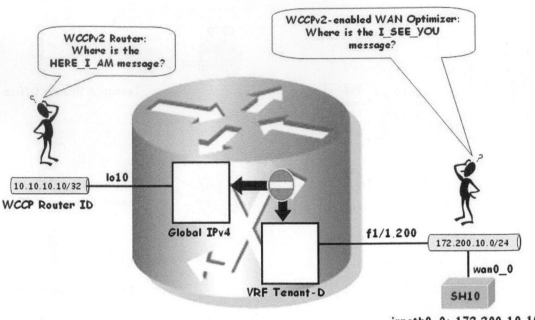

FIGURE 6.4

Reachability information in different routing tables

specific VRF address space, the router ID must be reachable by SH10 through the corresponding VRF routing table. The way to solve the problem is to have the router ID and SH10 in-path address reachable in both the VRF and the global IPv4 routing tables.

In addition, the IOS order of operations necessitates the following:

- For ingress traffic, WCCPv2 redirection is performed before VRF routing table lookup.
- For egress traffic, WCCPv2 redirection is performed after VRF routing table lookup.

Using Figure 6.4 as an illustration, four scenarios can be derived:

- The WCCPv2 redirect-in operation from the WAN to LAN direction needs to know the whereabouts of SH10 via the global IPv4 routing table.
- The WCCPv2 redirect-in operation from the LAN to WAN direction requires the location of SH10 in the global IPv4 routing table.
- The WCCPv2 redirect-out operation from the WAN to LAN direction needs to know the whereabouts of SH10 through the VRF Tenant-D routing table.
- The WCCPv2 redirect-out operation from the LAN to WAN direction requires the location of SH10 in the VRF Tenant-D routing table.

Any WCCPv2 redirect-in operation faces the same WCCPv2 two-way connectivity challenge mentioned earlier. Therefore, the best way out of this stalemate is to ensure that the WCCPv2 router ID and SH10 in-path address are reachable in both the global IPv4 routing table and the VRF Tenant-D routing table.

> **NOTE:**
>
> Ensuring the router ID and the WAN optimizer are reachable in both the global IPv4 routing table and the respective VRF routing table would immunize a solution against the IOS order of operations for WCCPv2 redirection and VRF routing table lookup.

The Not-So-VRF solution

The Not-So-VRF (NSV) solution solves the WCCPv2 two-way connectivity challenge brought up in the previous subsection, The WCCPv2 Two-Way Connectivity Challenge. The NSV solution relies on the VRF Select mechanism (for details, see VRF Select section) for the workaround. After the VRF Select mechanism is applied to loopback10 (the WCCP router ID), it becomes visible to the VRF Tenant-D table as illustrated in Figure 6.5.

Although the WCCP router ID is now reachable through the VRF Tenant-D table, there is one more missing link: How would the WCCPv2 router reach SH10 via the global IPv4 routing table? Figure 6.6 illustrates how this is achieved by defining a static route in the global IPv4 routing table pointing to the subnet where SH10 is residing.

> **NOTE:**
>
> The NSV solution uses the WCCP GRE redirection/return. NSV with WCCP L2 redirection/return is outside the scope of this book.

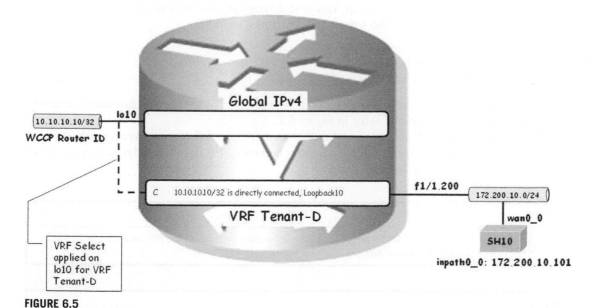

FIGURE 6.5

WCCP router ID in VRF routing table

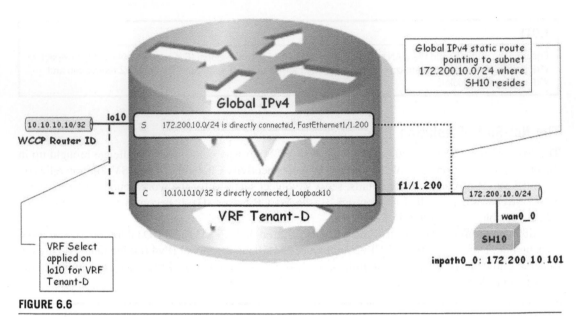

FIGURE 6.6

WAN optimizer subnet in global IPv4 routing table

The Not-So-VRF illustration

Figure 6.7 shows the NSV example setup. This base diagram and the NSV implementation steps that follow are referenced throughout the following subsections, including:

- Implementing NSV at the core or aggregation layer
- The alternative to VRF Select
- Implementing NSV at the WAN edge or peering layer

The NSV and WCCPv2 configurations (or code listings) implemented in the abovementioned subsections are based on the depicted setup in Figure 6.7.

R32 is the star of the NSV example setup as illustrated in Figure 6.7. It serves as a multi-VRF router at the DC core/aggregation layer for Tenant-E and it becomes a PE (Provider Edge) router at the DC WAN edge/peering layer for Tenant-F.

> **NOTE:**
>
> R32 is running on IOS version 12.4(15)T9. Although this version does not support the VRF-aware WCCPv2 feature, it does come with the VRF Select mechanism.

> **NOTE:**
>
> The DC WAN optimizers deployed in this example setup are Riverbed VSH-2050-H Virtual Steelhead appliances with WCCPv2 enabled. The branch WAN optimizers (not shown in the diagram for brevity) are Riverbed SH-1050-H Steelhead appliances deployed physically in-path at the remote branches.

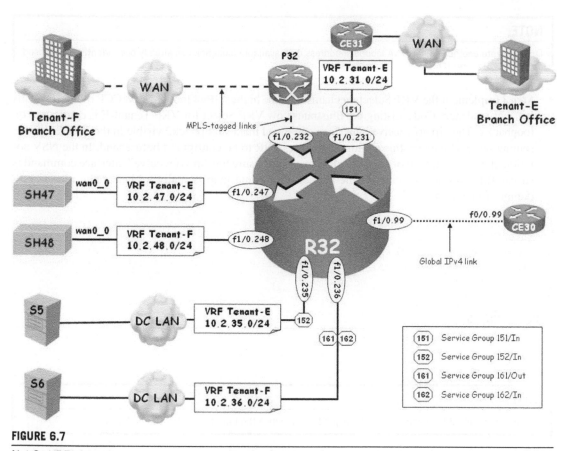

FIGURE 6.7

Not-So-VRF example

Implementing NSV at the core or aggregation layer

This subsection implements the NSV solution for Tenant-E where R32 is the multi-VRF router at the DC core/aggregation layer. There are six simple steps to follow:

- **Step 1** Identify WCCP router ID. This, by far, is the most primitive step as WCCPv2 will always choose the highest loopback IPv4 address (and if there is no loopback, the highest physical interface IPv4 address) on the router as the WCCP router ID.
- **Step 2** Optionally, create the highest IPv4 loopback if none is available. Perform this step with care as it might impact the attributes of other protocols that are running in the router (e.g., the router ID of a routing process and so on). Code Listing 6.4 illustrates how loopback2 is created on R32 as the WCCP router ID.

```
!
interface Loopback2
 ip address 10.2.100.32 255.255.255.255
!
```

CODE LISTING 6.4

Create highest IPv4 loopback

NOTE:

Do not create another higher IPv4 loopback address if an available loopback has already been identified and used as the WCCP router ID.

- *Step 3* Implement the VRF Select mechanism on the highest IPv4 loopback (WCCP router ID). This is the crucial step. Code Listing 6.5 illustrates how VRF Select for VRF Tenant-E is configured on loopback2. The "ip vrf receive" interface command makes loopback2 visible in the VRF Tenant-E routing table. However, this command requires PBR to be configured beforehand. In the NSV solution, the main purpose of the PBR route map is to ensure the "ip vrf receive" interface command is successfully applied. Therefore, the applied PBR route map is really a blank route map (i.e., a dummy route map).

```
!
interface Loopback2
 ip address 10.2.100.32 255.255.255.255
 ip policy route-map dummy
 ip vrf receive Tenant-E
!
```

CODE LISTING 6.5

Apply VRF Select on IPv4 loopback for Tenant-E

NOTE:

You are not required to construct a route map "dummy" since the intention is for it to be blank.

After configuring the VRF Select mechanism, the loopback will appear in the VRF Tenant-E routing table. Code Listing 6.6 illustrates how to verify this step by using the "show ip route vrf Tenant-E" exec command.

```
R32#show ip route vrf Tenant-E
[-----Snipped for brevity-----]
C 10.2.31.0/24 is directly connected, FastEthernet1/0.231
C 10.2.35.0/24 is directly connected, FastEthernet1/0.235
C 10.2.47.0/24 is directly connected, FastEthernet1/0.247
C 10.2.100.32/32 is directly connected, Loopback2
```

CODE LISTING 6.6

Verify IPv4 loopback is in VRF Tenant-E routing table

Code Listing 6.7 depicts the existing configurations on the subinterface that connects SH47 (see Figure 6.7).

```
interface FastEthernet1/0.247
 encapsulation dot1Q 247
 ip vrf forwarding Tenant-E
 ip address 10.2.47.2 255.255.255.0
```

CODE LISTING 6.7

VRF interface connecting the Tenant-E WAN optimizer

> **NOTE:**
>
> If a VLAN is unavailable for the out-of-path placement of the WAN optimizer, you can always create one with its corresponding 802.1Q subinterface.

- *Step 4* Complete the NSV solution by enabling global IPv4 route leaking. The global IPv4 routing table must know how to reach the WAN optimizer. This is achieved with VRF to global IPv4 route leaking. From Code Listing 6.7, we can gather that SH47 is in subnet 10.2.47.0/24 reachable via the VRF Tenant-E routing table through interface f1/0.247. Code Listing 6.8 illustrates how a global IPv4 static route leaks this reachability information to the global IPv4 routing table.

```
!
ip route 10.2.47.0 255.255.255.0 FastEthernet1/0.247
!
```

CODE LISTING 6.8

VRF to global-IPv4 route leaking for Tenant-E

Code Listing 6.9 verifies whether subnet 10.2.47.0/24 is now reachable via the global IPv4 routing table by executing the "show ip route" exec command.

```
R32#show ip route
S 10.2.47.0/24 is directly connected, FastEthernet1/0.247
C 10.2.100.32/32 is directly connected, Loopback2
```

CODE LISTING 6.9

Verify VRF Tenant-E subnet is in global IPv4 routing table

With the completion of all four steps, the WCCP router ID 10.2.100.32 that is initially visible only in the global IPv4 routing table, is now visible in the VRF Tenant-E routing table. Subnet 10.2.47.0/24 which at first is reachable only through the VRF Tenant-E routing table is now reachable through the global IPv4 routing table. Steps 1-4 wrap up the NSV workaround. The rest of the steps (Steps 5 and 6) are standard WCCPv2 configuration settings.

> **NOTE:**
>
> The VRF to global-IPv4 route leaking is local to R32 and is only between the WCCP router ID and SH47. It does not affect the integrity of the existing L3 path isolation implementation for Tenant-E. SH47 is a transparent proxy so the actual source and destination are still only reachable through the VRF Tenant-E routing tables.

- ***Step 5*** involves WCCPv2 global configurations on R32 for Tenant-E (see Figure 6.7), this is illustrated in Code Listing 6.10. The redirect ACLs in Code Listing 6.10 assume there is only a single TCP application running in server S5 (10.2.50.88) that requires optimization and is accessed by a remote client (10.2.10.78) at the branch office of Tenant-E.

```
!
ip wccp 151 redirect-list 151
ip wccp 152 redirect-list 152
!
access-list 151 permit tcp host 10.2.10.78 host 10.2.50.88
access-list 152 permit tcp host 10.2.50.88 host 10.2.10.78
!
```

CODE LISTING 6.10

WCCPv2 global configuration on R32 for Tenant-E

- ***Step 6*** enables WCCPv2 on the ingress of the respective interfaces (f1/0.231 and f1/0.235) as shown in Code Listing 6.11. Subinterface f1/0.231 is the WAN facing interface (i.e., towards the remote branch of Tenant-E) and subinterface f1/0.235 is the DC LAN facing interface (i.e., towards server S5). Both subinterfaces are VRF-based.

```
!
interface FastEthernet1/0.231
 encapsulation dot1Q 231
 ip vrf forwarding Tenant-E
 ip address 10.2.31.2 255.255.255.0
 ip wccp 151 redirect in
!
interface FastEthernet1/0.235
 encapsulation dot1Q 235
 ip vrf forwarding Tenant-E
 ip address 10.2.35.2 255.255.255.0
 ip wccp 152 redirect in
!
```

CODE LISTING 6.11

WCCPv2 interface configuration on R32 for Tenant-E

The configuration for SH47 (see Figure 6.7) is straightforward as illustrated in Code Listing 6.12. It basically enables logical in-path and reciprocates the WCCPv2 configuration with that of R32 for Tenant-E (see Figure 6.7).

```
#
interface inpath0_0 ip address 10.2.47.101 /24
ip in-path-gateway inpath0_0 10.2.47.2
#
in-path enable
in-path oop enable
#
wccp enable
wccp service-group 151 routers 10.2.100.32
wccp service-group 152 routers 10.2.100.32
#
```

CODE LISTING 6.12

WCCPv2 configuration on SH47 for Tenant-E

The alternative to VRF Select

What if the VRF Select mechanism is not supported on the IOS version or variant you are running? There is an unorthodox way to solve this problem but this method relies on another L3 device that is directly connected to the multi-VRF/WCCPv2 router. In Figure 6.7, this L3 device is router CE30. CE30 is the "boomerang" router that directly connects R32 (the multi-VRF/WCCPv2 router).

Code Listing 6.13 reenacts Step 3 above (see the Implementing NSV at the Core or Aggregation Layer section) but this time without using the VRF Select mechanism. Although Step 3 is cumbersome using this method, the relaxation of the IOS version requirement can be valuable. Only the usual WCCPv2 support is required. An alternate Step 3b is:

*   ***Step 3b*** Code Listing 6.13 illustrates how subinterface f1/0.99 on R32 is newly created to open up an IPv4 "crack" (or a direct IPv4 path) to CE30. This is followed by leaking the reachability information of the WCCP router ID into the VRF Tenant-E routing table using a VRF static route that points to CE30 (10.2.99.30) as the next-hop through subinterface f1/0.99.

```
!
hostname R32
!
interface Loopback2
 ip address 10.2.100.32 255.255.255.255
!
! - - - Create IPv4 crack to boomerang router CE30
interface FastEthernet1/0.99
 encapsulation dot1Q 99
 ip address 10.2.99.32 255.255.255.0
!
! - - - Bounce the location of WCCP Router ID to boomerang router CE30
ip route vrf Tenant-E 10.2.100.32 255.255.255.255 FastEthernet1/0.99 10.2.99.30
!
```

CODE LISTING 6.13

The alternative configuration to VRF Select

Code Listing 6.14 shows the configurations of the boomerang router, CE30 that reciprocates its subinterface (f0/0.99) configuration with that (f1/0.99) of R32. The IPv4 static route simply boomerangs any IP packet with destination 10.2.100.32 (the WCCP router ID) back to R32 (10.2.99.32).

```
!
hostname CE30
!
! – Create corresponding IPv4 crack to CE32
interface FastEthernet0/0.99
 encapsulation dot1Q 99
 ip address 10.2.99.30 255.255.255.0
!
! – Boomerang back
ip route 10.2.100.32 255.255.255.255 10.2.99.32
!
```

CODE LISTING 6.14

Boomerang router configuration

> **NOTE:**
>
> This alternative method only affects Step 3 (see Implementing NSV at the Core or Aggregation Layer section). The rest of the steps remain the same. The configuration changes are only made at R32 (see Code Listing 6.13) and CE30 (see Code Listing 6.14).

Implementing NSV at the WAN edge or peering layer

This subsection implements the NSV solution for Tenant-F at the DC WAN edge/peering layer using the same router, R32 (see Figure 6.7). With the addition of Tenant-F, there are now two VRFs: VRF Tenant-E and VRF Tenant-F. Recall that WCCPv2 only recognizes its router ID in the global IPv4 address space. The NSV workaround does not change this fact. In multi-VRF scenarios (i.e., VRF Tenant-E and VRF Tenant-F), the WCCP router ID will still have to be shared among the WCCPv2-enabled WAN optimizers residing at the various VRF address spaces. Thus, new steps 3-6 are required, see Steps 3c-6c below.

- **Step 3c** As the WCCP router ID (Loopback2) has already been defined in Code Listing 6.4, we can jump straight to Step 3 as described in Implementing NSV at the Core or Aggregation Layer section. Since the PBR route map is already in place from the previous Tenant-E VRF Select configuration (see Code Listing 6.5), only the "ip vrf receive" interface command is required for Tenant-F. This is depicted in Code Listing 6.15.

```
!
interface Loopback2
 ip address 10.2.100.32 255.255.255.255
 ip policy route-map dummy
 ip vrf receive Tenant-E
 ip vrf receive Tenant-F
!
```

CODE LISTING 6.15

Apply VRF Select on IPv4 loopback for Tenant-F

After configuring the VRF select mechanism, the loopback should appear in the VRF Tenant-F routing table. Code Listing 6.16 illustrates how to verify this by using the "show ip route vrf Tenant-F" exec command.

```
R32#show ip route vrf Tenant-F
[----- Snipped for brevity-----]
C 10.2.36.0/24 is directly connected, FastEthernet1/0.236
C 10.2.48.0/24 is directly connected, FastEthernet1/0.248
C 10.2.100.32/32 is directly connected, Loopback2
```

CODE LISTING 6.16

Verify IPv4 loopback is in VRF Tenant-F routing table

Code Listing 6.17 depicts the existing configurations on the subinterface that connects SH48 (see Figure 6.7).

```
interface FastEthernet1/0.248
 encapsulation dot1Q 248
 ip vrf forwarding Tenant-F
 ip address 10.2.48.2 255.255.255.0
```

CODE LISTING 6.17

VRF interface connecting Tenant-F WAN optimizer

- *Step 4c* From Code Listing 6.17, we can gather that SH48 is in subnet 10.2.48.0/24 reachable via the VRF Tenant-F routing table through interface f1/0.248. Code Listing 6.18 (Step 4c) illustrates how a global IPv4 static route leaks this reachability information to the global IPv4 routing table.

```
!
ip route 10.2.48.0 255.255.255.0 FastEthernet1/0.248
!
```

CODE LISTING 6.18

VRF to global-IPv4 route leaking for Tenant-F

Code Listing 6.19 verifies whether subnet 10.2.48.0/24 is now reachable via the global IPv4 routing table by using the "show ip route" exec command.

```
R32#show ip route
S 10.2.47.0/24 is directly connected, FastEthernet1/0.247
S 10.2.48.0/24 is directly connected, FastEthernet1/0.248
C 10.2.100.32/32 is directly connected, Loopback2
```

CODE LISTING 6.19

Verify VRF Tenant-F subnet is in global IPv4 routing table

With the completion of Step 3c (see Code Listing 6.15) and Step 4c (see Code Listing 6.18), the WCCP router ID 10.2.100.32 is now visible in the VRF Tenant-F routing table and subnet 10.2.48.0/24 is now reachable via the global IPv4 routing table.

- **Step 5c** involves WCCPv2 global configurations on R32 for Tenant-F as illustrated in Code Listing 6.20. The redirect ACLs in Code Listing 6.20 assume there is only a single TCP application running in server S6 (10.2.60.88) that requires optimization and is accessed by a remote client (10.2.20.78) at the branch office of Tenant-F.

```
!
ip wccp 161 redirect-list 161
ip wccp 162 redirect-list 162
!
access-list 161 permit tcp host 10.2.20.78 host 10.2.60.88
access-list 162 permit tcp host 10.2.60.88 host 10.2.20.78
!
```

CODE LISTING 6.20

WCCPv2 global configuration on R32 for Tenant-F

NOTE:

You can use a different pair of service groups for different VRFs as a workaround for the IOS versions or variants that do not support VRF-aware WCCPv2.

- **Step 6c** enables bidirectional WCCPv2 redirection on the same DC LAN facing VRF interface, f1/0.236 as shown in Code Listing 6.21. This particular type of redirection is known as the service isolation mode. It is predominantly used to restrict redirection to a particular interface so that only traffic traversing that interface and matching the WCCP redirect ACLs will be redirected.

As shown in Figure 6.7, R32 is acting as a PE router at the DC WAN edge/peering layer for Tenant-F. Subinterface f1/0.232, the WAN facing interface of R32, connects to P32 (i.e., the P router) and is MPLS-tagged. The service isolation mode is adopted in Code Listing 6.21 because we want to skip implementing WCCPv2 redirection on R32f1/0.232 that is MPLS-tagged.

In Code Listing 6.21, the "ip wccp redirect exclude in" interface command is applied on R32f1/0.248, the subinterface connecting SH48 (see Figure 6.7). This is to prevent the redirect-out operation at R32f1/0.236 from reintercepting a previously redirected traffic flow (i.e., double redirection), creating a redirection loop.

```
!
interface FastEthernet1/0.236
 encapsulation dot1Q 236
 ip vrf forwarding Tenant-F
 ip address 10.2.36.2 255.255.255.0
 ip wccp 161 redirect out
 ip wccp 162 redirect in
!
interface FastEthernet1/0.248
 encapsulation dot1Q 248
 ip vrf forwarding Tenant-F
 ip address 10.2.48.2 255.255.255.0
 ip wccp redirect exclude in
!
```

CODE LISTING 6.21

WCCPv2 interface configuration on R32 for Tenant-F

> **NOTE:**
>
> The trade-off when using the service isolation mode or WCCP egress redirection is higher CPU utilization. This is because egress redirection must perform a routing table lookup to reach the outbound interface for the egress redirection.

The configuration for SH48 (see Figure 6.7) is straightforward as illustrated in Code Listing 6.22. It enables logical in-path and reciprocates the WCCPv2 configuration with that of R32 for Tenant-F.

```
#
interface inpath0_0 ip address 10.2.48.101 /24
ip in-path-gateway inpath0_0 10.2.48.2
#
in-path enable
in-path oop enable
#
wccp enable
wccp service-group 161 routers 10.2.100.32
wccp service-group 162 routers 10.2.100.32
#
```

CODE LISTING 6.22

WCCPv2 configuration on SH48 for Tenant-F

> **NOTE:**
>
> For the NSV solution to support overlapping addressing schemes, a dedicated WAN optimizer is allocated per VRF. In this case, a WAN optimizer with a virtual form-factor is the most appropriate. Note the WAN optimizer must be on a unique IP subnet because this information has to be leaked out to the global IPv4 routing table that is "shared" among the various VRFs (e.g., VRF Tenant-E and VRF Tenant-F).

INTERCEPTION AT THE SERVICES AGGREGATION LAYER

The services aggregation layer (see Figure 2.1 in Chapter 2) is the ideal place to integrate firewalls and server load-balancers (SLBs) in the cloud-based service-oriented infrastructure (SOI). The services aggregation layer is typically the demarcation between L2 and L3 in the DC. It allows intelligent service devices (i.e., firewalls and SLBs) to be shared across multiple switches in the access layer. For more details, see Service Integration in the Data Center section in Chapter 3.

Why implement interception at the services aggregation layer? The short answer is: pass the control over the interception process in the cloud to the tenants or end-users. In other words, implementing interception at the services aggregation layer allows the cloud service providers to stay hands-off as far as cloud interception is concerned.

From the discussion conducted in the preceding sections, WCCPv2 is most likely the de facto interception mechanism in private clouds. But when it comes to end-user control using WCCPv2, a particular tenant would need to have direct access to the L3 device that is implementing the WCCPv2 server. In most cases, the L3 device will implement multiple VRFs to facilitate L3 path isolation for the various tenants. If access to this L3 device is given to a particular tenant for configuration purposes, the tenant will be able to see all the existing multi-VRF configurations on the L3 device, posing a security breach. The use of virtual device contexts (VDCs) is one way out of this dilemma.

The NX7K switch and ACESM support VDCs. At the time of writing, the NX7K switch supports only a maximum of four VDCs including the default VDC. This limited number of VDCs poses a scalability issue for the NX7K switch as a self-managed WCCPv2 server platform. The other alternative is to use the ACESM located at the services aggregation layer. Rather than performing SLB function, an ACESM VDC is instantiated for intercepting and redirecting traffic for each tenant. In this case, the tenant manages the ACESM VDC.

The focus of this section is on the ACESM as the interception mechanism at the services aggregation layer for WAN optimization in the private cloud.

The topics for discussion in the subsequent subsections include:

- Services chassis requirements
- Admin context
- User context
- ACESM interception: bridged mode
- ACESM interception: routed mode
- Health monitoring with probes
- WAN optimizer farm redundancy

Services chassis requirements

The Application Control Engine (ACE) comes in two form-factors: service module and physical appliance. The ACE appliance is beyond the scope of this book. The services chassis requirements for the ACESM include:

- Any Catalyst 6500 Series chassis:
  - Catalyst 6500 Series Supervisor Engine 720 or Supervisor Engine 720-10GE.
  - IOS 12.2(18)SXF4 onward for Supervisor Engine 720.
  - IOS 12.2(33)SXH onward for Supervisor Engine 720-10GE.
- Any Cisco 7600 Series chassis:
  - Cisco 7600 Series Supervisor Engine 720 and Route Switch Processor 720.
  - IOS 12.2(18)SXF4 onward and IOS 12.2(33)SRB onward for Supervisor Engine 720.
  - IOS 12.2(33)SRC onward for Route Switch Processor 720.

The ACESM works as a fabric-enabled line card and takes up one slot in the switch chassis.

Admin context

The ACESM supports virtualization through the configuration of VDCs (or virtual contexts). Network resources are dedicated to a single context or shared among contexts. The following equipment is used in the ACESM discussion (Figure 6.8 may be useful as an example):

- The Catalyst 6506-E data center switch (hostname "tl-tsw2") is the services chassis and it runs on IOS version 12.2(33)SXH2a.

• An ACESM (hostname "ACESM-123") running software version 3.0(0)A1(4a) is housed at slot 5 of the Catalyst 6506-E switch (tl-tsw2). ACESM-123 can be accessed through the "session slot 5 processor 0" exec command through tl-tsw2 before IP connectivity and management access are configured. The default username/password pair is admin/admin, which will log in directly to the Admin context.

NOTE:

The admin and www users are present in the Admin context by default and provide default access. The admin is for administration while the www user account is for supporting the XML interface. If the www user is deleted, the XML interface will be disabled for the entire ACESM.

Code Listing 6.23 illustrates the information of the ACESM with the "show module 5" exec command on the switch.

```
tl-tsw2#show module 5
Mod Ports Card Type                          Model            Serial No.
- - - - - - - - - - - - - - - - - - - - - -  - - - - - - - - - - - - - - - - - - -
  5    1   Application Control Engine Module  ACE20-MOD-K9     SAD111505C2

Mod MAC addresses                     Hw     Fw          Sw         Status
- - - - - - - - - - - - - - - - - - - - -   - - -  - - - - - - -  - - - - - - - -  - - - - - - -
  5  001b.2a65.faac to 001b.2a65.fab3  2.1    8.6(0.252-En 3.0(0)A1(4a) Ok

Mod Online Diag Status
- - - - - - - - - - - - - - - -
  5  Pass
```

CODE LISTING 6.23

Services chassis ACESM information

There are two main types of contexts: Admin and User. The Admin context is created by default and cannot be renamed or deleted. User contexts, and the corresponding resource allocations, are administered from the Admin context. In other words, to provision a User context for the respective tenant, the cloud service providers will need to configure this from the Admin context.

NOTE:

The default setting for ACESM base code is one Admin context and five User contexts. The Admin context cannot be renamed or deleted. The number of default User contexts can be increased by purchasing additional licenses to can expand the number of contexts to 250 per module.

The preliminary configurations that are required on the Admin context include:

• Management VLAN for Admin context
• Management access for Admin context
• Access VLAN for User context
• Resource allocation for User context

Management VLAN for Admin context

To establish IP connectivity, a management VLAN, in which the ACESM Admin context will be managed, needs to be created first on the switch, tl-tsw2, and the same management VLAN is then replicated on the Admin context of ACESM-123. This is accomplished in six steps:

- *Step 1* enables multiple SVIs on tl-tsw2 as depicted in Code Listing 6.24. The IOS code by default checks that only one SVI that is defined for MSFC-routing functionality is assigned to a service module. The command "svclc multiple-vlan-interfaces" turns off this default behavior or to enable multiple SVIs for the service module (i.e., ACESM-123).

> **NOTE:**
>
> Multiple SVIs are required for routed links between the ACESM and the MSFC in the routed mode deployment.

```
!
svclc multiple-vlan-interfaces
!
```

CODE LISTING 6.24

Enable multiple SVIs for ACESM

- *Step 2* is straightforward. Create the management VLAN (e.g., VLAN 41) and its corresponding SVI on tl-tsw2 as depicted in Code Listing 6.25.

```
!
vlan 41
!
interface Vlan41
 ip address 10.41.1.1 255.255.255.0
 !
```

CODE LISTING 6.25

Create management VLAN and SVI for ACESM

- *Step 3* assigns the newly created management VLAN (i.e., VLAN 41) to a SVCLC VLAN-group ("123") on tl-tsw2 as depicted in Code Listing 6.26. VLANs are assigned to a service line card (SVCLC) VLAN-group using the "svclc vlan-group <group_number> <vlan_list>" command.

```
!
svclc vlan-group 123 41
!
```

CODE LISTING 6.26

Assign management VLAN to SVCLC VLAN-group

> **NOTE:**
>
> Each SVCLC VLAN-group can contain multiple VLANs but each VLAN can only be a member of one SVCLC VLAN-group.

- **Step 4** associates SVCLC VLAN-group "123" to ACESM-123 as depicted in Code Listing 6.27. The SVCLC VLAN-group "123" is assigned to slot 5 of tl-tsw2 where ACESM-123 is located using the "svclc module <slot-number> vlan-group <group-list>" command.

```
!
svclc module 5 vlan-group 123
!
```

CODE LISTING 6.27

Associate SVCLC VLAN-group to ACESM

> **NOTE:**
>
> A VLAN-group is shared by multiple ACESM.

- **Step 5** creates the management SVI in the Admin context of ACESM-123 as depicted in Code Listing 6.28.

```
!
interface vlan 41
 ip address 10.41.1.100 255.255.255.0
 no shutdown
!
```

CODE LISTING 6.28

Create management SVI in Admin context of ACESM

> **NOTE:**
>
> Any SVI created on the ACESM is "shut down" by default. Remember to use the "no shutdown" command to undo this default behavior.

- **Step 6** defines the default route in the Admin context of ACESM-123 as depicted in Code Listing 6.29. The next hop of the defined default route points to the corresponding SVI IP (10.41.1.1) on tl-tsw2 (see Code Listing 6.25).

```
!
ip route 0.0.0.0 0.0.0.0 10.41.1.1
!
```

CODE LISTING 6.29

Define default route in Admin context of ACESM

Management access for Admin context

All management traffic destined for the Admin context of ACESM-123 must be permitted explicitly by a management service policy. This is accomplished in three steps:

- **Step 1** creates the class map in the Admin context of ACESM-123. As depicted in Code Listing 6.30, class map "REMOTE_ACCESS" defines the management traffic allowed for the Admin context of ACESM-123. This includes SSH, TELNET, ICMP, SNMP, and HTTP.

```
!
class-map type management match-any REMOTE_ACCESS
 2 match protocol ssh any
 3 match protocol telnet any
 4 match protocol icmp any
 5 match protocol snmp any
 6 match protocol http any
 !
```

CODE LISTING 6.30

Create class map in Admin context of ACESM

- **Step 2** creates the policy map in the Admin context of ACESM-123. As depicted in Code Listing 6.31, the policy map "REMOTE_MGMT_ALLOW_POLICY" defines the "permit" action for conforming traffic matching the class map defined in Step 1 (see Code Listing 6.30). For management access, a policy map of type "management" is required.

```
!
policy-map type management first-match REMOTE_MGMT_ALLOW_POLICY
 class REMOTE_ACCESS
  permit
 !
```

CODE LISTING 6.31

Create policy map in Admin context of ACESM

- **Step 3** applies the policy map "REMOTE_MGMT_ALLOW_POLICY" (see Code Listing 6.31) to the management SVI (see Code Listing 6.28) in the Admin context of ACESM-123 using the "service-policy input" command as depicted in Code Listing 6.32.

```
!
interface vlan 41
 service-policy input REMOTE_MGMT_ALLOW_POLICY
 !
```

CODE LISTING 6.32

Apply policy map to mgmt SVI in Admin context of ACESM

> **NOTE:**
>
> Currently, the ACESM software version only supports the inbound direction for any service-policy.

Access VLANs for User context

In general, three access VLANs are required on the services chassis switch to provision a User context in the ACESM:

- A client-facing VLAN.
- A server-facing VLAN.
- A dedicated VLAN for the WAN optimizer farm or cluster.

For illustration purposes, VLANs 7, 19, and 30 are created on tl-tsw2. They are depicted in Code Listing 6.33. VLAN 19 is the client-facing VLAN, VLAN 7 is the server-facing VLAN, and VLAN 30 is for the WAN optimizer farm. These VLANs are assigned to SVCLC VLAN-group 123, which in turn is associated to ACESM-123.

```
!
svclc multiple-vlan-interfaces
!
vlan 7,19,30
!
svclc vlan-group 123 7,19,30
!
svclc module 5 vlan-group 123
!
```

CODE LISTING 6.33

Access VLAN configurations for User context

Resource allocation for User context

The ACESM system resources are allocated to individual User contexts through resource classes that are configured in the Admin context. Each User context is then assigned to a single resource class.

> **NOTE:**
>
> Every User context is a member of a resource class named *default*, which has unlimited access to the system resources only when available (i.e., no guarantee). This default resource class comes into effect if no user-defined resource class has been specified for the User context. A maximum of 100 resource classes can be configured.

Individual resource classes define a minimum and maximum resource allocation that is configured as a percentage of the overall system resources. Minimum resource allocations imply a guaranteed resource allocation while maximum resource allocations can either be specified as unlimited or equal to the minimum. Defining a resource class with a maximum resource allocation of "unlimited" (i.e., 100%) allows unused resources to be accessed by User contexts that are members of this resource class.

In Code Listing 6.34, a resource-class named "Tenant-G-RA" is created to be used by the "Tenant-G" user context at a later stage (see the User Context section). This resource-class guarantees the 2% ("minimum 2.00") of the ACESM system resources and allows User contexts belonging to this resource-class to access any unused or de-allocated resources ("maximum unlimited").

```
!
resource-class Tenant-G-RA
  limit-resource all minimum 2.00 maximum unlimited
!
```

CODE LISTING 6.34

Resource allocation configurations for User context

Code Listing 6.35 illustrates how the resource-class information is verified with the "show resource allocation" exec command in the Admin context of ACESM-123.

```
ACESM-123/Admin# show resource allocation.
- - - - - - - - - - - - - - - - - - - - - - - - - - - - - - - - - - - - - - -
Parameter            Min           Max           Class
- - - - - - - - - - - - - - - - - - - - - - - - - - - - - - - - - - - - - - -
acl-memory           0.00%         100.00%       default
                     2.00%         100.00%       Tenant-G-RA

syslog buffer        0.00%         100.00%       default
                     2.00%         100.00%       Tenant-G-RA

conc-connections     0.00%         100.00%       default
                     2.00%         100.00%       Tenant-G-RA

mgmt-connections     0.00%         100.00%       default
                     2.00%         100.00%       Tenant-G-RA

proxy-connections    0.00%         100.00%       default
                     2.00%         100.00%       Tenant-G-RA

bandwidth            0.00%         100.00%       default
                     2.00%         100.00%       Tenant-G-RA

connection rate      0.00%         100.00%       default
                     2.00%         100.00%       Tenant-G-RA

inspect-conn rate    0.00%         100.00%       default
                     2.00%         100.00%       Tenant-G-RA

syslog rate          0.00%         100.00%       default
                     2.00%         100.00%       Tenant-G-RA

regexp               0.00%         100.00%       default
                     2.00%         100.00%       Tenant-G-RA
```

```
sticky               0.00%       100.00%      default
                     2.00%       100.00%      Tenant-G-RA

xlates               0.00%       100.00%      default
                     2.00%       100.00%      Tenant-G-RA

ssl-connections rate 0.00%       100.00%      default
                     2.00%       100.00%      Tenant-G-RA

mgmt-traffic rate    0.00%       100.00%      default
                     2.00%       100.00%      Tenant-G-RA

mac-miss rate        0.00%       100.00%      default
                     2.00%       100.00%      Tenant-G-RA
```

CODE LISTING 6.35

Resource allocation verification

User context

The following items (see the Admin Context section) have to be administered by the cloud service provider in the Admin context:

- Management VLAN
- Management access
- Access VLANs for User context
- Resource allocation for User context

In addition, the cloud service provider has to provision the User context for the respective tenant in the Admin context before handing over the interception and redirection configurations to the tenant.

For illustration purposes, the User context for Tenant-G is created in the Admin context of ACESM-123. Code Listing 6.36 illustrates the User context configurations for Tenant-G. The "context <context_name>" command creates a User context with a name, in this case, "Tenant-G."

VLANs 7, 19, and 30 (see Code Listing 6.33) are allocated to context "Tenant-G" using the "allocate-interface vlan" command. The resource-class "Tenant-G-RA" (see Code Listing 6.34) is added to context "Tenant-G" with the "member <resource_class_name>" command.

```
!
context Tenant-G
  allocate-interface vlan 7
  allocate-interface vlan 19
  allocate-interface vlan 30
  member Tenant-G-RA
!
```

CODE LISTING 6.36

User context configurations

> **NOTE:**
>
> The User context names are case-sensitive.

Code Listing 6.37 illustrates how the User context information is verified with the "show context <context_name>" exec command in the Admin context of ACESM-123.

```
ACESM-123/Admin# show context Tenant-G

Name: Tenant-G, Id: 1
Description:
Resource-class: Tenant-G-RA
Vlans: Vlan7, Vlan19, Vlan30
```

CODE LISTING 6.37

User context verification

After defining the User context, the next step for the cloud service provider is to configure the management access for the User context.

Management access for User context

The Tenant-G user context has already been created in Code Listing 6.36. However, the management IP has yet to be configured by the cloud service provider to facilitate end-user (tenant) log in. To access this user context initially, you can use the "changeto <context_name>" exec command at the Admin context.

After gaining access to Tenant-G context, an administrative user must be created for this context because there is no default user for User contexts. You have to explicitly create one as shown in Code Listing 6.38. The password length is at least 8 alphanumeric characters (up to a maximum of 24) and the selected role should be "Admin."

```
!
username admin password 12345678 role Admin
!
```

CODE LISTING 6.38

Create administrative user in Tenant-G context

Just like the Admin context, all management traffic destined for Tenant-G context must be permitted explicitly by a management policy map. The class map and policy map defined in Code Listings 6.30 and 6.31 can be reused for Tenant-G context. This is illustrated in Code Listing 6.39. In bridged mode, as illustrated in the next subsection (for details, see ACESM Interception: Bridged Mode), the BVI (bridge-group virtual interface) can be used as the management interface. However, a policy map cannot be applied directly onto the BVI so in Code Listing 6.39, the policy map is applied globally instead.

```
!
class-map type management match-any REMOTE_ACCESS
  2 match protocol ssh any
  3 match protocol telnet any
  4 match protocol icmp any
  5 match protocol snmp any
  6 match protocol http any
!
policy-map type management first-match REMOTE_MGMT_ALLOW_POLICY
  class REMOTE_ACCESS
   permit
!
service-policy input REMOTE_MGMT_ALLOW_POLICY
!
```

CODE LISTING 6.39

Tenant-G management access configurations

> **NOTE:**
>
> It is easier to provision another VLAN in the User context for out-of-band management purposes rather than utilizing the existing in-band VLANs. That way, the hand-over from the cloud service provider to the end-user is more clear-cut. For brevity, this is not illustrated in the ACESM configuration examples.

ACESM interception: bridged mode

The IaaS end-user, or tenant, will take over the ACESM-123 Tenant-G user context (ACESM-123/Tenant-G) configurations from this subsection onward.

Figure 6.8 depicts the logical interconnections between tl-tsw2 (MSFC), the Tenant-G context (ACESM-123/Tenant-G), SERVER71, and the WAN optimizer farm that consists of SHS31 and SH32. VLAN 19 is the client-facing VLAN that interconnects the SVI of tl-tsw2 (MSFC) for VLAN 19. VLAN 7 is the server-facing VLAN that interconnects SERVER71. VLAN 30 interconnects WAN optimizers, SH31 and SH32, to the Tenant-G context.

> **NOTE:**
>
> The DC WAN optimizers shown in Figure 6.8 are the Riverbed VSH-2050-H Virtual Steelhead appliances with logical in-path enabled. The branch WAN optimizer (not shown in the diagram for brevity) is the Riverbed SH-1050-H Steelhead appliance deployed physically in-path at the branch office of Tenant-G.

In bridged mode, the Tenant-G context is physically in-path between the client-facing VLAN 19 and server-facing VLAN 7. All traffic between these VLANs must be transparently bridged. Since the Tenant-G context is deployed physically in-path, it will play the role of intercepting and redirecting traffic flows between the clients at Tenant-G branch office and SERVER71 for WAN optimization. For more details on the ACESM bridged mode see the SLB Bridged and Routed Modes section in Chapter 3.

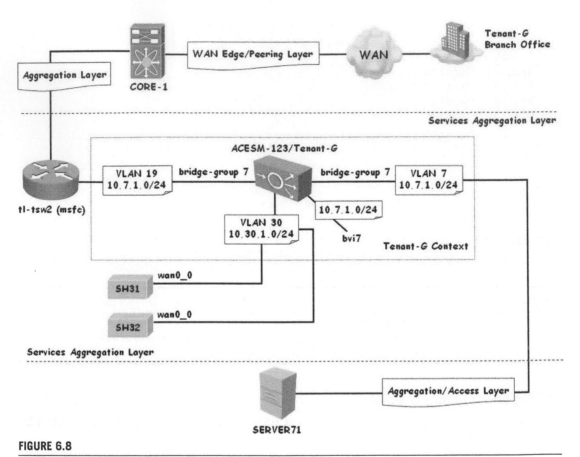

FIGURE 6.8

ACESM interception with bridged mode

The topics pertaining to ACESM interception using bridged mode are discussed in the following subsections:

- Bridged mode interface configurations
- Integrated Routing and Bridging
- Configuring real servers and server farm
- ARP interval
- Configuring service policy for interception and redirection

The configurations (or Code Listings) implemented in the following subsections are based on the setup depicted in Figure 6.8.

Bridged mode interface configurations
In bridged mode, SVIs are typically the interfaces used by the ACESM. The bridged mode interface configurations for the Tenant-G context (see Figure 6.8) are divided into six steps:

- *Step 1* creates the server-facing SVI that belongs to VLAN 7. This is depicted in Code Listing 6.40. In a bridged mode implementation, the server-facing SVI is a bridged interface (for more details, see the Integrated Routing and Bridging section). A bridged interface is L2-based and does not require an IP address.

```
!
interface vlan 7
 no shutdown
!
```

CODE LISTING 6.40

Bridged mode server-facing SVI configuration

- *Step 2* creates the client-facing SVI belonging to VLAN 19. This is depicted in Code Listing 6.41. The client-facing SVI is also a bridged interface (for more details, see the Integrated Routing and Bridging section).

NOTE:

The bridging domain encompasses only the server-facing and client-facing SVIs.

```
!
interface vlan 19
 no shutdown
!
```

CODE LISTING 6.41

Bridged mode client-facing SVI configuration

- *Step 3* creates the SVI belonging to VLAN 30 for the WAN optimizer farm. This is depicted in Code Listing 6.42. The SVI for the WAN optimizer farm is L3-based so it requires an IP address (10.30.1.123).

```
!
interface vlan 30
 ip address 10.30.1.123 255.255.255.0
 no shutdown
!
```

CODE LISTING 6.42

SVI for WAN optimizer farm configuration

- *Step 4* creates an access-control list (ACL) that allows all flows through the ACESM. This is depicted in Code Listing 6.43. The ACL named "any" explicitly allows all traffic to flow through the Tenant-G context. This ACL is applied globally at the inbound direction with the "access-group input <ACL_name>" command.

```
!
access-list any line 8 extended permit ip any any
!
access-group input any
!
```

CODE LISTING 6.43

Access-list configurations for Tenant-G context

NOTE:

The ACL can also be used on a per-interface basis.

- **Step 5** disables TCP normalization on all the newly created SVIs. This is depicted in Code Listing 6.44. TCP normalization is enabled by default on the ACESM and will interfere with the auto-discovery process (such as TCP option values and TCP sequence number changes) of the WAN optimizers. This ACE security function needs to be disabled for WAN optimization to work properly.

```
!
interface vlan 7
 no normalization
!
interface vlan 19
 no normalization
!
interface vlan 30
 no normalization
!
```

CODE LISTING 6.44

Disable TCP normalization on SVIs of Tenant-G context

NOTE:

The auto-discovery process for Riverbed Steelhead appliances uses TCP options 76 and 78.

- **Step 6** enables mac-sticky on the SVI that is associated to the WAN optimizer farm. This is depicted in Code Listing 6.45. The mac-sticky feature ensures that flows coming back through the Tenant-G context are forwarded to the same WAN optimizer. It establishes an L2 adjacency from the Tenant-G context to the WAN optimizer that handles the original SYN packet. The mac-sticky feature is typically configured on the SVI where a WAN optimizer farm (i.e., more than one WAN optimizer) is deployed.

```
!
interface vlan 30
 mac-sticky enable
!
```

CODE LISTING 6.45

Enable mac-sticky on SVI for WAN optimizer farm

> **NOTE:**
>
> The connection forwarding feature on the Riverbed Steelhead appliance can be used as an alternative to the mac-sticky feature of the ACESM.

Integrated Routing and Bridging

Bridged mode implements Integrated Routing and Bridging (IRB). IRB provides the ability to route between a bridged domain and a routed domain with the help of a BVI. The BVI is a virtual interface within the ACESM that represents a bridge-group as a routed interface. The interface number of the BVI is the link between the BVI and the configured bridge-group.

Inbound packets on a routed interface destined to a host on a segment in a bridge-group are routed to the BVI. From the BVI, the packet is in turn forwarded through a bridged interface associated with the bridge-group. Similarly, inbound packets on a bridged interface destined to a host on a routed network first go to the BVI. The BVI then forwards the packets out of the routed interface. The BVI is an L3 interface while the bridged interface is simply L2.

Interface vlan 7 (see Code Listing 6.40) and interface vlan 19 (see Code Listing 6.41) are the bridged interfaces. These SVIs are associated with bridge-group 7. This is depicted in Code Listing 6.46. With the bridge-group in place, all traffic between VLANs 7 and 19 are transparently bridged.

```
!
interface vlan 7
 bridge-group 7
!
interface vlan 19
 bridge-group 7
!
```

CODE LISTING 6.46

Associate bridge-group with the relevant SVIs

Code Listing 6.47 illustrates the BVI configurations. Since the BVI is itself a routed interface, an IP address is required. The BVI interface number is 7, which is derived from bridge-group 7 (see Code Listing 6.46). As this is a bridged (transparent) mode implementation, BVI 7, the SVI belonging to VLAN 19, and the SVI belonging to VLAN 7 will all belong to the same subnet, 10.7.1.0/24.

> **NOTE:**
>
> The default gateway of SERVER71 points to the IP address 10.7.1.1 (not shown in Figure 6.8 for brevity) of the SVI that belongs to VLAN 19 at tl-tsw2 (MSFC).

```
!
interface bvi 7
 ip address 10.7.1.123 255.255.255.0
 no shutdown
!
```

CODE LISTING 6.47

Define the bridge-group virtual interface

> **NOTE:**
>
> Any BVI created on the ACESM is shut down by default. Remember to use the "no shutdown" command to undo this default behavior.

The ACESM is not a router. It needs the help of a default route (or more specific static routes) for destinations beyond its reach. In Figure 6.8, the subnets of SERVER71, SH31, and SH32 are stub networks with no further hops downstream. A default route is required to forward traffic from these subnets to the "outside world." Code Listing 6.48 illustrates how this is done on the Tenant-G context with a default route pointing upstream to the IP address 10.7.1.1 (not shown in Figure 6.8 for brevity) of the SVI that belongs to VLAN 19 at tl-tsw2 (MSFC).

```
!
ip route 0.0.0.0 0.0.0.0 10.7.1.1
!
```

CODE LISTING 6.48

Bridged mode default route configuration

Configuring real servers and server farm

When setting up a server load-balancing configuration in an ACESM User context, real server instances, known as rservers, have to be defined. From the WAN optimization perspective, the rservers are really WAN optimizers.

As depicted in Code Listing 6.49, SH31 and SH32 (see Figure 6.8) are defined as the rservers. The "inservice" command is required to place the rserver in service. Since the WAN optimizers (i.e., SH31 and SH32) are functioning as transparent TCP proxies, NAT should not be used with them. In other words, IP address information must be preserved for traffic being redirected/load-balanced to the WAN optimizers. This particular functionality (dispatch mode) is enabled by the "transparent" keyword in the server farm definition. The rservers are added to the server farm using the "rserver <rserver_host_name>" command. Remember to also "inservice" the rservers within the server farm definition.

```
!
rserver host SH31
 ip address 10.30.1.31
 inservice
rserver host SH32
 ip address 10.30.1.32
 inservice
!
serverfarm host SH-FARM-G
 transparent
 predictor hash address 255.255.255.255
 rserver SH31
  inservice
 rserver SH32
  inservice
!
```

CODE LISTING 6.49

Real servers and server farm configurations

> **NOTE:**
>
> You can use the "no inservice" command to gracefully shut down the rserver.

Load-balancing (LB) algorithms are known as predictors in the ACESM and are used to select an rserver to respond to an incoming connection. There are two types of predictors: load predictors and traffic-pattern predictors.

Load predictors include the following load-balancing algorithms:

- Least connections with optional slow start
- Response time
- Least loaded
- Least bandwidth

Traffic-pattern predictors comprise the following load-balancing algorithms:

- Hash address: source or destination or both with optional mask
- Hash cookie (for L7 LB)
- Hash header (for L7 LB)
- Hash HTTP URL (for L7 LB)
- Hash HTTP content (for L7 LB)
- Hash Layer 4 payload
- Round robin with optional weight (the default if no predictor is explicitly specified in the server farm definition)

The hash address is the recommended predictor for load-balancing TCP connections to the WAN optimizers. It can load-balance based on either the same source or destination IP address or the same pair of source and destination IP addresses. This is to ensure that the same WAN optimizer is selected for each traffic flow instance. Hash source and destination addresses are used in Code Listing 6.49. The /32 (255.255.255.255) mask implies that the algorithm will examine and use all four octets of the IPv4 address for the hash.

Code Listing 6.50 illustrates how the state of the rservers within the server farm are verified with the "show serverfarm <serverfarm_name>" exec command. As depicted in Code Listing 6.50, the rservers SH31 and SH32 are in the "OPERATIONAL" state, which means so far so good.

```
ACESM-123/Tenant-G# show serverfarm SH-FARM-G
  serverfarm    : SH-FARM-G, type: HOST
  total rservers : 2
- - - - - - - - - - - - - - - - - - - - - - - - - - - - -
                                   - - - - - - - - - connections- - - - - - - -
          real             weight state   current   total
    ----+----------------+-----+---------+--------+-----------------
      rserver: SH31
          10.30.1.31:0       8      OPERATIONAL 0        0
      rserver: SH32
          10.30.1.32:0       8      OPERATIONAL 0        0
```

CODE LISTING 6.50

Verify real server state within server farm

ARP interval

The "arp interval" command specifies the interval (in seconds) that the ACESM sends ARP requests to the configured hosts (i.e., gateway, rservers, and learned hosts). The default is 300 sec. This interval is reduced to 15 sec as depicted in Code Listing 6.51 to speed up the host discovery process in the bridged domain.

```
!
arp interval 15
!
```

CODE LISTING 6.51

Reduce default ARP interval

The "show arp" exec command shows how the ACESM populates its ARP table. From the command output in Code Listing 6.52, there exists an ARP entry for each of the rservers (i.e., SH31 and SH32), the default gateway (i.e., next-hop of the default route), and the learned host (i.e., SERVER71).

```
ACESM-123/Tenant-G# show arp

Context Tenant-G
==================================================================
IP ADDRESS     MAC-ADDRESS       Interface  Type       Encap  NextArp(s) Status
==================================================================
10.7.1.1       00.19.07.b8.5d.c0  vlan19     GATEWAY    26     11 sec      up
10.7.1.123     00.1b.2a.65.fa.ad  bvi7       INTERFACE  LOCAL    _          up
10.7.1.71      00.50.56.a7.1b.13  vlan7      LEARNED    34     9997 sec    up
10.30.1.31     00.0e.b6.84.eb.22  vlan30     RSERVER    32     13 sec      up
10.30.1.32     00.0e.b6.85.50.54  vlan30     RSERVER    33     6 sec       up
10.30.1.123    00.1b.2a.65.fa.ad  vlan30     INTERFACE  LOCAL    _          up
==================================================================
Total arp entries 6
```

CODE LISTING 6.52

ARP table verification

Configuring service policy for interception and redirection

The WAN optimization traffic interception and redirection functions are provisioned by the ACESM load-balancing operation. In other words, the interception and redirection configurations are equivalent to defining the ACESM load-balancing action with the WAN optimizers acting as the "servers." The service policy configurations for interception and redirection should include class maps and policy maps.

The main criterion for L4 load-balancing is the requirement for a virtual IP (VIP) address. However, from the WAN optimization interception and redirection perspective, there will not be an actual VIP address since the WAN optimizer farm is in dispatch mode (for more details, see the Configuring Real Servers and Server Farm section). By not restricting the match condition to any particular VIP, TCP sessions to and from the actual server (i.e., SERVER71) will be load balanced (i.e., intercepted and redirected) to the WAN optimizer farm (i.e., SH31 and SH32) for optimization.

Code Listing 6.53 illustrates how the class map "TCP-ANY" is defined with the condition to match any TCP traffic to any VIP address.

```
!
class-map match-all TCP-ANY
   8 match virtual-address 0.0.0.0 0.0.0.0 tcp any
!
```

CODE LISTING 6.53

Bridged mode class map configuration

NOTE:

The match condition of the class map in Code Listing 6.53 assumes there is only a single TCP application running in the respective server that requires optimization. In most cases, it is recommended to refine the match condition based on the number of TCP applications and the types of TCP applications (e.g., based on TCP destination ports) that require WAN optimization.

To load balance (i.e., intercept and redirect) TCP sessions, a policy map of type "loadbalance" is required. Code Listing 6.54 illustrates how the load-balance policy map "LB-SH-G" is created. The built-in class named "class-default" is used, as there is only a single server farm named SH-FARM-G (see Code Listing 6.49) that requires load balancing.

```
!
policy-map type loadbalance first-match LB-SH-G
  class class-default
    serverfarm SH-FARM-G
!
```

CODE LISTING 6.54

Bridged mode load-balance policy map configuration

In addition, another policy map of type "multi-match" is required. Code Listing 6.55 illustrates how the multi-match policy map "INTERCEPT" is created. The main function of the multi-match policy map is to associate an incoming session that matches class map "TCP-ANY" (see Code Listing 6.53) to load balance policy map "LB-SH-G" (see Code Listing 6.54). This is done using the "loadbalance policy LB-SH-G" command. For the load-balancing operations to function properly, the VIP must be initialized with the "loadbalance vip inservice" command. The multi-match policy map is then applied to the intercepting SVIs. The intercepting SVIs of concern are the server-facing SVI for VLAN 7 and the client-facing SVI for VLAN 19. The multi-match policy map "INTERCEPT" is applied on these interfaces with the "service-policy input" command.

```
!
policy-map multi-match INTERCEPT
  class TCP-ANY
    loadbalance vip inservice
    loadbalance policy LB-SH-G
!
interface vlan 7
  service-policy input INTERCEPT
!
interface vlan 19
  service-policy input INTERCEPT
!
```

CODE LISTING 6.55

Bridged mode multi-match policy-map configuration

The service policy configurations are verified using the "show service-policy <multi-match_policy-map_name>" exec command. From the command output in Code Listing 6.56, the configured service policy is in the "ACTIVE" state and the VIP is "INSERVICE," that means the Tenant-G context is ready to intercept and redirect TCP traffic to the WAN optimizer farm for optimization.

```
ACESM-123/Tenant-G# show service-policy INTERCEPT

Status: ACTIVE
--------------------------------
Interface: vlan 7 19
  service-policy: INTERCEPT
class: TCP-ANY
    loadbalance:
      L7 loadbalance policy: LB-SH-G
      VIP Route Metric     : 77
      VIP Route Advertise  : DISABLED
      VIP ICMP Reply       : DISABLED
      VIP State: INSERVICE
      curr   conns    : 0    , hit count        : 0
      dropped conns   : 0
      client pkt count : 0   , client byte count: 0
      server pkt count : 0   , server byte count: 0
```

CODE LISTING 6.56

Bridged mode service-policy verification

ACESM interception: routed mode

Besides bridged mode, the end-user can also use routed mode for the ACESM interception deployment. For more details on the ACESM routed mode see the SLB Bridged and Routed Modes section in Chapter 3.

In routed mode implementation, the client-facing SVI and server-facing SVI belong to a different broadcast domain or subnet. As illustrated in Figure 6.9, the client-facing SVI of VLAN 19 is in subnet 10.19.1.0/24 and the server-facing SVI of VLAN 7 is in subnet 10.7.1.0/24. Subnet 10.19.1.0/24 is now the transit subnet to reach the WAN optimizer farm subnet 10.30.1.0/24 and the SERVER71 subnet 10.7.1.0/24. In other words, the Tenant-G context becomes an L3 next-hop for traversing traffic to and from SERVER71 so that interception and redirection can take place.

Figure 6.9 is the base diagram for the ACESM routed mode interception deployment and is referenced throughout the later subsections, including:

• Routed mode interface configurations
• Health monitoring with probes
• Configuring TCP probes
• WAN optimizer farm redundancy
• WAN optimizer farm redundancy example

The configurations (or code listings) implemented in the abovementioned subsections are based on the depicted setup in Figure 6.9.

Most of configurations for ACESM routed mode are similar to those described in the preceding subsections for bridged mode. For brevity, only the routed mode interface configurations are elaborated on in the next subsection.

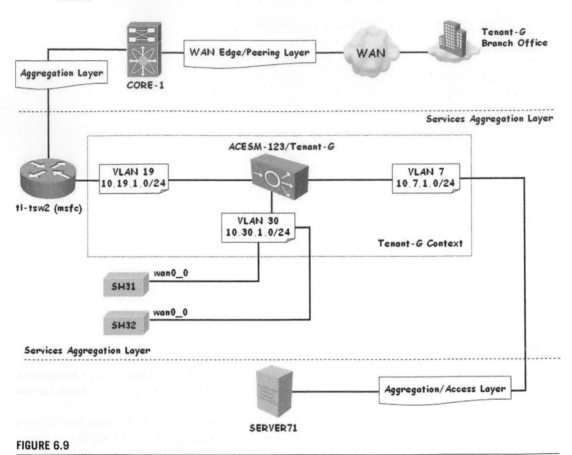

FIGURE 6.9

ACESM interception with routed mode

Routed mode interface configurations

The routed mode interface configurations require some additional configurations on the client-facing and server-facing SVIs that were previously configured for bridged mode (for more details, see the Bridged Mode Interface Configurations section).

As illustrated in Figure 6.9, the BVI is not required in routed mode deployment. The client-facing SVI of VLAN 19 is configured with an IP address of 10.19.1.123 and the server-facing SVI of VLAN 7 is configured with an IP address of 10.7.1.123. The revised configurations for these SVIs in the Tenant-G context are depicted in Code Listing 6.57. With the defined IP addresses, these SVIs become routed interfaces. The next-hop of the default route is now 10.19.1.1 (not shown in Figure 6.9 for brevity), the IP address of the SVI that belongs to VLAN 19 at tl-tsw2 (MSFC).

> **NOTE:**
>
> In routed mode, the directly reachable L3 next-hop or default gateway for the server would be on the ACESM itself. The default gateway of SERVER71 points to the IP address 10.7.1.123 (not shown in Figure 6.9 for brevity) on the server-facing SVI of VLAN 7 at the Tenant-G context.

```
!
interface vlan 7
  ip address 10.7.1.123 255.255.255.0
  no normalization
  service-policy input INTERCEPT
  no shutdown
!
interface vlan 19
  ip address 10.19.1.123 255.255.255.0
  no normalization
  service-policy input INTERCEPT
  no shutdown
!
ip route 0.0.0.0 0.0.0.0 10.19.1.1
!
```

CODE LISTING 6.57

Routed mode interface configurations

Health monitoring with probes

The ACESM supports two types of health monitoring: passive and active. The focus of this subsection is on the active health monitoring functions in the ACESM, which sends out periodic requests, known as probes, to the real servers (rservers). If the server does not respond within a defined interval, it is removed from service. Passive health check is outside the scope of this book.

Probes define what types of requests to send, what corresponding responses to look out for, as well as the time intervals for retries and timeout. It is associated with an rserver or a server farm. Currently, the ACESM has 17 different built-in probe types:

- DNS
- Echo
- Finger
- FTP
- HTTP
- HTTPS
- ICMP
- IMAP
- POP3
- RADIUS
- RTSP
- SIP
- SMTP
- SNMP
- TCP
- Telnet
- UDP

Additional customized probes (i.e., a.k.a. scripted probes) can be created using the Tool Command Language (TCL). The TCP probe configurations are covered in the next subsection. The rest of the probes are beyond the scope of this book.

Configuring TCP probes

The TCP probe can be used to monitor the health status of the WAN optimizers. Code Listing 6.58 illustrates how the TCP probe "CHK-PORT-7800" is created and applied to "SH-FARM-G" (see Code Listing 6.49) that is comprised of SH31 and SH32 (see Figure 6.9). As port 7800 is the TCP optimization service port of the Riverbed Steelhead appliances (SH31 and SH32), it is defined in TCP probe "CHK-PORT-7800" as the port to be monitored.

A TCP probe is sent to port 7800 of SH31 and SH32 at an interval of 5 seconds (default is 120 seconds) set by the "interval" command. The "passdetect interval" command specifies the time interval to send a probe to a failed WAN optimizer that is set to 2 seconds (default is 300 seconds). The "passdetect count" command sets the number of consecutive successful probe responses (required to mark the failed WAN optimizer as "SUCCESS") to 2 (default is 3). When the ACESM sends a probe, it expects a response within a default time period of 10 seconds. In Code Listing 6.58, this value is set to 15 seconds using the "receive" command.

```
!
probe tcp CHK-PORT-7800
  port 7800
  interval 5
  passdetect interval 2
  passdetect count 2
  receive 15
!
serverfarm host SH-FARM-G
  transparent
  predictor hash address 255.255.255.255
  probe CHK-PORT-7800
  rserver SH31
    inservice
  rserver SH32
    inservice
!
```

CODE LISTING 6.58

TCP probe configurations for WAN optimizers

NOTE:

Before the ACESM marks a WAN optimizer as "FAILED," it must detect that the probes have failed a consecutive number of times. By default, when three consecutive probes have failed, the ACESM marks the WAN optimizer as "FAILED." This value is changed by the "faildetect <retry-count>" command. The default retry-count of three is used in Code Listing 6.58 so that no fail-detect configuration is required.

The "show probe" exec command determines the health status of SH31 and SH32. To simulate an outage, disable the WAN optimization function on SH32 and issue the "show probe" exec command. From the command output shown in Code Listing 6.59, the health status of SH32 is reflected as "FAILED."

```
ACESM-123/Tenant-G# show probe CHK-PORT-7800
probe       : CHK-PORT-7800
type        : TCP, state : ACTIVE
- - - - - - - - - - - - - - - - - - - - - - - - - - - - - -
   port     : 7800    address    : 0.0.0.0        addr type : -
   interval : 5       pass intvl : 2              pass count : 2
   fail count : 3     recv timeout : 15
                  - - - - - - - - - - - - - probe results - - - - - - - - - - - - - - - - - - -
   probe association   probed-address   probes   failed   passed    health
- - - - - - - - - - - - - - - - - - - - - - - - - +- - - - - - - +- - - - - - - +- - - - - - - +- - - - - -
   serverfarm  : SH-FARM-G
     real      : SH31[0]
                     10.30.1.31        6        0        6          SUCCESS
     real      : SH32[0]
                     10.30.1.32        13       13       0          FAILED
```

CODE LISTING 6.59

Health status of WAN optimizers

NOTE:

Disabling the WAN optimization function does not affect IP. In fact, IP connectivity still remains intact in this case. Therefore, the probe response will still be successful if ICMP probes are used. This is also the main reason why TCP probes are preferred over ICMP probes when it comes to monitoring the WAN optimizers because TCP probes can detect both L3 and L4 connectivity issues.

WAN optimizer farm redundancy

Besides providing redundant WAN optimizers as a value-added (or premium) service option, the cloud service provider might also want to take into consideration the scenario when the entire WAN optimizer farm fails. In other words, what happens when both SH31 and SH32 (see Figure 6.9) in "SH-FARM-G" (see Code Listing 6.58) become unavailable? With no backup farm specified, the actual server farm (SERVER71) will become inaccessible if the WAN optimizer farm is down. There are three ways to alleviate this type of outage:

- **Multiple WAN optimizer farms:** For instance, "SH-Farm-G-1" performs WAN optimization for "Server-Farm-1," and "SH-Farm-G-2," for "Server-Farm-2." "SH-Farm-G-1" is configured as the backup for "SH-Farm-G-2" and the reverse applies. This particular backup method is cost effective if there are multiple server farms requiring different WAN optimizer farms for optimization.

It will not be applicable in cases where there is only a single WAN optimizer farm or there are multiple server farms relying on a single WAN optimizer farm.

- **Dedicated WAN optimizer backup farm:** Using a dedicated WAN optimizer farm to back up an existing one is technically the best solution but the end-user needs to absorb the additional costs.
- **Actual server farm:** The actual server farm itself can be used as the backup. The assumption here is the actual server farm remains available when the WAN optimizer farm is down. This is the most cost effective backup solution, although the trade-off is there will be no WAN optimization during the period the WAN optimizer farm remains down.

In Figure 6.9, the actual server farm (SERVER71) is used as the WAN optimizer backup farm. For more details, see the following subsection.

> **NOTE:**
> Implementing redundancy (or fault-tolerance) through a pair of ACESMs is outside the scope of this book.

WAN optimizer farm redundancy example

Code Listing 6.60 illustrates the configuration of using the actual server farm (SERVER71) as the backup when the WAN optimizer farm (SH-FARM-G) becomes unavailable. The configuration is a continuation of Code Listing 6.58. SERVER71 (see Figure 6.9) is defined as the rserver and is defined in server farm "BACKUP-G." Since "SERVER71" is acting as the backup for the WAN optimizer farm "SH-FARM-G" (see Code Listing 6.58), the "transparent" keyword is still applicable. The backup server farm is then defined using the "backup" keyword within the "serverfarm" command line under "policy-map type loadbalance first-match LB-SH-G" as shown in Code Listing 6.60.

```
!
rserver host SERVER71
  ip address 10.7.1.71
  inservice
!
serverfarm host BACKUP-G
  transparent
  rserver SERVER71
    inservice
!
policy-map type loadbalance first-match LB-SH-G
  class class-default
      serverfarm SH-FARM-G backup BACKUP-G aggregate-state
!
```

CODE LISTING 6.60

WAN optimizer backup farm configuration

The current status of the WAN optimizer backup farm is verified using the "show serverfarm" exec command. The command output in Code Listing 6.61 does not register any current connections at the moment because the WAN optimizer farm "SH-Farm-G" is still available.

```
ACESM-123/Tenant-G# show serverfarm BACKUP-G
  serverfarm     : BACKUP-G, type: HOST
  total rservers : 1
  - - - - - - - - - - - - - - - - - - - - - - - - - - - -

                                        - - - - - - - - connections- - - - -
           real          weight state      current    total
  - - -+- - - - - - - - - - - - -+- - - - - -+- - - - - - - - - -+- - - - - - - - -+- - - - - - - - - - - -
     rserver: SERVER71
        10.7.1.71:0    8       OPERATIONAL  0          0
```

CODE LISTING 6.61

Backup farm status before WAN optimizer farm failure

To simulate the WAN optimizer farm outage, disable the WAN optimization function on both SH31 and SH32 and issue the "show probe" exec command. As shown in Code Listing 6.62, the TCP probe configured in Code Listing 6.58 reflects the health status of SH31 and SH32 as "FAILED." The entire WAN optimizer farm is down now.

```
ACESM-123/Tenant-G# show probe CHK-PORT-7800

  probe       : CHK-PORT-7800
  type        : TCP, state : ACTIVE
  - - - - - - - - - - - - - - - - - - - - - - - - - - - - - - - - - - - -
    port      : 7800   address   : 0.0.0.0      addr type : -
    interval  : 5      pass intvl : 2           pass count : 2
    fail count : 3     recv timeout: 15
                        - - - - - - - - - - - - - - - - probe results - - - - - - - - - - - - - - - - - -
    probe association     probed-address  probes   failed   passed    health
    - - - - - - - - - - - - - - - -  - - - - - - - - - - - - -+- - - - - - - +- - - - - - - - -+- - - - - - - - - -+- - - - - -
    serverfarm : SH-FARM-G
      real    : SH31[0]
                  10.30.1.31      19919    780      19139     FAILED
      real    : SH32[0]
                  10.30.1.32      21361    3181     18180     FAILED
```

CODE LISTING 6.62

Verify health status after WAN optimizer farm failure

For verification purposes, an HTTP session is invoked from a client in the branch office of Tenant-G (see Figure 6.9) to SERVER71, which establishes successfully.

> **NOTE:**
>
> The web server is the single TCP application running in SERVER71 that requires WAN optimization.

Code Listing 6.63 provides another glance at the current status of the backup server farm using the "show serverfarm" exec command. The command output registers a current connection, confirming that the WAN optimizer backup farm "BACKUP-G" has come into action.

```
ACESM-123/Tenant-G# show serverfarm BACKUP-G
 serverfarm     : BACKUP-G, type: HOST
 total rservers : 1
 - - - - - - - - - - - - - - - - - - - - - - - - - - -
                                            - - - - - - - - - connections- - - - - - -
      real                weight state    current    total
 - - -+- - - - - - - - - - - - - - - -+- - - - -+- - - - - - - - -+- - - - - - - - -+- - - - - - - - - - - - - -
      rserver: SERVER71
        10.7.1.71:0        8      OPERATIONAL 1         1
```

CODE LISTING 6.63

Backup farm status after WAN optimizer farm failure

> **NOTE:**
>
> The WAN optimizer backup farm configurations as illustrated in Code Listing 6.60 work with TCP sessions that initiate from the client. Additional configurations (not illustrated for brevity) are required for TCP sessions that initiate from the server.

SUMMARY

WAN optimization has become a vital component in cloud-based service delivery architectures, or the SOI, because it alleviates the negative impacts of WAN latency, in turn expediting cloud adoption. In terms of implementation flexibility, it is important to ensure that WAN optimization is deployable at the various hierarchical layers of the cloud infrastructure. These layers include:

- Virtual machine level
- Core/aggregation layer
- WAN edge/peering layer
- Services aggregation layer

This chapter focused on the intercepting mechanisms at the various infrastructure layers for identifying and redirecting traffic to and from end-hosts that need to be optimized, to the respective

WAN optimizers for optimization. A special interface driver or host agent can be used for interception at the VM level that scales with the infrastructure due to centralized configuration but it adds a requirement for the server-installs, breaking organizational boundaries.

WCCPv2 and the ACESM are the more conventional ways of intercepting and redirecting traffic in private cloud deployments. WCCPv2 is positioned for the core/aggregation and WAN edge/peering layers since it is readily supported on the L3 devices that are located at these layers. In most cases, the ACESM is deployed at the services aggregation layer to provide server load-balancing services. In the WAN optimization context, the traffic interception and redirection functions are provisioned by the ACESM load-balancing operation. Finally, the chapter also covered the deployment details of WCCPv2 and the ACESM interception with their associated layers in the private cloud.

SAN Extensions and IP Storage

7

Always have a backup plan.
—**Mila Kunis**

INFORMATION IN THIS CHAPTER:

- SAN Extension Overview
- Optical Networking Solutions
- SONET/SDH Services
- FCIP
- iSCSI
- Putting It All Together
- Summary

INTRODUCTION

In Chapters 4 to 6, we covered WAN optimization in the private cloud. Chapter 7 looks at a different private computing building block—the storage module (see Figure 2.1). This chapter discusses SAN extension designs and solutions for interconnecting multiple storage modules in a private cloud computing environment. As the famous saying goes, "Do not put all your eggs (data/databases) in a single basket (DC)." A single DC (or "cloud computer") will sooner or later exhaust its resources as the number of end-users peaks. Just imagine the load impact on the various components of the DC when an entire global community is accessing it. In an era full of uncertainties, a sole DC is highly susceptible to disasters whether natural (e.g., hurricanes, earthquakes, floods, and so on) or human-made. There is certainly a need to have more than one DC in a private cloud computing environment to distribute the global user load regionally, ensure business continuity (BC), and provide disaster recovery (DR). BC and DR cannot be excluded with private cloud computing. In fact, BC and DR are part and parcel of the service-oriented infrastructure (SOI) and are mandated by cloud IaaS.

The geographical distance plays a vital role in terms of BC, DR, and end-user population. As the physical distance increases, servicable user population goes up (as a result of larger geographical scope), user traffic-load increases, service quality can degrade, and the liability of an unforeseen outage is higher. One way to simultaneously provide BC, DR, and a more efficient load distribution of end-user traffic is to have more than one DC site.

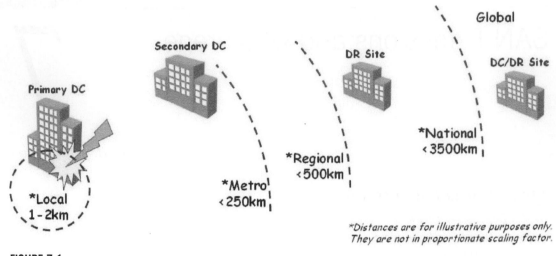

FIGURE 7.1

Approximate distance ranges for DC and DR sites

Figure 7.1 illustrates the approximate distance for DC and DR sites. The dilemma is always the same are these sites far enough for safety but still near enough for cost-effective performance? The secondary DC should be within close proximity (with the metro span radius) to the primary DC in order to support BC. A separate DR center is not always required. The secondary DC can be an active DC serving its population, doubling up as a DR site for another active DC at a different geographical location. For strict DR requirements (or regulatory compliance), a remote DC beyond the regional or national radius, in a different geographical location, is recommended.

With multiple DC sites, each site can have its own application servers, network equipment, storage devices, and so on. There is one more area that needs to be explored: data replication. The databases between the multiple DCs have to be consistent, bearing in mind that for proper BC and DR, these DCs are not supposed to stand alone. How can one achieve consistent remote replication? The answer is SAN extension.

NOTE:

The DC/DR sites referred to in this book are hot sites. A hot site holds a duplicate of the original site of the organization, with full computer systems as well as near-complete replicas of user data.

SAN EXTENSION OVERVIEW

SAN extension provides interconnectivity between multiple enterprise DCs over campus, metro, or WAN distances as well as extending the existing SAN segment between these DCs. SAN extension is also another consolidation technique to link multiple geographically distributed DCs together as one

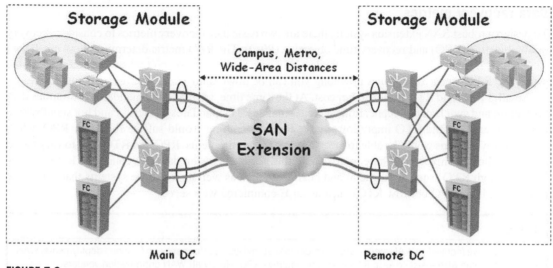

FIGURE 7.2

SAN extension for private cloud computing

virtual DC cluster, providing greater reach, as well as more reliability, availability, and serviceability (RAS) to the end-users.

Figure 7.2 (derived from Figure 1.2) illustrates the SAN extension for private cloud computing between two storage modules, each at a different location. The distance between the two enterprise DCs could be within a campus, metro, or wide-area span. SAN extension solutions include:

- Direct fiber or dark fiber
- Wavelength services such as Dense Wavelength Division Multiplexing (DWDM[1]) and Course Wavelength Division Multiplexing (CWDM[2])
- Synchronous Optical Networking (SONET) and Synchronous Digital Hierarchy (SDH[3]) services
- Fibre Channel over IP (FCIP)

Direct fiber (up to 10 km), DWDM (up to 200 km with amplification), and CWDM (up to 100 km) are typically meant for interconnecting SAN segments (or islands) within metro or regional span. SONET/SDH (thousands of kilometers) is meant for the national level and FCIP (tens of thousands of kilometers) is targeted toward the longer WAN ranges.

NOTE:

Wavelength services and SONET/SDH services are Layer-1 (L1) services. This allows a broad range of network protocols that operate at L2 or higher to be transported over these services transparently.

Data recovery metrics

To design a robust SAN extension system, there are two basic data recovery metrics to consider: recovery point objective (RPO) and recovery time objective (RTO). The RPO metric determines how much data can be lost. It is based on how far back the last backup occurred or the point where data are in a usable state. The RTO metric determines how long you can be down until your systems are recovered.

Smaller RPO and RTO imply higher cost. At the same time, smaller RPO mandates continuous data protection and synchronous replication whereas smaller RTO mandates clustering and hot standby systems. Larger RPO and RTO imply lower cost. Remote vaulting would suffice for larger RPO, while cold standby systems would be able to meet larger RTO requirements. RPO and RTO tend to vary based on the application involved. These metrics tend to fluctuate between data that cannot be lost (i.e., low RPO but high RTO) such as financial and healthcare data as well as real-time systems that cannot be down (i.e., high RPO but low RTO) such as an E-commerce web server.

> **NOTE:**
>
> In Chapter 4 we focused on WAN optimization in order to keep end-user performance up for cloud deployments. WAN optimization can also assist to keep RTO down and improve RPO. Nearly all WAN optimization vendors provide improvements for remote backup software, although performance will vary across vendors and models. Riverbed and Silver Peak are very strong for replication environments, with Riverbed providing application-layer improvements for SRDF/A, for example.

Preliminary design considerations

Besides the RPO and RTO metrics, other preliminary SAN extension design considerations include:

- Fibre Channel (FC) flow control over distance
- Application types such as:
  - Remote backup
  - Mirrors and snapshots
  - Synchronous and asynchronous replication

FC flow control over distance

The buffer-to-buffer credit (BB_Credit) mechanism provides FC link-level flow control. The fabric login (FLOGI) procedure informs the peer port of the number of BB_Credits each N_Port and F_Port has available for frame reception. Likewise, the exchange link parameters (ELP) procedure informs the peer port of the number of BB_Credits that each E_Port has available for frame reception.

> **NOTE:**
>
> For more information on terminologies, such as F_Port, N_Port, E_Port, FLOGI, and ELP, see the notes in the FCoE Data Plane section of Chapter 2.

Figure 7.3 illustrates the BB_Credit operation over a short distance optical link between an FC transmitter port and receiver port. Each time a transmitter port sends a frame, the port decrements the BB_Credit counter associated with the receiver port. The receiver port sends a receiver ready

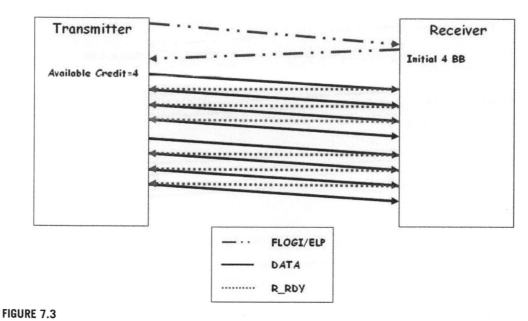

FIGURE 7.3

FC BB_Credit operation over short distance

(R_RDY) response to the transmitter port after it processes a received frame. Each time the transmitter port receives a R_RDY response, the port increments the BB_Credit counter associated with the receiver port. If the BB_Credit counter reaches zero at the transmitter port, frame transmission is stalled until an R_RDY response is received from the receiver port. This particular behavior of the BB_Credit mechanism ensures that frames are not dropped during link-level buffer overrun.

NOTE:

R_RDY is known as a primitive signal in FC terminologies.

Every FC frame sent by the transmitter port is assumed to occupy the receiver port interface buffer capacity until an R_RDY response is returned. For this reason, full (or line-rate) throughput is not sustained beyond a specific distance limit based on the buffer capacity or BB_Credits. This is reminiscent of the throughput-limiting TCP dynamics that we explored in Chapter 4. Determining the number of BB_Credits required to fully utilize the optical pipe over a specific distance is an important preliminary design consideration prior to the SAN extension implementation.

Figure 7.4 illustrates that when the distance increases, it takes time for the transmitter port to receive the R_DY responses from the receiver port, resulting in a "transmission stop-interval" at the transmitter port once the BB_Credit counter associated with the receiver port registers zero. Thus all available BB_Credits at the transmitter port have been exhausted while waiting for the respective R_RDY responses for the BB_Credit replenishment. Therefore, the maximum sustainable throughput degrades significantly when the optical link exceeds a particular distance limit. This phenomenon is

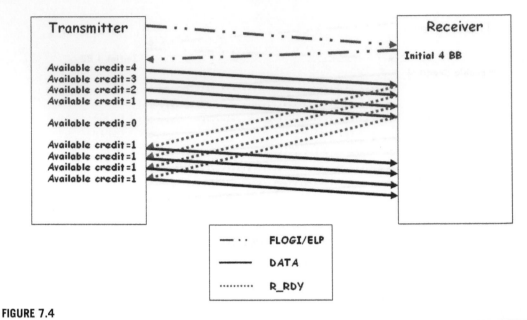

FIGURE 7.4

FC BB_Credit operation over long distance

also known as drooping. Drooping begins when the distance reaches a point where the time the light takes to make one round-trip exceeds the time it takes to transmit sufficient data to fill the receiver's link-level buffers. In other words, there must be sufficient BB_Credits in order to support line-rate throughput for a particular distance.

The following mathematical expressions are used to calculate the number of BB_Credits that is required to fully utilize the optical pipe over a specific distance:

- Drooping begins when BB_Credit < RTT/SF where:
  - RTT is the Round-trip time
  - SF is the Serialization delay for a data frame
- RTT is affected by the serialization, propagation, processing, and transmission delay:
  - RTT is the sum of SF, PF, SR, and PR, where:
    - SF is the Serialization of a data frame time
    - PF is the Propagation delay of data frame
    - SR is the Serialization of R_RDY time
    - PR is the Propagation delay of R_RDY

> **NOTE:**
>
> In the RTT calculation, the processing delay is omitted because it is considered to be insignificant compared to the other delays.

```
Distance = 80 Km
Fiber Channel Speed: 2G FC

SF = ((Frame size + 24 bytes for IDLE) * 8 bits/bytes *10/8 for 8b/10b encoding)  / (FC Speed ))* 1000000
   = ((2148+24)*10 / (2125000000 ))*1000000 [Maximum FC frame size is 2148 bytes]
   = (21720 / 2125000000 ) * 1000000
   = 10.221 µsec

SR = ((R_RDY Frame size + 8 bytes for 2 IDLE) * 8 bits/bytes *10/8 for 8b/10b encoding)
              / (FC Speed ))* 1000000
   = ((4+8)*10 /2125000000)*1000000
   = 0.056 µsec

PF = PR = (Distance in Km * 5 µsec) [It takes light 5 µsec to propagate through 1 km of optical fiber]
   = 80*5
   = 400 µsec


RTT = SF + SR + PF + PR
   = 10.221 + 0.056 + 400 + 400
   = 810.277 µsec


RTT/SF = 730.277/10.221 = 79.28 ~= 80
Therefore, 2G FC system requires 80 BB_Credits to reach 80 Km without drooping.
```

FIGURE 7.5

BB_Credit calculation to avoid drooping

Figure 7.5 shows the BB_Credit calculation to avoid drooping for a distance of 80 km based on a 2-G FC line rate. These calculations are for illustration purposes only. The other alternative is to use the industry's rule of thumb as a rough gauge:

- One BB_Credit supports up to 1 km of distance at full throughput for 2G FC, or
- One BB_Credit supports up to 2 km of distance at full throughput for 1G FC, or
- Two BB_Credit supports up to 1 km of distance at full throughput for 4G FC, and so on.

> **NOTE:**
>
> 1G FC = 1.0625 Gbps; 2G FC = 2.125 Gbps; 4G FC = 4.25 Gbps; 10G FC = 10.51875 Gbps.

The industry rule of thumb is actually derived from the mathematical formulas shown in Figure 7.5. Full line-rate throughput can be difficult to achieve over long distances due to the high BB_Credit count requirement on a physical port. Some FC switch vendors overcome this hardware constraint through the support of thousands of BB_Credits for each port on some of the FC switch's line cards.

> **NOTE:**
>
> R_RDY spoofing can be used to extend beyond what the negotiated buffer credit allows. In this case the R_RDY signal, normally used by the FC switches to indicate that a frame has been received, is intercepted and simulated by the interconnecting transit node for every frame the FC switch transmits.

Remote backup

Remote backup is sometimes known as remote vaulting, which is much faster than standard offsite vaulting, i.e., trucking in tapes. In this approach, data are backed up using standard backup applications, such as Symantec (formerly Veritas) NetBackup, but the backup site is situated at a remote location. Backup or archived copies of files can be stored on tape so that they can be restored when required.

Mirrors and snapshots

A mirror is a fully redundant 100% copy of the primary volume. The secondary volume is the same size as the primary volume and all data blocks are in the same place. For this reason, the metadata will be the same. After the data have been copied, it can be read from either the primary or secondary volume.

NOTE:

Metadata are pointers to the data blocks in a volume at any point in time. Metadata will be revised whenever any data blocks are written, modified, or deleted.

In terms of replication, once the mirroring completes, the secondary volume is desynchronized from the primary volume to create a split mirror that is then frozen in time. Data can then be replicated to a remote DC by reading data from the split mirror and writing to the replicated volume. Other applications continue to read and write to the primary volume during replication without any performance impact on the running applications.

To sum up, the properties of a mirror include:

- Full copy of data volume and metadata
- Creates redundant secondary data volume
- Utilizes more disk space
- Longer duration to copy
- Only available when full mirroring is completed

A snapshot is a point-in-time copy of the metadata together with a copy of any blocks that have been modified after the last snapshot was taken. A snapshot is not considered a redundant copy since it only involves one copy of the data. However, it consumes less disk space and is readily available.

The metadata are frozen in time after the snapshot is taken. The snapshot metadata contain the pointers to the original data blocks in the primary volume. In this case, applications continue to read and write to the primary volume, thus any changed data blocks are written to a different area. Data can be replicated to a remote DC by reading data from the primary volume and writing data to the replicated volume. However, both the running applications and the replication process access the primary volume during replication, reducing the application performance.

To sum up, the properties of a snapshot include:

- Point-in-time copy of metadata
- Only copy modified data blocks
- Uses only the primary data volume
- Utilizes less disk space
- Readily available
- Provides point-in-time roll back to the last snapshot

> **NOTE:**
>
> Continuous data protection (CDP) can roll back to any point in time because all data modifications are logged continuously, although only one copy of the data exists.

Synchronous and asynchronous replications

Replications are typically array-based. Some array-based replication schemes include:

- EMC Symmetrix Remote Data Facility (SRDF)
- Hitachi True Copy
- IBM Peer-to-Peer Remote Copy (PPRC)

Replication can be generally categorized into two modes: synchronous and asynchronous. When synchronous replication mode is used, the local host system is not notified that an SCSI write command has completed until the remote copy is done. Figure 7.6 illustrates an example of synchronous replication.

The advantage of synchronous replication is that it ensures both the local and remote FC disk arrays are updated before the local host system continues the next SCSI write. The disadvantage of synchronous replication is that the host must wait for the remote write to complete. If the remote array is distant, or connected through a high latency link, this will adversely impact performance.

Concisely, in synchronous replication mode:

- Data must be written to both arrays before an I/O operation is done.
- Data in both arrays is always fully synchronized and updated.

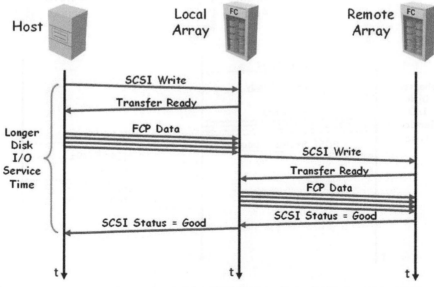

FIGURE 7.6

Synchronous replication example

- Distance between sites is a direct factor to consider in terms of application performance as latency increases with distance.

When asynchronous replication mode is used, the local host system is notified that an SCSI write command has completed before the remote copy is completed (the remote copy is updated asynchronously at a later point in time). Figure 7.7 gives an example of asynchronous replication.

The advantage of asynchronous replication is that the host system is acknowledged immediately by the local FC disk array and subsequent SCSI writes can follow without waiting for the completion of the remote copy. The disadvantage is that the local and remote copies of the data are not the same until the remote update completes. If there is a system or link outage during this time, the two copies might not match.

Concisely, in asynchronous replication mode:

- Modified data are cached until data can be replicated.
- Data in remote disk array is never completely synchronized or up-to-date.
- The increase in application performance at the cost of data protection.
- Longer geographical distances are covered and higher latencies are tolerated.

Private enterprises have to assess the pros and cons of each replication mode to determine which suits their DC cloud computing environment better. The factors to consider include:

- Implementation costs.
- DR site goals, including geographical proximity to the primary SAN.

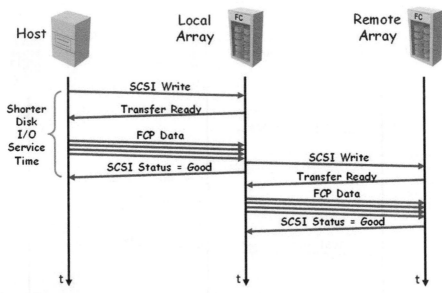

FIGURE 7.7

Asynchronous replication example

- The cost of losing data (high RPO).
- The cost of prolonged recovery time (high RTO).
- Application-dependent heterogeneous solutions.

A mix of synchronous and asynchronous solutions can achieve better results than relying solely on either one. That is, implement synchronous replication to a secondary site but use asynchronous replication instead to a more distant tertiary site. Using a relational database management system (RDBMS) as an example:

- The redo logs are synchronously replicated to the remote site.
- The archive logs are either asynchronously replicated or backed up at specific timings—for instance, nightly.
- Periodic point-in-time copies of data and control files are asynchronously replicated or backed up at intervals.

OPTICAL NETWORKING SOLUTIONS

This section discusses some of the optical networking solutions that can be used for SAN extension. They include:

- Dark fiber
- DWDM
- CWDM

Dark fiber

Dark fiber can provide direct optical interconnectivity between two FC SAN segments located within a campus range (<10 km). Dark fibers are typically spare or excess fibers installed in place, by an optical network provider, to accommodate future growth. Because these spare fibers are not carrying signal (no light) before leasing, they are also referred to as unlit fibers. The type of fiber used defines the maximum link distances for connecting FC ports over dark fiber:

- Single-mode 9-μm fiber supports 10-km distances at 1 Gbps, 2 Gbps, 4 Gbps, and 10 Gbps.
- Multimode 50-μm fiber supports 500-m distances at 1 Gbps, 300-m distances at 2 Gbps, 150-m distances at 4 Gbps, and 82-m distances at 10 Gbps.
- Multimode 62.5-μm fiber supports 350-m distances at 1 Gbps, 150-m distances at 2 Gbps, and 75-m distances at 4 Gbps.

NOTE:

The 9-μm core diameter of a single-mode fiber is small enough to allow only a single propagation mode (or path) through the fiber. The 50-μm or 62.5-μm core diameter of a multimode fiber is much larger resulting in modal dispersion or multiple propagation modes (or paths) through the fiber. This also explains why single-mode fibers can transmit for a much greater distance than multimode fibers.

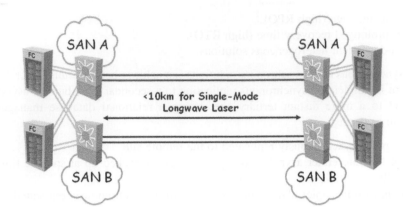

FIGURE 7.8

SAN extension with dark fibers

When two FC switches are connected together with an interswitch link (ISL), they merge fabrics and become part of the same fabric with a shared address space, shared services, and a single principal switch. This is considered a disruptive event at the point in time when the interconnection takes place. The FC routing protocol, Fabric Shortest Path First (FSPF[4]), can also disruptively reconstruct a new routing table that is distributed to all switches within the fabric.

When a link outage occurs, the single fabric is segmented into two separate fabrics, each with its own address space, FC services, and principal switch. In this case, FSPF must disruptively build a routing table for each segmented fabric again. Figure 7.8 illustrates the different paths or multiple dark fibers that are required in an SAN extension deployment to offset some of the mentioned constraints. For more details on HA techniques, see the FCIP HA section.

An enterprise that wishes to extend an FC SAN between DCs within a distance of approximately 10 km can lease dark fiber to avoid installation and right-of-way (or public throughway) issues that are associated with installing optical cables directly. Nevertheless, the cost of factoring in diverse paths for availability can be prohibitive in some cases.

DWDM

Transporting a single data stream through an optical fiber can be costly and inefficient. Wavelength-Division Multiplexing (WDM) can transmit multiple, independent data streams through a single optical fiber to better utilize the bandwidth of the given optical fiber. Each data stream adopts a different wavelength of light (aka lambda) and the data streams travel through a single fiber. With WDM, multiple cloud IaaS tenants can share the same optical fiber. Closely spaced wavelengths provide a higher number of channels (or bandwidth) per fiber. DWDM falls under this category.

The DWDM pitch

For many SAN engineers, DWDM is the ideal SAN extension mechanism since it provides:

- Very high scalability
- Very low, predictable latency
- Moderately long distances

In addition, DWDM can accommodate Enterprise System Connection (ESCON[5]) solutions as well as Fiber Connection (FICON[6]) and FC. Although DWDM supports FC SAN extension with longer ranges, the distance capacity is still limited by the application (for more details, see the Synchronous and Asynchronous Replications section) and the FC flow control mechanism (for more details, see the FC Flow Control over Distance section). Synchronous replication requires high bandwidth and low latency over long distances. DWDM fulfils these requirements, making it an ideal fit for synchronous replication applications.

NOTE:

Besides DWDM, FCIP also supports FICON.

Nevertheless, financial controllers might find the cost (the main trade-off) for DWDM somewhat prohibitive:

- DWDM equipment is more expensive than other solutions.
- Dark fiber can be costly to lease.
- DWDM services are not as widely available as SONET or SDH. If DWDM is adopted, the enterprises might need to implement and manage their own DWDM solutions.
- DWDM does not have the same robust management capabilities as SONET/SDH and this can also increase the cost of management.

DWDM functional overview

A single fiber pair connecting two FC switches together through an ISL uses only a single channel wavelength of light between the two switches. With DWDM, multiple channels can share a single fiber pair by dividing the light up into discrete wavelengths or lambdas (λ), separated by approximately 0.4-nm (50-GHz) spacing around the 1550-nm wavelength region of the infrared spectrum. Each DWDM lambda can support a full-duplex FC, ESCON, FICON, or Ethernet channel (port channel).

NOTE:

DWDM systems primarily use C- and/or L-band ranges, which start around 1500 nm and go higher. The formula to calculate wavelength (λ) is $\lambda = c/\text{frequency}$ where c is the speed of light in meters per second, frequency is in Hertz, and λ is in meters.

The basic DWDM components include transponders and (de)multiplexers. Figure 7.9 illustrates a simple DWDM setup. The DWDM transponders convert each channel into its dedicated lambda and multiplex it onto a 2.5-Gbps, 10-Gbps, or 40-Gbps link between the DWDM (de) multiplexers.

NOTE:

It is expected that 100G wavelengths will debut on some production networks in 2011, and by 2012, the first-generation 100G DWDM optical network transport deployments will be commercially available.

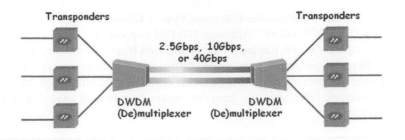

FIGURE 7.9

Simplified DWDM network

DWDM distance capacity

Before discussing the various factors that will limit the DWDM capacity, it is worthwhile to examine some of the optional DWDM components that can play a pivotal role in the enhancement or deterioration of the distance capacity. The optional DWDM components include:

- **Optical amplifier:** For longer distances, flat-gain optical amplifiers can boost the signal on longer ranges or to preamplify the signal before it leaves the local site. The most common type of optical amplifier is the Erbium-doped fiber amplifier (EDFA). Conventional EDFAs operate in the 1530-nm to 1563-nm wavelength range.

> **NOTE:**
>
> An example of an EDFA is the Cisco ONS 15501, which has a wavelength range of 1530 nm to 1563 nm.

- **Dispersion Compensation Units (DCUs):** DCUs are used to prevent signal degradation due to dispersion of the optical signals over long distances. DCUs might need to be deployed for 10-G Ethernet and FC at distances over 50 km.
- **Optical add drop multiplexers (OADMs):** OADMs can be deployed for added signal grooming flexibility. OADMs allow a particular wavelength on the fiber to be demultiplexed (or dropped) and remultiplexed (or added) while at the same time bypassing all other wavelengths. The wavelengths that pass through an OADM filter will experience a small amount of signal attenuation.
- **Variable Optical Attenuators (VOAs):** VOAs are required for DWDM ring topologies when OADMs are used. When the OADM injects a new wavelength into the ring, the signal strength of that wavelength can be stronger than other wavelengths at that point on the ring. The VOA attenuates (or reduces) the strength of the new wavelength so that it matches the strength of the other wavelengths.

Although DWDM distances are typically grouped into three categories: interoffice (0–300 km), long haul (300–600 km), and extended long haul (600–2000 km), the actual distance capacity is still limited by a number of factors:

- Optical signals can travel about 100 km before they need to be amplified or regenerated.
- With amplification, the point-to-point distance for a DWDM link is about 200 km. At longer distances, further amplification will distort the optical signal.

- With regeneration, the point-to-point distance for a DWDM link can be extended further. However, additional latency is incurred during the regeneration process.
- The maximum distance for a DWDM link is dependent on the components used along the link, such as optical amplifiers, DCUs, VOAs, OADMs, and so on.

As a rule of thumb, the maximum point-to-point distance is about 200 km with amplification only (i.e., no regeneration).

DWDM linear topologies

The most straightforward way to implement DWDM is through a point-to-point topology. The top diagram of Figure 7.10 shows a simple unprotected point-to-point topology. The point-to-point topology interconnects the primary DC to a remote DC for data mirroring or snapshot applications to support backup and DR applications. For a protected point-to-point topology (or operation), the two sites must be connected by two fiber pairs instead of a single pair.

The bottom diagram of Figure 7.10 shows a bus topology where multiple sites are connected in a linear model. Specific wavelengths (or lambdas) are used between the central site and each remote site. This topology can interconnect multiple campuses in an MAN. The bus topology offers only limited protection.

DWDM ring topologies

DWDM ring topologies are typically deployed in MANs. DWDM rings can span tens of kilometers. The ring topologies can support any-to-any traffic (as in meshed ring) or they can be configured with a hub and satellite nodes (as in hubbed ring). Traffic can be unidirectional or bidirectional.

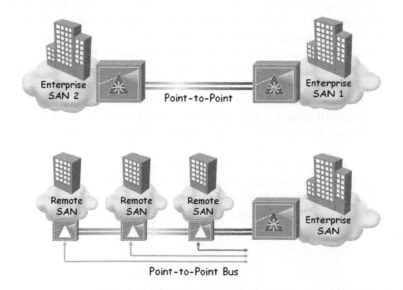

FIGURE 7.10

DWDM linear topologies

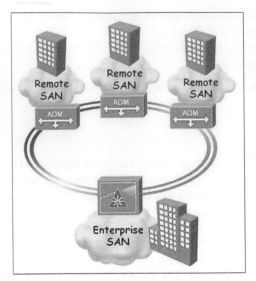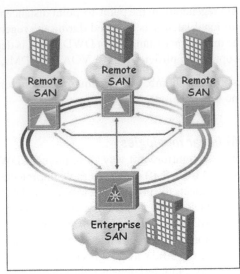

FIGURE 7.11

DWDM ring topologies

The left diagram in Figure 7.11 shows a hubbed ring topology that interconnects an enterprise DC to three remote sites using DWDM as the transport. This type of topology is also known as hub and spoke, because each of the spoke nodes is logically connected to only the hub node. In a hubbed ring, the hub can use terminal mux/demux modules, while each of the spoke nodes must be equipped with OADM modules. In the left diagram of Figure 7.11, the corporate HQ site is the hub and OADMs are used at the remote sites to add and drop specific wavelengths. At the spoke nodes, one or more wavelengths can be dropped off or added while the others are passed through transparently.

This network topology also enhances reliability and availability with its ring switching capability. Ring protection is supported using per-channel unidirectional path switching or bidirectional path switching. If there is a fiber cut between any of the sites, communications are not disrupted between the sites. However, cost still plays a major factor here. Ring topologies are normally confined to an MAN or campus situation but they can also be extended to very long distances with amplification and regeneration.

The right diagram of Figure 7.11 shows a mesh ring topology where each site is connected to a DWDM (de)multiplexer. In this configuration, specific wavelengths (or lambdas) are used between each pair of sites. Meshed rings provide a full logical mesh whereby every site can communicate with every other site. If this is not a requirement, individual nodes can be connected only to other specific nodes or groups of nodes through specific lambdas and a partial mesh is formed instead.

CWDM

CWDM, just like DWDM, uses multiple light wavelengths to transmit signals over a single optical fiber. Nevertheless, the two technologies vary in many ways:

- CWDM uses a 20-nm wavelength spacing that is much wider than the 0.4 nm for DWDM. The wider wavelength spacing in CWDM means lower product development costs. This is one reason why CWDM is less costly than DWDM.

> **NOTE:**
>
> Most CWDM devices operate in the 1470-nm to 1610-nm range. The frequency grid for DWDM and the wavelength grid for CWDM systems are defined by the International Telecommunications Union (ITU) standards G.694.1 and G.694.2, respectively.

- CWDM provides a maximum of 8 lambdas between two CWDM multiplexers over a single fiber pair as compared to DWDM, which support up to 32 lambdas (based on 0.8-nm or 100-GHz wavelength spacing) over a single fiber pair.

> **NOTE:**
>
> Some long-haul DWDM systems can support up to 160 lambdas per fiber pair.

- Each CWDM channel uses a specialized gigabit interface converter (GBIC[7]) or small form-factor pluggable (SFP[8]) transceivers. These specialized transceivers are commonly known as colored GBIC and SFP. Each CWDM channel uses a different "color" GBIC or SFP because each lambda represents a different color in the spectrum. In this case, the native GBIC or SFP in the client devices are substituted with a colored GBIC or SFP.
- CWDM multiplexers are usually passive (i.e., not powered) devices containing a very accurate prism to multiplex eight separate wavelengths of light along a single fiber pair. Passive devices cannot generate or repeat optical signals.
- No amplification is possible with CWDM because CWDM uses wavelengths that cannot be amplified with EDFA amplifiers. Therefore, the maximum distance for a CWDM link is approximately 100 km.

> **NOTE:**
>
> The Cisco ONS 15501 EDFA, which has a wavelength range of 1530 nm to 1563 nm, can only amplify two signals (1530 nm and 1550 nm) out of the eight signals that are multiplexed onto the fiber pair.

CWDM provides an alternative solution to DWDM for low-latency and high-bandwidth requirements associated with synchronous replication applications. However, DWDM is more scalable than CWDM. DWDM also has a longer distance capacity than CWDM because DWDM can be amplified. The main benefit of CWDM is its low cost. It is a cheaper solution than DWDM. In other words, CWDM is optimized for cost, while DWDM is optimized for bandwidth. For enterprises that have access to dark fiber and have only limited scalability requirements, CWDM is a relatively inexpensive way to achieve low-latency and high-bandwidth interconnections between DCs. The CWDM implementation also results in less complex installation, configuration, and operation as compared to DWDM.

CWDM topologies

CWDM can be deployed in point-to-point, linear, or fiber protected ring topologies. It is limited to a distance of up to 120 km for Gigabit Ethernet and 100 km for 2-G FC in a point-to-point topology. It is typically used only for extension of the FC fabric in a metro or campus application. As CWDM carries only eight lambdas on a single fiber pair, there are limits to the number of possible drops and the number of sites that can be interconnected. A ring or linear topology reduces the distance depending on the number of OADMs traversed by the CWDM channels because each OADM introduces additional power loss in the network.

CWDM can also be used to enable multiple ISL connections between the switches over a single fiber since it requires less fiber for interconnecting two metro sites. The same benefit applies to port channel implementation between the switches.

In short, DWDM is a solution that provides a higher number of connections and longer reach, or extension, at a much higher cost while CWDM is a more cost-effective solution for metro or campus solutions where the distance is limited.

SONET/SDH SERVICES

SONET/SDH is a TDM-based technique for framing data (or voice) onto a single wavelength on fiber. SONET is an ANSI specification. SDH is the SONET-equivalent specification proposed by the ITU-T (originally defined by the ETSI). The primary differences between the SONET and SDH specifications are the basic transmission rate and some header information. With a few exceptions, SDH can be thought of as a superset of SONET. From the enterprise perspective, SONET/SDH typically forms the L1 transport underlying some other form of upper layer connections. SONET/SDH offers the following advantages:

- SONET/SDH services have a significant installed base and are readily available in many areas. Although a point-to-point SONET/SDH link (without repeaters) is typically 50 km or less, many long-haul fiber connections are still SONET/SDH-based due to the fact that repeaters are widely deployed in many SP networks to boost signals that are carried across long distances. For this reason, SONET/SDH services allow longer distances at a lower cost than purely optical transports like DWDM and CWDM.
- While FCIP is another SAN extension option for longer distances, SONET/SDH services tend to have lower latencies than FCIP. For the best of both worlds, FCIP can ride on top of the L1 SONET/SDH services.
- SONET/SDH provides various protection schemes, including N+1 protection, which is a more cost-effective protection scheme than 1+1 protection schemes. DWDM and CWDM do not offer N+1 protection capability. In addition, SONET/SDH has a subsecond failover time of 50 ms that is transparent to the upper layer protocols. For instance, the 50-ms failover recovery time is considered negligible to the FC Receiver Transmitter Timeout Value (R_T_TOV) of 100 ms (the default).

NOTE:

In 1+1 protection, a working card is paired with a protect card of the same type. If the working card fails, the traffic from the working card switches to the protect card. N+1 protection allows a single card to protect multiple working cards.

- SONET/SDH provides a wide range of transmission rates which include OC-3 (155.52 Mbps), OC-12 (622.08 Mbps), OC-48 (2.49 Gbps), OC-192 (9.95 Gbps), and OC-768 (39.81 Gbps).

> **NOTE:**
>
> OC-192 rate and above is required if there is more than one 2-G FC or FICON channel.

SONET/SDH supports FC and FICON with the help of the Generic Framing Procedure (GFP[9]) that allows mapping of 8b/10b[10] encoded data streams over a transport network like SONET/SDH. GFP can also carry gigabit Ethernet, ESCON, or any other 8b/10b encoded data. The details of GFP are beyond the scope of this book.

> **NOTE:**
>
> Next-generation SONET/SDH extends the utility of the existing SONET/SDH network by leveraging the existing Layer-1 networking. It also includes technologies, such as Virtual Concatenation (VCAT), Generic Framing Procedure (GFP), and the Link Capacity Adjustment Scheme (LCAS).

SONET/SDH Topologies

SONET/SDH can be deployed using various topologies:

- Point to point
- Linear add/drop multiplexer (ADM)
- Two-fiber unidirectional path switch ring (UPSR)
- Two-fiber bidirectional line switch ring (BLSR)
- Four-fiber BLSR
- Path-protected mesh

Any of these topologies can be used in the MAN or for larger geographical areas. The incremental way is to begin with a point-to-point deployment with two sites and gradually evolve to a ring as more sites are included. A ring is defined as a set of nodes interconnected to form a closed loop, where fiber cables serve as links.

A UPSR protects against fiber cuts and node failures by providing duplicate, geographically diverse paths for each circuit. UPSR provides dual fiber paths around the ring. Working traffic flows clockwise in one direction and protection traffic flows anticlockwise in the opposite direction. UPSR uses path (or span) switching. In the event that a fiber or node failure takes place in the working traffic path, the receiving node switches to the path coming from the opposite direction. A connection/circuit on a UPSR uses the capacity of the entire ring. Because each traffic path is transported around the entire ring, UPSRs are more appropriate for a hub-and-spoke network with traffic flowing through one central hub.

A BLSR uses bidirectional line (or ring) switching protection mechanisms. Line-switched rings use the SONET/SDH line level indications to initiate protection switching. BLSR nodes can terminate traffic that is fed from either side of the ring. They are suited for distributed node-to-node traffic applications such as interoffice networks and access networks. This protection system is more costly but allows bandwidth to be reused around the ring and can carry more traffic than a UPSR because a connection/circuit on a BLSR uses only the capacity between the nodes.

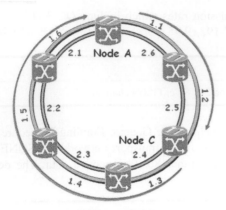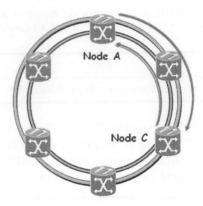

2-Fiber UPSR   **2-Fiber BLSR**

FIGURE 7.12

SONET/SDH ring topologies

A 4-fiber BLSR differs from a 2-fiber BLSR in that it allows path (or span) switching as well as line (or ring) switching, thereby adding another layer of protection but at a more expensive cost. Hence, 4-fiber BLSRs are usually used for higher bandwidth applications and when the most protection of the traffic is required.

The nodes on a SONET/SDH ring are really add/drop multiplexers (ADMs). Two fiber spans are required to complete a connection between two nodes and in a ring configuration this results in two available paths. The left diagram of Figure 7.12 illustrates a UPSR. Spans 1.1, 1.2, 1.3, 1.4, 1.5, and 1.6 is the primary path of the ring. Spans 2.1, 2.2, 2.3, 2.4, 2.5, and 2.6 is the protection path.

If node A sends data to node C the traffic travels clockwise across span 1.1 and 1.2. If node C sends data to node A, the traffic still travels clockwise across spans 1.3, 1.4, 1.5, and 1.6. Thus there will be a latency difference between sending a message from node A to node C and sending a message from node C to node A.

The right diagram of Figure 7.12 illustrates a BLSR. If a user connected to node A would like to communicate with a user connected to node C, the request traffic travels clockwise from node A to node C. If the user on node C would like to respond back to node A, the response traffic travels anticlockwise back to node A.

As for a path-protected mesh network (PPMN), it is an interconnected hybrid mix of linear and ring topologies. If route diversity is part of the design, PPMN would be the ideal choice as compared to other network topologies.

FCIP

FCIP is a tunneling protocol that allows SAN segments (or islands) to be interconnected over IP networks. The connection is transparent to native FC and the result of an FCIP link between two different SAN fabrics is a fully merged FC fabric. FCIP encapsulates FC frames and uses TCP/IP as the underlying transport to provide congestion control and in-order delivery of error-free data. With FCIP, organizations are able to leverage their current IP infrastructure and management resources to interconnect and extend existing native FC SANs for private cloud computing. In addition, long geographical distances are no longer a constraint when using FCIP.

FCIP primer

This section discusses the following FCIP concepts:

- FC frame encapsulation
- Virtual expansion ports (VE_Ports)
- FCIP links and virtual interswitch links (virtual ISLs)

FC frame encapsulation

The IETF FC frame encapsulation specification (RFC3643) defines the encapsulation header for FC frames. It is not specific only to the FCIP protocol as it is also used for the Internet Fibre Channel Protocol (iFCP[11]). The header is 28 bytes (or 7 words) and includes a time stamp, a cyclic redundancy check (CRC), and provisions for FCIP special frames (FSF).

NOTE:

FSF negotiation (optional) provides an additional authentication security mechanism by determining whether a newly created TCP connection is associated with the correct FCIP link before FC fabric initialization of the connection commences. The first bytes sent from the TCP connect request initiator to the receiver are an FSF identifying both the sender and who the sender thinks is the receiver. If the contents of this FSF are correct and acceptable to the receiver, the unchanged FSF is echoed back to the sender. This send/echo process is the only set of actions that allows the TCP connection to be used to carry FC fabric traffic.

Figure 7.13 illustrates the nesting of the various upper layer protocol data units (PDUs) of an encapsulated FC frame in an IP packet.

NOTE:

All frame data for FC, including FC flag header information and CRC, remain intact for use on the FC network after the IP capsule is removed.

VE_Ports

An FCIP link connects two separate portions of an FC fabric together to form a single FC fabric, using an IP network as the transport. Each end of an FCIP link is associated with a virtual expansion port (VE_Port). A VE_Port behaves exactly like a standard FC E_Port, except that the transport in this case is FCIP (which is TCP/IP based) rather than native FC. A VE_Port is uniquely identified by an 8-byte VE_Port_Name.

NOTE:

The terms FCIP link and FCIP tunnel are synonymous.

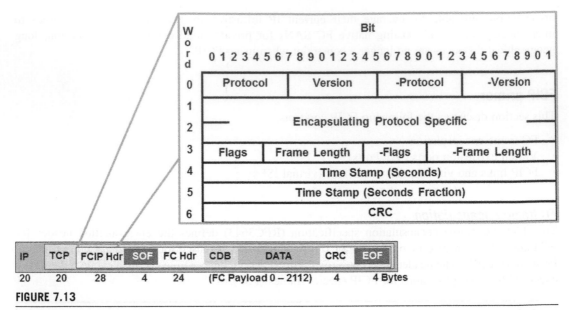

FIGURE 7.13

IETF FC frame encapsulation

The VE_Port interfaces with the FCIP link endpoint (FCIP_LEP). The FCIP_LEP formats, encapsulates, and forwards encapsulated FC frames. Encapsulated FC frames are sent as TCP segments over the IP network. The FCIP_LEP receives byte-encoded start-of-frame (SOF) or end-of-frame (EOF) delimited FC frames and a time stamp from its VE_Port.

The FCIP data engine (FCIP_DE) is the data forwarding component of the FCIP_LEP. It handles all encapsulation/de-encapsulation and transmission/reception of the encapsulated FC frames on the FCIP link. The FCIP_LEP contains one or more FCIP_DEs, each corresponding to a TCP connection.

FCIP links and virtual ISLs

The FCIP link is composed of one or more TCP connections between two FCIP_LEPs. Each link carries encapsulated FC frames. When the FCIP link is established, a virtual ISL (Inter-Switch Link) is also established between the VE_Ports at both ends of the FCIP link. Figure 7.14 provides a simple illustration on the FCIP link and virtual ISL.

> **NOTE:**
>
> The FC-BB-3 specification defines two functional models for Fibre Channel Backbone (FC-BB) devices that connect to IP networks: VE_Port and B_Access. The VE_Port model is implemented by FC switches with integrated FCIP functionality. The B_Access model is implemented by FCIP devices that are external to the FC switches. Devices that implement the B_Access functional model are known as FCIP bridges. The interface within an FCIP bridge to which an FC switch connects is called a B_Port. The term virtual ISL, when used unqualified, refers to VE_Port virtual ISL and B_Access virtual ISL.

The VE_Port initialization behavior is identical to a normal E_Port. This behavior is independent of the link being FCIP or native Fibre Channel. The VE_Ports communicate between themselves using

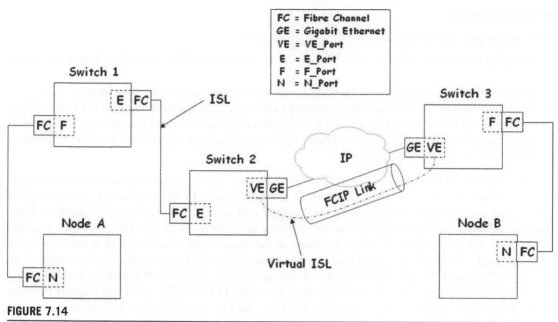

FIGURE 7.14

FCIP link and virtual ISL

Switch Internal Link Services (SW_ILS[12]), such as Exchange Link Parameter (ELP[12]), Exchange Switch Capabilities (ESC[12]), Build Fabric (BF[12]), Reconfigure Fabric (RCF[12]), Fabric Shortest Path First (FSPF), and so on.

The FCIP link carries encapsulated FC traffic between FCIP_LEPs over an IP network using TCP port 3225 which is the default TCP well-known port (WKP) for FCIP. More than one TCP connection between two FCIP_LEPs is possible. An example is the Cisco MDS 9000 Series storage switch which creates two TCP connections for each FCIP link:

- One connection is used for data frames (Class 3).
- The other connection is used only for FC control frames, that is, interswitch frames (Class F). This arrangement provides low latency for all control frames (ELP, ESC, and so on).

NOTE:

Class F is used between FC switches to communicate fabric-related traffic on ISLs. Class 3 is a connectionless class of service with no confirmation of delivery or notification of nondelivery.

NOTE:

The FC-BB-3 specification requires all FC backbone networks (this includes FCIP) to support Class F frames. Class 2, 3, and 4 frames can be optionally supported. Class 1 and 6 frames are not supported. FC primitive signals, primitive sequences, and Class 1 FC frames are not transmitted across an FCIP link because they cannot be encoded using FC frame encapsulation. In practice, only Class 3 (for data) and Class F (for control) are used.

FCIP topologies

FCIP topologies are fairly straightforward. They include:

- **Point-to-point:** The point-to-point topology uses a dedicated FCIP tunnel to interconnect two sites. This topology is commonly associated with an initial deployment involving just two sites. This deployment can grow to a hub-and-spoke topology as more sites are added.
- **Hub-and-spoke:** The hub-and-spoke topology can extend the corporate SAN at the hub site (i.e., enterprise DC) over an IP-based WAN to multiple remote spoke sites. This topology is an ideal fit with the DMVPN-based WAN solutions that were discussed earlier in The Next-Generation Enterprise WAN section of Chapter 3.

The MDS 9000 IP Storage Services (IPS) Module, particularly the IPS-8 module, is as an example to further examine hub-and-spoke FCIP configurations. FCIP tunnels are established by connecting exactly two FCIP interfaces together in a peer-to-peer fashion over an IP network. Each Gigabit Ethernet port on the IPS-8 module supports up to three FCIP interfaces, so each one can form an FCIP tunnel with an FCIP interface at the remote site, thus creating a hub-and-spoke configuration. As there are eight Gigabit Ethernet ports on the IPS-8 module, it can support up to 24 FCIP tunnels. Figure 7.15 illustrates a simple example of an FCIP hub-and-spoke topology using the IPS-8 modules on the MDS switches. The three FCIP interfaces on one Gigabit Ethernet port of the IPS-8 module at the enterprise DC (i.e., the hub site) are fully utilized to extend the corporate SAN to the three remote spoke sites. Each of the remote spoke sites reciprocates with a single FCIP interface.

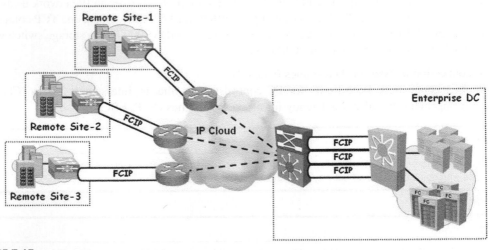

FIGURE 7.15

FCIP hub-and-spoke topology

> **NOTE:**
>
> The IP Storage Services 8-port (IPS-8) modules provide eight Gigabit Ethernet ports to support iSCSI and FCIP. The ports are hot-swappable, SFP LC-type Gigabit Ethernet interfaces. You can configure modules with either short- or long-wavelength SFPs for connections up to 550 m and 10 km, respectively. Each port can be configured in software to support iSCSI protocol and FCIP protocol simultaneously. In other words, it serves as an integrated multiprotocol (iSCSI and FCIP) gateway on the MDS switch.

From the flexibility perspective, an FCIP deployment surpasses those of optical networking. So long as FCIP is implemented over an IP network, it is independent of any underlying L1/L2 services and physical distance limitations. Potential FCIP deployment environments include:

- **Synchronous replication:** This type of application requires high bandwidth and low latency. FCIP over a metro Ethernet will be the preference. FCIP over SONET/SDH can serve as the secondary option if the SONET/SDH infrastructure provides the high bandwidth and low latency (<1–5 ms) that are mandatory for synchronous replication.
- **Asynchronous replication:** This type of application devours less bandwidth and can tolerate more latency (approximately 100 ms). In this case, FCIP over SONET/SDH can provide a more cost-effective solution, while at the same time supporting longer distances.
- **Remote vaulting:** Remote vaulting applications are typically standard backup applications with the backup device located at a remote site. These backup applications do not have stringent latency requirements and the remote backup site can be situated at a longer distance. In this case, FCIP over SONET/SDH is the most cost-effective solution.
- **Host-based mirroring:** Host-based mirroring applications have less stringent bandwidth and latency requirements. FCIP over SONET/SDH or FCIP over IP-based WAN can be considered for these applications.

FCIP HA

A resilient FCIP deployment begins with two IPS modules on two separate MDS switches. Parallel FCIP tunnels interconnect the different switches across two SAN islands. This solution relies on FSPF, the standard path selection or routing protocol used by FC fabrics. FSPF is specifically used to:

- Dynamically compute routes throughout an FC fabric by establishing the shortest and fastest path between any two FC switches.
- Decide on an alternative path when a given path is no longer available. FSPF supports multiple paths and automatically computes an alternative path around a failed link. It provides a preferred route when two equal paths are available.

Figure 7.16 shows an FSPF-based HA solution. Traffic is load balanced over two FCIP tunnels per switch. Upon a port or link failure, FSPF reroutes all traffic over to the remaining tunnel.

By creating multiple FCIP tunnels and using FSPF for load balancing, the FC fabric connectivity is maintained during port or link failure. However, FSPF needs to recalculate routes when a path is lost due to port/link outage resulting in a disruption of the FC fabric.

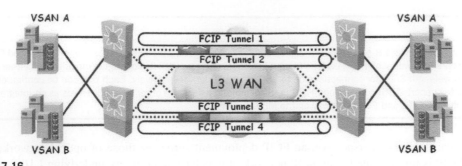

FIGURE 7.16

FSPF-based HA solution

Aggregating FCIP tunnels in a port channel obviates FSPF recalculation that is caused by a port or a link failure. In other words, port channels can be used in conjunction with the FSPF-based solution to achieve nondisruptive failover. A port channel offers the following functionalities:

- Provides a point-to-point connection over ISL or FCIP tunnel. Multiple links can be combined into a port channel, which increases the overall aggregated bandwidth because traffic is distributed among all the functional links in the channel.
- Load balances across multiple links and sustains optimal bandwidth utilization. The load balancing itself is based on the source ID (S_ID[13]), destination ID (D_ID[13]), and originator exchange ID (OX_ID[13]).
- Incorporates HA functionality. If one link fails, traffic previously carried on this link is switched to the remaining links transparent to the upper layer protocol, even though the bandwidth is reduced. The FSPF routing tables are not affected by this link failure. Moreover, port channels can span multiple modules for added HA so that a failure of a switching module will not bring down the port channel link.

> **NOTE:**
>
> Port channel load balancing can also be set to S_ID and D_ID only. This is required in FICON implementations.

> **NOTE:**
>
> In some cases, a port channel link failover results in an out-of-order delivery. FC protocols or applications such as FICON cannot handle out-of-order frame delivery. The workaround is to enable the in-order delivery feature on the MDS switch for an FICON-enabled VSAN.

In the port channel enhanced solution, recovery is done at the port channel level and not at the FSPF routing level, so recovery is nondisruptive and much faster. Figure 7.17 shows an example of an FSPF-based HA solution enhanced with port channels.

For a configuration example on FCIP HA, see the Simple FCIP Design Example section in Chapter 9.

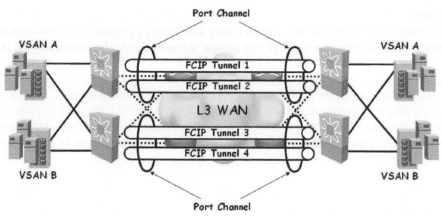

FIGURE 7.17

FSPF-based HA with port channels

NOTE:

To provide fault tolerance with respect to the IP layer, create FCIP tunnels over different subnet addresses with different physical paths. If a path goes down, the port channel containing the FCIP tunnels will continue to operate over the other path.

FCIP performance tuning

FCIP performance tuning parameters include:

- TCP timeouts
- TCP retransmissions
- TCP acknowledgments
- MTU size
- Flow control
- Packet shaping
- FCIP write acceleration
- FCIP tape acceleration
- FCIP compression
- IP QoS

The MDS switch with the IPS module is used as the example platform in the following subsections for these performance tuning parameters.

NOTE:

The term MDS switch used in the subsequent subsections refers to an MDS switch with the IPS module.

TCP timeouts

The TCP keepalive timeout defines the interval during which the TCP connection verifies that the FCIP link is working. This ensures that an FCIP link outage is detected quickly, even when the link is idle. If the TCP connection is idle for more than the specified interval, TCP keepalive packets are sent to verify whether the connection is active. The MDS switch uses the "tcp keepalive-timeout" command to specify the keepalive timeout in seconds (the range is from 1 to 7200 seconds, default 60). In an interval during which the connection is idle is for the configured interval, 8 keepalive probes are sent at 1-sec intervals. If no response is received for these 8 probes and the connection remains idle throughout, that FCIP link is automatically closed. Code Listing 7.1 illustrates a sample TCP keepalive timeout configuration template.

```
fcip enable
fcip profile 1
  tcp keepalive-timeout 30
```

CODE LISTING 7.1

TCP keepalive timeout configuration template

TCP retransmissions

TCP provides reliability by sending an acknowledgment for received data segments. However, data segments and acknowledgments can be lost. TCP handles this by setting a retransmission timeout when it sends data. If the data have not been acknowledged when the timeout expires, TCP retransmits the data. Two parameters determine whether TCP continues or terminates sending data:

- TCP minimum retransmit time
- TCP maximum retransmissions

The "tcp minimum-retransmit-time" command controls the minimum amount of time TCP waits before retransmitting. The default is 200 ms and the range is from 200 to 5000 ms. The "tcp max-retransmissions" command specifies the maximum number of times a packet is retransmitted before TCP decides to close the connection. The default is 4 and the range is from 1 to 8 retransmissions. Code Listing 7.2 illustrates a sample TCP retransmission timeout configuration template.

```
fcip profile 1
  tcp max-retransmissions 6
  tcp min-retransmit-time 500
```

CODE LISTING 7.2

TCP retransmission timeout configuration template

NOTE:

In the case of a "dirty" WAN link, reduce "tcp max-retransmissions" to "1" in the FCIP profile to speed up flap detection. Use this option with caution.

TCP acknowledgments

TCP, in general, uses a cumulative acknowledgment scheme where only in-sequence data segments are acknowledged. In case of packet loss, subsequent segments that are successfully received are not acknowledged by the receiver. Thus the sender has no way of knowing which segments within the current window of transmission were successfully received when there is a packet loss. Consequently, the sender has no choice but to retransmit all segments after the packet loss is detected by a retransmission timeout. This behavior leads to retransmission of segments that were actually successfully received, incurring unnecessary network bandwidth utilization. The retransmission timeout also causes the congestion window to reduce in size drastically, and further transmissions have to be made at a slower rate than before.

By using the selective acknowledgment (SACK) mechanism, a receiver is able to selectively acknowledge segments that were received after a packet is lost. The sender, having been notified beforehand through the selective acknowledgments, needs only to retransmit the lost segments. The "tcp sack-enable" command enables SACK (enabled by default).

MTU size

With regard to maximum transmission unit (MTU) size, there is a dilemma:

- Too large an MTU size brings about retransmissions when the packet encounters a downstream device that is unable to handle the large packet.
- Too small an MTU size give rise to higher header overhead and more acknowledgments.

The maximum FC frame size is 2148. Using the standard Ethernet MTU size of 1518 results in the fragmentation of the FC frame. Using jumbo frames, the FCIP payload can accommodate a full-size FC frame without fragmenting the frame into smaller packets. However, for this solution to be effective, the entire IP infrastructure between the two FCIP-connected MDS switches must support jumbo frames.

Path MTU (PMTU) is the minimum MTU on the IP network between the two endpoints of the FCIP link. PMTU discovery (PMTUD[14]) is a mechanism by which TCP dynamically discovers the PMTU size and adjusts the maximum TCP segment accordingly. Ideally, PMTUD must be used in conjunction with jumbo frames. PMTUD is enabled on MDS switches with a default reset timeout of 3600 sec. The "tcp pmtu-enable" command enables PMTUD (enabled by default).

Flow control

Flow control for FCIP tunnels is slightly different from native FC. Although they carry FC traffic, they do not use, and are therefore not restricted by, BB_Credits. Instead, TCP flow control is used, which has an end-to-end sliding-window, flow control mechanism. The ability to keep the pipe full or maintain the data flow is determined by the window size. In FC networks, BB_Credits apply to every hop except FCIP hops. FC flow control terminates at the VE_Port of an FCIP tunnel.

On the MDS switch, the optimal TCP window size is automatically calculated using the maximum bandwidth parameter, the minimum available bandwidth parameter, and the dynamically measured round-trip–time parameter. The defaults are as follows:

- Maximum bandwidth = 1 Gbps
- Minimum available bandwidth = 500 Mbps
- Round-trip time (RTT) = 1 ms

The TCP maximum window size (MWS) is derived from the product of the (max-bandwidth / 8) × RTT × 0.9375 + 4-KB.

Packet shaping

FC traffic can be very bursty and classic TCP can amplify that burstiness. With classic TCP, the network must absorb these bursts through buffering in switches and routers. Packet drops happen when there is not enough buffering at these transit points. To lower the probability of drops, the FCIP TCP implementation on the MDS switch uses packet shaping to reduce the burstiness of the TCP traffic leaving the GE interface.

When packet shaping is properly configured, packets are sent over the GE interface with sufficient spacing so they can be forwarded with little or no buffering at each intermediate point in the FCIP path. Since bursts are controlled through per-flow shaping and TCP congestion window monitoring (CWM), TCP is less likely to overrun the downstream network devices and this in turn reduces the probability of drops.

A minimum available bandwidth (consumable by the downstream path) is required when configuring the packet shaper. This value is used as the TCP slow start threshold. The packet shaper then ramps up to this threshold within 1 RTT. From there onward, the MDS FCIP TCP stack uses linear congestion avoidance, increasing throughput at the rate of two segments per RTT until the MWS is reached. During congestion, the congestion window drops to the minimum available bandwidth value. The degree of aggressiveness during recovery is therefore proportional to the minimum available bandwidth configuration. In other words, the minimum available bandwidth parameter determines how aggressively FCIP should behave. A higher value would be more aggressive while a lower value would make FCIP behave more fairly.

NOTE:

The shaper is active only during the first RTT after an idle period. After the first RTT, returning acknowledgments clock the transmission of further packets.

NOTE:

If the FCIP path has 1 Gbps (or more) of dedicated bandwidth available end to end, the sender can send at gigabit speed without overrunning buffers in the downstream routers or switches.

The configuration requirements for the packet shaper to work properly include:

- Minimum available bandwidth must be at least 1/20 maximum bandwidth.
- SACK must be enabled.

When configuring packet shaping, it is important to know the minimum and maximum bandwidth available to FCIP. If the minimum value is correctly chosen, there is little chance of overrunning the downstream routers and switches. Code Listing 7.3 illustrates a sample packet shaping configuration template.

```
fcip profile 1
   tcp max-bandwidth-mbps 900 min-available-bandwidth-mbps 300 round-trip-time-ms 10
```

CODE LISTING 7.3

Packet shaping configuration template

FCIP write acceleration

A normal SCSI FC protocol (FCP) write operation requires two round-trips between the host initiator and the target array or tape:

- **Round-trip 1:** The host initiator issues an SCSI write command (FCP_WRITE) and the target responds with an FCP transfer-ready command (FCP_XFER_RDY).
- **Round-trip 2:** The initiator sends FCP data frames up to the amount specified in the previous ready command and the target responds with an SCSI status response (FCP_RSP) frame if the I/O is completed successfully.

The two round-trips double the latency. This issue is even more obvious for applications that limit the number of outstanding I/O operations, such as tape backup. The number of FCIP WAN round-trips per SCSI FCP write are reduced with FCIP write acceleration.

FCIP write acceleration is an SCSI protocol-spoofing mechanism that is designed to improve application performance by reducing the overall service time for SCSI write I/Os and replicated write I/Os over distance. The FCIP write acceleration spoofs XFER_RDY:

1. After the initiator issues an SCSI FCP write, an FCP_XFER_RDY is immediately returned to the initiator by the MDS switch (proxying as the target to the initiator).
2. The initiator can immediately send data to its target across the FCIP tunnel. The data are received by the remote MDS switch (proxying as the initiator to the target) and are buffered.
3. At the remote end, the target, which has no knowledge of write acceleration, responds with an FCP_XFER_RDY. The remote MDS switch does not allow this to pass back across the WAN.
4. When the remote MDS switch receives FCP_XFER_RDY, it allows the data to flow to the target.
5. When all data have been received, the target issues an FCP_RSP response or status, acknowledging the end of the operation (i.e., the FC Exchange).

FCIP write acceleration is able to reduce the two round-trips required by a normal FCP_WRITE to just one. It allows the host (initiator) to begin sending the write data without waiting for the long latency of the returning XFER_RDY over the WAN.

> **NOTE:**
>
> The MDS switch proxying as the initiator/target modifies the OX_ID and RX_ID fields of the FC header and create a new RX_ID, but this will invalidate the original FC CRC. Therefore, in conjunction with the new RX_ID, a new FC CRC must also be applied.

In Figure 7.18, the top diagram illustrates a normal SCSI write operation without write acceleration while the bottom diagram shows the SCSI write operation with write acceleration.

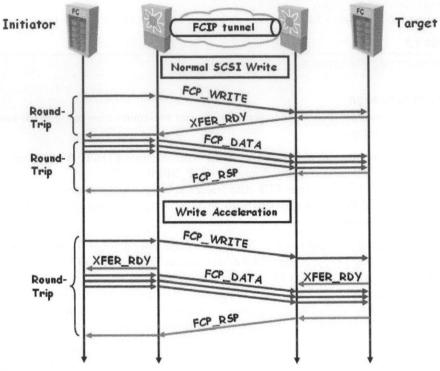

FIGURE 7.18

FCIP write acceleration before and after

Code Listing 7.4 illustrates a sample FCIP write acceleration configuration template.

```
interface fcip1
  write-accelerator
```

CODE LISTING 7.4

FCIP write acceleration configuration template

FCIP tape acceleration

One common issue with tape drives is that they have limited buffering, which is often not enough to handle WAN latencies. Even with write acceleration, each drive can support only one outstanding I/O. Write acceleration alone is insufficient to keep the tape streaming. It halves the total RTT for a write I/O, but the initiator must still wait to receive FCP_RSP before sending the next FCP_WRITE. If the latency is too high and the tape drive does not receive the next data block in time, it must stop and rewind the tape. This shoe-shining effect not only increases the time it takes to complete the backup job, but it also potentially reduces the lifespan of the tape drive.

FCIP tape acceleration is an enhancement to write acceleration that extends tape buffering to the MDS switches. It also includes a flow control scheme to avoid overflowing the buffers. Figure 7.19

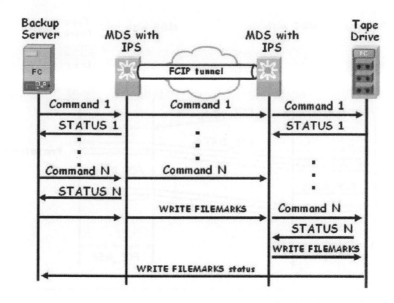

FIGURE 7.19

FCIP tape acceleration for write operations

illustrates an example of FCIP tape acceleration for write operations. The backup server issues a write command to a drive in the tape library. Acting as a proxy for the remote tape drives, the local MDS switch buffers the command and proxies an XFER_RDY to signal the host (the actual backup server) to begin sending data. After receiving and buffering all data, the local MDS switch proxies the successful completion of the SCSI write operation by sending the appropriate STATUS message. This response allows the host to start the next SCSI write operation. Unlike write acceleration, tape acceleration provides local acknowledgment of the write command by proxying the STATUS message and the XFER_RDY. This enhancement (tape acceleration for write operation) results in more data being sent over the FCIP tunnel in the same duration compared to the time taken to send data without write acceleration for tapes. The remote MDS switch buffers the command and data and emulates the backup server by listening for an XFER_RDY from the tape drive before forwarding the data.

NOTE:

Tape acceleration for write operations maintains write data integrity by requiring the WRITE FILEMARKS operation to complete end to end without proxying. The WRITE FILEMARKS operation signals the synchronization of the buffer data with the tape library data. While tape media errors are returned to backup servers for error handling, tape busy errors are retried automatically by the remote MDS switch.

The performance issues are different when dealing with data restoration or read operation from tape drives across a WAN. Figure 7.20 illustrates an example of FCIP tape acceleration for read operations. The restore server issues read operations to a drive in the tape library. During the restore process, the remote MDS switch at the tape end, while awaiting more SCSI read operations from the host

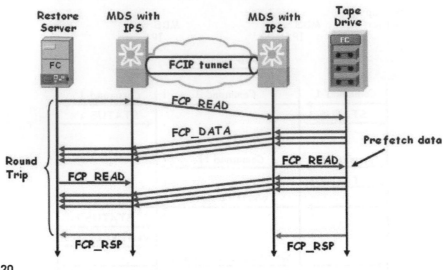

FIGURE 7.20

FCIP tape acceleration for read operations

(restore server), sends out SCSI read operations on its own to the tape drive. The prefetched read data are then cached at the local MDS switch. The local MDS switch sends out the cached data upon receiving SCSI subsequent read operations from the host.

By prefetching data and keeping the tape moving, FCIP tape read acceleration significantly improves the performance for tape reads over a WAN. Code Listing 7.5 illustrates a sample FCIP tape acceleration configuration template.

```
interface fcip1
  write-accelerator tape-accelerator flow-control-buffer-size auto
```

CODE LISTING 7.5

FCIP tape acceleration configuration template

Tape acceleration requires write acceleration to be enabled. The default flow control buffering uses the automatic (auto) option. This option takes the WAN latencies and the speed of the tape into consideration to provide optimum performance. You can also specify a flow control buffer size (64–12,288 KB) instead.

NOTE:

In tape acceleration, after a certain amount of data have been buffered at the remote MDS switch, the write operations from the host are flow controlled by the local MDS switch, by not proxying the XFER_RDY. Upon completion of a write operation where some data buffers are freed, the local MDS switch resumes the proxying.

FCIP compression

Compression can increase overall throughput on slow-speed WAN links. The MDS switches adopt the IP payload compression using the Lempel-Ziv-Stac (IPPCP LZS[15]) lossless compression algorithm for compressing data. The IPPCP LZS compresses the IP payload that contains the TCP header and its corresponding payload in which the entire FCIP frame is nested. By compressing only the IP payload and keeping the IP header intact, this particular IP packet can be routed through an IP network and still be subjected to access-control lists (ACLs) and quality-of-service (QoS) mechanisms based on the IP header fields. For IPPCP LZS, typical data mixes should achieve about a 2:1 compression ratio subject to the type of the data in the data stream.

The FCIP compression can be configured using one of the following modes:

- **Mode1:** A fast compression mode for high bandwidth links (>25 Mbps)
- **Mode2:** A moderate compression mode for moderately low bandwidth links (10–25 Mbps)
- **Mode3:** A high compression mode for low bandwidth links (<10 Mbps)
- **Auto (the default):** Selects the appropriate mode based on the bandwidth of the link (gathered from the bandwidth information configured for the TCP parameters in the FCIP profile)

Code Listing 7.6 illustrates a sample FCIP compression configuration template.

```
interface fcip1
  ip-compression mode3
```

CODE LISTING 7.6

FCIP compression configuration template

The deduplication in WAN acceleration (Chapter 4) provides greater data reduction than LZS and should be used wherever possible in preference to these compression settings.

IP QoS

The MDS switches support QoS through the classification and prioritization of FCIP control traffic and data traffic. The QoS implementation is based on the DiffServ model as defined in RFC2474 and RFC2475. The QoS parameter uses the Differentiated Services Code Point (DSCP) value to mark IP packets as follows:

- The control DSCP value applies to all FCIP frames in the control TCP connection.
- The data DSCP value applies to all FCIP frames in the data TCP connection.
- If the FCIP tunnel has only one TCP connection, the data DSCP value is applied to all packets in that connection.

Code Listing 7.7 illustrates a sample FCIP IP QoS configuration template.

```
interface fcip1
  qos control 34 data 26
```

CODE LISTING 7.7

FCIP IP QoS configuration template

FCIP security

DWDM/CWDM and SONET/SDH links are considered relatively secure due to the inherent difficulty of tapping into optical fiber. FCIP itself does not support any IP-related security mechanisms. Thus transporting data on FCIP tunnels that are routed over the Internet or public networks poses a big security risk. FCIP needs to rely on IPSec for IP-based security services. Users can enable IPSec on existing routers or VPN appliances at the WAN edge to encrypt the FCIP traffic. This is in line with the DMVPN-based WAN solutions mentioned in Chapter 3. The other alternative is to utilize built-in IPSec capabilities (if supported) on the FCIP gateway products.

> **NOTE:**
>
> The MDS 14/2-port Multiprotocol Services (MPS-14/2) module has built-in IPSec hardware acceleration.

> **NOTE:**
>
> After FCIP link establishment, the FC virtual ISL is secured by FC Security Protocols (FC-SP) such as the Diffie Hellman-Challenge Handshake Authentication Protocol (DH-CHAP).

iSCSI

iSCSI brings the discussion back to the technical world that we are familiar with—Ethernet and TCP/IP. With iSCSI, SANs typically become IP-based and are referred to as iSCSI SANs. Ideally, iSCSI initiators (hosts) and iSCSI targets (storage arrays) are plugged into existing Ethernet switches. Communication and data transfers then take place over iSCSI sessions running on top of the TCP/IP stack. Sound simple? Think again: What are the main reasons behind using iSCSI over FC? The primary reasons include:

- iSCSI integrates seamlessly with existing Ethernet infrastructures.
- iSCSI leverages on TCP/IP as the I/O transport.
- iSCSI uses block I/O access so that iSCSI storage arrays can be accessed via an SAN.

On top of all of these advantages, and often even more important, iSCSI is much cheaper. If this is the case, why would an enterprise have implemented the more costly FC in the first place? The deterring factor at that time was because Ethernet had a maximum speed of only 1 Gbps whereas FC HBAs had 2 Gbps and 4 Gbps ports. Although 10GE has removed this limitation, enterprise customers with a large FC installed base still have difficulty implementing iSCSI since it does not preserve the existing FC management and deployment model. Therefore, iSCSI is more aligned with greenfield setups and the SMB market segment. That said, it is still worthwhile to consider iSCSI for:

- Storage consolidation as an alternative to FCoE (for more details, see Chapter 2).
- Host-based mirroring or backup for BC and DR purposes.
- Block I/O access from remote IP-based users.
- Remote network boot.

iSCSI protocol overview

This section discusses the following iSCSI concepts:

- iSCSI packet format
- iSCSI components
- iSCSI naming schemes
- iSCSI session types
- iSCSI security authentication
- iSCSI solicited and unsolicited data transfer
- iSCSI initiator mechanisms and server virtualization

iSCSI packet format

iSCSI facilitates direct block-level access between an initiator and a target over TCP/IP networks. SCSI commands, data, and status are encapsulated within an iSCSI PDU. Transporting SCSI (I/O) over TCP ensures that high volume storage transfers have in-order delivery and error-free data with congestion control. This also overcomes distance limitations and allows IP hosts to gain access to previously isolated FC-based storage targets. Figure 7.21 illustrates the nesting of the various levels of protocol PDUs in an Ethernet frame during an iSCSI session establishment.

The TCP payload of an iSCSI packet contains iSCSI PDUs. All iSCSI PDUs begin with one or more header segments followed by zero or one data segment. The first segment is the basic header (BH) segment, a fixed-length 48-byte header segment. This can be followed by a number of optional additional header segments (AHSs), an optional header digest, an optional data segment, and an optional data digest.

All the headers are optional other than the BH. The optional digests are CRC-32 (32-bit cyclic redundancy check) values used to validate the contents of the respective segments (headers and data). Apart from a specific TCP destination port of 3260, an iSCSI packet looks just like any other IP packet. From the L2 perspective, the iSCSI packet looks like any ordinary Ethernet frame.

NOTE:

The header overhead in iSCSI encapsulation results in a lower effective throughput. For better effective throughput, jumbo frame support should be enabled.

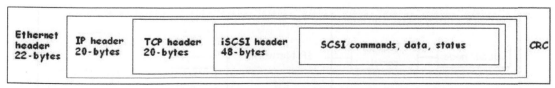

FIGURE 7.21

iSCSI encapsulation

iSCSI components

Figure 7.22 illustrates the iSCSI architecture and components. They include:

- **Network entity:** A network entity represents a device or gateway that is accessible from the IP network. It must have one or more network portals, each of which can be used by some iSCSI nodes contained in that network entity to gain access to the IP network.
- **iSCSI node:** An iSCSI node represents a single iSCSI initiator or iSCSI target. There can be one or more iSCSI nodes within a network entity. The iSCSI node is accessible through one or more network portals and is identified by a unique iSCSI name. The separation of the iSCSI name from the IP addresses for the iSCSI node allows multiple iSCSI nodes to use the same IP addresses and the same iSCSI node to use multiple IP addresses.
- **Network portal:** A network portal is responsible for implementing the TCP/IP stack and is used by an iSCSI node within that network entity for the connection(s) within one of its iSCSI sessions. In an iSCSI initiator entity, the network portal is identified by its IP address. In an iSCSI target entity, the network portal is identified by its IP address and its listening TCP port.
- **Portal groups (not shown in diagram):** A portal group is a set of network portals identified within an iSCSI node by a portal group tag between 0 and 65535. It supports multiple TCP connections over multiple links per iSCSI session and provides multiple paths to the same iSCSI node. Both iSCSI initiators and iSCSI targets have portal groups although only the iSCSI target portal groups are used directly in the iSCSI protocol.

> **NOTE:**
>
> An iSCSI session is composed of one or more TCP connections from an initiator to a target. These TCP connections can be logically separated on the same physical link or they can be different connections on different physical links.

iSCSI naming schemes

Each iSCSI node, whether an initiator or target, requires an iSCSI name for the purpose of identification. An iSCSI node name is also the SCSI device name of an iSCSI device. The iSCSI name of an SCSI device is the principal object used in authentication of targets to initiators and initiators to targets. This name is also used to identify and manage iSCSI storage resources.

iSCSI names are associated with iSCSI nodes and not iSCSI network adapter cards. This ensures that the replacement of network adapter cards does not require reconfiguration of all SCSI and iSCSI resource allocation information. This also enables iSCSI storage resources to be managed independent of location (or address). iSCSI names must be globally unique and permanent (i.e., the iSCSI initiator node or iSCSI target node has the same name for its lifetime).

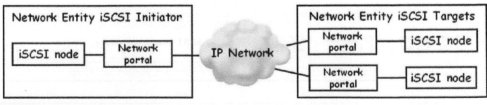

FIGURE 7.22

iSCSI architecture and components

Three types of iSCSI node names are currently defined: iSCSI Qualified Name (IQN), Extended Unique Identifier (EUI), and Network Address Authority (NAA).

The IQN string is variable in length up to a maximum of 223 characters. It consists of the following in ascending order (from left to right):

1. The string "iqn"
2. A date code, in "yyyy–mm" format
3. A dot (.)
4. The reversed Fully Qualified Domain Name (FQDN) of the naming authority (person or organization) creating this iSCSI name
5. An optional colon (:) or dot (.) prefixed qualifier string within the character set and length boundaries that the owner of the domain name deems appropriate. This can contain product types, serial numbers, host identifiers, or software keys (e.g., it can include colons to separate organization boundaries). With the exception of the colon prefix, the owner of the domain name can assign everything after the reversed domain name as desired. It is the responsibility of the entity, that is the naming authority, to ensure that the iSCSI names it assigns are unique worldwide. The colon separates the reversed domain name from its subgroup (i.e., subgroup naming authority) to prevent naming conflicts.

For instance, "Example Storage Arrays, Inc." might own the domain name "example.com." The following are examples of IQNs that might be generated by this organization:

- iqn.2001-04.com.example:storage:diskarrays-sn-a8675309
- iqn.2001-04.com.example
- iqn.2001-04.com.example:storage.tape1.sys1.xyz
- iqn.2001-04.com.example:storage:tape1.sys1.xyz
- iqn.2001-04.com.example:storage.disk2.sys1.xyz

The length of an iSCSI node name of type EUI is fixed at 20 characters. The EUI format consists of two components: the type designator "eui." followed a valid IEEE EUI-64 string. The length of an EUI-64 string is 8 bytes and is expressed in hexadecimal, for example:

eui.02004567A425678D

The length of an iSCSI node name of type NAA is either 20 or 36 characters. The iSCSI NAA naming format is "naa." followed by an NAA identifier represented in hexadecimal. An example of an iSCSI name with an 8-byte NAA value follows:

naa.52004567BA64678D

An example of an iSCSI name with a 16-byte NAA value follows:

naa.62004567BA64678D0123456789ABCDEF

> **NOTE:**
> The iSCSI protocol does not use the iSCSI fully qualified address. Instead, it is used by management applications. The fully qualified address of an iSCSI node is specified as a URL (uniform resource locator):<domain-name> [:<port >]/<iSCSI-name>.

iSCSI session types

iSCSI implements two types of sessions: normal and discovery. Each discovery session uses a single TCP connection. Each normal session can use multiple TCP connections for load balancing and better fault tolerance. All iSCSI sessions proceed in two main phases: login and full-feature. The login phase always comes first and it consists of two subphases: security parameter negotiation and operational parameter negotiation. Each subphase is optional but at least one of the two subphases must occur.

There are three ways the iSCSI initiator can discover iSCSI targets:

- Manual configuration (no discovery).
- Using the "SendTargets" command (semi-manual configuration).
- "Zero configuration" (or automated configuration) methods such as Service Location Protocol (SLPv2[16]) and Internet Storage Name Service (iSNS[17]).

For brevity and simpler illustrations, only the "SendTargets" command is covered in this section. To establish a discovery session using the "SendTargets" command, the initiator needs to be manually configured with the IP address and TCP port number of the target entity. In discovery sessions, the purpose of login is to identify the initiator node to the target entity so that security filters can be applied to the responses. The initiator node name is required in the login request and not the target node name, because the target node name is not known to the initiator before discovery. Upon completion of login, the discovery session changes to the full feature phase. The "SendTargets" command is the only command that can be issued in the full feature phase. After initial discovery, the discovery session can be maintained or closed. Figure 7.23 illustrates a discovery session example.

For normal sessions, the initiator is required to specify the target node name in the login request. After the login phase, the normal session transits to the full feature phase where the initiator can issue iSCSI commands, as well as send SCSI commands and data. Figure 7.24 illustrates a normal session example.

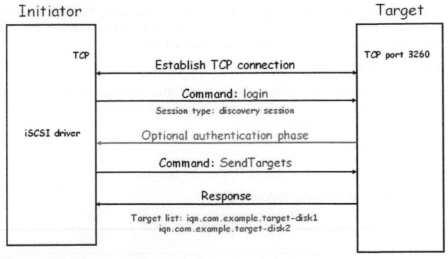

FIGURE 7.23

Discovery session example

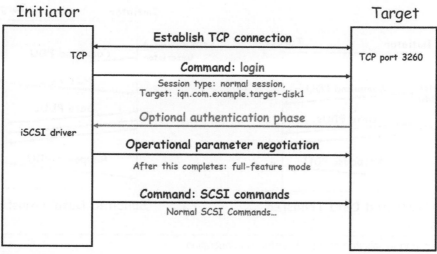

FIGURE 7.24

Normal session example

iSCSI security authentication

When the initiator enters the security authentication phase, its login request PDU specifies its supported authentication methods using the AuthMethod keyword-value pair in the data segment. All supported methods are listed in order of preference, including "none," which means that the initiator is willing to skip the authentication phase. The target selects the first authentication protocol that it supports in the list of protocols provided by the initiator.

iSCSI requires support for the Challenge Handshake Authentication Protocol (CHAP), which is widely supported by most iSCSI vendors. Nevertheless, iSCSI can also support Secure Remote Password (SRP), Kerberos version 5, and the Simple Public Key Mechanism (SPKM-1 or SPKM-2).

> **NOTE:**
>
> The MDS IPS module supports the use of a local password database, a RADIUS server, or a TACACS+ server for CHAP authentication.

iSCSI solicited and unsolicited data transfer

After successful login and authentication, the initiator and target enter the full-feature phase. In this phase, the devices exchange normal command and data PDUs. There are two basic types of data transfers:

- **Unsolicited data transfer:** A write command in which the initiator sends a write command PDU followed immediately by data-out PDUs. The initiator does not wait for an R2T (ready to transfer) PDU from the target. Targets can limit the size of unsolicited writes that they will accept by setting the FirstBurstLength key value in the login data segment. The left diagram of Figure 7.25 illustrates an example of an unsolicited data transfer.

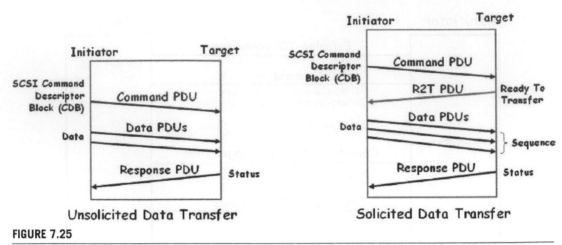

FIGURE 7.25

iSCSI solicited and unsolicited data transfer for write operation

---

NOTE:

Besides unsolicited data transfer, data can be included as part of the write command PDU. This is known as immediate data transfer.

- **Solicited data transfer:** A write command in which the initiator sends a write command PDU and then waits for an R2T PDU from the target, or in which the initiator sends a read command PDU and waits for data-in PDUs. Initiators and targets can limit the size of solicited writes by setting the MaxBurstLength key value in the login data segment. The right diagram of Figure 7.25 illustrates an example of a solicited data transfer.

NOTE:

In solicited data transfer, iSCSI uses the R2T PDU as the primary flow control mechanism to control the flow of SCSI data during write commands.

---

iSCSI initiator mechanisms and server virtualization

In general, there are three different iSCSI initiator mechanisms:

- iSCSI software driver with a standard NIC
- NIC with a TCP offload engine (TOE) to reduce CPU utilization
- iSCSI HBAs that offload both TCP and iSCSI operations

Revisiting server virtualization (for details, see Chapter 2), an iSCSI hardware implementation (TOE or iSCSI HBA) can reside in the hypervisor where iSCSI is terminated. The hypervisor uses a single iSCSI session for the entire physical server or one per VM. In iSCSI software implementation (iSCSI driver), iSCSI can run in the VM over a virtual NIC. In this case, the iSCSI traffic is transparent to the hypervisor, which only "sees" the TCP segments that carry the iSCSI PDUs.

iSCSI deployments

There are two main iSCSI deployment scenarios: native IP SANs and heterogeneous IP SANs. Native IP SANs are deployed end-to-end without gateways. The required components, such as IP hosts, iSCSI HBAs, gigabit Ethernet switches, TCIP/IP networks, and so on are all iSCSI-friendly. However, this implementation does not integrate with existing FC infrastructure.

On the other hand, heterogeneous IP SANs consist of components that transmit SCSI over both TCP/IP and over FC interconnections. To accomplish this, an iSCSI gateway device is required at a demarcation point between IP and FC. The iSCSI gateway has two roles to play. At the iSCSI end, it presents the FC targets as virtual iSCSI targets to the IP hosts. At the FC end, it presents each iSCSI host as an FC HBA (FC initiator). The deployment of iSCSI for heterogeneous IP SANs is described in more detail in the following subsections.

The iSCSI view

The MDS IPS module has integrated iSCSI gateway functionality. It is used as the example platform for further elaboration. At the iSCSI end, the IPS module presents physical FC targets as virtual iSCSI targets, allowing them to be accessed by iSCSI hosts. It accomplishes this in one of two ways:

- **Dynamic target mapping:** This approach automatically imports all the FC target devices/ports as iSCSI devices. The IPS module maps each physical FC target port as one iSCSI target (subject to VSAN and zoning). In other words, all logical units (LUs) accessible through the physical storage target port are made available as iSCSI LUs with the same logical unit number (LUN) as in the FC storage target. This mapping creates automatic iSCSI target names. Figure 7.26 illustrates an example of dynamic target mapping.
- **Static target mapping:** This approach manually creates iSCSI target devices and maps them to the whole FC target port or a subset of FC LUNs. Unique iSCSI target names are required with this mapping. Static mappings are used when iSCSI hosts must be restricted to subsets of LUs in the FC targets and/or when iSCSI access control is required. This static importing also allows transparent failover if the LUs of the FC targets are reachable by redundant FC ports.

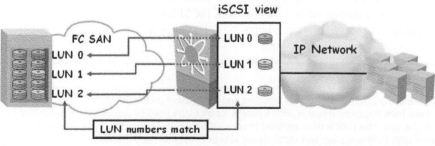

FIGURE 7.26

Dynamic target mapping example

The FC view

At the FC end, the IPS module can present the iSCSI hosts to the FC targets in the FC fabric in two different modes:

- **Transparent mode:** In this mode, each iSCSI host is presented as one virtual FC host. The benefit of transparent mode is that it allows a granular level of access-control configuration. Because of the one-to-one mapping from iSCSI to FC, each host can have different zoning or LUN access-control on the FC target. By presenting iSCSI hosts in transparent mode, the iSCSI hosts are mapped to virtual FC hosts in either one of the following:
    - **Dynamic mapping (default):** With dynamic mapping, an iSCSI host is mapped to a dynamically generated port World Wide Name (pWWN[18]) and node World Wide Name (nWWN[18]). However, each time the iSCSI host connects, it can be mapped to a different WWN. This mode is used when no access control is required on the FC target device.

> **NOTE:**
> You can use the "iscsi save-initiator" command to convert a dynamic iSCSI initiator to a static iSCSI initiator. This permanently retains the automatically assigned nWWN/pWWN mapping so the initiator can use the same mapping the next time it logs in.

- **Static mapping:** With static mapping, an iSCSI host is mapped to a specific pWWN and nWWN. This mapping is maintained in persistent storage and each time the iSCSI host connects, the same WWN mapping is used. This mode is used when access-control is required on the target device. Static mapping can be implemented in one of two ways:
    - **User assignment:** In this method, the user specifies the unique WWN during the configuration process.
    - **System assignment (recommended):** In this method, the switch provides the WWN from the switch's FC WWN pool and keeps the mapping permanent.
- **Proxy-initiator mode:** In this mode, only one virtual host N_Port (HBA port) is created per IPS port. All iSCSI hosts connecting to this IPS port are multiplexed using the same virtual host N_Port to access FC targets. In the event the FC storage device requires explicit LUN access-control for every host, using the transparent initiator mode (presenting one iSCSI host as one FC host) implies that every iSCSI host has to be configured statically. This can involve several configuration tasks for each iSCSI host. In this case, using the proxy initiator mode simplifies the configuration. Figure 7.27 illustrates a proxy-initiator example.

> **NOTE:**
> When using the proxy-initiator mode, LUN mapping and assignment on the FC storage array must be configured to allow access from the proxy virtual N_Port's pWWN for all LUNs used by each iSCSI initiator that connects through this IPS port. The LUN is then assigned to each iSCSI initiator by configuring static target mapping (iSCSI virtual targets with LUN mapping) and iSCSI-based access-control on the MDS switch.

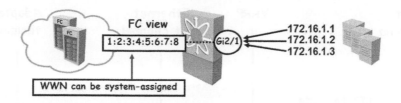

FIGURE 7.27

Proxy-initiator example

iSCSI HA

HA for iSCSI deployments uses features that are more readily available and less costly as compared to the HA solutions for FC. Some of the common HA features for iSCSI include:

- **Adapter teaming:** The adapter teaming feature allows two Ethernet network interfaces to act as one logical interface, using only one IP address and one MAC address. The adapter teaming feature can run in two modes, either with both adapters active or with one adapter active and the other passive.
- **VRRP:** VRRP provides redundant router gateway services (or first-hop redundancy). If a Gigabit Ethernet port on the IPS module fails, another Gigabit Ethernet port on a redundant IPS module resumes the iSCSI service (and its attributes) and continues to provide access for affected iSCSI sessions.
- **Ethernet port channel:** An Ethernet port channel combine two physical Gigabit Ethernet links into one logical link with higher bandwidth.

> **NOTE:**
>
> An Ethernet port channel on the IPS module is restricted in that it allows only two contiguous IPS ports, such as ports 1–2, 3–4, and so on, to be combined in one Ethernet port channel. This restriction applies only to Ethernet port channels.

- **Target multipathing:** Target multipathing (aka pWWN aliasing) is accomplished with the help of statically imported iSCSI targets (static target mapping), which have an additional option to provide a secondary pWWN for the FC target. This can be used when the physical FC target is configured to have an LU visible across redundant ports. When the active port fails, the secondary port becomes active and the iSCSI session switches to use the new active port.

A cost-effective and robust iSCSI HA solution can be achieved with adapter teaming, VRRP, and Ethernet port channel implemented at the front end in conjunction with target multipathing for FC redundancy implemented at the back end. Figure 7.28 illustrates an iSCSI HA example using all these features in unison.

iSCSI security

Since iSCSI security authentication has already been discussed earlier, the main focus of this section is on iSCSI access-control. Access-control can be implemented on iSCSI devices in two different angles:

- FC zoning-based access-control (at the FC end)
- iSCSI ACL-based access-control (at the iSCSI end)

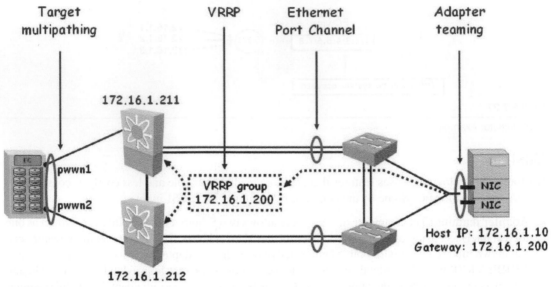

FIGURE 7.28

iSCSI HA example

The FC zoning can be extended from the FC domain to the iSCSI/IP domain. This concept allows both FC and iSCSI features to provide a uniform access-control across a heterogeneous SAN. The iSCSI ACL-based and FC zoning-based access-control mechanisms are enforced during iSCSI discovery, iSCSI session creation, and the FC virtual N_Port creation.

> **NOTE:**
>
> FC zoning is a mechanism that provides access-control in an FC fabric. It defines which ports can access one another and limits the ability of an FC device to discover other FC devices.

There are two FC zoning access-control mechanisms:

- Statically map the iSCSI host to FC virtual N_Port(s) to create permanent nWWNs and pWWNs. Next, configure the assigned pWWN into zones just like adding a regular FC host pWWN to a zone.
- For iSCSI hosts that do not have a static WWN mapping, the iSCSI host initiator IP address or iSCSI node name can be added as a member of a zone. IP address-based zone membership allows multiple devices to be specified in one command line by providing the subnet mask. iSCSI hosts that have static WWN mapping can also specify the iSCSI host initiator IP address or iSCSI node name instead as zone members.

In proxy initiator mode, all iSCSI devices connecting to an IPS port gain access to the FC fabric through a single virtual FC N_Port. For this reason, zoning based on the iSCSI node name or IP address will not have any effect. If the zoning is based on pWWN, then all iSCSI devices connecting to that IPS port are put into the same zone. In this case, iSCSI-based access control is required on the virtual target to implement individual initiator access-control in the proxy initiator mode.

iSCSI-based access-control is applicable only if static iSCSI virtual targets are created. For a static iSCSI target, a list of iSCSI initiators can be configured to allow access to the virtual targets. The iSCSI initiator access list can consist of one or more initiators identified by one of the following mechanisms:

- iSCSI node name
- IPv4 address and subnet
- IPv6 address

NOTE:

By default, static iSCSI virtual targets are not accessible to any iSCSI host. You must explicitly configure accessibility to allow an iSCSI virtual target to be accessed by all hosts.

Other than authentication and access-control, iSCSI, just like FCIP, needs to rely on IPSec for IP-based security services. The detailed discussion of IPSec is beyond the scope of this book.

PUTTING IT ALL TOGETHER

Figure 7.29 illustrates what has been covered so far in this chapter to interconnect multiple private cloud computing storage modules together or to extend them, over a specific geographical range for BC and DR purposes.

Four important factors govern the use of a particular solution: bandwidth, latency, distance, and cost. Bandwidth and latency requirements depend on the application requirements. For instance, synchronous replication requires high bandwidth and low latency, while asynchronous replication

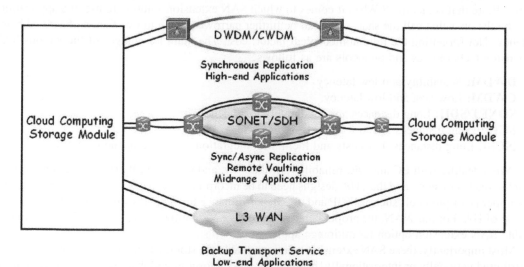

FIGURE 7.29

SAN extension solutions for private cloud computing

consumes less bandwidth and can tolerate more latency. On the other hand, as physical distance increases, available bandwidth tends to be smaller, at the same time latency increases. Cost becomes the decisive factor since high bandwidth and low latency are more expensive solution or unavailable.

Solution-wise, L3 WAN would be suitable for low-end applications, SONET/SDH is more aligned to midrange applications, and DWDM/CWDM is geared toward high-end applications. Although FCIP and iSCSI are TCP/IP based, the physical media could still be SONET/SDH and/or DWDM/CWDM, which are really L1 services. In addition, L3 WANs could be chosen for midrange applications, with proper WAN optimization techniques and deployments in place (for more details, see Chapters 4 and 5).

NOTE:

VMware VMotion is another application that has sensitive bandwidth and latency requirements. It requires a minimum bandwidth of 622 Mbps between DCs and at least 1-Gbps links within a DC. In addition, the maximum round-trip latency between the source and destination VMware ESX servers cannot exceed 5 ms. Based on the speed of light over fiber and certain guard bands for network delays, a maximum distance of 400 km is supported today.

SUMMARY

Chapter 7 covers various SAN extension designs and solutions for interconnecting multiple storage modules together in a private cloud computing environment. BC and DR are inevitable factors to be taken into considerable for any DC setup, including those DCs that are involved in private cloud computing.

The SAN extension technologies and protocols include: DWDM/CWDM, SONET/SDH, FCIP, and iSCSI. Which technologies or protocols are the most prevalent? Which one gives the best value for the expenditure that is incurred? When it comes to which SAN extension solution to use, the applications will be the ones that call the shots. This can be further narrowed down to two factors: bandwidth and latency. Not forgetting the third nontechnical factor: cost. The main advantages of the various SAN extension technologies and protocols are as follows:

- **DWDM:** Scalability and low latency.
- **CWDM:** Low cost and low latency.
- **SONET/SDH:** Long distances and moderately low latency.
- **FCIP:** Long distances and low cost.
- **iSCSI:** Long distances, low costs and facilitates integration with heterogeneous SANs.

When dealing with BC and DR, reliability, availability, and serviceability (RAS) are other important factors to consider, and thus, HA designs need to be incorporated into the SAN extension solutions. For upper layer protocols such as FCIP and iSCSI, performance tuning and security have to be handled on top of HA. For the WAN, the proper deployment of WAN optimizers can render L3 WANs to be a viable SAN extension option for midrange applications.

Most importantly, these SAN extension solutions enable the storage fabrics or SAN segments to be distributed nationally or internationally, bringing us a step closer to a global private cloud computing service-oriented infrastructure (SOI) for cloud IaaS offerings.

Cloud Infrastructure as a Service

You cannot stay on the summit forever; you have to come down again. So why bother in the first place? Just this: What is above knows what is below, but what is below does not know what is above. One climbs, one sees. One descends, one sees no longer, but one has seen. There is an art of conducting oneself in the lower regions by the memory of what one saw higher up. When one can no longer see, one can at least still know.
—**Rene Daumal**

INFORMATION IN THIS CHAPTER:

- Cloud Security
- Unified Computing System
- Cloud Management
- Cloud IaaS: The Big Picture
- Summary

INTRODUCTION

The sheer determination required to closely follow the past seven chapters is itself an amazing feat. Kudos if you have come this far. Chapter 7 looked at the implementation of SAN extension to interconnect multiple private cloud-computing SANs over a specific geographical range for BC and DR purposes. Chapter 8 discusses three more prerequisite areas: cloud security, Unified Computing System (UCS), and cloud management.

Chapter 8 covers the various security considerations from the server virtualization perspective when implementing cloud IaaS offerings. The chapter also discusses how UCS resolves the current server deployment constraints in enterprise DCs and how UCS is the ideal compute platform for private cloud computing and cloud IaaS offerings. Chapter 8 covers cloud management in relation to server virtualization and cloud IaaS. The chapter also discusses the various components of the SOI and how cloud IaaS offerings can be directly overlaid on top of this SOI.

CLOUD SECURITY

The term *cloud security* might sound like an entirely new thing, but in reality, it is not. The good news is that existing security infrastructure and techniques can be reused in cloud IaaS with some minor restructuring and additions. The restructuring basically pertains to server virtualization (for more information, see the Server Virtualization section in Chapter 2). Existing firewalls, network intrusion prevention systems, web application firewalls, endpoint security, and so on still remain applicable in cloud security. These security devices and mechanisms provide the same protection as they do for physical servers. For brevity, the main focus of this section is on the various security considerations from the server virtualization perspective when implementing cloud IaaS offerings.

Through the implementation of server virtualization many server locations will change. In particular, some applications previously residing in the demilitarized zone (DMZ) will now reside on virtual machines (VMs), and in turn, multiple VMs will reside within the same physical server. In the traditional DMZ model, each physical server is connected to an access port and any communication to and from a particular server, or between servers, goes through a physical access switch, as well as any associated appliances such as a firewall or a load balancer. In a virtualized server environment, multiple VLANs, IP subnets, and access ports can all reside within the same physical server as part of a virtual access layer. Traffic does not need to leave the physical server and go through a physical access switch for one VM to communicate with another. Instead, a virtual switch that shares the same basic functionality as a traditional physical access-layer switch, is configured to provide connectivity for all the VMs.

This virtual access layer poses some security challenges because conventional methods can no longer gather visibility information for inter-VM traffic flows that reside within a physical server. To overcome these security challenges, the existing DMZ must be aligned with the server virtualization. One way is to design a virtual DMZ based on the virtual access layer. Another way is through the implementation of virtual security appliances.

A virtual security appliance is designed with virtual network security in mind and it runs inside virtual environments. It is prepackaged with a security application (e.g., a virtual firewall) and runs on hardware that is virtualized using a hypervisor. The fact that the virtual security appliance runs in a virtual environment also means it can directly address security isolation, protection, and monitoring within the virtual environment without relying on physical security and monitoring devices external to the virtual access network. A detailed discussion of virtual security appliances is beyond the scope of this book.

NOTE:

Examples of a virtual firewall or a virtual security appliance include VMware vShield Zones and Cisco Virtual Security Gateway (VSG) for the NX1KV switch.

In addition, the physical server or hardware platform that is involved in the server virtualization process needs to be "hardened" as all the applications are now residing on multiple VMs within the same physical server. Examples of platform security include:

- **Type 1 hypervisor (or bare-metal hypervisor):** Type 1 hypervisor does not require an underlying OS for installation onto a physical server making attacks in this aspect difficult because it is bare-metal.
- **Thin-hypervisor strategy:** The thin-hypervisor's compact footprint ensures fewer patches and smaller attack area making it less prone to threats due to the absence of arbitrary code. An example of a thin-hypervisor is the VMware ESXi.

- **Memory protection:** The use of the no execute (NX) bit and address space layout randomization (ASLR) provide memory protection:
  - **NX bit:** The NX bit is used in CPUs to segregate areas of memory used by either storage of processor instructions (or code) or for storage of data. An OS with support for the NX bit can mark certain areas of memory as nonexecutable. The processor then refuses to execute any code residing in these areas of memory. The general technique, known as executable space protection, prevents certain types of malicious software from taking over computers by inserting their code into another program's data storage area and running their own code from within this section.
  - **ASLR:** ASLR randomly arranges the positions of key data areas, usually including the base of the executable, as well as the position of libraries, heap, and stack, in a process's address space. It makes attacks that involve the prediction of target addresses more difficult as the related memory addresses are obscured from the attackers.
- **Kernel module integrity:** The use of digital signing that ensures the integrity and authenticity of modules, drivers, and applications as they are loaded by the kernel (e.g., VMkernel).
- **Trusted Execution Technology (TXT):** Intel TXT[1] uses a mix of processor, chipset, and Trusted Platform Module (TPM) to detect and/or prevent software-based attacks such as:
  - Attempts to insert rootkit hypervisor (e.g., the "blue pill" malware).
  - Attacks designed to compromise platform secrets in memory.
  - BIOS and firmware update attacks.

NOTE:

TXT is implemented in Westmere-EP. Westmere-EP is the code name for the 1–2 socket, and up to six core server/workstation processors, targeted for the Intel 5520 chipset-based platform (compatible with Intel Xeon 5500 platform). Westmere-EP is part of the family of 32-nm processors, based on Intel microarchitecture (code name Nehalem).

Besides platform security, secure isolation must also be assured between the multitenants subscribing to cloud IaaS. This is generally achieved through the virtualization of the infrastructure computing resources, such as servers (for details, see Chapter 2), storage (for details, see Chapter 2), and networks (for details, see Chapter 3).

Because virtual access networks are no different from physical networks, they end up with the same kinds of vulnerabilities typically associated with a physical network such as:

- Users on VMs within the virtual network have access to all other VMs on the same virtual network.
- Compromising one VM on a virtual network is sufficient to provide a platform for additional attacks against other VMs on the same network segment.
- If a virtual network is interconnected to the physical network or the Internet then the VMs on the virtual network might have access to external resources (and to external exploits as well) that could leave them open to exploitation.
- Network traffic that passes directly between VMs without passing through security devices is unmonitored.

The problems created by the near invisibility of direct inter-VM (or VM-to-VM) traffic on a virtual network are exactly like those found in physical networks, complicated by the fact that the packets are moving entirely within the hardware of a single physical host:

- Because the virtual network traffic never leaves the physical host hardware, security administrators have no means to examine direct VM-to-VM traffic. They cannot intercept it nor have any knowledge on what that traffic is for.
- Logging of direct VM-to-VM network activity within a single host and verification of VM access for regulatory compliance purposes becomes difficult.
- Inappropriate usage of virtual network resources and bandwidth consumption by direct VM-to-VM traffic activities are difficult to discover or rectify.
- Inappropriate services running on or within the virtual network can go undetected.
- A rogue VM overpowering the host physical resources (e.g., CPU cycles, memory, and so on) can bring down the entire virtualized environment and all the other VMs with it.

Virtual switch security

The Nexus 1000V (NX1KV) switch is used as an example in this chapter to denote the virtual access-layer switch. Besides the advantages mentioned in Chapter 2, the NX1KV switch also inherited most of the security features that can be derived from a physical access-layer switch. These features include:

- VLANs
- Private VLANs
- Access-control lists (ACLs)
- Anti-spoofing features such as:
    - Dynamic Host Configuration Protocol (DHCP) snooping
    - IP Source Guard
    - Dynamic ARP Inspection (DAI)
- Port mirroring
- NetFlow version 9

> **NOTE:**
>
> The NX1KV is an L2 switch. It is however equipped with L3/L4 awareness to support features such as ACLs, NetFlow, QoS, and IGMP snooping.

VLANs

The concept of VLAN is supported on the virtual access layer. VLAN support on the virtual access-layer switch provides a reliable method for segmenting traffic flows from the L2 perspective. This helps to maintain and extend L3 isolated paths to the virtual access layer. VLANs with applied ACLs control traffic to different VMs and applications. Existing VLAN security best practices for physical access-layer switches still hold true and should be adopted in the virtual environment.

Private VLANs

Just as in a physical environment, VMs residing in the same VLAN can still directly access one another. This can wreak security havoc if one of the VMs is compromised. Secondary attacks can be launched from the compromised VM to other VMs in the VLAN. These can be application-specific attacks, man-in-the-middle attacks, or network-based attacks targeted at compromising systems and capturing data.

Private VLANs (PVLANs) are used in the virtual switching environment to isolate VMs within the same VLAN. PVLANs are further divided into primary and secondary VLANs. The primary VLAN is usually the existing VLAN used for access. The secondary VLAN is local to the physical or virtual switch in which it is configured. Each secondary VLAN is associated with a primary VLAN. Multiple secondary VLANs are associated with a single primary VLAN in a common subnet. Three types of ports are available when configuring PVLANs:

- **Promiscuous ports:** These are the "open ports" of the PVLANs. They communicate with all other ports. The promiscuous port is usually the uplink port for the switch and carries the primary VLAN. The purpose of the promiscuous port is to move traffic between ports in community or isolated VLANs. The promiscuous port can be a trunk port or an access port.
- **Community ports:** These ports communicate with other ports in the same community and with the promiscuous port. Ports in different communities cannot communicate with one another. Put another way, a port that is assigned to a community VLAN is a community port.
- **Isolated ports:** These ports only communicate with the promiscuous port. Traffic from the isolated port is forwarded only to the promiscuous port and no other. Put another way, a port that is assigned to an isolated VLAN is an isolated port.

The primary VLAN carries traffic from a promiscuous port to the isolated and community ports according to their associations. The secondary VLAN is assigned either an isolated port or a community port. In other words, the secondary VLAN can either be an isolated VLAN or a community VLAN. An isolated VLAN is useful when isolation needs to be maintained between VMs within the virtual infrastructure. A community VLAN plays a crucial role when direct VM-to-VM machine communication is required or when server clustering is being used.

In Figure 8.1, port Eth3/3 is the promiscuous port and is part of primary VLAN 80. Eth3/3 leads to a default gateway (not shown in the diagram for brevity). Ports vEth1 and vEth2 are community ports and they belong to the same community VLAN 81. Thus VM1 and VM2 can directly communicate with each other and with the default gateway. Ports vEth3 and vEth4 are isolated ports belonging to isolated VLAN 82. In this case, VM3 only communicates with the default gateway. The same applies to VM4.

Access-control lists

Direct communication should not be allowed between VMs in the same subnet but belonging to different cloud IaaS tenants or end-users. Since this inter-VM traffic might not leave the physical server, implementing IP ACL on the respective virtual switch ports provides another alternative to segment this traffic from the L3 perspective.

As mentioned in the previous section, a port in an isolated VLAN cannot communicate directly with a port in another isolated VLAN. Likewise, ports in different community VLANs cannot communicate directly with one another. To do so, they need to use L3 means, through a router or another

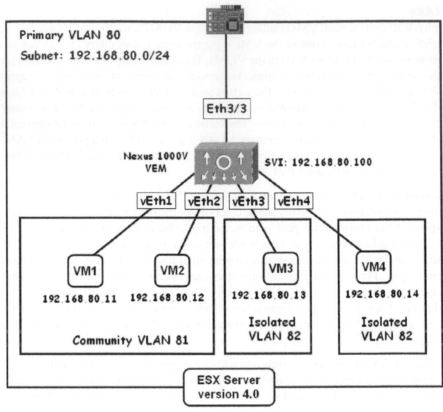

Primary VLAN 80
Subnet: 192.168.80.0/24

Eth3/3

Nexus 1000V
VEM   SVI: 192.168.80.100

vEth1   vEth2   vEth3   vEth4

VM1   VM2   VM3   VM4

192.168.80.11   192.168.80.12   192.168.80.13   192.168.80.14

Isolated   Isolated
VLAN 82   VLAN 82

Community VLAN 81

ESX Server
version 4.0

FIGURE 8.1

VM isolation using PVLANs

L3 device. In this case, the application of the necessary ACLs can be done to either permit or deny communication between these VLANs.

In cases where the communication between VMs in different subnets needs to be restricted an ACL would be the appropriate mechanism. ACLs can also ensure the secure isolation between production and management networks (or VLANs).

> **NOTE:**
>
> On the NX1 KV switch, ACL processing for IP packets are typically processed on the I/O modules (VEMs). Management interface traffic is always processed on the supervisor module (VSM), which will take a slightly longer time.

DHCP snooping

The DHCP snooping feature provides network protection from bogus DHCP servers. It creates a logical firewall between untrusted hosts and DHCP servers. The switch builds and maintains a DHCP binding database (aka DHCP snooping table). The DHCP binding database keeps track of DHCP addresses that are assigned to ports. It can also filter DHCP messages from untrusted ports. Inbound packets received on untrusted ports are dropped if the source MAC address does not match any MAC address in the DHCP binding database.

IP Source Guard

The IP Source Guard feature restricts IP traffic on untrusted L2 ports by filtering traffic based on the DHCP snooping binding database or statically configured IP source bindings. An entry in the IP source binding table contains the IP address along with the associated MAC and VLAN numbers. The IP source guard feature is enabled in combination with the DHCP snooping feature on untrusted L2 ports. It prevents IP spoofing attacks when a host tries to spoof the IP address of another host. Any IP traffic coming into the untrusted L2 port with a source IP address other than that assigned through DHCP or static configuration will be filtered out. The IP Source Guard feature is supported on L2 ports only, including access and trunk ports.

Dynamic ARP Inspection

A malicious user could intercept traffic intended for other hosts on the LAN segment and poison the ARP caches of connected host systems by broadcasting forged ARP responses. To prevent such attacks, the L2 switch must have a mechanism to ensure that only valid ARP requests and responses are forwarded.

DAI is a security feature on the switch that validates ARP packets in a network. It performs an ARP validity check on packets by inspecting the IP-to-MAC address binding entries stored in a trusted database (the DHCP snooping binding database) before forwarding the packet to the appropriate destination. DAI drops all ARP packets with invalid IP-to-MAC address bindings. DAI does not check outbound packets; it inspects only inbound packets.

Since the DHCP snooping binding database is not available in non-DHCP environments, the DAI can validate ARP packets against a user-defined ARP ACL that maps hosts with a statically configured IP address to their MAC addresses. It is recommended to enable the DAI feature on the switch because it safeguards the network from many of the commonly known man-in-the-middle (MITM) attacks.

Port mirroring

With server virtualization, traffic flows occur within the physical server between VMs without the need to traverse a physical access-layer switch. As the visibility of the virtual access layer is obscured, administrators can have a tough time identifying a VM that is infected or compromised without the forwarding of traffic through the relevant physical security appliances.

Switched Port Analyzer (SPAN) and Encapsulated Remote SPAN (ERSPAN) are very useful traffic monitoring tools for gaining visibility into network traffic flows at the virtual access layer. In local SPAN, the source interface and destination interface are on the same device. The network analyzer is attached directly to the SPAN destination port. The SPAN source can be a port or a VLAN interface. The destination, usually a port, can also be a VLAN. Local SPAN can monitor all traffic received on the source interface including BPDUs.

Local SPAN cannot forward traffic through the IP network but this is possible with ERSPAN. ERSPAN monitors traffic in multiple network devices across an IP network and carries that traffic using a GRE tunnel to destination analyzers. In other words, ERSPAN monitors traffic remotely and ERSPAN sources can be ports or VLANs.

ERSPAN can be enabled on the NX1KV switch, and traffic flows can then be exported from the VMs to external devices, such as Intrusion Protection System (IPS) appliances and Network Analysis Modules (NAMs).

> **NOTE:**
>
> ERSPAN uses separate source and destination sessions. The source and destination sessions are configured on different switches. The ERSPAN source session copies traffic from the source ports or source VLANs and forwards the traffic using routable GRE-encapsulated packets to the ERSPAN destination session. The ERSPAN destination session switches the traffic to the destinations.

In Figure 8.2, ERSPAN source sessions on the NX1KV switch forward copies of the VM4 traffic (with ERSPAN-ID 104) to the IPS appliance, and copies of the VM1 (with ERSPAN-ID 101) traffic to the NAM, through ERSPAN destination sessions configured on a services aggregation-layer switch

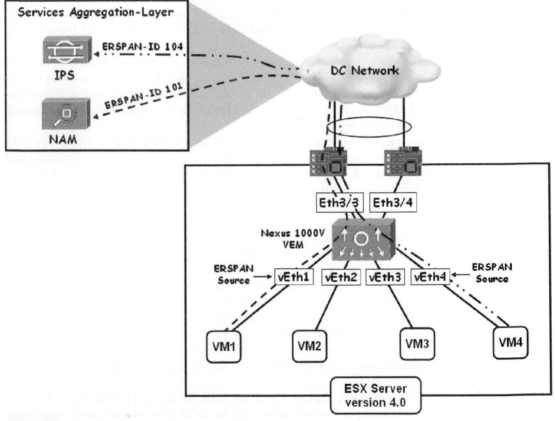

FIGURE 8.2

Visibility with ERSPAN

(not shown in diagram for brevity). Both the IPS and the NAM are connected to this services aggregation-layer switch. The ERSPAN destination sessions on the services aggregation-layer switch upon receiving the traffic from the ERSPAN source sessions, forwards the traffic to the respective destinations, in this example, the IPS appliance and the NAM.

An ERSPAN ID (1-1023) can be added to the ERSPAN header of the encapsulated frame to differentiate between various ERSPAN streams of traffic at the destination (in this example, ERSPAN ID 101 for NAM and ERSPAN ID 104 for IPS). The application of a different ERSPAN ID for each session provides distinction between multiple aggregated ERSPAN sessions. This is particularly useful when many aggregated ERSPAN sessions terminate at a dedicated device residing in a central location, for instance, the services chassis (e.g., the Cat6K switch) at the services aggregation layer. For more details on ERSPAN deployment, see the ERSPAN Design Study section in Chapter 9.

> **NOTE:**
>
> Cisco has an NX1KV NAM Virtual Service Blade (VSB) that resides on the Nexus 1010 Virtual Services Appliance. This means that ERSPAN and NetFlow from the NX1KV switch can be directed to a NAM VSB located within the virtual access network rather than to a physical NAM located on the services aggregation layer.

NetFlow

NetFlow is typically used to gather data for network monitoring, accounting, and planning. The NX1KV switch provides this capability in the virtual access layer. This provides the desired visibility on the network traffic generated by the resident VMs that in turn facilitates the proper security monitoring and accounting of these VMs.

A flow is a unidirectional stream of packets that arrives on a source interface (or subinterface), matching a set of conditions. All packets with the same source/destination IP address, source/destination ports, protocol interface, and class-of-service are grouped into a flow in which packets and bytes are then tallied. This condenses a large amount of network information into a database called the NetFlow cache.

A flow record defines the information that NetFlow gathers, such as packets in the flow, and the types of counters gathered per flow. Either newly defined flow records or predefined flow records are used. The NX1KV switch supports NetFlow version 9 and includes the following predefined flow records:

- NetFlow-Original: Predefined traditional IPv4 input NetFlow with origin AS numbers.
- NetFlow IPv4 Original-Input: Predefined traditional IPv4 input NetFlow.
- NetFlow IPv4 Original-Output: Predefined traditional IPv4 output NetFlow.
- NetFlow IPv4 Protocol-Port: Predefined protocol and ports aggregation scheme.

> **NOTE:**
>
> Why NetFlow version 9? NetFlow version 9 is preferred because NetFlow version 5 is limited by fixed field specifications, a 16-bit representation of the 32-bit interface index used in NX-OS, and there is no support for IPv6, L2, or MPLS fields.

> **NOTE:**
>
> At the time of this writing, NetFlow Exporter format version 5 is not supported on the NX1KV switch. Although NetFlow Exporter format version 9 is supported, L2 and IPv6 match fields are not supported.

A flow exporter defines where and when the flow records are sent from the NetFlow cache to the reporting server, called the NetFlow Collector. An exporter definition includes the following:

- Destination IP address
- Source interface
- UDP port number (this is where the collector is listening)
- Export format

A flow monitor is then created to associate the flow record with the flow exporter. The flow monitor is applied to a specific interface in a specific direction.

> **NOTE:**
>
> There are two modes for NetFlow on NX-OS: full and sampled. Full-mode analyzes all packets on the interface, while sample-mode adopts a user-defined sampling algorithm and rate, to analyze packets on interfaces with NetFlow configured. However, at the time of this writing, NetFlow Sampler is not supported on the NX1KV switch.

The NetFlow Collector assembles the exported flows and combines them to produce reports used for traffic and security analysis. NetFlow export pushes information periodically to the NetFlow Collector. The NetFlow cache is constantly filling with flows. Timers determine when a flow is exported to the NetFlow Collector Server. A flow is ready for export when one of the following conditions occurs:

- The flow is inactive for a certain time during which no new packets are received for the flow.
- The flow has lived longer than the active timer—for instance, a large FTP download.
- A TCP flag (i.e., an FIN or RST flag) indicates the flow is terminated.
- The flow cache is full and some flows must be aged out in order to make room for new flows.

> **NOTE:**
>
> On the NX1KV switch, the default active timer is 1800 sec (configurable from 60 to 4092 sec) and the default inactive timer is 15 sec (configurable from 15 to 4092 sec).

The NetFlow Collector generates reports to display details, such as packets per second, on the virtual Ethernet interfaces residing on the NX1KV switch. The flow monitor on the NX1KV switch also monitors flows from the physical interfaces associated with the switch and VMkernel interfaces (vmknics), including VMotion traffic.

NetFlow traffic is forwarded to collectors in both in-band and out-of-band deployments. In in-band deployment, the collector is located on the production network so the NetFlow traffic will be forwarded through the production interface of the switch. In out-of-band deployment, the collector is located on a dedicated out-of-band management network so the NetFlow traffic will be forwarded through the management interface of the switch instead.

Endpoint security

Recall from the Port Mirroring section, traffic generated by VMs is forwarded to network IPS appliances by configuring ERSPAN on the virtual switch. An alternative to this is host-based IPS. Host-based IPS is one of the most effective ways to protect an endpoint against exploitation attempts and malicious software. It mitigates most known attacks and is also effective at preventing zero-day attacks.

NOTE:

The term "zero-day" is derived from the age of the exploit. When a developer becomes aware of a security hole, there is a race to close it before attackers discover it or the vulnerability goes public. A "zero-day" attack occurs on or before the first or "zero-th" day of developer awareness, meaning that the developer has not had any opportunity to distribute a security fix to users of the software.

Host-based IPS thwarts new attacks by examining the behavioral aspects of the attack. This is possible without requiring the installation of an IPS attack signature. Host-based IPS is typically used in conjunction with network IPS in most DMZ and server-farm environments. The details of network IPS and host-based IPS are beyond the scope of this book.

Virtual DMZ

Concisely, a virtual DMZ solution requires the use of:

- Physical network segmentation with firewalls to maintain stateful traffic inspection of production and nonproduction traffic (for more information, see the Firewall Virtualization section in Chapter 3)
- Port profiles to maintain separation of duties (between server and network administrators) and policy enforcement (for more information, see the Whose Turn, Server or Network Administrator? section in Chapter 2)
- Authentication, authorization, and accounting (i.e., AAA) model to define access rights and maintain accurate logs
- VLANs and PVLANs for isolation of VMs and applications (for details see the VLANs and Private VLANs sections)
- ACLs to limit access between DMZ VMs, production networks, and management networks (for details see the Access-Control Lists section)
- ERSPAN and NetFlow to increase operational visibility in the virtual DMZ environment (for details see the Port Mirroring and NetFlow sections)
- Rate limiting to reduce the effect of malicious traffic generated by denial-of-service (DoS) attacks mounted from compromised VMs or hosts elsewhere

In addition, some general rules-of-thumb to bear in mind are as follows:

- Maintain security (e.g., intrusion detection and prevention, firewalling to prevent unwanted traffic, DoS prevention, and so on) as in a physical nonvirtualized environment.
- Maintain detailed documentation for virtual and physical network interconnections
- Enforce clearly defined change management controls
- Enforce a clear separation of roles and responsibilities
- Perform ongoing auditing (i.e., logging and audit trails) and monitoring

UNIFIED COMPUTING SYSTEM

In the current server deployment landscape, there are generally two approaches: scale up or scale out. The scale-up (or scale vertically) approach is based on increasing the computing power of a single server by adding resources in terms of more processors, memory, I/O devices, and so on. The scale-out (or scale horizontally) approach is based on increasing the number of servers. The latter approach is preferred by most enterprise DCs because standard computing components are used. However, the more favored scale-out approach introduces another interesting DC phenomenon—server sprawl.

So enters server virtualization, which is instrumental in reducing server sprawl and has since been widely adopted by organizations worldwide. With virtualization, a physical server is a container of multiple logical servers. The virtualization software even comes with a virtual access layer switch (e.g., NX1KV switch) that is equivalent to a physical one. Scale up or scale out now? How about both, or better still, a paradigm shift instead? The focus should be on addressing the current deployment constraints rather than betting on which approach is better. The Cisco Unified Computing System (UCS) is used as the example platform for further development of this topic.

With private cloud computing adoption increasing, "anonymous" servers that can be quickly repurposed are fast becoming a common requirement from enterprise customers. These new servers must also be capable of supporting a large number of VMs, facilitate ease of moving them from one server to another, have a management system that is policy driven and offers a rich API to interface with the cloud software.

A physical server may well run out of RAM long before it runs out of CPU while supporting multiple tenants, each with their own VMs. The capability to add lots of RAM to a server has become a key requirement for many enterprise DCs contemplating cloud IaaS offerings. To this end, the UCS blade server, using next-generation CPUs, memory expansion technologies, and I/O techniques, can support a large memory footprint of up to 384 GB of RAM.

To facilitate the ease of migrating server configurations from one DC to another, the identity of the various components (MAC addresses, UUIDs, WWNs, and so on) of the UCS are not burned in the hardware. Instead, they are contained in a configuration file. This means that recreating an identical UCS in a DR site is as simple as moving the configuration file.

Management tools often come as a late addition in the product development life cycle and, consequently, might not be tightly integrated with the managed entities. UCS has an embedded management processor that has global visibility on all the managed entities (or elements) that make up the UCS. This enhances coordinated control and provides integrated management as well as diagnostics.

Moreover, UCS is designed according to the ToR approach (for more details, see the Rack Topologies section in Chapter 2). All the servers that belong to a UCS are connected to two fabric interconnects that are placed at the top of one or every few racks, and they communicate by using a unified fabric (network-centric) approach (for more details, see the Unified Data Center Fabric section in Chapter 2), which significantly reduces the cabling.

To summarize, UCS is a niche solution in resolving the current server deployment constraints in enterprise DCs. UCS would be the ideal compute platform for private cloud computing and cloud IaaS offerings.

> **NOTE:**
>
> The UCS section in this chapter explains its applicability with respect to private cloud computing. This is just an ad hoc discussion session and not an authoritative guide. The reader is advised to refer to appropriate official documents when evaluating products, designing solutions, or conducting businesses that have to do with UCS. The authors do not provide any guarantee of the correctness of the content and are not liable for any mistake or ambiguity.

UCS Enabling Technologies

UCS is a system and not just a server chassis. The UCS's aggregation point in the DC is the network. In other words, UCS uses the network as the pivotal platform. Some of its enabling technologies include:

- FCoE (for more details, see the Unified Data Center Fabric section in Chapter 2)
- Virtual NIC Tag (VNTag)
- Memory expansion
- Unified management

These enabling technologies help to remove unnecessary switches, adapters, cables, and management modules, resulting in a better streamlined server deployment for private cloud computing environments.

VNTag

The VNTag is a 6-byte Ethernet tag inserted into the Ethernet frame immediately after the destination and source MAC address pair (MAC-DA and MAC-SA). Traditional Ethernet switches do not support the forwarding of frames where the source and destination MAC are on the same port, thus they do not forward frames between two VMs connected on the same switch port. VNTag resolves this issue by creating a virtual Ethernet (vEth) interface for each VM on the switch.

> **NOTE:**
>
> The IEEE MACsec (authentication and encryption) tag can precede the VNTag.

In other words, the VNTag binds a vNIC to a vEth interface and the reverse applies too. A "VNTag-aware" switch is capable of forwarding between vEth interfaces so frames are forwarded between VMs connected on the same physical port. These VMs are identified by the destination virtual interface identifier (dst_vif [14 bits]) and source virtual interface identifier (src_vif [12 bits]) fields in the VNTag. The implementation of VNTag can be done either as a VNTag-capable NIC or in the software by the hypervisor. It can also be implemented as a separate box commonly referred as a fabric extender that acts as a remote multiplexer toward an Ethernet switch. Figure 8.3 illustrates two fabric extenders connected to two Ethernet switches. Each fabric extender has 4 × 10GE uplinks to the Ethernet switches and 48 × 1GE down-facing ports toward the servers. The uplinks from the fabric extenders to the Ethernet switches use the VNTag header, and 48 virtual interfaces (vifs) are used to identify each down-facing 1GE port.

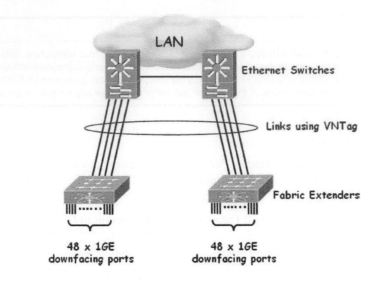

FIGURE 8.3

Fabric extenders

> **NOTE:**
>
> Palo, a CNA developed by Cisco, supports VNTag.

Memory expansion

The need for virtualization software to run multiple OS instances mandates large amounts of memory. In order to achieve a larger memory footprint, most IT organizations have to scale up to four-socket servers that are typically more expensive, require more power, and involve higher licensing costs.

The Cisco Extended Memory Technology expands the capabilities of CPU-based memory controllers by logically changing the geometry of main memory while still using standard double-data-rate three (DDR3[2]) memory. The technology makes every four dual in-line memory module (DIMM[3]) slots in the expanded memory blade server appear to the CPU's memory controller as a single DIMM that is four times the size. For example, using standard DDR3 DIMMs, the technology makes four 8-GB DIMMS appear as a single 32-GB DIMM. This unique memory expansion technique allows incremental memory scale-up in a two-socket server, rather than a forklift upgrade to a four-socket server.

For virtualized environments that require significant amounts of main memory, but not the full 384-GB extent, smaller-sized DIMMs can be used in place of 8-GB DIMMs, with resulting cost savings. For instance, eight 1-GB DIMMS should be less expensive than one 8-GB DIMM.

Unified management

The UCS Manager (UCSM) is an embedded device-management software that manages the UCS as a single logical entity through GUI, CLI, or XML API. It creates a unified management domain with centralized management capabilities. The UCSM implements policy-based and role-based management using service profiles and templates.

UCS resources are abstract in the sense that their identities, I/O configuration, MAC addresses, as well as WWNs, firmware versions, BIOS boot order, and network attributes (such as QoS settings, ACLs, pin groups, and threshold policies) are all programmable using a just-in-time deployment model. The UCSM stores this identity, connectivity, and configuration information in service profiles. A service profile is applied to any resource to provision it with the characteristics required to support a specific software stack. The service profile allows server and network definitions to move within the management domain, enabling flexibility in the use of system resources. Service profile templates allow different classes of resources to be defined and applied to a number of resources, each with its own unique identities assigned from predetermined pools.

> **NOTE:**
>
> The UCSM resides in the fabric interconnect (see the Fabric Interconnect section). UCSM is an NX-OS module (plug-in); thus, it is supervised, monitored, and controlled by the NX-OS running on the fabric interconnect.

In addition, the UCSM supports multitenant environments that serve internal clients, or end-users, as separate business entities. The system can be logically partitioned and allocated to different clients or customers to administer as their own.

UCS components

It would be a great challenge to pull off a UCS-like solution without having complete control over the hardware. It is worthwhile to briefly discuss the UCS components for a clearer view of this solution. Cisco has attempted to keep UCS open from a software and management perspective, which is a mandatory requirement in today's DC. The UCS consists of the following components:

- UCS Manager (for more details, see the Unified Management section)
- Fabric interconnect
- Blade server chassis
- Fabric extender
- I/O adapters
- Blade servers

Figure 8.4 illustrates a typical UCS topology.

Fabric interconnect

The UCS 6100 Series fabric interconnects provide a unified network fabric as the aggregation point that connects every server resource in the system using "wire once" 10GE/FCoE/SFP+ ports (for more details, see the Cable Considerations section in Chapter 2) and/or 2/4/8G FC uplinks (via an expansion module). Fabric interconnects are typically deployed in active–active redundant pairs providing uniform access to storage arrays and other network resources.

The UCS 6100 Series fabric interconnect is based on the Nexus 5000 product line with the additional functionality of managing the UCS chassis with the embedded UCS Manager. In terms of Ethernet connectivity, the fabric interconnect supports vPC, MAC pinning, and so on (for more details, see the vPC and Nexus 1000V section in Chapter 2).

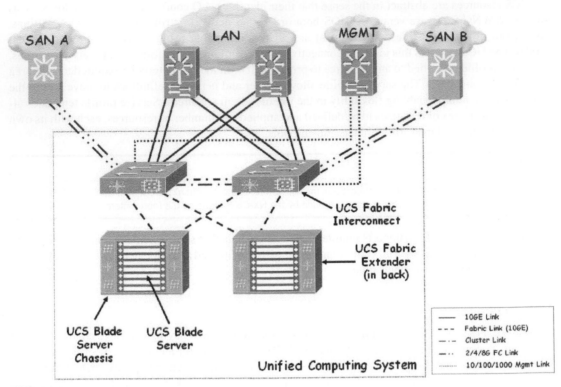

FIGURE 8.4

Simplified UCS topology

NOTE:

The UCS 6120XP fabric interconnect (1RU) comes with 20 10GE/FCoE/SFP+ ports, whereas the UCS 6140XP fabric interconnect (2RU) comes with 40 10GE/FCoE/SFP+ ports.

Blade server chassis

The UCS 5108 blade server chassis (of the UCS 5100 Series) is six rack units (6RU) high. On the front of the chassis are eight half-slots for the server blades and four slots for power supplies. The chassis can accommodate both half-width and full-width server-blade form-factors. On the back of the chassis, there are slots for eight fans, two fabric extenders, and the power entry module.

Each pair of half-slots can become a full slot by removing a metal sheet separator. The following are the various blade server installation combinations based on the eight half-slots:

- Eight half-slot server blades
- Six half-slot server blades and one full-slot server blade

- Four half-slot server blades and two full-slot server blades
- Two half-slot server blades and three full-slot server blades
- Four full-slot server blades

> **NOTE:**
>
> At the time of this writing, there is only a single UCS blade server chassis available, the UCS 5108.

Fabric extender

The UCS 2100 Series fabric extenders (FEXs) bring the unified fabric into the blade server enclosure, providing 10GE connections between blade servers and the fabric interconnect. It also simplifies diagnostics, cabling, and management.

In other words, the UCS 2100 Series FEX extends the I/O fabric between the UCS 6100 Series fabric interconnects and the UCS 5100 Series blade server chassis, enabling a lossless and deterministic FCoE fabric to connect all blades and chassis together. Because the FEX is similar to a distributed line card, it does not do any switching and is managed as an extension of the fabric interconnect. This approach removes switching from the chassis, reduces overall infrastructure complexity, scales the UCS to multiple chassis without multiplying the number of switches required, and allows all chassis to be managed as a single management domain. The UCS 2100 Series FEX also manages the chassis environment (i.e., the power supplies and fans as well as the blades) in conjunction with the fabric interconnect so that separate chassis management modules are not required.

The UCS 2104XP FEX has eight 10GE downlink ports that connect through the midplane to each half-width slot in the chassis. It has four 10GE/FCoE/SFP+ uplink ports that connect the blade chassis to the fabric interconnect. The uplinks from the FEX to the fabric interconnect use the VNTag header (see the VNTag section). VNTag can also be used between the adapter and the FEX on the downlink ports if the adapter is VNTag-capable. Just like fabric interconnects, FEXs are typically configured in pairs for redundancy.

> **NOTE:**
>
> At the time of this writing, there is only a single UCS FEX available, the UCS 2104XP.

The mezzanine I/O adapters (for more details, see the I/O Adapters section) that are installed on the server blades are pre-pinned to the uplinks by default. Figure 8.5 shows the server blade slots prepinning based on the number of available uplinks. At the time of this writing, these settings are not user configurable.

I/O adapters

The UCS I/O adapters are really CNAs (for more details, see the FCoE Data Plane section in Chapter 2). CNAs help to reduce the number of adapters, cables, and access-layer switches that are required for LAN and SAN connectivity. This in turn brings down capital and operational expenditure, real estate power and cooling, as well as administrative overheads. The CNAs used by UCS blade servers are in mezzanine form-factor. These CNAs are also 10GBASE-KR based. Please refer to the appropriate UCS product documentation for the various supported I/O adapters.

Number of Links from FEX to Fabric Interconnect = 1	
Uplink	Slots pinned to uplink
1	1, 2, 3, 4, 5, 6, 7, 8
Number of Links from FEX to Fabric Interconnect = 2	
Uplink	Slots pinned to uplink
1	1, 3, 5, 7
2	2, 4, 6, 8
Number of Links from FEX to Fabric Interconnect = 4	
Uplink	Slots pinned to uplink
1	1, 5
2	2, 6
3	3, 7
4	4, 8

FIGURE 8.5

Uplink prepinning

> **NOTE:**
>
> 10GBASE-KR is part of the backplane Ethernet standard used in backplane applications, such as blade servers.

Blade servers

The UCS B-Series two-socket blade servers include:

- **UCS B200 two-socket blade server:** The UCS B200 is a half-slot blade server with 12 DIMM slots for up to 96 GB of memory. It supports one mezzanine adapter.
- **UCS B250 two-socket extended memory blade server:** The UCS B250 is a full-slot blade server with 48 DIMM slots for up to 384 GB of memory. It supports up to two mezzanine adapters.

> **NOTE:**
>
> The two-socket UCS blades are based on Nehalem-EP and Westmere-EP processors.

> **NOTE:**
>
> There is also a UCS B440 four-socket blade server and the UCS C-Series rack servers. The UCS C-Series rack servers can be used either as stand alone servers or interconnected in a UCS with hybrid configuration (both blade and rack servers).

CLOUD MANAGEMENT

Just like cloud security, the term *cloud management* sounds like new subject matter, but in fact, it is not. Existing network management strategies and techniques are still applicable in cloud IaaS. The additional inclusion, once again, pertains to server virtualization. For brevity, the scope of this section is narrowed down to network management pertaining to cloud IaaS offerings and the discussion will be conducted in a generic manner.

From the workflow perspective, management is a task that has to be distributed beyond the basic manager-agent management topologies in order to be in line with the exponential growth of networks that must be managed. In large-scale cloud IaaS deployments, qualities such as hierarchical management model, policy-based management, management mediation, automation, user self-service portals, and standardization with XML should be taken into consideration.

Hierarchical management

Hierarchical management requires information-gathering hierarchies that lead to more compact, aggregated, and even more abstracted information being collected. From the scalability perspective, hierarchical management is a core function. It provides a more efficient deployment of management when the links between the network operations center (NOC[4]) and remote locations are made up of small bandwidth pipes. A management hierarchy, when properly deployed, can decouple management functionality from a central NOC to the branch locations of an enterprise, nearer to devices that are need to be managed.

Figure 8.6 illustrates a simplified hierarchical management model. A subordinate management (submanagement) system can relieve the central management system from some of its management tasks. In certain aspects, a subordinate management system can be viewed as element management that involves managing the individual network elements (i.e., managed devices) in the network. The functions of element management include viewing and modifying the configurations of network elements, monitoring alarm messages generated from the network elements, the maintenance of hardware/software, and so on. Some form of "management helper" can also be embedded into the device. The capability to include additional management functionality on the device is commonly termed as embedded management intelligence or an autonomic system. A good example of an embedded device-management software implementation is the UCSM (for more information, see the Unified Management section). The main idea for the embedded subordinate management system or management helper is to include management functionalities on the managed device that would otherwise need to be provided by external management applications.

NOTE:

Element management is derived from the Telecommunication Management Network (TMN) model that consists of the layers (in bottom most to top most order): network elements, element management, network management, service management, and business management.

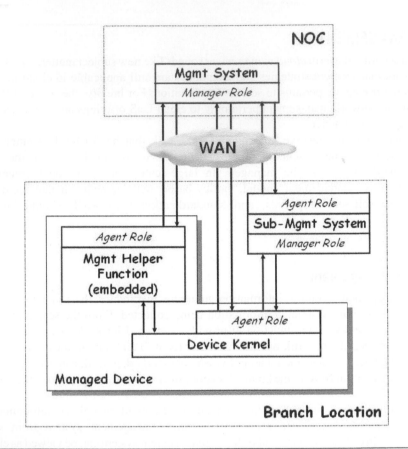

FIGURE 8.6

Simplified hierarchical management model

Policy-based management

There are a number of approaches to implement management tasks. For cloud IaaS offerings, one of the more appropriate ways is policy-based management. What is policy-based management? For starters, it is a management system that establishes specific goals for a subordinate management (or submanagement) system. The submanagement system, in turn, translates those goals into the required lower-level actions to ensure that the goals are met. In this case, the upper-layer management system can simply focus on setting overall policy, while the submanagement system converts the policy into actions. This approach is geared toward distributing management tasks, as close to the edges of the management network as possible.

Figure 8.7 illustrates a simplified policy-based management model. The basic components of policy-based management include:

- **Policy enforcement point (PEP):** This is the point where policy is enforced—that is, conditions that are subjected to policy are identified and the respective policy actions are taken.

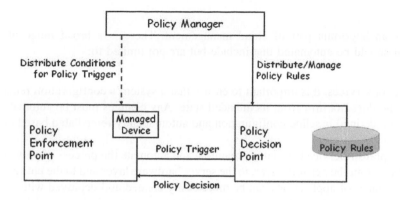

FIGURE 8.7

Simplified policy-based management model

- **Policy decision point (PDP):** This is the point where a decision is made on what to do when a policy trigger is received by the PEP. Based on the conditions reported by the PEP, the PDP takes the action (if any) that is inferred from the policy rules and conveys the decision back to the PEP, which then in turn executes it. The PDP typically can reside on the same system (or device) as the PEP or it can be an external (or separate) controller instead.
- **Policy manager:** The policy manager is responsible for managing and defining the policies. Policy rules must be established and distributed to the PDPs. The conditions that will trigger a policy rule must be distributed to the PEPs so that the PEPs are aware of the types of events and actions that are subjected to the defined policy.

Management mediation

As the variety of management interfaces and protocols proliferates, management mediation becomes a necessity. Management mediation leads to special variation of management hierarchies, where the subordinate management system (in the middle) must be further enhanced with a gateway function to bridge the gap between the manager at the top and the agent that it manages at the bottom.

One aspect of management mediation involves the translation of management messages of one protocol into the management messages of another. A simple way to achieve this is through the use of templates. Templates are really a collapsed form of rules. Templates define one rule for each type of message that can occur rather than analyzing the messages in terms of their syntax. In other words, the template approach is based on pattern matching and text substitution. This approach is suitable for management mediation that involves responses to CLI commands or syslog messages.

Management mediation becomes a complex topic that involves significant application complexity when an in-depth analysis of the management information is required before making a valid translation. Management mediation discussion is beyond the scope of this book.

> **NOTE:**
>
> The simplest form of management mediation is syntactic whereby an in-depth analysis of management information is not required in order to make the translation. On the other hand, semantic mediation would need to be in place if the translation operation requires an in-depth analysis of the management information before making the conversion.

Automation

Automation is an important part of cloud management. There is a broad range of essential DC operations that should be automated that include but are not limited to:

- **Change and configuration management:** To optimize the availability and performance of applications or services, it is important to ensure that a system's configuration remains consistent over time and does not drift from its intended state. Any changes must be automatically detected based on a predefined baseline configuration and automatically remediated based on a predefined policy action.
- **Service templates:** Service templates streamline and automate the process of provisioning an end-to-end service from the network layer, to the server hardware layer and to the entire software stack. Multiple instances of applications can be more easily created and deployed without requiring the user to replicate common configuration specifications.
- **Automated provisioning to handle increased application workload:** If an application requires additional resources, due to a heavy workload, additional resources must be automatically provisioned to improve the application performance. In most cases, application provisioning is policy-based, rather than based on dedicated resources. The main idea is to allow application services to dynamically scale up and down based on usage/performance. Similarly, resources can be freed and made available to other services as they become unused.
- **Automated service-level management:** With the help of service templates, the types of resources required by a service, such as processor speed, amount of memory, and other performance-related parameters, can be predefined. Thus, the level of service can be stipulated, providing high-performance or even low-performance services, as required by the service-level agreements.
- **Automated failover:** To reduce the downtime for critical applications, failover must be automated. If a device stops working, another device should be automatically provisioned to take over the role of the failing device.

User self-service

So far this chapter has covered cloud management from the perspective of the cloud IaaS provider. What about the subscribers, end-users, or tenants? The answer is: user self-service. Actually, the relationship between the IaaS provider and the IaaS user is analogous to the relationship between the landlord and the tenant. In simple terms, when real estate is leased by the landlord to the tenant, the tenant is responsible for the housekeeping of the property. The landlord can lease out the entire building or just apartments in the building according to the preference of the tenants. From the tenant's perspective, renting an entire building would mean better control but with more housekeeping responsibilities, whereas renting individual apartments would mean a smaller housekeeping role but with a lesser scope of control. Obviously, the price would also make a big difference between the two.

Assuming a landlord has buildings and apartments for lease, in this case, an end-user self-service reservation system is handy for interested tenants. Recall that in cloud IaaS (for more details, see the Service Models section in Chapter 1), the user does not really manage or control the underlying cloud infrastructure but has control over OS, deployed applications, system requirements, and so on. As such, compute platforms are made available as a part of the end-user self-service reservation system that allows users to select the OS, the system requirements, the applications, and so on without the need to directly involve IT support staff. This is illustrated by the following example sequence:

1. Select an OS.
2. Select the application(s).
3. Specify the system requirements.
4. Specify the reservation period.

> **NOTE:**
> The sequence of the OS and application will reverse when the choice of application dictates the choice of OS. For example, an application might only be supported running on Windows.

Just like a lease is valid for a limited period in real estate, at the end of the IaaS reservation period, the resources involved with the existing user can be reallocated to the new users. During the lease period, the user is responsible for managing the applications running on the compute platform while the provider is responsible for the maintenance of the underlying infrastructure including the hardware of the compute platform.

Selected networking components, such as firewalls and load balancers, can be made available in the self-service reservation system to the IaaS user as well. In this case, the firewalls and load balancers would typically be virtual device contexts, solely leased to that particular user (for more information, see the Service Integration in the Data Center section in Chapter 3).

XML-ization

Standardizing machine-readable interfaces across the various types of equipment and software in the cloud is crucial as extensive user interaction will become a pitfall in the long term. In most cases, extensible markup language (XML) is the de facto encoding scheme.

XML provides tags that are used to delimit different pieces of information with an XML document. The information that goes into an XML document can simply consist of a set of XML tags that are used to delimit, for example, a complete configuration file. An XML document can also be sophisticated in the sense that every parameter and attribute is represented with its own standardized tag. "XML-encoded" management information is recognizable throughout the cloud by different management software from different vendors.

CLOUD IaaS: THE BIG PICTURE

Private cloud computing is a generic term and along with it are three different service models: SaaS, PaaS, and IaaS (for more information, see the Service Models section in Chapter 1). SaaS or PaaS fulfillment typically requires applications or software development expertise. IaaS, on the other hand, is application-independent and provides a quick and easy entry point into the private cloud computing world. IaaS is a cloud service "superset" wherein SaaS overlays PaaS that in turn overlays IaaS (for more information, see the Service Models section in Chapter 1).

Most enterprise infrastructure-based services are pegged on physical infrastructure making it an uphill task for any kind of restructuring. Private cloud computing and cloud IaaS shift the focus from the physical infrastructure to a virtual infrastructure. The buzzword is virtualization. Consolidation is typically achieved through virtualization. Services are no longer built around real-estate floor space, physical servers, or ports. Instead, they are built around VM images, application instances, virtualized storage, and virtualized networks. In other words, cloud IaaS enables users to run workloads on the enterprise's infrastructure; that is, with some restructuring and add-ons, it can transform the existing physical infrastructure to a service-oriented infrastructure (SOI) that supports virtual environments. The main idea is to construct cloud IaaS offerings in a modular fashion on top of the SOI, so that they can be adaptively repurposed to support a substantially different service in response to changing user requirements. The SOI is also equipped with capabilities to support non-cloud and nonvirtual environments in cases where private cloud computing and cloud IaaS will coexist with traditionally delivered services using the same infrastructure. Using some preexisting equipment can reduce overall capital as well as operational expenditure required for the private cloud creation. It can also increase the utilization of the infrastructure and sometimes simplify the DC environment operationally.

The discussion thus far has covered most of the "pieces" of the IaaS jigsaw puzzle. Let's recap and assemble all these "pieces" together to produce a complete picture. Recall in Chapter 1, we mentioned the building blocks for private cloud computing that include:

- Server module
- Storage module
- Fabric module
- WAN module

For further illustrations in the subsequent subsections, these modules are further refined as follows:

- Server module:
    - Application software submodule
    - Virtual machine submodule
    - Virtual access-layer submodule
    - Compute submodule
- Storage module:
    - Storage array submodule
    - SAN submodule
    - SAN extension submodule
- Fabric module:
    - Access-layer submodule
    - Aggregation-layer submodule
    - Core-layer submodule
- WAN module:
    - Peering submodule
    - Next-generation WAN submodule

Figure 8.8 illustrates the various submodules that make up the SOI. These submodules form the underlying baseline infrastructure for cloud IaaS offerings in enterprises.

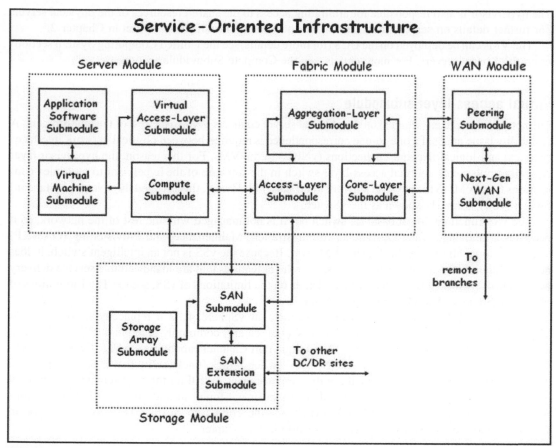

FIGURE 8.8

Service-oriented infrastructure expanded view

Application software submodule

Applications still call the shots in the virtualized world of cloud computing. In most cases, the applications are supplied by (or to) the end-users as a preconfigured VM image. However, applications can also include the software that the enterprise uses to provision and manage the cloud IaaS service. These applications include resource allocation automation, user self-service portals, cloud infrastructure management platform (CIMP), and so on.

Virtual machine submodule

VMs are the kingpins in virtual environments. They are the "offsprings" of server virtualization. Applications now run on top of these VMs (or logical servers), sharing the common resources of a physical server. The hypervisor (e.g., VMware ESX) is responsible for abstracting the virtual computing environment presented to end-users from the physical servers that implement the environment.

The hypervisor is also responsible for arbitrating access to the shared resources of the physical server. For further details on server virtualization, see the Server Virtualization section in Chapter 2.

The VMs can be deployed on the UCS (for more details, see the Unified Computing System section) or on third-party servers. For more details, see the Compute Submodule section.

Virtual access-layer submodule

The network interfaces (vmnics) on the physical server connects VMs to the rest of the environment. A scalability issue arises if a one-to-one correspondence is required between physical network interfaces (vmnics) and logical network connections (vNICs) to the VMs. For this reason, the hypervisor layer typically implements a virtual access-layer switch in the software of the hypervisor to multiplex connections from VMs to the physical network interfaces. In VMware, this is called the vNetwork Standard Switch (vSS), formerly known as the vSwitch.

The vSS functions like a basic L2 switch but it is not managed with the rest of the network, so it becomes a challenge when Operations, Administration, Maintenance, and Provisioning (OAM&P) tasks have to go all the way back to the VM level. Because the vSS is not an intelligent switch, it does not come equipped with the security and service-level features that are mandated in a service delivery environment such as cloud IaaS. For more details on the limitations of vSS, see the The Limitations of vNetwork Standard Switch section in Chapter 2.

The Nexus 1000V (NX1KV) Switch, available in vSphere 4, is a replacement for the vSS. The NX1KV switch comes with some of the essential features commonly found in intelligent physical access-layer switches that include PVLANs, unique Port Channel capabilities, ACLs, QoS, ERSPAN, NetFlow, and so on. In other words, the NX1KV switch brings functionality that is expected for the physical network into the realm of the virtual environment, fulfilling the requirements of the IaaS end-users. In fact, it establishes the virtual access layer not found in traditional nonvirtual environments. For more details on the NX1KV switch, see the The Cisco Nexus 1000V Switch section in Chapter 2 and the Virtual Switch Security section in this chapter.

Compute submodule

Cloud IaaS offerings give the end-users the impression that the computing capacity can be provisioned on demand, at variable scale, and transparent to the physical infrastructure that is required to deliver it. In order to fulfill these capabilities, the IaaS providers must still deploy real servers and deal with real processors, memory, and network interfaces. These physical assets are what the compute submodule encompasses.

The UCS supports a wide range of environments, including very demanding ones. UCS is a pre-integrated system that uses the network to aggregate server virtualization software, memory, storage, and the internal server architecture together. It also supports FCoE (on the CNAs) for I/O consolidation in the DC and works transparently with the NX1KV switch for extension of network intelligence into the virtual realm. For more details on the UCS, see the Unified Computing System section in this chapter. However, UCS is just an option. UCS makes life easier in terms of integration and management within the compute submodule. Besides the UCS, existing server infrastructure or DC-focused servers with strong DC features from other vendors can also be used in building out the private cloud DC. New initiatives like the Open Compute Project[5] also offer radically new ways of looking at the DC design that might apply to private clouds after more development on the management side.

Storage array submodule

This submodule includes equipment designed to decouple storage from the compute submodule and consolidate it for maximum efficiency. The process of decoupling storage capacity from compute resources is crucial in the virtualized environment of cloud IaaS. In order for end-users to run their workloads on a VM that is located on a physical server anywhere in the DC of an enterprise, it is essential that storage capacity is not limited to storage devices (such as hard drives) that are directly connected to a particular server. This would severely hamper the IaaS provider's ability to scale processing capacity on demand, to scale storage capacity beyond the limits of a few devices, to provide VM mobility to other facilities, and so on. In most cases, storage virtualization is the solution. For more details on storage virtualization, see the Storage Virtualization section in Chapter 2.

SAN submodule

The SAN submodule consists of the FC switched fabric that is required to connect the now decoupled storage capacity (for more details, see the Storage Array Submodule section) from the processing unit in the compute submodule. The FC switched fabric is typically constructed from FC directors and switches, such as the MDS 9000 Series storage switches, forming the SAN that interconnects the storage array and compute submodules.

An SAN environment is traditionally made up of a multitier or core-edge architecture. The core-edge model has two or more core switches at the center of the fabric to interconnect two or more edge switches at the edge of the fabric. The other option is the collapsed-core architecture. A collapsed-core model is a core-edge topology that replaces core and edge switches with high port-count directors. The storage devices are directly attached to these directors. From the unified DC fabric perspective, the collapsed-core architecture is preferred because it permits the access-layer submodule to serve both the storage and application environments. For more details, see the Access-Layer Submodule section.

SAN extension submodule

The SAN extension submodule provides interconnectivity between multiple enterprise DCs over campus, metro, or WAN distances as well as extending existing SAN segments between these DCs. SAN extension is a consolidation technique that links up multiple geographically distributed DCs together as one virtual DC cluster, providing greater reach and more reliability, availability, and serviceability (RAS) to the IaaS end-users. SAN extension also serves as a talisman to the IaaS providers because it ensures business continuity (BC), and provides disaster recovery (DR) during unforeseen circumstances. For more details on SAN extension, see Chapter 7.

Access-layer submodule

The access-layer submodule implements a distributed switching infrastructure to provide scale-out capabilities for the cloud IaaS offerings. One of the challenges in delivering cloud IaaS involves the deployment of diverse networks to accommodate both storage and application networking. Therefore, the implementation of a unified fabric is essential at the access-layer submodule as this allows both storage and application traffic to use a single form of I/O or transport. The unified fabric has to ensure that the traditional performance characteristics of both environments are maintained. This is where technologies such as 10GE, lossless Ethernet, and FCoE come into play. With FCoE, a separate access layer for the SAN is no longer required thereby collapsing two networks (i.e., FC and Ethernet) into a single unified fabric. For more details on FCoE enabling technologies, see the Unified Data Center Fabric section in Chapter 2.

Aggregation-layer submodule

The aggregation-layer submodule plays a pivotal role in providing a highly reliable, scalable "middle layer" for bringing together the traffic from the access-layer submodule, while at the same time ensuring the optimal use of physical resources. The aggregation layer is also where STP streamlining with vPC takes place. For more information on vPC and other L2 enhancements, see the Layer 2 Evolutions section in Chapter 2.

In addition, network-based virtual services, such as firewall services, server load balancing, intrusion, and anomaly-detection deep packet inspection, WAN optimization, and other upper-layer services, are typically integrated at the aggregation-layer submodule. These network services are implemented within a services chassis such as the Catalyst 6500 Series switch chassis. For details on service integration, see the Service Integration in the Data Center section in Chapter 3.

Core-layer submodule

The core-layer submodule is required to sustain the massive scalability projected as a requirement for large cloud IaaS deployments. The core-layer submodule is separated from the aggregation layer as well as the peering submodule. In environments that require lesser scale, the core-layer submodule is physically collapsed with the aggregation-layer submodule, the peering submodule, or potentially both.

Within this submodule, L3 segmentation is extended from the next-generation WAN submodule into the DC using virtual device contexts (VDCs) or VRFs on the core-layer switches. This ensures that traffic remains partitioned over the L3 infrastructure. L3 segmentation is also extended into the aggregation-layer submodule. The L3 isolated paths are eventually associated to their respective VLANs in the access-layer module. For details on L3 segmentation, see the Infrastructure Segmentation section in Chapter 3.

Peering submodule

The peering submodule is situated between the edge of the enterprise's DC and the WAN. Essential L2 and L3 feature sets are required here, as well as a variety of LAN and WAN interface options, and protocols. The peering submodule is specifically set aside to accommodate peering applications, such as BGP, GRE tunnels, IPSec, and so on across service providers' networks, or the Internet at large, to the remote branch offices or end-users. For more details on some of the peering applications related to the SOI for cloud IaaS, see the The Next-Generation Enterprise WAN section in Chapter 3.

In cases where cloud IaaS offerings are deployed into environments already supporting existing non-cloud services, physical and logical separation must be implemented at this submodule. For instance, two logical networks or more, one supporting the existing non-cloud environment, and the rest for private cloud computing and cloud IaaS, can be consolidated within the peering submodule.

Next-generation WAN submodule

The next-generation WAN is not a submodule within the enterprise DC. Instead, it consists of a series of networks that include the service providers' networks, the partners' networks, and the Internet. To maintain end-to-end isolated paths to the remote sites or end-users, it is necessary to extend L3 segmentation from the enterprise DC over these WANs. This brings up a list of next-generation WAN refurbishment techniques such as:

- Multi-VPN service from a service provider
- MPLS over L2 circuits
- DMVPN per VRF
- MPLS VPN over DMVPN (hub and spoke only)

For details on these techniques, see the The Next-Generation Enterprise WAN section in Chapter 3.

WAN Optimization

The deployment for WAN optimization is not restricted to just one of the above mentioned submodules. The submodules that cloud interception can take place includes:

- Virtual Machine Submodule
- Aggregation-Layer Submodule
- Core-Layer Submodule
- Peering Submodule
- Next Generation WAN
- The link the Remote Branches

For more details on WAN Optimization, see Chapters 4-6.

Cloud infrastructure management platform

The cloud infrastructure management platform (CIMP) is a crucial element of a cloud IaaS offering. This platform enables the IaaS provider to offer portions of the virtual environment to end-users on-demand, at variable scale, and independent of the physical infrastructure, as though the environment were dedicated to that particular end-user.

Nevertheless, the infrastructure management platform is not a single piece of hardware or software, but rather a combination of offerings from various vendors, third parties, and the IaaS provider's own internal management capabilities. It incorporates operational support systems, billing systems, self-provisioning tools, element managers, and so on.

The infrastructure management platform can be loaded as management applications onto the VMs in the VM submodule on the same SOI that is used to deliver the cloud IaaS offering to the end-users. This helps to improve the overall efficiency and scalability of the environment and removes unnecessary complexity that might arise from a separate management infrastructure. For a generic overview on cloud management, see the Cloud Management section in this chapter.

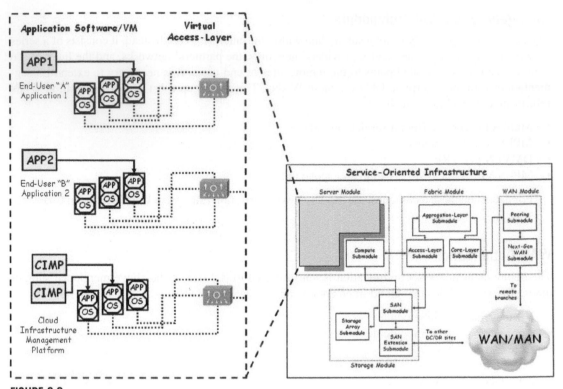

FIGURE 8.9

Cloud IaaS offering overlay with SOI

End-user workloads and applications

Beyond the cloud infrastructure management platform, no additional elements are needed to deliver a cloud IaaS offering because at its core the offering is simply providing the infrastructure on which end-users can run their own workloads or applications. To the end-users, the environment appears as if it is dedicated to their applications alone.

The cloud IaaS overlay

A cloud IaaS offering can be deployed on top of the SOI to leverage on the functional submodules as described in the previous subsections. Figure 8.9 shows an example cloud IaaS offering overlaying with the SOI submodules.

We started our private cloud computing voyage by setting our sights on the consolidation of server, storage, and network resources. This is achieved with the help of virtualization that decouples the underlying physical devices from their logical representation to enhance resource utilization and provisioning. Together with WAN optimization functionality, the existing process-oriented DC infrastructure is transformed into a service-oriented infrastructure (SOI). This SOI is where private cloud computing services, specifically cloud IaaS offerings, can be overlaid.

With the cloud IaaS overlay presented in Figure 8.9, we are reaching the closing stage of this expedition, but we are not finished. The concluding episode is in Chapter 9 where the discussion will revisit what has been covered so far, but this time in the form of case studies. After digesting Chapter 9, you will have a good conceptual grasp on consolidation, virtualization, and SOI, leading to the deployment of private cloud computing and the provisioning of cloud IaaS offerings.

SUMMARY

This chapter discusses cloud security. It goes through existing security infrastructures and techniques that are still applicable and can be reused accordingly in cloud security environments. The additional items within private cloud security purview are really the by-products of server virtualization— the VMs and the additional virtual access layer where the VMs reside. The virtual access-layer switch is a good place to extend existing security mechanisms from the physical infrastructure onto the virtual domain. For instance, using the NX1KV switch, features such as VLANs, PVLANs, DHCP snooping, IP Source Guard, DAI, port mirroring, and NetFlow can be implemented.

Due to the massive scaling requirement that is anticipated in private cloud computing and cloud IaaS offerings, the need for highly powered servers becomes a strategic imperative. This is where the UCS comes into play. While UCS does not come cheap, it does provide flexibility and high service levels. In the long term, the total cost of ownership (TCO) of UCS should be considerably lower, especially after factoring in reduced cabling, memory, and labor costs that are derived from a fully virtualized, integrated management infrastructure. UCS, in fact, facilitates the rack-and-roll deployment model for modularity at the rack level as well as rapid server provisioning in existing DC or greenfield environments.

Cloud management, is not as overly complex as one might think, because existing network management strategies and integration techniques are still fully applicable in cloud IaaS offerings. This chapter discussed cloud management in a generic manner in lieu of the actual cloud infrastructure management platform. In large-scale private cloud computing deployments, qualities such as hierarchical management model, policy-based management, management mediation, automation, user self-service portals, and standardization with XML should be taken into consideration.

Last but not least, with the SOI comprising submodules such as application software, virtual machine, virtual access layer, compute, storage array, SAN, SAN extension, access layer, aggregation layer, core layer, peering, and next-generation WAN in place, cloud IaaS offerings can be directly overlaid on top of this SOI. To the end-users, the environment appears as if it is dedicated to their applications alone.

Case Studies

In theory, theory and practice are the same; in practice they are not.
—Lawrence Peter Berra and Albert Einstein attributed alternately

INFORMATION IN THIS CHAPTER:

- Virtual Access–Layer Design Study
- ERSPAN Design Study
- WAN Optimization Study
- Unified Fabric Design Study
- Top-of-Rack Architecture Design Study
- Basic vPC Design Study
- SAN Extension Design Study
- Service-Oriented Infrastructure Design Study
- Summary

INTRODUCTION

Chapter 9 is the grand finale—the concluding chapter on the design and deployment of private cloud computing based on the consolidation and virtualization processes discussed in the previous chapters as well as the provisioning of cloud IaaS offerings over a service-oriented infrastructure (SOI).

This chapter is slightly different from the earlier chapters in that the topics are presented in the form of case studies. These case studies include design as well as deployment topics, basic configurations, and tutorials on some of the more complex concepts covered in the previous chapters.

VIRTUAL ACCESS–LAYER DESIGN STUDY

The Nexus 1000V (NX1KV) switch is an essential element in the server virtualization process. It brings the functionality of a physical switch into the virtual environment and interconnects VMs to the physical network. In other words, the NX1KV switch establishes the virtual access layer, that in turn "multiplexes" connections from VMs to the physical network, achieving the scalability factor mandated in private cloud computing environments. For more details on the functionality of the virtual access-layer, see the Virtual Access-Layer Submodule section in Chapter 8.

> **NOTE:**
>
> The NX1KV switch supports VN link (virtual network link) that is based on the concept of virtual Ethernet (vEth) interfaces.

Nexus 1000V components

Before examining the various NX1KV design examples, the following sections briefly describe the NX1KV components:

- Virtual Supervisor Module (VSM)
- Virtual Ethernet Module (VEM)
- VMware vCenter

Virtual Supervisor Module

The VSM is really an ESX VM with three vNICs (for the control, management, and packet interfaces). Each VSM requires dedicated (not shared) resources with 2GB RAM and 1.5GHz CPU reservation. The VSM runs NX-OS release 4.0.4 and later, which is compiled for the x86 CPU. It performs management, monitoring, and configuration functions. Two VSMs can be set up in an HA active/standby configuration. The primary (active) and secondary (standby) VSMs should be implemented on different ESX hosts.

Virtual Ethernet Module

The VEM is a software module running in the VMware hypervisor on an ESX host. It provides the distributed virtual switch (DVS) capability in the hypervisor. The data-path component of the VEM functions as an L2 switch that is configured by the VSM. In general, VEMs need to be L2-adjacent to the VSMs for the control path. Once configured, the VEM can continue to forward traffic without VSM connectivity until the next reboot. Other interactions between the VEM and VSM include:

- Each VEM is represented as a line card in the VSM.
- A VEM is uniquely identified by the VSM using the UUID of the ESX server.
- A slot number is assigned to each VEM by the VSM during its registration.
- The VSM preserves a slot number associated with a VEM mapping across reboots by storing it in persistent storage.
- Slots 1–2 are reserved for the VSMs, whereas slots 3–66 are for the VEMs.
- The VSM broadcasts heartbeat messages on its control interface:
  - To detect any new VEMs inserted into the DVS.
  - To check the connectivity status of those VEMs that have already registered with the VSM.

VMware vCenter

The vCenter is a VM application for managing ESX hosts. It has a control channel to each ESX host. The VSM connects to the vCenter using an SSL connection and a self-signed certificate is used for the connection. The VSM generates one NX1KV DVS in the vCenter, while the vCenter administrator adds ESX hosts to this DVS to make them members of the NX1KV DVS. The VSM also downloads some configurations to the VEM through the vCenter.

The VSM configures the vCenter using Simple Object Access Protocol/Web Services Description Language (SOAP[1]/WSDL[2]) APIs to:

- Generate NX1KV DVS and dvPortGroups in the vCenter.
- Store DVS data to be transferred to ESX hosts that have become members of the NX1KV DVS.
- Retrieve information (e.g., DC, DVS, VM, and so on) from vCenter.
- Maintain periodic connectivity check.

Design examples

When dealing with NX1KV design, keep the following guidelines in mind:

- **Connectivity to the physical access-layer switch:** This is usually in terms of the number of interconnecting NICs on the ESX host.
- **Availability, redundancy, and load balancing:** This involves the use of PortChannel (EtherChannel) and its corresponding hashing algorithms. There are two main PortChannel hashing categories:
  - **Source-based hashing:** This particular hashing algorithm hashes all traffic from a single source down the same link. Examples include source MAC, VLAN, Virtual Port, and so on.
  - **Flow-based hashing:** Each flow might take a different path for this type of hashing. It also requires EtherChannel to be configured upstream. Examples include any hash using packet destination, L4 port, or combinations of source address, destination address, and L4 port.
- **VMware and NX1KV traffic:**
  - **VM Data:** This includes all data from VMs including the VSMs. Multiple VLANs are usually involved.
  - **VMkernel:** This is used for VMotion and IP storage.
  - **Server console:** This is used for ESX management.
  - **Control:** The NX1KV switch control traffic.
  - **Packet:** Carries CDP and IGMP control packets.

Based on the above design attributes, we can examine the following design examples:

- Two-NIC configuration
- Four-NIC configuration
- Six-NIC configuration

Two-NIC configuration

Enterprise "A" has small rack servers and blade servers with 1-Gbps NICs. Enterprise "A" would like to kick-start server virtualization using these existing servers as the interim ESX hosts. On the other hand, Enterprise "B" has already gone through the DC fabric unification process with FCoE and has blade servers with 10-Gbps CNAs readily available. Enterprise "B" would like to take on the rack-and-roll approach. Figure 9.1 illustrates the two-NIC configuration that would meet the requirements for both Enterprise "A" and Enterprise "B."

The two-NIC configuration setup includes:

- Physical access-layer switch configuration:
  - Trunk port.
  - No EtherChannel is configured.

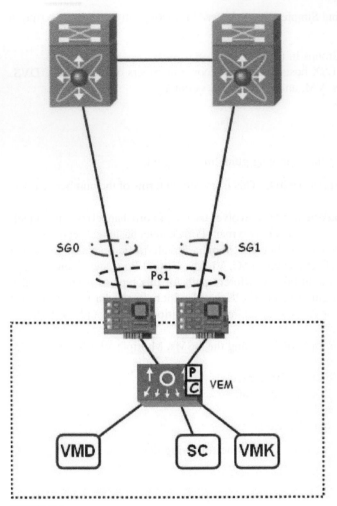

FIGURE 9.1

Two-NIC configuration example

- NX1KV PortChannel 1 (Po1):
  - Single PortChannel (PC) using vPC Host Mode (vPC-HM). For more information on vPC-HM, see the vPC Host Mode section in Chapter 2.
  - Carries VM data, service console, VMkernel, control, and packet traffic.
- VEM configuration:
  - Source-based hashing.

This design is the simplest from the perspective of the NX1KV switch because with two NICs there is little configuration variation, thus reducing the overall design complexity. Source-based hashing is used as well, with source MAC address hashing preferred over VLAN hashing.

VLAN hashing could create the tendency for the VM Data VLAN and the VMotion (VMkernel) VLAN to be hashed to the same uplink port. If VMotion is initiated, all VMs might contend for the same bandwidth as the VMotion session. On 1-Gbps NICs, this could lead to undesirable load balancing, but with 10-Gbps NICs the impact is negligible because of the substantial bandwidth available.

Source MAC address hashing would distribute the load of the VMs across both uplinks more evenly so that when VMotion is initiated, it will be contending for bandwidth among a smaller number of VMs.

Four-NIC configuration option 1

Enterprise "C" has medium rack servers as well as blade servers with 1-Gbps NICs. However, the requirements of Enterprise "C" differ from Enterprises "A" and "B" in that VMotion traffic needs to be separated from VM Data. Figure 9.2 illustrates the four-NIC configuration option 1 that would meet the requirements for Enterprise "C."

The four-NIC configuration option 1 setup includes:

- Physical access-layer switch configuration:
  - Trunk port.
  - No EtherChannel is configured.
- NX1KV PortChannel 1 (Po1):
  - vPC-HM is enabled.
  - Carries VM data.
- NX1KV PortChannel 2 (Po2):
  - vPC-HM is enabled.
  - Carries service console, VMkernel, control, and packet traffic.
- VEM configuration:
  - Source-based hashing.

The main advantage of this design is that VMotion does not affect the performance of VM data traffic. Po1 carries all VM data and Po2 carries VMotion (VMkernel), service console, control, and packet traffic.

Four-NIC configuration options 2 and 3

Both Enterprise "D" and Enterprise "E" have implemented vPC between two of their Nexus 7010 switches, acting as the physical access layer in the DC. For more details on vPC, see the Virtual Port Channels: The STP Makeover section in Chapter 2.

Enterprise "D" would like to maximize the VM bandwidth and can accept shared links for VM Data and VMotion traffic. Enterprise "E," on the other hand, has strict requirements to separate VMotion traffic from VM data. The four-NIC configuration option 2 shown in the left diagram of Figure 9.3 would meet the requirements of Enterprise "D," whereas the four-NIC configuration option 3 illustrated in the right diagram of Figure 9.3 would meet those of Enterprise "E."

NOTE:

The four-NIC configuration options illustrated in this subsection are for clustered switches implementing vPC.

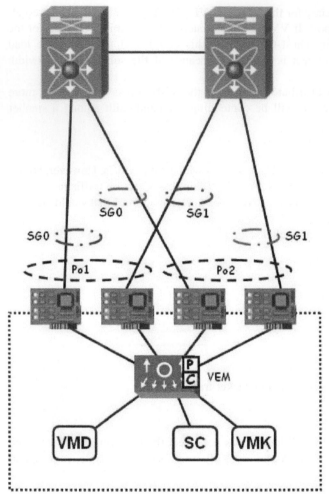

FIGURE 9.2

Four-NIC configuration option 1

The four-NIC configuration option 2 setup includes:

- Physical access-layer switch configuration:
    - Trunk port.
    - Single EtherChannel that spans across both physical access-layer switches.
- NX1KV PortChannel 1 (Po1):
    - Standard EtherChannel is configured.
    - Carries VM data, service console, VMkernel, control, and packet traffic.
- VEM configuration
    - Flow-based hashing.

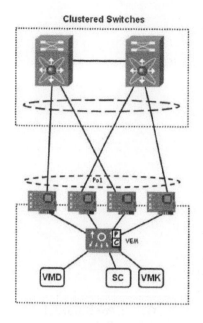

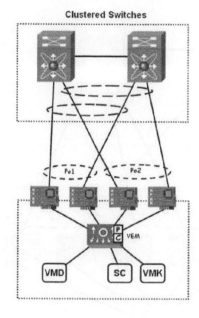

FIGURE 9.3

Four-NIC configuration options 2 and 3

The four-NIC configuration option 3 setup includes:

- Physical access-layer switch configuration:
  - Trunk port.
  - Two EtherChannels that span across each physical access-layer switch.
- NX1KV PortChannel 1 (Po1):
  - Standard EtherChannel is configured.
  - Carries VM data.
- NX1KV PortChannel 2 (Po2):
  - Standard EtherChannel is configured.
  - Carries service console, VMkernel, control, and packet traffic.
- VEM configuration:
  - Flow-based hashing.

Six-NIC configuration

Enterprise "F" has high performance servers (with 1-Gbps NICs) that require the VM bandwidth to be greater than 1 Gbps and separate links for VM data and VMotion traffic. Figure 9.4 illustrates the six-NIC configuration that would meet these requirements.

NOTE:

To simplify the overall design, you should consider migrating to 10GE connectivity beyond four NICs.

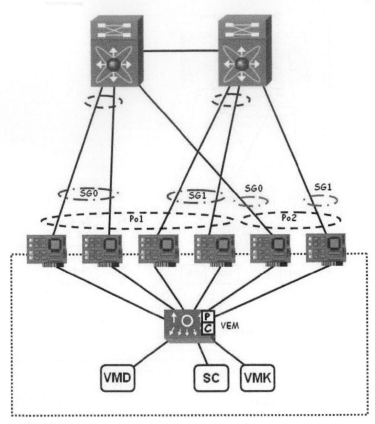

FIGURE 9.4

Six-NIC configuration example

The six-NIC configuration setup includes:

- Physical access-layer switch configuration:
  - Trunk port.
  - Separate EtherChannels from each physical access-layer switch to Po1 only.
- NX1KV PortChannel 1 (Po1):
  - vPC-HM is enabled.
  - Carries VM data.
- NX1KV PortChannel 2 (Po2):
  - vPC-HM is enabled.
  - Carries service console, VMkernel, control, and packet traffic.
- VEM configuration:
  - Flow-based hashing.

NOTE:

In the original release, NX1KV supported only two subgroups: 0 and 1. In release 4.0.4.SV1.2 onward, the subgroup IDs are extended to 32.

ERSPAN DESIGN STUDY

Encapsulated Remote Switch Port Analyzer (ERSPAN), discussed in Chapter 8, facilitates the remote monitoring of traffic on the NX1KV switch that constitutes the virtual access layer. It is a crucial traffic monitoring tool for gaining visibility into network traffic flows at the virtual access layer. ERSPAN monitors traffic either on a port or VLAN. It helps to mirror traffic in the virtual access layer to existing network analyzers (e.g., the NAM and the IPS appliance) at the services aggregation layer. ERSPAN is used by the IaaS provider to perform internal auditing and security monitoring functions in a cloud IaaS environment.

> **NOTE:**
>
> A local SPAN session must be on the same host VEM as the destination port. ERSPAN is local SPAN extended with the capability to send packets outside the local host VEM to a remote destination IP address.

ERSPAN source interfaces

The source interfaces that are monitored by ERSPAN are as follows:

- Ethernet
- Virtual Ethernet
- PortChannel
- VLAN

The characteristic of these source interfaces include:

- The source interface cannot be a destination port in a local SPAN session.
- The source interface are configured to monitor the direction of traffic:
  - Receive (ingress)
  - Transmit (egress)
  - Both
- Source ports are in the same or different VLANs.
- For VLAN SPAN sources, all active ports in the source VLAN are included as source ports. These source ports might be across multiple VEMs.

ERSPAN design example

Enterprise "G" has just started a small-scale server virtualization initiative using the NX1KV switch as the virtual access layer while retaining the existing Cat6K switches at the services aggregation layer. Enterprise "G" is implementing ERSPAN to gain visibility into the network traffic flows of the newly created virtual access layer.

Figure 9.5 shows the ERSPAN deployment for Enterprise "G" in which the destination IP belongs to a Cat6K switch. In this case, an ERSPAN destination session is configured on the Cat6K switch to forward the GRE-decapsulated packets to another port where a sniffer device (can also be an NAM or IPS appliance) is attached.

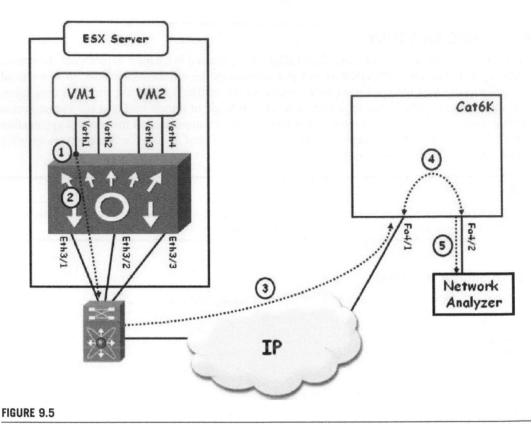

FIGURE 9.5

ERSPAN with remote L3 switch as destination

Figure 9.5 illustrates the ERSPAN operation to the destination Cat6K switch in five simple steps:

Step 1: An ERSPAN source port is configured as Veth1 that connects VM1.

Step 2: Packets received on the depicted ERSPAN source port are GRE encapsulated and are sent to the destination IP.

Step 3: The packets are routed to the destination IP configured on the Cat6K.

Step 4: An ERSPAN destination session is configured on Cat6K to GRE-decapsulate packets received on port Fa4/1 and to forward the decapsulated packets to port Fa4/2.

Step 5: An external network analyzer attached to port Fa4/2 captures the packets for analysis.

NOTE:

For security monitoring purposes, you can substitute the external network analyzer with an IDS/IPS appliance instead.

ERSPAN basic configurations

Consider the following checklist when configuring ERSPAN:

- An "l3control"-capable port profile is required. A sample "l3control"-capable port profile configuration is shown in Code Listing 9.1. The "capability l3control" command indicates that the interface (vmknic) created usees L3 (IP) control function. The VEM usees this L3 port to send out packets.

```
port-profile erspan
 capability l3control
 vmware port-group
 switchport mode access
 switchport access vlan 123
 no shutdown
 system vlan 123
 state enabled
```

CODE LISTING 9.1

L3 control–capable port-profile configuration example

- A vmknic must be configured on the VEM host(s).
  - The vmknic is added on the NX1KV DVS.
  - The vmknic is created using the "l3control"-capable port profile.
  - The vmknic is configured with a source IP address for ERSPAN.
- Ensure that the destination IP is reachable from the VEM host.
- Configure an ERSPAN source session on the VSM. Code Listing 9.2 shows a sample ERSPAN source session configuration.

```
monitor session 1 type erspan-source
 source interface vethernet23
 destination ip 10.123.123.1
 erspan-id 123
 no shut
```

CODE LISTING 9.2

ERSPAN source session configuration example

- Last but not least, configure a corresponding ERSPAN destination session on the destination switch (e.g., Cat6K).

Deployment guidelines and restrictions

Consider the following guidelines and restrictions for the ERSPAN deployment on the NX1KV switch:

- The total number of SPAN and ERSPAN sessions that can be configured on the NX1KV is 64; this is also the total number of SPAN and ERSPAN sessions that can be run simultaneously.

- A port can be configured in a maximum of 4 SPAN sessions.
- The maximum number of source VLANs per session is 32.
- The maximum number of source interfaces per session is 128.
- The destination IP address has to be reachable from the host(s).
- When sourcing VLANs, beware not to overload the uplink ports.

WAN OPTIMIZATION STUDY

As discussed in Chapter 4, WAN optimization is the technology that enables the private cloud to be usable, and thus, a success for the enterprise deploying it. Enterprise "Q" implemented WAN optimization in deploying an engineering-focused cloud. For brevity, we will examine the business and overall technical issues, but not the LAN/WAN design.[3]

Enterprise "Q" seeks to solve two problems with their cloud deployment: internal and external. They have offices spread over the state, up to 1000 km away from their DC, to centralize files. In addition to offering services to internal users, they also want to offer services to ecosystem partners of theirs, but privately, not as a public cloud. The remote engineers use digital model file sets of approximately 600 MB in size for their projects spread across multiple files and directories in a PLM system. Even nearby offices with good connectivity (10 Mbps and 15 ms latency) saw significant delays accessing the resources centralized to the DC, such as a 14-MB file taking 15 min to access from the application. Remote offices saw 30- to 60-sec delays between mouse click and action in the application finding it unusable. They investigated two different VDI solutions and WAN optimization.

The first VDI solution was found to have vastly greater bandwidth requirements than their existing offices had available. This could have been addressed with bandwidth increases, at a recurring cost, but this would not be practical for their ecosystem partners, who are much smaller than Enterprise "Q." The second VDI solution did not perform adequately for the task with demanding engineering users, even given additional bandwidth.

They pursued a dual strategy for WAN optimization, placing Riverbed Steelhead appliances in 15 offices in the first phase and using Riverbed Steelhead appliances Mobile for the ecosystem engineers and their internal remote or mobile workers. They leveraged both the bandwidth reduction and application acceleration features to bring success to the project; the combination nets the expected performance increases:

- A 17 MB transfer at a central office sped from 1 min and 25 sec to 8 seconds.
- A single office used 48.6 GB of remote material, but due to deduplication and compression, only transferred 2.2 GB over their WAN connection.
- A remote construction site saw an effective 500 Mbps over their 10-Mbps connection during a peak use.
- The various office applications measured saw 10 to 25× speed up due to the combination of the two technologies (1000% to 2500% faster).

The cloud centralization resulted in nontechnical benefits as well. They saw fewer engineering errors as offices used cloud-based authoritative copies of files rather than locally saved ones (which previously were sometimes out of date). They also achieved faster engineering cycles because of the increased collaboration and sharing. An estimated $1.5 million in savings were realized by implementing this design as well as improved cycle time and error reduction.

UNIFIED FABRIC DESIGN STUDY

The most pragmatic approach toward a unified DC fabric typically starts at the physical access layer without introducing any additional changes to the configuration of the FC directors or the aggregation-layer switches in the enterprise DC. Figure 9.6 illustrates a simplified example of an enterprise DC without server I/O consolidation. The server is connected to two separate network infrastructures—the Ethernet LAN and the FC SAN. The primary objective of this case study is to add an access layer that "merges" both of these independent fabrics together.

FCoE access-layer design

Enterprise "I" has an existing DC setup similar to the one shown in Figure 9.6. This DC setup has gone through one facelift with the introduction of 10 GE into the existing infrastructure (core and aggregation layers) using Nexus 7000 switches. The management of Enterprise "I" has just approved another next-generation DC initiative, this time the introduction of FCoE at the access layer. Full-blown FCoE implementation was found to be too costly and to a certain extent, disruptive. The objective is to exercise caution in terms of new equipment purchases so that the life cycle of the new equipment can last for the next 5 years before becoming obsolete. As far as existing native FC gear is concerned, it should be utilized until no depreciation value remains. The new FCoE access layer should also provide room for future extension and expansion, as well as interoperability with new innovations such as cloud IaaS.

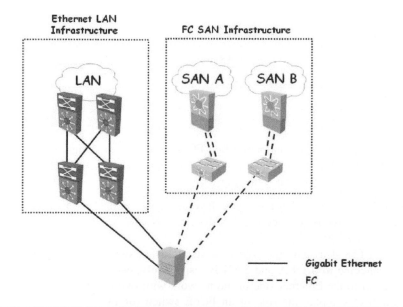

FIGURE 9.6

DC with disparate LAN and SAN infrastructures

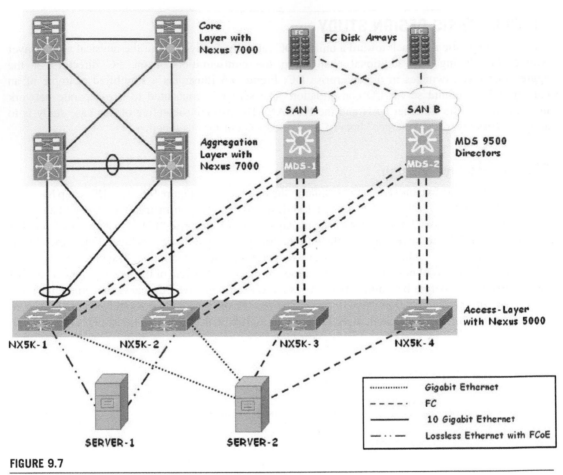

FIGURE 9.7

FCoE access-layer design

Figure 9.7 shows the proposed and simplified FCoE access-layer design.

The Nexus 5000 (NX5K) switches form the new access layer. These NX5K switches (NX5K-1 to NX5K-4) are also designed in the following ways:

- The NX5K switches deployed at the access layer are either part of SAN A (connecting NX5K-1 and NX5K-3) or SAN B (connecting NX5K-2 and NX5K-4). SAN A is in VSAN 100 and SAN B is in VSAN 200.
- NX5K-3 and NX5K-4 assume the role of a standard FC switch. In this case, SERVER-2 has two HBAs connected to SAN A and SAN B respectively, each with a 4G FC link. SERVER-2 is also connected to the Ethernet side of the network with two GE NICs.
- NX5K-1 and NX5K-2 play the role of an FCoE switch (or FCoE forwarder). SERVER-1 has a dual-port CNA, providing two 10GE links on which both LAN and SAN traffic is forwarded.

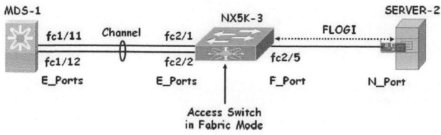

FIGURE 9.8

Access switch in fabric mode

Access layer to FC SAN

NX5K-3 and NX5K-4 assume the role of a standard FC access switch. They interconnect SERVER-2 to the core FC directors MDS-1 (for SAN A) and MDS-2 (for SAN B). Since native FC uplinks are used on these Nexus 5000 switches, either fabric mode or N-Port virtualization (NPV) mode can be used. These two options involve different configurations on the director and access switch.

Figure 9.8 illustrates the access switch in fabric mode. The ports between the FC director (MDS-1) and access switch (NX5K-3) are expansion ports (E_Ports). The attached FC host (SERVER-2) logs onto the fabric by contacting the fabric port (F_Port) on the access switch. It also retrieves an FC Identifier (FCID) directly from this F_Port.

Because FC traffic between node ports (N_Ports) is directly forwarded by the access switch, this mode is recommended when there is a combination of FC initiators and targets at the access layer. In fabric mode, each access switch is assigned an FC domain ID that typically ranges from 1 to 239. This presents a limitation on the fabric mode in terms of scalability issues that would incur at the access layer during large deployments.

When deploying the access switch in fabric mode, some best practices to consider include:

- The use of SAN PortChannel to provide redundant connections between the access switch and the FC director as well as load balancing between the uplinks. It also minimizes disruption to the fabric if a link were to fail.
- Rather than letting the switch automatically negotiate on the port mode (e.g., E_Port, F_Port, and so on), it is be better to hardcode the port mode to ensure that a link will remain down and will not come up unnecessarily because of improper cabling.

Code Listing 9.3 illustrates a sample fabric mode configuration template on the access switch (NX5K-3).

```
vsan database
 vsan 100 interface san-port-channel 1

interface san-port-channel 1
 switchport mode E
 switchport trunk off
```

```
interface fc2/1
  switchport mode E
  channel-group 1
  no shutdown

interface fc2/2
  switchport mode E
  channel-group 1
  no shutdown
```

CODE LISTING 9.3

Access switch fabric mode configuration template

> **NOTE:**
> _____
> By default, the NX5K switches operate in the fabric mode.

The NPV mode alleviates the domain ID limit (of the fabric mode) by sharing the domain ID of the FC director among multiple access switches. In NPV mode, the access switch relays all traffic from server-side ports (N_Ports) to the FC director. The FC director provides F_Port functionality (such as login and port security) and all the FC switching capabilities. In this case, the edge switch (access switch) appears as an FC host to the FC director and as a regular FC switch to its connected devices.

In short, NPV simplifies the deployment and management of large-scale server environments as follows:

- The number of FC domain IDs required is reduced.
- Interoperability issues with the FC core switch (FC director), especially in a mixed-vendor SAN environment, are minimized.
- Coordination and interaction between the server and SAN administrator are cut down.

Figure 9.9 illustrates the access switch in NPV mode.

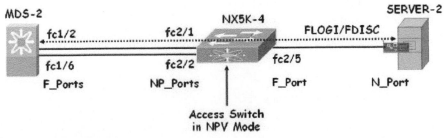

FIGURE 9.9

Access switch in NPV mode

NPV has the following components:

- **Server interfaces:** Server interfaces are F_Ports on the access switch (NX5K-4) that connect to the end devices (SERVER-2 in our example). The server interfaces are automatically distributed among the NP uplinks to the FC director (MDS-2). All of the end devices connected to a server interface are mapped to the same NP uplink.
- **NP uplinks:** All interfaces from the access switch to the FC director are configured as proxy N_Ports (NP_Ports). An NP uplink is a connection from an NP_Port on the access switch (NX5K-4) to an F_Port on the FC director (MDS-2). When an NP uplink is established, the access switch sends a fabric login (FLOGI) message to the FC director. If the FLOGI is successful, the access switch registers itself with the name server on the FC director. Subsequent FLOGIs from end devices (e.g., SERVER-2) are converted to fabric discovery (FDISC) messages instead.

NOTE:

In NX5K switches, server interfaces can be physical or virtual FC (VFC) interfaces.

NOTE:

A server interface can support multiple end devices by enabling the N_Port Identifier Virtualization (NPIV) feature. NPIV is defined by the T11 committee as part of the FC Link Services (FC-LS) specification. It provides a means to assign multiple FCIDs to a single N_Port, enabling multiple logins per physical port, rather than a one-to-one, login-to-port mapping.

Code Listing 9.4 illustrates a sample NPV configuration template on the FC director (MDS-2). The FC director must support the NPIV feature. In the configuration template shown, the two F_Ports of the FC director are assigned to VSAN 200, representing SAN B in our example.

```
npiv enable

vsan database
 vsan 200 interface fc1/2
 vsan 200 interface fc1/6

interface fc1/2
 switchport mode F
 no shutdown

interface fc1/6
 switchport mode F
 no shutdown
```

CODE LISTING 9.4

FC director NPV configuration template

Code Listing 9.5 illustrates a sample NPV mode configuration template on the access switch (NX5K-4). The uplinks (fc2/1 and fc2/2) are configured as NP ports and are also assigned to VSAN 200.

```
npv enable

vsan database
 vsan 200 interface fc2/1
 vsan 200 interface fc2/2

interface fc2/1
 switchport mode NP
 no shutdown

interface fc2/2
 switchport mode NP
 no shutdown
```

CODE LISTING 9.5

Access switch NPV mode configuration template

> **NOTE:**
> The "npv enable" configuration command automatically triggers a switch reboot. The NPV mode is applied to the entire switch and cannot be configured on a per-interface basis.

> **NOTE:**
> When the access switch is running in NPV mode, it is not an FC switch. As a result, there are no local FLOGI and name server registration databases on the access switch. Details about these databases need to be viewed from the FC director instead.

Consider the following guidelines and restrictions when configuring NPV on the access switch:

- In-order data delivery is not required in the NPV mode because the exchange between two end devices always takes the same uplink from the access switch to the FC director.
- Zoning can be configured for end devices that are connected to access switches using all available member types on the FC director.
- Access switches can connect to multiple FC directors. In other words, different NP ports can be connected to different FC directors.
- NPV supports NPIV-capable servers. This capability is called nested NPIV.
- NPV supports only F, NP, and SD (SPAN Destination) ports.
- NPV uses a load-balancing algorithm to automatically assign end devices in a VSAN to one of the NP uplinks (in the same VSAN) upon initial login. If an uplink fails, all the end devices that were associated with it are disconnected and will need to log in again.

- If a server interface goes down and comes back into service, the interface is not guaranteed to be assigned to the same NP uplink.
- The server interface is only operational when the assigned NP uplink is operational.
- The NP uplink between the FC director and the access switch currently does not support channeling or trunking. If these features are critical, fabric mode is required.
- FC switching is not performed in the access switch. All traffic is switched in the FC director instead. If two end devices need to connect to each other, they do so through the FC director.

Access layer to Ethernet LAN

Figure 9.10 illustrates the FCoE connection between the CNA on SERVER-1 and the access switch, NX5K-1. SERVER-1 is connected via 10GE to NX5K-1. A VLAN dedicated to FCoE is defined on NX5K-1 and then automatically advertised by FCoE Initialization Protocol (FIP) to the FCoE End Node (ENode). The VN_Ports on the ENode must then connect to the VF_Ports of an FCF (or FCoE switch) on this VLAN. For more details on FCoE terminologies and concepts such as CNA, FIP, ENode, VN_Ports, VF_Ports, FCF, and so on, see the Unified Data Center Fabric section in Chapter 2.

NX5K-1 is the FCF (FCoE forwarder). It allows the creation of virtual FC (VFC) interfaces for this purpose.

To associate a VFC to a particular end device (or ENode), it is defined in the following two ways:

- **Server-provided MAC addresses (SPMAs):** A VFC is bound to the MAC address of a particular ENode. In this case, only traffic transmitted on the FCoE VLAN and originating from the CNA is forwarded to the VFC. This method is configuration-intensive because an MAC address must be manually configured on the FCoE switch (NX5K-1).

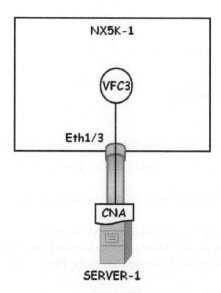

FIGURE 9.10

FCoE connectivity between access switch and end device

- **Fabric-provided MAC addresses (FPMAs):** A VFC is bound to a physical Ethernet interface on the FCoE switch. In this case, any FCoE traffic (identified by VLAN and Ethertype) received on the associated physical Ethernet port is forwarded to the VFC. In this method, the MAC address is assigned by the FCoE switch (NX5K-1) during the FIP login process. Hence, it does not require an MAC address to be configured on the FCoE switch, making the solution more flexible because the CNA in the end device (SERVER-1) can be swapped with no additional configuration. FPMA is typically the preferred method.

For more details on SPMAs and FPMAs, see the Virtual Link Instantiation section in Chapter 2. Code Listing 9.6 illustrates a sample configuration template on the definition of an FCoE VLAN and a VFC.

```
feature fcoe

vlan 100
 fcoe vsan 100

interface vfc3
 bind interface Ethernet1/3
 no shutdown

vsan database
 vsan 100 interface vfc3

fcoe fcmap 0xefc0a

interface Ethernet1/3
 switchport mode trunk
 spanning-tree port type edge trunk
```

CODE LISTING 9.6

FCoE VLAN and VFC configuration template

Consider the following configuration guidelines when configuring FCoE on the access switch:

- Bind VFCs to physical interfaces. In other words, for less manual configuration overhead, use FPMAs instead of SPMAs.
- Configure an FCoE MAC Address Prefix (FC-MAP) on the switch depending on the fabric to which it is connected.
- The recommended range for the 24-bit FC-MAP is from 0EFC00h to 0EFCFFh (default is 0EFC00h). For more details on FC-MAP, see the Virtual Link Instantiation section in Chapter 2.
- For better security in the data plane, limit the span of the FCoE VLAN to where ENodes are directly connected.
- Use only the FCoE VLANs for FCoE traffic.
- For an FCoE VLAN, do not use the default VLAN, VLAN 1.

- Different fabrics (e.g., SAN A and SAN B) should use separate FCoE VLANs.
- FCoE traffic must be 802.1Q tagged because the 802.1Q tag includes a field for the class-of-service (CoS) value that is required by lossless Ethernet mechanisms such as the Priority-based Flow Control (PFC) and Enhanced Transmission Selection (ETS). Therefore, the Ethernet interfaces involved should be configured as trunks. For more details on PFC and ETS, see the Ethernet Reloaded section in Chapter 2.
- To ensure that FCoE traffic is 802.1Q tagged, the native VLAN must not be the FCoE VLAN on the Ethernet interfaces.
- Configure the Ethernet interface connecting to the ENode as the edge interface (PortFast or TrunkFast) for the spanning tree protocol (STP) using use the "spanning-tree port type edge trunk" command. This configuration is essential because STP could attempt to synchronize (i.e., put in a temporary discarding state) this Ethernet interface during convergence, which would have undesirable impact on the FCoE traffic.

> **NOTE:**
>
> The NX5K switch expects frames from an FIP T11-compliant CNA to be tagged with the VLAN tag for the FCoE VLAN. Frames that are not correctly tagged are discarded. The switch expects frames from a pre-FIP CNA to be priority tagged with the FCoE CoS value but will still accept untagged frames from the pre-FIP CNA.

Design comments

FCoE is still very much a FC. It does not change the fundamental rules for designing and administering an FC SAN. Since FCoE mandates a lossless Ethernet, this functionality can be easily achieved at the access layer.

Server I/O consolidation over Ethernet with FCoE results in a unified DC fabric that eliminates the cost associated with the maintenance of multiple parallel networks. The savings in terms of the reduction of adaptors, cables, and switch ports helps to bring down both CAPEX and OPEX. In turn, this generates an economy of real-estate floor space, power, and cooling. The unified DC fabric also provides a "wire-once" model, reducing deployment cycles, which is a critical goal when rolling out cloud IaaS offerings.

Most importantly, the introduction of FCoE does not require a complete overhaul of the DC. Deploying FCoE at the access layer not only realizes most of the benefits of a unified fabric, but it also fits in seamlessly without causing disruption to existing FC-attached end devices.

TOP-OF-RACK ARCHITECTURE DESIGN STUDY

With private cloud computing initiatives looming on the horizon, enterprises can no longer shy away from the need for flexibility and mobility in their DCs. When it comes to DC infrastructure expansion or extension, the days are numbered for more equipment or forklift upgrades, more power and cooling drain, more cable spaghetti, more real-estate floor space to acquire, and so on. What next-generation enterprises need is a modular DC infrastructure with "rack-at-a-time" deployments that can be commissioned within hours and not days or weeks. To achieve such feat, racks should come with preconfigured servers (e.g., in rack and/or blade form factor) as well as preinstalled power, network, and storage cablings.

The top-of-rack (ToR) architecture defines a rack-and-roll deployment model that places ToR switches into each rack so that server connectivity is aggregated and interconnected with the rest of the DC infrastructure through a small number of cables connected to end-of-row (EoR) or middle-of-row (MoR) access or aggregation-layer switches. Copper cabling is typically used to connect the servers to the ToR switches that are located within the same or an adjacent rack.

ToR design with Nexus 5000 and 2000

The ToR switch plays an important role in the ToR model. If the ToR switch is just another access switch, it will probably be assimilated into existing STP topologies, creating a larger setup than before. Consequently, operational issues, such as manageability and maintenance, will start to creep in. In this case, the ToR model solves one problem by creating another. Is there a better way out? Yes, through the use of fabric extender (FEX) instead of an access switch.

For a brief discussion of FEX, see the UCS Enabling Technologies section of Chapter 8. However, you do not need a UCS to implement the FEX functionality. In this case study, the ToR architecture is constructed with Nexus 5000 (NX5K) switches and Nexus 2000 (NX2K) FEXs in concert. From the L2 perspective, the NX5K switch and NX2K FEX together form one logical access switch, providing ToR flexibility without incurring a larger STP topology.

NOTE:

The UCS adopts the same NX5K and NX2K combination except that the NX2K FEX is a module at the back of the UCS chassis. For more information, see the Blade Server Chassis and Fabric Extender sections in Chapter 8.

The FEX combines the benefits of both ToR and EoR architectures. Physically, it distributes the access layer across DC racks by residing on the top of each rack. Logically, it acts like an EoR access device that is managed by the NX5K switch. From the management perspective, the FEX functions as a remote line card for the NX5K switch, transforming it into a virtualized chassis. The FEX is not a separate management entity and no configuration is stored locally. Centralized management and configuration are performed on the NX5K that communicates with the FEX through in-band connectivity. As the FEX is an extension of the NX5K switch, it offers massive scale with no increase in management complexity and management points.

By deploying the NX5K/NX2K combination at the access layer, DCs can build self-contained racks of servers with 1GE connectivity requirements using a small number of 10GE fiber or CX-1 copper connections to an EoR or an MoR switch (the NX5K), reducing unnecessary horizontal cable runs.

NOTE:

The FEX does not support local switching. Forwarding is based on VNTag, which can be considered as an identifier carrying "source/destination interface" information. For more details on VNTag, see the VNTag section in Chapter 8.

ToR design example: 1GE-attached servers

The NX5K is a 10-Gbps switch. To accommodate older LAN environments that continue to employ 1 Gbps for LAN traffic and a separate FC storage environment, the NX2K FEX can be used to extend the LAN switching fabric of the NX5K to 1-Gbps ports housed in external FEXs. This effectively transforms the NX5K switch into a high-density, 1GE access-layer switch, providing a smooth migration path for existing enterprise LAN infrastructures that are incorporated into the service-oriented infrastructure (SOI) required by cloud IaaS offerings.

Enterprise "J" has just started their private cloud computing initiative and would like to offer cloud IaaS within the organization to channel partners and external customers. However, the stumbling block seems to be the existing pools of 1-Gbps servers in the DC that have been acquired less than 2 years ago. Specifically, there are 24 racks, each housing 20 servers, totaling 480 servers. The IT management fully understands the benefits of FCoE and a unified DC fabric, but at this point in time, they are able to live with a separate LAN and FC infrastructure. Modularizing/mobilizing the existing 24 racks of servers to facilitate a soft cloud IaaS rollout within 3 months is at the top of their agenda.

In this case study, Enterprise "J" adopts the FEX straight-through (i.e., single-homed) deployment method. The left diagram in Figure 9.11 shows a single NX5020 switch connecting with 12 NX2148T FEXs (equivalent to $12 \times 48 = 576$ host interfaces). The right diagram of Figure 9.11 illustrates the typical redundant deployment using two sets of the same setup (2×567 host interfaces) depicted in the left diagram as well as a dual-homed server with one active link and one standby link.

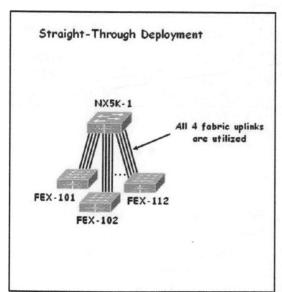
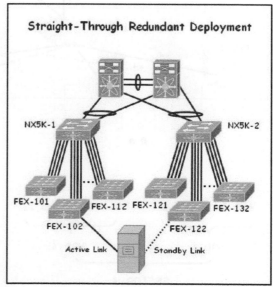

FIGURE 9.11

FEX straight-through deployment

> **NOTE:**
>
> The NX2148T FEX provides up to four SFP+ 10G uplinks supporting either 10G SFP+ optical transceivers, or CX-1 direct-attach copper cable assemblies if the distance to the NX5K switch is less than 10 meters. Twelve FEXs utilizing all the uplinks will require 48 10-Gbps ports on the NX5020. The NX5020 comes with 40 fixed 10-Gbps ports and 2 expansion modules. To support this scenario, the 2 expansion modules must be filled up. For example, extend each expansion slot with a 6-port 10G Ethernet module (N5K-M1600).

Besides the modularity and redundancy requirement, the IT management of Enterprise "J" wants only a single FEX on top of each rack to reduce additional hardware acquisition costs. Figure 9.12 illustrates the physical topology of the proposed ToR FEX design. The 24 racks are split into two sectors: SECTOR-A and SECTOR-B. Each sector comprises 12 racks and is further subdivided into six pods: POD-1 to POD-6. Each pod contains two racks with one FEX per rack.

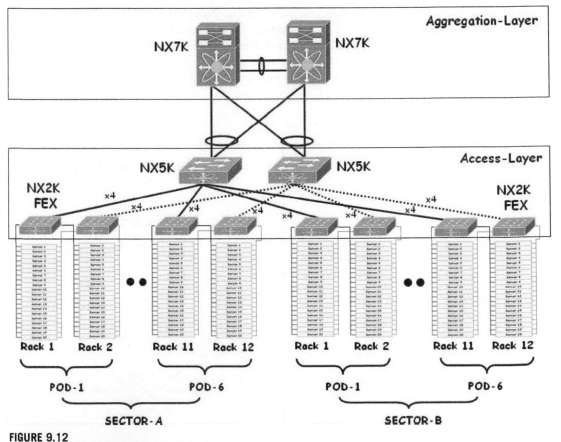

FIGURE 9.12

ToR FEX deployment example

The active 1-Gbps links belonging to the servers of each pod terminate at the FEX associated with the odd-numbered rack in the pod. On the other hand, the standby 1-Gbps links belonging to the servers of each pod terminate at the FEX associated with the even-numbered rack in the pod. Each FEX is effectively supporting 40 servers per pod but there will not be any oversubscription because all four 10GE uplinks on the FEX are utilized.

> **NOTE:**
>
> The servers in each rack are connected to the FC SANs (SAN A and SAN B) through a separate ToR FC switch (MDS 9148). For brevity, this is not shown in the diagrams.

Figure 9.13 depicts the rack layout of the ToR FEX deployment. The NX2148T FEX in each rack is connected to one of the two NX5020 switches installed at the EoR/MoR rack. The 1GE attached servers are connected to the ToR FEX using Cat5e RJ-45 patch cables (not shown in the diagram for brevity). Fiber uplinks provide connectivity between the FEXs and the upstream NX5020 switches. Since all four FEX uplinks are used, a total of four fiber strands are utilized from each rack to the EoR/MoR rack.

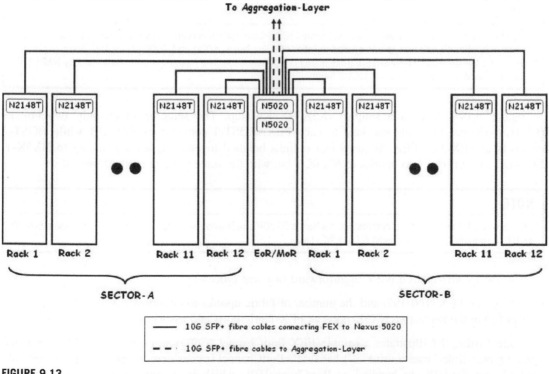

FIGURE 9.13

ToR FEX deployment rack layout

> **NOTE:**
>
> In case you are wondering, other than the UCS, is there a specific external FEX that supports 10GE/FCoE host interfaces? Yes, it is the Nexus 2232PP FEX. This particular FEX provides 32 1/10GE/FCoE/SFP+ host interfaces and 8 10GE/FCoE/SFP+ uplinks or fabric interfaces.

FEX basic configurations

There are two methods to connect the NX2K FEX and the NX5K switch together:

- **PortChannel:** Bundle all uplinks (up to four) between the NX2K FEX and the NX5K switch as a PortChannel. All the 1G server ports (or host interfaces) on the FEX are pinned to the PortChannel. In the event a link failure occurs within the PortChannel, traffic automatically uses the remaining uplinks based on the PortChannel hash. PortChannel must be used if link resiliency and link availability are part of the design requirements.
- **Static pinning:** Each of the uplinks between the NX2K FEX and the NX5K switch carries traffic for a group of 1G server ports (or host interfaces) on the FEX. When the uplink goes down, the corresponding server ports remain down until the uplink comes back up again.

> **NOTE:**
>
> Load sharing in previous generations of PortChannel (EtherChannel) implements only eight hash buckets, this can lead to nonoptimal load sharing with an odd number of links. Nexus 5000 and 2000 utilize 256 hash buckets, minimizing the imbalance between the links in any link failure case. The hashing (particularly used by NX2148T) could be based on a combination of L2/L3 fields.

Figure 9.14 illustrates a simple NX5K/NX2K setup. The setup involves only two uplinks (Eth1/17–18) per FEX and one host to each FEX. HOST-1 connects to FEX-101 while HOST-2 connects to FEX-121. FEX-101 uses two uplinks bundled together as a PortChannel to NX5K-1. FEX-121 also utilizes two uplinks to NX5K-2 but with the static pinning method instead.

> **NOTE:**
>
> In Figure 9.14, the hardware platforms are the Nexus 5020P switch and the Nexus 2148T FEX. The Nexus 5020P switch is running on NX-OS version 4.0(1a)N2(1a).

The FEX configuration is a straightforward two-step process:

- Define the FEX (100-199) and the number of fabric uplinks to be used by that FEX (1–4).
- Configure the respective NX5K ports as FEX-fabric ports and associate the desired FEX.

Code Listing 9.7 illustrates a sample FEX PortChannel configuration template. The command "pinning max-links" uses a value of 1 because a PortChannel is considered to be a single logical link. Eth1/17 and Eth1/18 are bundled as PortChannel101, which is in turn associated to FEX 101. The host interface Ethernet101/1/1 on FEX 101 connects HOST-1 in VLAN 101.

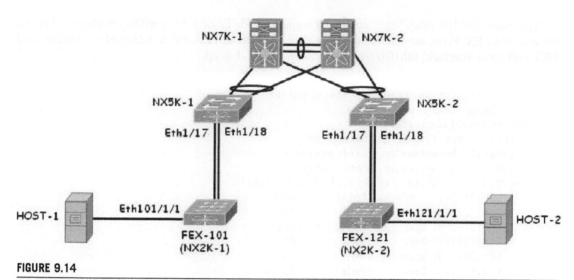

FIGURE 9.14

Simple NX5K/NX2K setup

```
vlan 101

feature fex

fex 101
  pinning max-links 1

interface port-channel101
  switchport mode fex-fabric
  fex associate 101

interface Ethernet1/17
  switchport mode fex-fabric
  fex associate 101
  channel-group 101

interface Ethernet1/18
  switchport mode fex-fabric
  fex associate 101
  channel-group 101

interface Ethernet101/1/1
  switchport access vlan 101
```

CODE LISTING 9.7

FEX PortChannel configuration template

The "show fex 101 detail" exec command output in Code Listing 9.8 verifies the current status of the attached FEX. From the command output trace, the state of FEX 101 is reflected as "Online" and FEX port (host interface) Eth101/1/1 that connects HOST-1 is up.

```
NX5K-1# show fex 101 detail
FEX: 101 Description: FEX0101    state: Online
[-----Snipped for brevity-----]
  Fabric interface state:
    Po101 - Interface Up. State: Active
    Eth1/17 - Interface Up. State: Active
    Eth1/18 - Interface Up. State: Active
  Fex Port        State  Fabric Port  Primary Fabric
      Eth101/1/1   Up      Po101        Po101
      Eth101/1/2   Down    Po101        Po101
      Eth101/1/3   Down    Po101        Po101
      Eth101/1/4   Down    Po101        Po101
      Eth101/1/5   Down    Po101        Po101
      Eth101/1/6   Down    Po101        Po101
      Eth101/1/7   Down    Po101        Po101
      Eth101/1/8   Down    Po101        Po101
      Eth101/1/9   Down    Po101        Po101
     Eth101/1/10   Down    Po101        Po101
     Eth101/1/11   Down    Po101        Po101
     Eth101/1/12   Down    Po101        Po101
     Eth101/1/13   Down    Po101        Po101
     Eth101/1/14   Down    Po101        Po101
     Eth101/1/15   Down    Po101        Po101
     Eth101/1/16   Down    Po101        Po101
     Eth101/1/17   Down    Po101        Po101
     Eth101/1/18   Down    Po101        Po101
     Eth101/1/19   Down    Po101        Po101
     Eth101/1/20   Down    Po101        Po101
     Eth101/1/21   Down    Po101        Po101
     Eth101/1/22   Down    Po101        Po101
     Eth101/1/23   Down    Po101        Po101
     Eth101/1/24   Down    Po101        Po101
     Eth101/1/25   Down    Po101        Po101
     Eth101/1/26   Down    Po101        Po101
     Eth101/1/27   Down    Po101        Po101
     Eth101/1/28   Down    Po101        Po101
     Eth101/1/29   Down    Po101        Po101
     Eth101/1/30   Down    Po101        Po101
     Eth101/1/31   Down    Po101        Po101
     Eth101/1/32   Down    Po101        Po101
     Eth101/1/33   Down    Po101        Po101
     Eth101/1/34   Down    Po101        Po101
```

```
    Eth101/1/35  Down      Po101       Po101
    Eth101/1/36  Down      Po101       Po101
    Eth101/1/37  Down      Po101       Po101
    Eth101/1/38  Down      Po101       Po101
    Eth101/1/39  Down      Po101       Po101
    Eth101/1/40  Down      Po101       Po101
    Eth101/1/41  Down      Po101       Po101
    Eth101/1/42  Down      Po101       Po101
    Eth101/1/43  Down      Po101       Po101
    Eth101/1/44  Down      Po101       Po101
    Eth101/1/45  Down      Po101       Po101
    Eth101/1/46  Down      Po101       Po101
    Eth101/1/47  Down      Po101       Po101
    Eth101/1/48  Down      Po101       Po101
[-----Snipped for brevity-----]
```

CODE LISTING 9.8

FEX status verification

The "show interface po101 fex-intf" exec command output in Code Listing 9.9 verifies the traffic mapping between the fabric interface and FEX interfaces (service-facing interfaces, aka host interfaces). From the command output trace, all 48 NX2K FEX interfaces are carried over the fabric interface PortChannel 101.

```
NX5K-1# show interface po101 fex-intf
Fabric          FEX
Interface       Interfaces
---------------------------------------------------------
Po101          Eth101/1/48   Eth101/1/47   Eth101/1/46   Eth101/1/45
               Eth101/1/44   Eth101/1/43   Eth101/1/42   Eth101/1/41
               Eth101/1/40   Eth101/1/39   Eth101/1/38   Eth101/1/37
               Eth101/1/36   Eth101/1/35   Eth101/1/34   Eth101/1/33
               Eth101/1/32   Eth101/1/31   Eth101/1/30   Eth101/1/29
               Eth101/1/28   Eth101/1/27   Eth101/1/26   Eth101/1/25
               Eth101/1/24   Eth101/1/23   Eth101/1/22   Eth101/1/21
               Eth101/1/20   Eth101/1/19   Eth101/1/18   Eth101/1/17
               Eth101/1/16   Eth101/1/15   Eth101/1/14   Eth101/1/13
               Eth101/1/12   Eth101/1/11   Eth101/1/10   Eth101/1/9
               Eth101/1/8    Eth101/1/7    Eth101/1/6    Eth101/1/5
               Eth101/1/4    Eth101/1/3    Eth101/1/2    Eth101/1/1
```

CODE LISTING 9.9

Traffic mapping for PortChannel method

Code Listing 9.10 illustrates a sample FEX static pinning configuration template. The command "pinning max-links" uses a value of 2 because FEX 121 utilizes two uplinks (Eth1/17 and Eth1/18) to NX5K-2 with the static pinning method. The host interface Ethernet121/1/1 on FEX 121 connects HOST-2 in VLAN 121.

```
vlan 121

feature fex

fex 121
  pinning max-links 2

interface Ethernet1/17
  switchport mode fex-fabric
  fex associate 121

interface Ethernet1/18
  switchport mode fex-fabric
  fex associate 121

interface Ethernet121/1/1
  switchport access vlan 121
```

CODE LISTING 9.10

FEX static pinning configuration template

Code Listing 9.11 shows the traffic mapping for static pinning between the fabric interfaces and FEX interfaces using the "show interface eth1/17 fex-intf" and "show interface eth1/18 fex-intf" exec commands. From the command output traces, FEX interfaces Eth121/1/1 to Eth121/1/24 are carried over fabric interface Eth1/17, whereas FEX interfaces Eth121/1/25 to Eth121/1/48 are carried over fabric interface Eth1/18. In this case, Eth121/1/1 that connects HOST-2 is "pinned" to fabric interface Eth1/17. This means that Eth121/1/1 will be down when uplink Eth1/17 is down and will remain down until Eth1/17 comes back up again.

```
NX5K-2# show interface eth1/17 fex-intf
Fabric       FEX
Interface    Interfaces
- - - - - - - - - - - - - - - - - - - - - - - - - - - - - - - - - -
  Eth1/17      Eth121/1/24   Eth121/1/23   Eth121/1/22   Eth121/1/21
               Eth121/1/20   Eth121/1/19   Eth121/1/18   Eth121/1/17
               Eth121/1/16   Eth121/1/15   Eth121/1/14   Eth121/1/13
               Eth121/1/12   Eth121/1/11   Eth121/1/10   Eth121/1/9
               Eth121/1/8    Eth121/1/7    Eth121/1/6    Eth121/1/5
               Eth121/1/4    Eth121/1/3    Eth121/1/2    Eth121/1/1
```

```
NX5K-2# show interface eth1/18 fex-intf
Fabric          FEX
Interface       Interfaces
- - - - - - - - - - - - - - - - - - - - - - - - - - - - - - - - - - - - - - - - - - -
  Eth1/18       Eth121/1/48   Eth121/1/47   Eth121/1/46   Eth121/1/45
                Eth121/1/44   Eth121/1/43   Eth121/1/42   Eth121/1/41
                Eth121/1/40   Eth121/1/39   Eth121/1/38   Eth121/1/37
                Eth121/1/36   Eth121/1/35   Eth121/1/34   Eth121/1/33
                Eth121/1/32   Eth121/1/31   Eth121/1/30   Eth121/1/29
                Eth121/1/28   Eth121/1/27   Eth121/1/26   Eth121/1/25
```

CODE LISTING 9.11

Traffic mapping for static pinning method

BASIC vPC DESIGN STUDY

Large-scale virtual PortChannel (vPC) designs are fairly complex so in this case study the scope is narrowed down to the vPC design fundamentals. All complex setups are based on simple building blocks and the same applies to vPC. For more information on the basic concepts of vPC, see the Virtual Port Channels: The STP Makeover section in Chapter 2. This section dives straight into the configuration aspects of vPC, but before that, a quick review on some of the vPC terminology pertaining to this design study:

- **vPC:** The combined PortChannel between the vPC peer devices and the downstream device.
- **vPC peer device:** One of a pair of devices that are connected with a special PortChannel known as the vPC peer link.
- **vPC peer link:** The link used to synchronize states between the vPC peer devices. Both ends must be on 10GE interfaces.
- **vPC domain:** This domain is formed by the two vPC peer devices. It is also a configuration mode for configuring some of the vPC peer-keepalive link parameters.
- **vPC peer-keepalive link:** The peer-keepalive link is an L3 link between the vPC peer devices that is used to ensure that both devices are up. This backup or fault-tolerant (FT) link sends configurable, periodic keepalive messages on an out-of-band management network between the vPC peer devices.
- **vPC member port:** Physical interfaces on the vPC peer devices that belong to the vPCs.

The above vPC terms are depicted accordingly in the later subsections.

In short, vPC overcomes the spanning tree protocol (STP) limitations (for more details, see the Layer 2 Evolutions section in Chapter 2). The migration of the existing DC topology from an STP-based one to a vPC-based one yields the following benefits:

- Allows a downstream device to use a single PortChannel across two upstream devices.
- Provides a loop-free topology without the help of STP.
- Eliminates STP blocked ports.
- Uses all available uplink bandwidth which was previously not possible with STP.
- Provides a faster convergence time if either a link or a device (node) goes down (as compared to STP).
- Ensures link-level resiliency and high availability.

Basic vPC configurations

Enterprise "K" would like to tackle their private cloud computing initiative from a different angle. Rather than proceeding straight to the virtual and physical access layers, they would like to start from the aggregation layer and the physical access layer instead. The IT management favors the idea of overhauling STP from their DC with vPC. STP has been their long-standing nightmare and this is the day they have been waiting for. Enterprise "K" has acquired a pair of Nexus 7010 (NX7010) and Nexus 5020 (NX5020) switches. The intention is to swap their existing pair of Cat6K aggregation-layer switches with the NX7010 switches incorporating vPC and build a 10GE/FCoE-capable physical access layer with the NX5020 switches. The Cat6K switches will eventually be utilized as services chassis in the services aggregation layer (for more details, see the Service Integration in the Data Center section in Chapter 3).

> **NOTE:**
>
> Besides the aggregation layer, vPC can also be implemented at the core or access layer.

Figure 9.15 shows a simple vPC setup with two NX7010 and two NX5020 switches. This base diagram is referenced throughout the later subsections, which include:

- Configuring the vPC domain
- Configuring the vPC peer link
- Configuring vPC

The configurations (or code listings) in the abovementioned subsections are based on the depicted setup in Figure 9.15.

> **NOTE:**
>
> The two Nexus 7010 switches in Figure 9.15 are running on NX-OS version 5.0(3).

In Figure 9.15, NX7K-1 and NX7K-2 are the vPC peer devices. PortChannel 1000 is the vPC peer link between NX7K-1 and NX7K-2 that bundles interfaces Eth2/1 and Eth2/2 from each of these switches. The vPC peer-keepalive link is established between the management interface (mgmt0) of NX7K-1 and NX7K-2 through an out-of-band management network. The vPC member ports are made up of interfaces Eth3/1 and Eth3/2 from each of these switches.

> **NOTE:**
>
> In a vPC implementation, the maximum number of vPC peer devices or physical nodes is two.

The basic configuration steps to deploy a vPC include:

1. Globally configure a vPC domain on both vPC peer switches (NX7K-1 and NX7K-2).
2. Configure and bring up a peer-keepalive link on both vPC peer switches.
3. Reuse or create an interswitch PortChannel between the vPC peer switches.

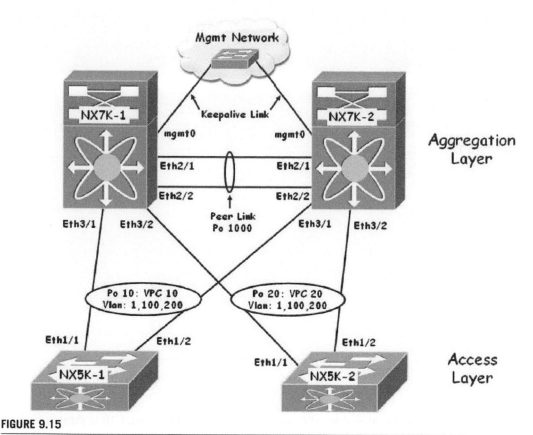

FIGURE 9.15

Simple vPC setup

4. Configure the interswitch PortChannel as a peer link on both vPC peer switches (ensure that this is working).
5. Reuse or create PortChannels to dual-attach downstream devices (NX5K-1 and NX5K-2).
6. Configure a unique logical vPC and join these access-layer-facing PortChannels across the vPC peer switches.

NOTE:

In order for a vPC domain to establish successfully, the peer-keepalive link must be operational.

Configuring the vPC domain

Code Listings 9.12 and 9.13 depict the vPC domain configurations for NX7K-1 and NX7K-2, respectively.

```
feature vpc

vpc domain 10
  role priority 1000
  peer-keepalive destination 10.10.10.2 source 10.10.10.1

interface mgmt0
  ip address 10.10.10.1/24
```

CODE LISTING 9.12

NX7K-1 vPC domain configuration

```
feature vpc

vpc domain 10
  role priority 2000
  peer-keepalive destination 10.10.10.1 source 10.10.10.2

interface mgmt0
  ip address 10.10.10.2/24
```

CODE LISTING 9.13

NX7K-2 vPC domain configuration

The "feature vpc" command enables vPC on the switch. The vPC domain 10 is created on both switches with the "vpc domain 10" command.

> **NOTE:**
>
> The vPC domain ID differentiates multiple vPC tiers (multilayer vPC), allowing for a unique L2 link aggregation ID for LACP-based configurations.

The vPC domain is also the configuration mode for configuring role priority and peer keepalive. In a vPC implementation, the pair of vPC peer switches appears as a single STP entity. The vPC role defines which of the two vPC peers processes BPDUs: the lower priority wins. For a tiebreaker, the lower system MAC address wins. In the example, NX7K-1 is configured as the primary vPC peer with a role priority of 1000 while NX7K-2 is configured as the secondary vPC peer with a role priority of 2000. The subsequent behavior with peer-link failures is determined by the vPC role of the peer switches (for more details, see the vPC Peer Keepalive section in Chapter 2).

> **NOTE:**
>
> The primary vPC peer device is typically the same device as the STP root and the active HSRP peer.

In the setup, the out-of-band management network through the management interface (mgmt0) of the supervisor module is used as the peer-keepalive (or fault-tolerant) link connection. This is achieved through the peering of the respective management IP addresses of NX7K-1 and NX7K-2 using the "peer-keepalive" command.

> **NOTE:**
>
> A separate port, preferably 1GE, is recommended for the peer-keepalive link between the vPC peer devices (not necessarily a direct link). This port should belong to a separate VRF. The management interface (mgmt0) is by default part of the management VRF, and is the only interface allowed to be part of this VRF. The NX-OS creates this management VRF by default.

The peer keepalive is a UDP message on port 3200, 96 bytes long (32-byte payload), and includes version, timestamp, domain ID, and local and remote IP addresses. It forms the heartbeat between the two vPC peer switches and is used for dual-active (no peer-link) detection.

There are three timers associated with the vPC peer keepalive:

- **Keepalive interval:** The default interval time for the vPC peer-keepalive message is 1 sec and can be configured between 400 ms and 10 seconds.
- **Keepalive hold-timeout:** The default hold-timeout value is 3 seconds (with a configurable range of 3 to 10 seconds). This timer starts when the vPC peer link goes down. During this hold-timeout period, the secondary vPC peer device ignores vPC peer-keepalive messages. This ensures that network convergence occurs before vPC action takes place. The purpose of the hold-timeout period is to prevent false-positive cases.
- **Keepalive timeout:** The default timeout value is 5 seconds (with a configurable range of 3 to 20 seconds). This timer starts at the end of the hold-timeout interval. During the timeout period, the secondary vPC peer device checks for vPC peer-keepalive hello messages from the primary vPC peer device. If the secondary vPC peer device receives a single hello message, it disables all vPC interfaces on the secondary vPC peer device.

> **NOTE:**
>
> The default keepalive timers can be modified and are optional parameters appended after the destination and source fields in the "peer-keepalive" command.

As shown in Code Listing 9.14, the "show vpc peer-keepalive" exec command to verifies whether the peer keepalive link is operational and for examining some of the vPC keepalive parameters.

```
NX7K-2# show vpc peer-keepalive

vPC keep-alive status          : peer is alive
--Peer is alive for            : (8) seconds, (886) msec
--Send status                  : Success
--Last send at                 : 2010.11.29 12:20:47 5 ms
--Sent on interface            : mgmt0
```

```
--Receive status            : Success
--Last receive at           : 2010.11.29 12:20:46 753 ms
--Received on interface     : mgmt0
--Last update from peer     : (0) seconds, (807) msec

vPC Keep-alive parameters
--Destination               : 10.10.10.1
--Keepalive interval        : 1000 msec
--Keepalive timeout         : 5 seconds
--Keepalive hold timeout    : 3 seconds
--Keepalive vrf             : management
--Keepalive udp port        : 3200
--Keepalive tos             : 192
```

CODE LISTING 9.14

vPC keepalive status and parameters

Some other considerations to keep in mind when deploying the vPC peer-keepalive link include:

- The keepalive message must not be routed over the peer link.
- In the case of redundant supervisors, when using supervisor management interfaces to carry the vPC peer keepalive, do not connect them back to back between the two peer switches. This is because only one management port is active at a given point in time and a supervisor switchover may break the peer-keepalive link connectivity.
- Use the management interface with an out-of-band management network, for instance, with a management switch in between (see Figure 9.15).

Configuring the vPC peer link

Code Listings 9.15 depicts the vPC peer link configuration that is used for both NX7K-1 and NX7K-2. The peer link configuration is symmetrical on both peer switches. It involves the usual PortChannel configuration with the addition of the "vpc peer-link" command.

The Link Aggregation Control Protocol (LACP) is used for graceful failover and misconfiguration protection over static link aggregation. It is enabled with the "feature lacp" global command and the "channel-group" command with the keyword "active" in the interface configuration (for more details on LACP, see the vPC Initiation section in Chapter 2).

```
feature lacp

interface port-channel1000
    switchport
    switchport mode trunk
    vpc peer-link
    switchport trunk allowed vlan 1,100,200
    spanning-tree port type network
```

```
interface Ethernet2/1
   switchport
   switchport mode trunk
   switchport trunk allowed vlan 1,100,200
   channel-group 1000 mode active
   no shutdown

interface Ethernet2/2
   switchport
   switchport mode trunk
   switchport trunk allowed vlan 1,100,200
   channel-group 1000 mode active
   no shutdown
```

CODE LISTING 9.15

vPC peer link configurations

> **NOTE:**
>
> The "spanning-tree port type network" command enables the Bridge Assurance (BA) feature on that link. BA causes the switch to send BPDUs on all operational ports that carry a port type setting of "network," including alternate and backup ports for each hello time period. If a neighbor port stops receiving BPDUs, the port is moved into the blocking state. If the blocked port begins receiving BPDUs again, it is removed from BA blocking and goes through normal Rapid-Per-VLAN-Spanning-Tree (RPVST) transition. This bidirectional hello mechanism helps to avoid looping conditions caused by unidirectional links or a malfunctioning switch.

In Code Listing 9.16, the "show vpc brief" exec command invoked at NX7K-1 verifies the status of the vPC peer link. From the command output trace, the status of PortChannel 1000 (Po1000) is reflected as up.

```
NX7K-1# show vpc brief
[------Snipped for brevity------]

vPC domain id                     : 10
Peer status                       : peer adjacency formed ok
vPC keep-alive status             : peer is alive
Configuration consistency status: success
[------Snipped for brevity------]
vPC role                          : primary
[------Snipped for brevity-----]

vPC Peer-link status
---------------------------------------------------------------
id   Port   Status Active vlans
---  -----  --------------------------------------------------
1    Po1000 up     1,100,200
```

CODE LISTING 9.16

vPC peer link status

Some considerations and recommendations to keep in mind when deploying the vPC peer link include:

- Although the vPC peer link is a standard 802.1Q trunk that can carry both vPC and non-vPC VLANs, it is highly recommended to split vPC and non-vPC VLANs on different inter switch PortChannels.
- No other device should be inserted between the vPC peers since a peer link is point-to-point based.
- For best resiliency, a minimum of two 10GE ports on separate modules in each peer switch is recommended.
- For oversubscribed modules (e.g., the 32-port 10GE Ethernet Module) on the NX7K switch, the 10GE ports should be in the dedicated mode rather than in the shared mode (Code Listing 9.15 uses the shared mode).

For more details on vPC peer link, see the vPC Peer Link section in Chapter 2.

> **NOTE:**
> _____
>
> The NX7K 32-Port 10GE Ethernet Module can deliver 8 ports at line rate, or allow up to 32 ports to share 80Gbps of bandwidth. The 32 ports are organized into eight groups of 4 ports. In dedicated mode, the first port in each group is active, delivering line rate performance, while the other 3 ports are disabled. In shared mode, all 4 ports in the group are active. The NX-OS allows each group to be individually configured for dedicated mode or shared mode. You can use the "show interface EthX/Y capabilities | include Members" (where X is the module number and Y is the port number) command to determine the other port group members that are associated with EthX/Y as well as the first port in this port group.

Configuring vPC

Code Listing 9.17 depicts the vPC configuration that is applied to both NX7K-1 and NX7K-2. Just like the peer link configuration, the vPC configuration is symmetrical on both peer switches. It involves the standard PortChannel configuration with the addition of the "vpc <number>" command. In Code Listing 9.17, PortChannel 10 (Po10) is associated with VPC 10 while PortChannel 20 (Po20) is associated with VPC 20.

Eth3/1 is added to Po10 with the "channel-group 10" command and becomes a vPC member port associated with VPC 10. Likewise, Eth3/2 is added to Po20 with the "channel-group 20" command and becomes a vPC member port associated with VPC 20.

> **NOTE:**
> _____
>
> vPC member ports should be 10GE interfaces.

```
interface port-channel10
  switchport
  switchport mode trunk
  vpc 10
  switchport trunk allowed vlan 1,100,200

interface port-channel20
  switchport
```

```
      switchport mode trunk
      vpc 20
      switchport trunk allowed vlan 1,100,200

  interface Ethernet3/1
      switchport
      switchport mode trunk
      switchport trunk allowed vlan 1,100,200
      channel-group 10 mode active
      no shutdown

  interface Ethernet3/2
      switchport
      switchport mode trunk
      switchport trunk allowed vlan 1,100,200
      channel-group 20 mode active
      no shutdown
```

CODE LISTING 9.17

vPC configurations

> **NOTE:**
>
> To avoid inconsistencies, the vPC member port configurations on both vPC peers need to match. However, the number of member ports on each vPC peer is not required to be the same.

Code Listings 9.18 and 9.19 depict the standard PortChannel configurations for NX5K-1 and NX5K-2, respectively. Eth1/1 and Eth1/2 are associated with PortChannel 10 in NX5K-1 and PortChannel 20 in NX5K-2. Both NX5K-1 and NX5K-2 are dual-attached to the vPC domain, Eth1/1 to NX7K-1 and Eth1/2 to NX7K-2, even though these interfaces are bundled by the same PortChannel. This ensures minimal disruption with peer-link failover and consistent behavior for vPC dual-active scenarios (for more details on dual-active situations, see the vPC Peer Keepalive section in Chapter 2).

```
  interface port-channel10
      switchport mode trunk
      switchport trunk allowed vlan 1,100,200

  interface Ethernet1/1
      switchport mode trunk
      switchport trunk allowed vlan 1,100,200
      channel-group 10 mode active

  interface Ethernet1/2
      switchport mode trunk
      switchport trunk allowed vlan 1,100,200
      channel-group 10 mode active
```

CODE LISTING 9.18

NX5K-1 PortChannel configuration

```
interface port-channel20
  switchport mode trunk
  switchport trunk allowed vlan 1,100,200

interface Ethernet1/1
  switchport mode trunk
  switchport trunk allowed vlan 1,100,200
  channel-group 20 mode active

interface Ethernet1/2
  switchport mode trunk
  switchport trunk allowed vlan 1,100,200
  channel-group 20 mode active
```

CODE LISTING 9.19

NX5K-2 PortChannel configurations

As shown in Code Listing 9.20, the "show port-channel summary" exec command verifies the status of the vPC member ports on NX7K-1 and NX7K-2. Likewise, to verify the vPC status, repeat the "show vpc brief" exec command again on NX7K-1 and NX7K-2. From the command output traces, the statuses of vPC10/Po10 and vPC20/Po20 are reflected as up.

```
NX7K-1# show port-channel summary
Flags:  D - Down          P - Up in port-channel (members)
        I - Individual    H - Hot-standby (LACP only)
        s - Suspended     r - Module-removed
        S - Switched      R - Routed
        U - Up (port-channel)
--------------------------------------------------------------------------------

Group Port-       Type    Protocol    Member Ports
      Channel
--------------------------------------------------------------------------------

10    Po10(SU)    Eth     LACP        Eth3/1(P)
20    Po20(SU)    Eth     LACP        Eth3/2(P)
1000  Po1000(SU)  Eth     LACP        Eth2/1(P)    Eth2/2(P)


NX7K-1# show vpc brief
[----Snipped for brevity----]

vPC domain id                    : 10
Peer status                      : peer adjacency formed ok
vPC keep-alive status            : peer is alive
Configuration consistency status: success
[----Snipped for brevity----]
vPC role                         : primary
Number of vPCs configured        : 2
[----Snipped for brevity----]
```

```
vPC Peer-link status
- - - - - - - - - - - - - - - - - - - - - - - - - - - - - - - - - - - - - - - - - - - - - - - -
id    Port    Status Active vlans
- - -  - - - - -  - - - - - - - - - - - - - - - - - - - - - - - - - - - - - - - - - - - - - - -
1     Po1000  up     1,100,200

vPC status
- - - - - - - - - - - - - - - - - - - - - - - - - - - - - - - - - - - - - - - - - - - - - - - -
id    Port    Status Consistency Reason                    Active vlans
- - -  - - - - -  - - - - - - - - - - - - - - - - - - - - - - - - - - - - - - - - - - - - - - -
10    Po10    up     success     success                   1,100,200
20    Po20    up     success     success                   1,100,200
```

CODE LISTING 9.20

vPC status verification

SAN EXTENSION DESIGN STUDY

The main focus of this SAN extension design study is on FCIP. The idea is to leverage an enterprise's current IP infrastructure and management resources to interconnect and extend existing native FC SANs for private cloud computing and cloud IaaS offerings. The FCIP solution also nullifies the long geographical distance (>10,000 km) constraint. For an overview of FCIP, see the FCIP Primer section in Chapter 7.

Simple FCIP design example

Enterprise "L" decides to take a different approach pertaining to private cloud computing. There is a directive from top management that there could be a corporate HQ swap in 6 months between their current corporate HQ in London and the regional HQ in Hong Kong.

From the organization perspective, business continuity (BC) and disaster recovery (DR) are more important than everything else. IT management would like to first focus on the DC migration from London to Hong Kong, or rather extend the existing FC SAN from the corporate DC to the regional DC. The private cloud computing and cloud IaaS rollout will follow right after the SAN extension implementation. The initial target IaaS users will be from the Asia Pacific (APAC) region.

The FCIP topology between the corporate DC and the regional DC will initially be point-to-point. This should transit to a hub-and-spoke topology (for more details, see the FCIP Topologies section in Chapter 7) as more APAC sites are added at a later stage. The preliminary bandwidth and latency requirements between the two sites are not restrictive since the existing applications involved are mainly remote vaulting and host-based mirroring. Asynchronous replication might come in at some future stage so this is not an immediate concern.

Nevertheless, Enterprise "L" is obligated to keep a stringent low recovery time objective (for more details, see the Data Recovery Metrics section in Chapter 7). In other words, the FCIP design must include robust HA mechanisms that have minimal downtime. Moreover, in the early stage, the SAN extension will only involve FC initiators at the regional DC but FC initiators and FC targets at the corporate DC.

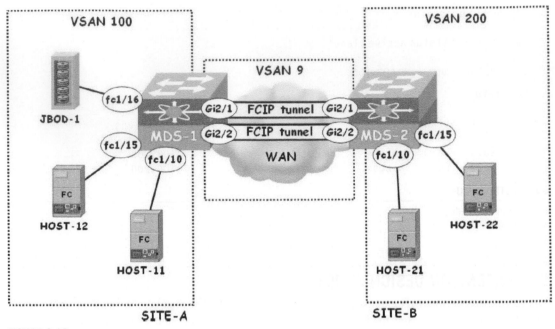

FIGURE 9.16

Simple point-to-point FCIP setup

Figure 9.16 illustrates the point-to-point FCIP simulation setup between Site-A (corporate DC) and Site-B (regional DC). JBOD-1 (with six disks), HOST-11, and HOST-12 are in VSAN 100. They are all connected to FC switch MDS-1. HOST-21 and HOST-22 are in VSAN 200. They are both connected to FC switch MDS-2. This base diagram is referenced throughout the later subsections, which include:

- Configuring FCIP HA
- Configuring VSANs and inter-VSAN routing

The configurations (or code listings) in the abovementioned subsections are based on the setup depicted in Figure 9.16.

NOTE:

A pair of MDS 9216A switches are used as the FC switches in Figure 9.16 and they are running on SAN-OS version 3.3(3). Each switch also has an 8-port IP Storage Services Module in addition to a 16-port Fibre Channel Switching Module.

Configuring FCIP HA

Code Listings 9.21 and 9.22 show the FCIP HA configurations for MDS-1 and MDS-2, respectively.

```
interface GigabitEthernet2/1
   ip address 172.16.100.1 255.255.255.0
   no shutdown

interface GigabitEthernet2/2
   ip address 172.16.200.1 255.255.255.0
   no shutdown

interface port-channel 10
   channel mode active

fcip enable

fcip profile 1
   ip address 172.16.100.1

fcip profile 2
   ip address 172.16.200.1

interface fcip1
   channel-group 10 force
   use-profile 1
   peer-info ipaddr 172.16.100.2
   no shutdown

interface fcip2
   channel-group 10 force
   use-profile 2
   peer-info ipaddr 172.16.200.2
   no shutdown
```

CODE LISTING 9.21

MDS-1 FCIP HA configuration

```
interface GigabitEthernet2/1
   ip address 172.16.100.2 255.255.255.0
   no shutdown

interface GigabitEthernet2/2
   ip address 172.16.200.2 255.255.255.0
   no shutdown

interface port-channel 10
   channel mode active

fcip enable
```

```
fcip profile 1
  ip address 172.16.100.2

fcip profile 2
  ip address 172.16.200.2

interface fcip1
  channel-group 10 force
  use-profile 1
  peer-info ipaddr 172.16.100.1
  no shutdown

interface fcip2
  channel-group 10 force
  use-profile 2
  peer-info ipaddr 172.16.200.1
  no shutdown
```

CODE LISTING 9.22

MDS-2 FCIP HA configuration

The standard configuration steps (in order) are as follows:

- Configure the Gigabit Ethernet interfaces to be assigned to the respective FCIP profiles. In Code Listings 9.21 and 9.22, they are Gig2/1 and Gig2/2.
- Create the PortChannel. In Code Listings 9.21 and 9.22, it will be PortChannel 10 (Po10). Set the channel mode for Po10 to active with the "channel mode active" command.
- Enable the FCIP feature with the "fcip enable" command.
- Configure the FCIP profiles. You can configure various parameters within an FCIP profile. Code Listings 9.21 and 9.22 associate FCIP profile 1 with the local IP address of Gig2/1 and FCIP profile 2 with the local IP address of Gig2/2.
- Configure the FCIP interfaces. In Code Listings 9.21 and 9.22, they are interfaces fcip1 and fcip2 with the following interface configurations:
  - Add fcip1 and fcip2 to Po10 using the "channel-group 10" command.
  - Assign FCIP profile 1 to interface fcip1 and FCIP profile 2 to interface fcip2 with the "use-profile" command.
  - Assign the corresponding peer IP address information to interface fcip1 and interface fcip2 accordingly, using the "peer-info ipaddr" command.
  - Remember to enable interfaces fcip1 and fcip2 with the "no shutdown" command.

> **NOTE:**
>
> FCIP interfaces are the local endpoints of the FCIP link (or FCIP tunnel) and a VE_Port interface. All the FCIP and E_Port parameters are configured in the context of the FCIP interface. For more details, see the VE_Ports section and the FCIP Links and Virtual ISLs section in Chapter 7.

As shown in Code Listing 9.23, the "show fcip profile <id>" exec command displays the status of the configured FCIP profiles for verification purposes.

```
MDS-1# show fcip profile 1
FCIP Profile 1
    Internet Address is 172.16.100.1  (interface GigabitEthernet2/1)
    Tunnels Using this Profile: fcip1
    Listen Port is 3225
[-----Snipped for brevity-----]

MDS-1# show fcip profile 2
FCIP Profile 2
    Internet Address is 172.16.200.1  (interface GigabitEthernet2/2)
    Tunnels Using this Profile: fcip2
    Listen Port is 3225
[-----Snipped for brevity-----]

MDS-2# show fcip profile 1
FCIP Profile 1
    Internet Address is 172.16.100.2  (interface GigabitEthernet2/1)
    Tunnels Using this Profile: fcip1
    Listen Port is 3225
[-----Snipped for brevity-----]

MDS-2# show fcip profile 2
FCIP Profile 2
    Internet Address is 172.16.200.2  (interface GigabitEthernet2/2)
    Tunnels Using this Profile: fcip2
    Listen Port is 3225
[-----Snipped for brevity-----]
```

CODE LISTING 9.23

FCIP profile verification

A quick way to verify the status of the FCIP interface status on each of the local MDS switches is through the "show fcip summary" exec command as shown in Code Listing 9.24. From the command output traces, both tunnel1 (fcip1) and tunnel2 (fcip2) are up with trunking (reflected as TRNK) enabled.

```
MDS-1# show fcip summary
-------------------------------------------------------------------------------
Tun  prof   Eth-if   peer-ip       Status T W T Enc Comp  Bandwidth   rtt
                                          E A A            max/min     (us)
-------------------------------------------------------------------------------
1    1      GE2/1    172.16.100.2   TRNK  Y N N  N   N     1000M/500M  1000
2    2      GE2/2    172.16.200.2   TRNK  Y N N  N   N     1000M/500M  1000
```

```
MDS-2# show fcip summary
- - - - - - - - - - - - - - - - - - - - - - - - - - - - - - - - - - - - - - - - - -
Tun   prof   Eth-if   peer-ip        Status T W T Enc Comp  Bandwidth   rtt
                                            E A A            max/min     (us)
- - - - - - - - - - - - - - - - - - - - - - - - - - - - - - - - - - - - - - - - - -
 1     1     GE2/1    172.16.100.1   TRNK   Y N N  N   N     1000M/500M  1000
 2     2     GE2/2    172.16.200.1   TRNK   Y N N  N   N     1000M/500M  1000
```

CODE LISTING 9.24

FCIP interface status summary

NOTE:

The TRNK status means that the tunnel is operating in TE mode. This also implies the FCIP interface is functioning as a trunking expansion port (TE_Port). The rest of the abbreviations such as WA (write acceleration), TA (tape acceleration), Enc (encryption), and Comp (compression) denote some of the advanced FCIP features that are not enabled in Code Listings 9.21 and 9.22. For more details of these features, see the FCIP Performance Tuning section in Chapter 7.

As illustrated in Code Listing 9.25, the "show port-channel database" exec command displays the PortChannel database for all the configured PortChannels on the local MDS switch. From the command output trace, both FCIP interfaces, fcip1 and fcip2, register an "up" status, indicating that they are successfully associated with Po10. The asterisk indicates the first operational port (fcip1) in Po10.

```
MDS-1# show port-channel database
port-channel 10
     Administrative channel mode is active
     Operational channel mode is active
     Last membership update succeeded
     First operational port is fcip1
     2 ports in total, 2 ports up
     Ports:   fcip1    [up] *
              fcip2    [up]
```

CODE LISTING 9.25

FCIP PortChannel database

Configuring VSANs and inter-VSAN routing

Bundling FCIP interfaces as a PortChannel not only load balances traffic across the FCIP tunnels and sustains optimal bandwidth utilization, but also incorporates HA functionality. If one link fails, traffic previously carried on this link is switched to the remaining link transparent to the upper layer protocol. The FSPF routing tables are not affected by this link failure, so recovery is nondisruptive and much faster.

It is recommended to put the configured PortChannel in a transit virtual storage area network (VSAN) rather than leaving it as a trunk. This is to ensure that any WAN-related outages (e.g., WAN link flaps/failures) are confined only to the transit VSAN and will not disrupt the local VSANs. Since the PortChannel is nontrunking and in a separate VSAN (transit VSAN), inter-VSAN routing (IVR) is required to route the FC frames between the different VSANs. In Figure 9.16, VSAN 9 is the transit VSAN and IVR needs to be implemented between VSAN 9 and VSAN 100 as well as VSAN 200.

> **NOTE:**
>
> A VSAN in FC is analogous to the VLAN concept in Ethernet. A VSAN is a collection of ports from a set of connected FC switches that form a virtual fabric. Ports within a single switch are partitioned into multiple VSANs, despite sharing hardware resources. On the other hand, multiple FC switches join a number of ports to form a single VSAN through an inter-switch link (ISL) or enhanced ISL (EISL). The EISL can be considered an FC trunk.

IVR requires a VSAN rewrite table. Each IVR-enabled switch maintains a VSAN rewrite table. The table can hold up to 4096 entries that are based on per switch domain, rather than per end device. Figure 9.17 illustrates a simplified VSAN rewrite table based on the example setup illustrated in Figure 9.16.

Using the VSAN rewrite table shown in Figure 9.17 as illustration, assume that an FC frame is traversing from FC domain 0x8f to FC domain 0x2c. MDS-1 performs a VSAN rewrite, changing the VSAN tag from 100 to 9 while MDS-2 rewrites the VSAN tag from 9 to 200. The process is reversed on the return path.

> **NOTE:**
>
> The actual VSAN rewrite table on the MDS switch is displayed with the "show ivr internal fcid-rewrite-list" exec command.

Back to the IVR implementation, the first thing is to set the trunk mode on Po10 and the FCIP interfaces (fcip1 and fcip2) from trunk to nontrunk. As illustrated in Code Listing 9.26, the "switchport trunk mode off" command is used to turn off trunking on Po10 and the FCIP interfaces (fcip1 and fcip2). This command is applied to both MDS-1 and MDS-2.

VSAN Rewrite Table				
Switch	Current VSAN	Source Domain	Destination Domain	Next-hop VSAN (rewritten VSAN)
MDS-1	100	0x8f	0x2c	9
MDS-1	9	0x2c	0x8f	100
MDS-2	200	0x2c	0x8f	9
MDS-2	9	0x8f	0x2c	200

FIGURE 9.17

Simplified VSAN rewrite table

```
interface port-channel 10
  switchport trunk mode off
[-----Snipped for brevity-----]

interface fcip1
  switchport trunk mode off
[-----Snipped for brevity-----]

interface fcip2
  switchport trunk mode off
[-----Snipped for brevity-----]
```

CODE LISTING 9.26

Non–trunk mode configurations

Code Listing 9.27 shows the VSAN configurations for MDS-1. In Code Listing 9.27, FC interfaces fc1/10, fc1/15, and fc1/16 go to VSAN 100 while Po10 goes to VSAN 9. The FC interfaces are enabled with the "no shutdown" command.

```
vsan database
  vsan 9
  vsan 100
  vsan 9 interface port-channel 10
  vsan 100 interface fc1/10
  vsan 100 interface fc1/15
  vsan 100 interface fc1/16

interface fc1/10
  no shutdown

interface fc1/15
  no shutdown

interface fc1/16
  no shutdown
```

CODE LISTING 9.27

MDS-1 VSAN configurations

Code Listing 9.28 shows the VSAN configurations for MDS-2. In Code Listing 9.28, FC interfaces fc1/10 and fc1/15 go to VSAN 200, while Po10 goes to VSAN 9. The FC interfaces are enabled with the "no shutdown" command.

```
vsan database
  vsan 9
  vsan 200
  vsan 9 interface port-channel 10
  vsan 200 interface fc1/10
  vsan 200 interface fc1/15

interface fc1/10
  no shutdown

interface fc1/15
  no shutdown
```

CODE LISTING 9.28

MDS-2 VSAN configuration

Now is a good time to take a quick look at the FLOGI and FCNS databases.

In an FC fabric, each host (N_Port) or disk (NL_Port) requires an FCID. If the required end device appears in the FLOGI database, the fabric login is considered successful. The FLOGI database displays all end devices that have logged into the fabric (i.e., the local MDS switch). The pWWNs for aliases and zoning are typically retrieved from this database.

Code Listing 9.29 illustrates the FLOGI database for MDS-1 and MDS-2, respectively, using the "show flogi database" exec command. From the command output traces, JBOD-1, HOST-11, and HOST-12 have successfully logged into MDS-1. The same applies to HOST-21 and HOST-22 for MDS-2.

```
MDS-1# show flogi database
---------------------------------------------------------------------------
INTERFACE    VSAN    FCID      PORT NAME                 NODE NAME
---------------------------------------------------------------------------
fc1/10       100     0x8f0000  21:00:00:e0:8b:1f:92:30   20:00:00:e0:8b:1f:92:30
fc1/15       100     0x8f0100  21:00:00:e0:8b:1f:92:31   20:00:00:e0:8b:1f:92:31
fc1/16       100     0x8f02e0  c5:f8:00:1b:2b:09:00:05   c6:81:00:1b:2b:02:00:05
fc1/16       100     0x8f02e1  c5:f8:00:1b:2b:09:00:04   c6:81:00:1b:2b:02:00:04
fc1/16       100     0x8f02e2  c5:f8:00:1b:2b:09:00:03   c6:81:00:1b:2b:02:00:03
fc1/16       100     0x8f02e4  c5:f8:00:1b:2b:09:00:02   c6:81:00:1b:2b:02:00:02
fc1/16       100     0x8f02e8  c5:f8:00:1b:2b:09:00:01   c6:81:00:1b:2b:02:00:01
fc1/16       100     0x8f02ef  c5:f8:00:06:0d:09:00:00   c5:f8:00:06:0d:09:00:00

Total number of flogi = 8.

MDS-2# show flogi database
---------------------------------------------------------------------------
INTERFACE    VSAN    FCID      PORT NAME                 NODE NAME
---------------------------------------------------------------------------
fc1/10       200     0x2c0000  21:01:00:e0:8b:3f:a9:ac   20:01:00:e0:8b:3f:a9:ac
fc1/15       200     0x2c0100  21:01:00:e0:8b:3f:a9:ad   20:01:00:e0:8b:3f:a9:ad

Total number of flogi = 2.
```

CODE LISTING 9.29

FLOGI database

The FC name server (FCNS) provides a simple database that contains information about each node (FC initiator and/or target), such as FCIDs, pWWNs, and so on, in a multiswitch fabric, as a topology-wide service.

Code Listing 9.30 illustrates the FCNS database for MDS-1 and MDS-2, respectively, using the "show fcns database" exec command. As IVR has not been implemented yet, the command output traces display only the respective end devices that are locally connected to MDS-1 and MDS-2.

```
MDS-1# show fcns database
VSAN 100:
-----------------------------------------------------------------------
FCID        TYPE  PWWN                      (VENDOR)    FC4-TYPE:FEATURE
-----------------------------------------------------------------------
0x8f0000    N     21:00:00:e0:8b:1f:92:30   (Qlogic)    scsi-fcp:init
0x8f0100    N     21:00:00:e0:8b:1f:92:31   (Qlogic)    scsi-fcp:init
0x8f02e0    NL    c5:f8:00:1b:2b:09:00:05               scsi-fcp:target
0x8f02e1    NL    c5:f8:00:1b:2b:09:00:04               scsi-fcp:target
0x8f02e2    NL    c5:f8:00:1b:2b:09:00:03               scsi-fcp:target
0x8f02e4    NL    c5:f8:00:1b:2b:09:00:02               scsi-fcp:target
0x8f02e8    NL    c5:f8:00:1b:2b:09:00:01               scsi-fcp:target
0x8f02ef    NL    c5:f8:00:06:0d:09:00:00               scsi-fcp:target

Total number of entries = 8

MDS-2# show fcns database

VSAN 200:
-----------------------------------------------------------------------
FCID        TYPE  PWWN                      (VENDOR)    FC4-TYPE:FEATURE
-----------------------------------------------------------------------
0x2c0000    N     21:01:00:e0:8b:3f:a9:ac   (Qlogic)    scsi-fcp:init
0x2c0100    N     21:01:00:e0:8b:3f:a9:ad   (Qlogic)    scsi-fcp:init

Total number of entries = 2
```

CODE LISTING 9.30

FCNS database before IVR

JBOD-1 (see Figure 9.16) has six disks (DISK-1 to DISK-6). The plan is to allocate one disk to each host and thus, some zoning configurations are required. Code Listing 9.31 illustrates the zone and zoneset configurations for VSAN 100 over at MDS-1. HOST-11 and DISK-1 are grouped into zone11. HOST-12 and DISK-2 are grouped under zone12. The zoneset "zonelocal" is then activated with zone11 and zone12 as members.

```
zone name zone11 vsan 100
    member pwwn 21:00:00:e0:8b:1f:92:30
    member pwwn c5:f8:00:06:0d:09:00:00

zone name zone12 vsan 100
    member pwwn 21:00:00:e0:8b:1f:92:31
    member pwwn c5:f8:00:1b:2b:09:00:01
```

```
zoneset name zonelocal vsan 100
    member zone11
    member zone12

zoneset activate name zonelocal vsan 100
```

CODE LISTING 9.31

MDS-1 zone and zoneset configurations

> **NOTE:**
>
> The "show zoneset active" exec command verifies the configured as well as activated zoneset(s).

Next, proceed to configure IVR on MDS-1 and MDS-2. Code Listings 9.32 and 9.33 depict the IVR configurations for MDS-1 and MDS-2, respectively.

```
ivr enable
ivr distribute
ivr nat
ivr vsan-topology auto


ivr zone name IvrZone21
  member pwwn 21:01:00:e0:8b:3f:a9:ac          vsan 200
  member pwwn c5:f8:00:1b:2b:09:00:02          vsan 100


ivr zone name IvrZone22
  member pwwn 21:01:00:e0:8b:3f:a9:ad          vsan 200
  member pwwn c5:f8:00:1b:2b:09:00:03          vsan 100

ivr zoneset name IvrZoneSet1
  member IvrZone21
  member IvrZone22


ivr zoneset activate name IvrZoneSet1 force
ivr commit
```

CODE LISTING 9.32

MDS-1 IVR configuration

```
ivr enable
ivr distribute
```

CODE LISTING 9.33

MDS-2 IVR configuration

The IVR configuration steps are as follow:

- Enable IVR on MDS-1 and MDS-2 with the "ivr enable" command.
- IVR uses the Cisco Fabric Services (CFS[4]) infrastructure for automatic IVR configuration distribution and to provide a single point of configuration for the entire (multiswitch) fabric. The master switch is MDS-1. Enable IVR configuration distribution on both MDS-1 and MDS-2 with the "ivr distribute" command.
- Enable IVR NAT and auto VSAN-topology discovery on master switch MDS-1 using the "ivr nat" and "ivr vsan-topology auto" commands. IVR NAT allows nonunique FC domain IDs across all VSANs and switches involved in the IVR topology.
- Configure IVR zones on the master switch MDS-1 with the "ivr zone" command. Add selected port members (pWWNs and associated VSANs) of HOST-21 and DISK-3 to a new IVRzone, IvrZone21. Likewise, add the pWWN and associated VSAN of HOST-22 and DISK-4 to a new IVRzone, IvrZone22. The related pWWNs and VSAN information are derived from the FLOGI database (see Code Listing 9.29).
- Configure IVR zonesets on the master switch MDS-1 with the "ivr zoneset" command. Add the newly created zones IvrZone21 and IvrZone22 to zoneset IvrZoneSet1.
- Activate zoneset IvrZoneSet1 on master switch MDS-1 with the "ivr zoneset activate" command.
- Issue commit on master switch MDS-1 with the "ivr commit" command to propagate the zone configurations to all IVR-enabled switches (MDS-2, in this case).

> **NOTE:**
> The Cisco Fabric Manager (FM) GUI is an easier and less error-prone alternative to configure IVR than using plain CLI commands.

A concise way to verify the trunk mode of Po10 is to use the "show interface brief" exec command. The command output trace as illustrated in Code Listing 9.34 reflects the trunk mode as "off" for Po10, fcip1, and fcip2. The operational mode on Po10, fcip1, and fcip2 is reflected as "E" instead of "TE." This further confirms that trunking has been successfully turned off.

```
MDS-1# show interface brief
[-----Snipped for brevity-----]
-----------------------------------------------------------------------

Interface       Vsan Admin Status    Oper  Oper   IP
                     Trunk           Mode  Speed  Address
                     Mode                  (Gbps)
-----------------------------------------------------------------------

port-channel 10  9   off   up        E     2      --
-----------------------------------------------------------------------

Interface Vsan Admin Admin Status   Oper Profile Eth Int    Port-channel
               Mode  Trunk          Mode
                     Mode
-----------------------------------------------------------------------

fcip1     9    auto  off   up        E    1 GigabitEthernet2/1  port-channel 10
fcip2     9    auto  off   up        E    2 GigabitEthernet2/2  port-channel 10
```

CODE LISTING 9.34

Non-trunk PortChannel verification

The "show ivr vsan-topology" exec command is used to verify the IVR VSAN topology configuration. The command output traces in Code Listing 9.35 show that transit VSAN 9 and VSAN 100 are associated with MDS-1, while transit VSAN 9 and VSAN 200 are associated with MDS-2. The asterisk indicates the World Wide Name (WWN[5]) of the local switch. The configured (Cfg) field displays "no" because the VSAN topology is automatically discovered rather than manually configured.

```
MDS-1# show ivr vsan-topology

AFID   SWITCH WWN                      Active   Cfg. VSANS
- - - - - - - - - - - - - - - - - - - - - - - - - - - - - - - - - - - - - - - - -
   1   20:00:00:0c:ce:6c:6c:40 *       yes      no  9,100
   1   20:00:00:0d:ec:0e:8e:80         yes      no  9,200

Total: 2 entries in active and configured IVR VSAN-Topology


MDS-2# show ivr vsan-topology

AFID   SWITCH WWN                      Active   Cfg. VSANS
- - - - - - - - - - - - - - - - - - - - - - - - - - - - - - - - - - - - - - - - -
   1   20:00:00:0c:ce:6c:6c:40         yes      no  9,100
   1   20:00:00:0d:ec:0e:8e:80 *       yes      no  9,200

Total: 2 entries in active and configured IVR VSAN-Topology
```

CODE LISTING 9.35

IVR VSAN topology status

The "show ivr zoneset active" exec command is used to verify the active IVR zoneset. This is shown in Code Listing 9.36. Note that the zone configurations put together at MDS-1 have successfully propagated to MDS-2.

```
MDS-2# show ivr zoneset active

zoneset name IvrZoneSet1
  zone name IvrZone21
    * pwwn 21:01:00:e0:8b:3f:a9:ac       vsan  200 autonomous-fabric-id  1
    * pwwn c5:f8:00:1b:2b:09:00:02       vsan  100 autonomous-fabric-id  1
  zone name IvrZone22
    * pwwn 21:01:00:e0:8b:3f:a9:ad       vsan  200 autonomous-fabric-id  1
    * pwwn c5:f8:00:1b:2b:09:00:03       vsan  100 autonomous-fabric-id  1
```

CODE LISTING 9.36

Active IVR zoneset verification

> **NOTE:**
>
> The autonomous fabric ID (AFID) distinguishes two VSANs that are logically and physically separate, but have the same VSAN ID. In the example, the AFIDs all have the same value of 1 (the default) because there are no overlapping VSAN IDs in the setup.

Code Listing 9.37 depicts the FCNS database of MDS-1 after the IVR configurations. The FCNS database for transit VSAN 9 displays the pWWN entries for DISK-3, DISK-4, HOST-21, and HOST-22. The FCNS database for VSAN 100 now registers the additional pWWN entries for HOST-21 and HOST-22. Thus IVR has successfully propagated this information over from VSAN 200 (to VSAN 9 and from VSAN 9 to VSAN 100).

```
MDS-1# show fcns database


VSAN 9:
- - - - - - - - - - - - - - - - - - - - - - - - - - - - - - - - - - - - - - - - -
FCID        TYPE  PWWN                       (VENDOR)      FC4-TYPE:FEATURE
- - - - - - - - - - - - - - - - - - - - - - - - - - - - - - - - - - - - - - - - -
0x58ce04    N     c5:f8:00:1b:2b:09:00:03                  scsi-fcp:target
0x58ce05    N     c5:f8:00:1b:2b:09:00:02                  scsi-fcp:target
0x8cdc35    N     21:01:00:e0:8b:3f:a9:ac    (Qlogic)      scsi-fcp:init
0x8cdd35    N     21:01:00:e0:8b:3f:a9:ad    (Qlogic)      scsi-fcp:init

Total number of entries = 4

VSAN 100:
- - - - - - - - - - - - - - - - - - - - - - - - - - - - - - - - - - - - - - - - -
FCID        TYPE  PWWN                       (VENDOR)      FC4-TYPE:FEATURE
- - - - - - - - - - - - - - - - - - - - - - - - - - - - - - - - - - - - - - - - -
0x8f0000    N     21:00:00:e0:8b:1f:92:30    (Qlogic)      scsi-fcp:init
0x8f0100    N     21:00:00:e0:8b:1f:92:31    (Qlogic)      scsi-fcp:init
0x8f02e0    NL    c5:f8:00:1b:2b:09:00:05                  scsi-fcp:target
0x8f02e1    NL    c5:f8:00:1b:2b:09:00:04                  scsi-fcp:target
0x8f02e2    NL    c5:f8:00:1b:2b:09:00:03                  scsi-fcp:target
0x8f02e4    NL    c5:f8:00:1b:2b:09:00:02                  scsi-fcp:target
0x8f02e8    NL    c5:f8:00:1b:2b:09:00:01                  scsi-fcp:target
0x8f02ef    NL    c5:f8:00:06:0d:09:00:00                  scsi-fcp:target
0xdbdc90    N     21:01:00:e0:8b:3f:a9:ac    (Qlogic)      scsi-fcp:init
0xdbdd90    N     21:01:00:e0:8b:3f:a9:ad    (Qlogic)      scsi-fcp:init

Total number of entries = 10
```

CODE LISTING 9.37

MDS-1 FCNS database after IVR

Code Listing 9.38 depicts the FCNS database of MDS-2 after the IVR configurations. Just like MDS-1, the FCNS database for transit VSAN 9 displays the pWWN entries for DISK-3, DISK-4, HOST-21, and HOST-22. The FCNS database for VSAN 200 now registers the additional pWWN entries for DISK-3 and DISK-4. This means that IVR has successfully propagated this information over from VSAN 100 (to VSAN 9 and from VSAN 9 to VSAN 200).

```
MDS-2# show fcns database
VSAN 9:
-------------------------------------------------------------------------------
FCID       TYPE  PWWN                        (VENDOR)      FC4-TYPE:FEATURE
-------------------------------------------------------------------------------
0x58ce04   N     c5:f8:00:1b:2b:09:00:03                   scsi-fcp:target
0x58ce05   N     c5:f8:00:1b:2b:09:00:02                   scsi-fcp:target
0x8cdc35   N     21:01:00:e0:8b:3f:a9:ac     (Qlogic)      scsi-fcp:init
0x8cdd35   N     21:01:00:e0:8b:3f:a9:ad     (Qlogic)      scsi-fcp:init

Total number of entries = 4


VSAN 200:
-------------------------------------------------------------------------------
FCID       TYPE  PWWN                        (VENDOR)      FC4-TYPE:FEATURE
-------------------------------------------------------------------------------
0x2c0000   N     21:01:00:e0:8b:3f:a9:ac     (Qlogic)      scsi-fcp:init
0x2c0100   N     21:01:00:e0:8b:3f:a9:ad     (Qlogic)      scsi-fcp:init
0xb0cec3   N     c5:f8:00:1b:2b:09:00:03                   scsi-fcp:target
0xb0cec4   N     c5:f8:00:1b:2b:09:00:02                   scsi-fcp:target

Total number of entries = 4
```

CODE LISTING 9.38

MDS-2 FCNS database after IVR

SERVICE-ORIENTED INFRASTRUCTURE DESIGN STUDY

This design study elaborates the various service-oriented infrastructure (SOI) submodules that are described in the Cloud IaaS: The Big Picture section of Chapter 8.

Enterprise "M" would like to launch a preliminary cloud IaaS trial with just two tenants (subscribers/end-users). More tenants could come in at a later stage. Tenant-A is comprised of internal end-users who belong to systems engineering team A located in Remote Branch Office A (RBO-A). Tenant-B is Subscriber-B (a valued channel partner) located in Remote Branch Office B (RBO-B). At this stage, the management team of Enterprise "M" has requested a high-level Project Initiation Design (PID). The PID should include the high-level design of the following:

- Virtual access layer
- Compute submodule
- Storage module
- Fabric module
- Services aggregation layer
- WAN module

Virtual access-layer high-level design

In the virtual access-layer design, the VMs connected to the virtual access-layer switches can be grouped into two main categories: infrastructure and tenant. Infrastructure VMs are used in configuring and maintaining the cloud IaaS environment. They are typically cloud infrastructure management platforms, such as VMware vCenter, NX1KV VSM, Data Center Network Manager (DCNM), Fabric Manager (FM), UCS Manager (UCSM), and so on. Tenant VMs are owned and leveraged by tenant applications and users. Figure 9.18 illustrates the high-level view of the virtual access-layer design.

> **NOTE:**
>
> The Cisco DCNM is a management platform for managing the Nexus switches. Similarly, the Cisco FM is for managing the MDS switches and the UCSM for managing the UCS.

The high-level, virtual access-layer design illustrated in Figure 9.18 includes the following:

- Eight tenant VMs, VM1 to VM8:
  - VM1, VM2, VM5, and VM6 are assigned to Tenant-A.
  - VM3, VM4, VM7, and VM8 are assigned to Tenant-B.

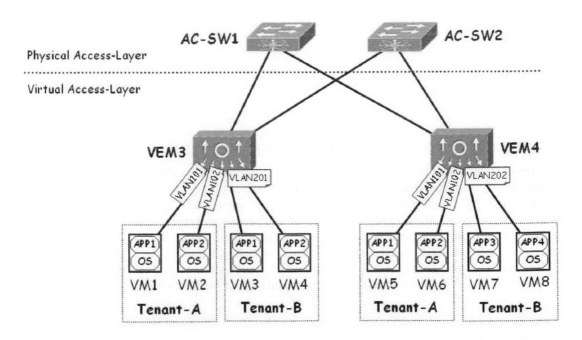

FIGURE 9.18

High-level virtual access-layer design

- Four different applications, APP1 to APP4:
  - APP1 runs on VM1, VM3, and VM5.
  - APP2 runs on VM2, VM4, and VM6.
  - APP3 runs on VM7.
  - APP4 runs on VM8.
- Two ESX hosts, ESX1 and ESX2 (not shown in diagram for brevity):
  - ESX1 contains VM1 to VM4.
  - ESX2 contains VM5 to VM8.
- Two physical access-layer switches: AC-SW1 and AC-SW2. These are either UCS 6140XP fabric interconnects or Nexus 5020 switches depending on whether the compute submodule is made up of the UCS or generic rack servers (for more details, see the Compute Submodule High-Level Design section).
- Two NX1KV VEMs, VEM3 and VEM4:
  - VM1 to VM4 connect to VEM3 in ESX1.
  - VM5 to VM8 connect to VEM4 in ESX2.
  - Each VEM has two 10GE uplinks, one to AC-SW1 and the other to AC-SW2.
  - The NX1KV design in the Two-NIC Configuration section is adopted by each VEM.
- Four VLANs, VLANs 101, 102, 201, and 202:
  - VM1 and VM5 are in VLAN 101. These VMs are running APP1 for Tenant-A. The intention is to distribute APP1 between the two ESX hosts to facilitate service chain or SLB (for more details, see the Services Aggregation-Layer High-Level Design section).
  - VM2 and VM6 are in VLAN 102. These VMs are running APP2 for Tenant-A. Similar to APP1, the intention is to distribute APP2 between the two ESX hosts to facilitate service chain or SLB (for more details, see the Services Aggregation-Layer High-Level Design section).
  - VM3 and VM4 are in VLAN 201.
  - VM7 and VM8 are in VLAN 202.

NOTE:

The service console and VMkernel also connect directly to the NX1KV VEM (they are not shown in the diagram for brevity).

Compute submodule high-level design

There are various ways to design the compute submodule. In this design study, we have narrowed it down to two, using either UCS or generic rack servers. The blade or rack server is where the virtual access layer "lives." Figure 9.19 shows the high-level view of the compute submodule design with UCS. Figure 9.20 depicts the compute submodule design using generic rack servers.

NOTE:

The UCS Manager (UCSM) runs on the UCS 6100 Series fabric interconnects and manages and configures the entire UCS system. The UCSM uses active/standby architecture, with an active instance called primary, and a standby instance called subordinate. All communication is handled by the primary instance that maintains the main configuration database. The main configuration database is stored on the primary instance and replicated on the subordinate instance. The primary instance sends updates to the subordinate when configuration changes occur. The UCSM instances communicate over the dual cluster links between the two fabric interconnects.

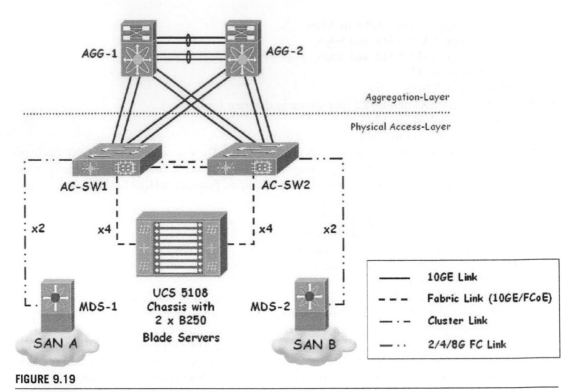

AGG-1

AGG-2

Aggregation-Layer

Physical Access-Layer

AC-SW1

AC-SW2

x2

x4

x4

x2

UCS 5108
Chassis with
2 x B250
Blade Servers

MDS-1

MDS-2

SAN A

SAN B

———— 10GE Link

— — — Fabric Link (10GE/FCoE)

— · — Cluster Link

— ·· 2/4/8G FC Link

FIGURE 9.19

High-level compute submodule design 1

The high-level compute submodule design 1 illustrated in Figure 9.19 includes the following components:

- Two UCS 6140XP fabric interconnects, AC-SW1 and AC-SW2 (for more details, see the Fabric Interconnect section in Chapter 8):
  - AC-SW1 has two pairs of 10GE uplinks: one pair to AGG-1 and the other to AGG-2. The same applies for AC-SW2.
  - AC-SW1 has four 10GE downlinks (fabric links) to FEX-1 (behind the UCS chassis). The same applies for AC-SW2 to FEX-2 (behind the UCS chassis). As only two blade servers are used in the design, two fabric links will suffice. However, all four fabric links are wired up (wire once) anyway for future expansion. For more details on UCS FEXs, see the Fabric Extender section in Chapter 8.
  - The abovementioned uplinks and downlinks for both fabric interconnects (AC-SW1 and AC-SW2) are 10GE/FCoE/SFP+ ports.
  - AC-SW1 has two native FC links to MDS-1 (SAN A). The same applies for AC-SW2 to MDS-2 (SAN B).
- Two UCS 2104XP FEXs: FEX-1 and FEX-2 (both located at the back of the UCS chassis).
- Two UCS B250 blade servers (for more details, see the Blade Servers section in Chapter 8): one for ESX1 and the other for ESX2.

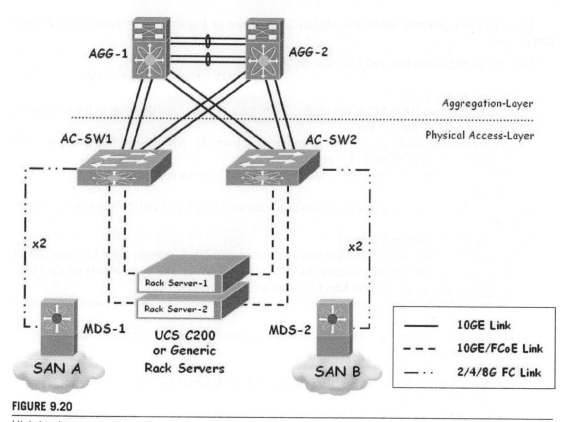

FIGURE 9.20

High-level compute submodule design 2

- Two CNAs, CNA-1 and CNA-2, per blade server (the UCS B250 is a full-slot blade server that supports up to two I/O adapters):
  - 10GE/FCoE connection is implemented on CNA-1 and CNA-2 between the ESX hosts (ESX1 and ESX2) and the fabric interconnects (AC-SW1 and AC-SW2). For more details on the FCoE configurations, see the Access Layer to Ethernet LAN section.
  - For each ESX host, CNA-1 is connected through FEX-1 to AC-SW1 and CNA-2 is connected through FEX-2 to AC-SW2.
  - The CNAs are used by the ESX hosts to access both the DC Ethernet LAN and the FC SANs (via FCoE).
- One UCS 5108 blade server chassis where the server blades and FEXs are housed (for more details, see the Blade Server Chassis section in Chapter 8).
- ToR architecture:
  - Since the UCS comes with FEXs that slot into the back of the UCS chassis, no other ToR devices are required. The fabric interconnects are located at an EoR rack.
  - The ToR layout is similar to Figure 9.13 except without the ToR FEX.
  - Since all four fabric uplinks are used on each UCS FEX in the design, a total of eight fiber strands are utilized from the UCS server rack to the EoR rack.

The high-level compute submodule design 2 illustrated in Figure 9.20 includes the following components:

- Two Nexus 5020 switches, AC-SW1 and AC-SW2:
  - AC-SW1 has two pairs of 10GE uplinks: one pair to AGG-1 and another to AGG-2. The same applies for AC-SW2.
  - AC-SW1 has two 10GE/FCoE downlinks: one to Rack Server-1 and the other to Rack Server-2. The same applies for AC-SW2.
  - The abovementioned uplinks and downlinks for both the NX5K switches (AC-SW1 and AC-SW2) are 10GE/FCoE/SFP+ ports.
  - AC-SW1 has two native FC links to MDS-1 (SAN A). The same applies for AC-SW2 to MDS-2 (SAN B).
- Two UCS C200 or generic rack servers: one (Rack Server-1) for ESX1 and the other (Rack Server-2) for ESX2.
- One dual-port CNA per rack server:
  - 10GE/FCoE connection is implemented on the dual-port CNA between the ESX hosts (ESX1 and ESX2) and the NX5K switches (AC-SW1 and AC-SW2). For more details on the FCoE configurations, see the Access Layer to Ethernet LAN section.
  - For each ESX host (rack server), one CNA port is connected to AC-SW1 and the other is connected to AC-SW2.
  - The dual-port CNA is used by the ESX hosts to access both the DC Ethernet LAN and the FC SANs (via FCoE).
- ToR architecture:
  - The two NX5K switches can be ToR switches within the server rack. The server rack layout is similar to Figure 2.26.
  - The two NX5K switches can also be located at an EoR rack. In this case, the ToR layout is similar to Figure 9.13 except without the ToR FEX.

Storage module high-level design

The SAN module design is based on the collapsed-core architecture where the storage devices are directly attached to high port-count FC directors. Figure 9.21 illustrates the high-level view of the storage module design.

The high-level storage module design illustrated in Figure 9.21 includes the following:

- Two MDS 9506 directors, MDS-1 and MDS-2:
  - One 48-port, 8-Gbps FC switching module per director for native FC connections.
  - One 16-port storage services node per director for FCIP connections.
- Two EMC CLARiiON AX4 drive arrays: EMC-1 and EMC-2.
- One pair of FCIP tunnels per director to extend the existing SANs (SAN A and SAN B) to other remote DC/DR sites over the WAN. For more details on the FCIP configurations, see the Simple FCIP Design Example section.

NOTE:

In most cases, the storage module is part of the existing DC SAN infrastructure.

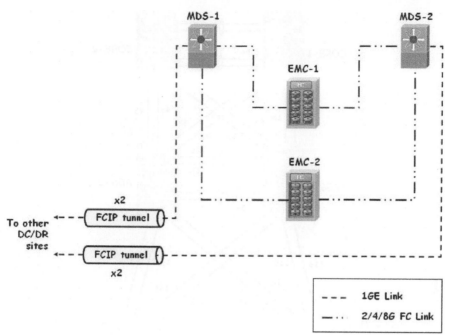

FIGURE 9.21

High-level storage module design

Fabric module high-level design

The fabric module is composed of the core layer, aggregation layer, and access layer. The DC LAN infrastructure is further segregated into different virtual contexts for Tenant-A and Tenant-B. This provides the necessary secure isolation between Tenant-A and Tenant-B. The overall physical topology is shown in Figure 9.22. Links 1a to 6a and 11a to 16a are allocated to Tenant-A. Links 1b to 6b and 11b to 16b are allocated to Tenant-B. In addition, the DC LAN is based on a multidomain multilayer vPC design with vPC extended from core to aggregation and from aggregation to access.

Because Tenant-A consists of only internal end-users, the IaaS provider (IT management) of Enterprise "M" would like these users to manage their own DC LAN infrastructure. The IaaS provider will only provision the aggregation-layer and core-layer switches with the minimal configurations. The end-users will then administer these switches themselves and extend on the existing configurations when necessary. Figure 9.23 illustrates the high-level view of the fabric module design for Tenant-A.

The high-level fabric module design for Tenant-A illustrated in Figure 9.23 includes the following:

- Four "logical" Nexus 7010 switches:
  - Core-layer switches: CORE-1A and CORE-2A
  - Aggregation-layer switches: AGG-1A and AGG-2A

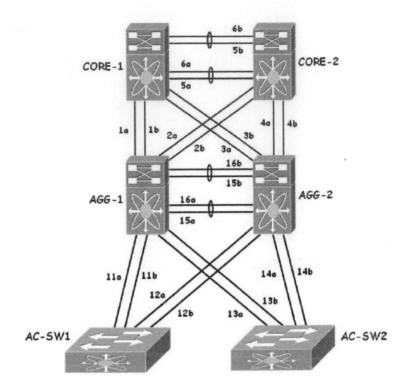

FIGURE 9.22

Fabric module physical topology

- Virtual Device Context (VDC) Tenant-A:
  - On CORE-1A and CORE-2A
  - On AGG-1A and AGG-2A
- VDC Tenant-A basically partitions out four more autonomous logical switches from the four existing physical switches so that Tenant-A can directly administer these switches:
  - CORE-1A is derived from physical switch CORE-1. It runs as an independent logical entity within CORE-1.
  - CORE-2A is derived from physical switch CORE-2. It runs as an independent logical entity within CORE-2.
  - AGG-1A is derived from physical switch AGG-1. It runs as an independent logical entity within AGG-1.
  - AGG-2A is derived from physical switch AGG-2. It runs as an independent logical entity within AGG-2.
- CORE-1A and CORE-2A vPC configurations:
  - In VPC Domain 101.
  - Peer link PortChannel 1002 for the two links (5a and 6a) between CORE-1A and CORE-2A.
  - VPC 100 (PortChannel 100) on CORE-1A and CORE-2A for the two uplinks (1a and 2a) from AGG-1A.

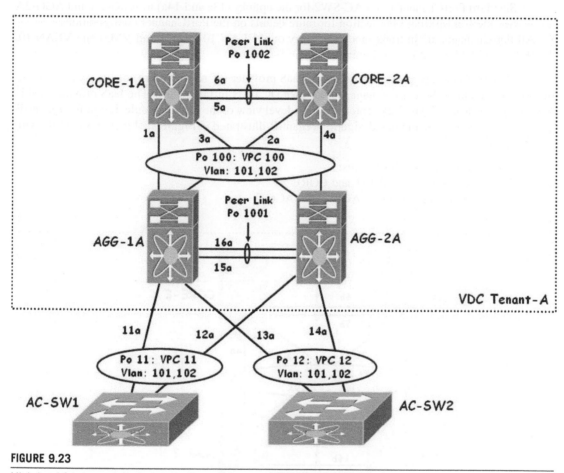

FIGURE 9.23

High-level fabric module design for Tenant-A

- VPC 100 (PortChannel 100) on CORE-1A and CORE-2A for the two uplinks (3a and 4a) from AGG-2A. For more details on the vPC configurations, see the Basic vPC Configurations section.
- AGG-1A and AGG-2A vPC configurations:
  - In VPC Domain 102.
  - VPC 100 (PortChannel 100) on AGG-1A for the uplinks (1a and 2a) to CORE-1A and CORE-2A.
  - VPC 100 (PortChannel 100) on AGG-2A for the uplinks (3a and 4a) to CORE-1A and CORE-2A.
  - Peer link PortChannel 1001 for the two links (15a and 16a) between AGG-1A and AGG-2A.
  - VPC 11 (PortChannel 11) on AGG-1A and AGG-2A for the two uplinks (11a and 12a) from AC-SW1.
  - VPC 12 (PortChannel 12) on AGG-1A and AGG-2A for the two uplinks (13a and 14a) from AC-SW2. For more details on the vPC configurations, see the Basic vPC Configurations section.
- AC-SW1 and AC-SW2 PortChannel configurations:
  - Standard PortChannel 11 on AC-SW1 for the uplinks (11a and 12a) to AGG-1A and AGG-2A.

- Standard PortChannel 12 on AC-SW2 for the uplinks (13a and 14a) to AGG-1A and AGG-2A. See the Configuring vPC section for more details on the PortChannel configurations.
- All PortChannels are in trunk mode and carry only VLAN 101 (VM1 and VM5) and VLAN 102 (VM2 and VM6) traffic (see Figure 9.18).

As Tenant-B belongs to external users, the IaaS provider (IT management) of Enterprise "M" has decided not to allow these users manage their own DC LAN infrastructure. The IaaS provider will be managing it instead. Figure 9.24 depicts the high-level view of the fabric module design for Tenant-B.

The high-level fabric module design for Tenant-B illustrated in Figure 9.24 includes the following components:

- Four physical Nexus 7010 switches:
  - Core-layer switches: CORE-1 and CORE-2
  - Aggregation-layer switches: AGG-1 and AGG-2

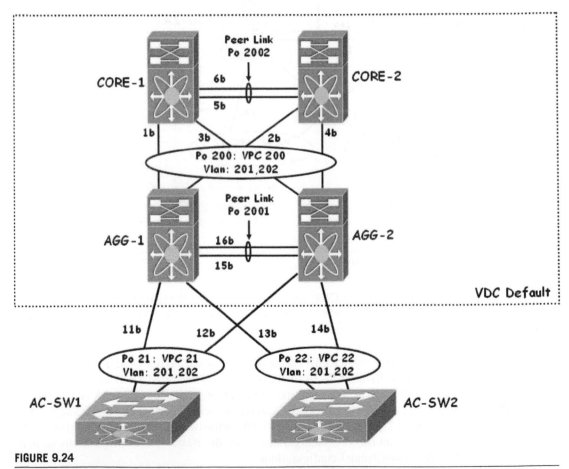

FIGURE 9.24

High-level fabric module design for Tenant-B

- The physical Nexus 7010 switch always has one VDC, the default VDC. In this design, all four switches are in the default VDC.
- As the physical switch itself and all VDCs are managed from the default VDC, there is a need to further segregate the default VDC virtually. This is achieved through VRF associations (for instance, using VRF-B) on L3 interfaces (or switch virtual interfaces) in CORE-1 and CORE-2 specific to Tenant-B. For more details, see the WAN Module High-Level Design section.

NOTE:

At the time of this writing, the Nexus 7000 Series switch supports only a maximum of four virtual device contexts (VDCs), including the default VDC. Enterprise "M" has no intention to exhaust all these VDCs but instead choses to use VRFs in Tenant-B's case for the logical segregation at L3.

- CORE-1 and CORE-2 vPC configurations:
  - In VPC Domain 201.
  - Peer link PortChannel 2002 for the two links (5b and 6b) between CORE-1 and CORE-2.
  - VPC 200 (PortChannel 200) on CORE-1 and CORE-2 for the two uplinks (1b and 2b) from AGG-1.
  - VPC 200 (PortChannel 200) on CORE-1 and CORE-2 for the two uplinks (3b and 4b) from AGG-2. For more details on the vPC configurations, see the Basic vPC Configurations section.
- AGG-1 and AGG-2 vPC configurations:
  - In VPC Domain 202.
  - VPC 200 (PortChannel 200) on AGG-1 for the uplinks (1b and 2b) to CORE-1 and CORE-2.
  - VPC 200 (PortChannel 200) on AGG-2 for the uplinks (3b and 4b) to CORE-1 and CORE-2.
  - Peer link PortChannel 2001 for the two links (15b and 16b) between AGG-1 and AGG-2.
  - VPC 21 (PortChannel 21) on AGG-1 and AGG-2 for the two uplinks (11b and 12b) from AC-SW1.
  - VPC 22 (PortChannel 22) on AGG-1 and AGG-2 for the two uplinks (13b and 14b) from AC-SW2. For more details on the vPC configurations, see the Basic vPC Configurations section.
- AC-SW1 and AC-SW2 PortChannel configurations:
  - Standard PortChannel 21 on AC-SW1 for the uplinks (11b and 12b) to AGG-1 and AGG-2.
  - Standard PortChannel 22 on AC-SW2 for the uplinks (13b and 14b) to AGG-1 and AGG-2. See the Configuring vPC section for more details on the PortChannel configurations.
- All PortChannels are in trunk mode and carry only VLAN 201 (VM3 and VM4) and VLAN 202 (VM7 and VM8) traffic (see Figure 9.18).

Services aggregation layer high-level design

In the design study, the L3 design begins at the core layer, which is also where L2 terminates. The services aggregation layer is built right below the core layer, adjacent to the aggregation layer. Figure 9.25 depicts the high-level view of the services aggregation-layer design and its overall physical topology.

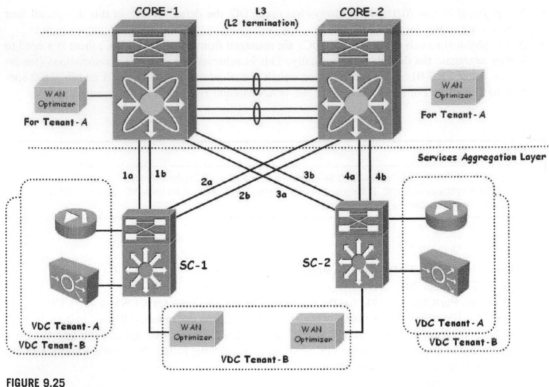

FIGURE 9.25

High-level services aggregation-layer design

The high-level services aggregation-layer design illustrated in Figure 9.25 has the following components:

- Two Cat6K service chassis: SC-1 and SC-2. Each comes with a Firewall Services Module (FWSM) and an Application Control Engine Service Module (ACESM). SC-1 and SC-2 are managed by the IaaS provider.
- Two VDCs are created on both the FWSM and ACESM:
  - VDC Tenant-A.
  - VDC Tenant-B.
  - Thus there are now separate "logical instances" of the FWSM and ACESM specifically assigned to each VDC or tenant.
  - For HA purposes, pairs of each FWSM and ACESM are allocated to each tenant.
  - The IaaS provider will only provision these FWSM and ACESM VDCs with the minimal configurations. The tenants will have to administer these VDCs themselves, and extend on the existing configurations (including HA configurations) when necessary. The tenants will also have to decide whether to use transparent mode or routed mode for the FWSM and ACESM VDCs.
- The FWSM VDCs provide the required base security for the respective tenants.

- The ACESM VDC for Tenant-A is used for server load balancing on APP1 service chain (VM1 and VM5) and on APP2 service chain (VM2 and VM6).
- The ACESM VDC for Tenant-B is used for traffic interception and redirection pertaining to WAN optimization.
- Four uplinks (in trunk mode) on SC-1:
  - Uplinks 1a and 2a are allocated to VDC Tenant-A.
  - Uplinks 1b and 2b are allocated to VDC Tenant-B.
  - If vPCs are configured for these pairs of links at the core-layer switches, configure the corresponding PortChannels.
- Four uplinks (in trunk mode) on SC-2:
  - Uplinks 3a and 4a are allocated to VDC Tenant-A.
  - Uplinks 3b and 4b are allocated to VDC Tenant-B.
  - If vPCs are configured for these pairs of links at the core-layer switches, configure the corresponding PortChannels.
- Two pairs of WAN optimizers (Riverbed Virtual Steelhead appliances VSH-2050-H):
  - CORE-1 and CORE-2 each have an attached WAN optimizer for optimizing APP1 and APP2 traffic of Tenant-A (see Figure 9.18). In this case, the interception and redirection functions are performed by WCCPv2 running within the VDC for Tenant-A on the core-layer switches (CORE-1A and CORE-2A).
  - SC-1 and SC-2 each have an attached WAN optimizer for optimizing APP1 to APP4 traffic of Tenant-B (see Figure 9.18). In this case, the interception and redirection functions are performed by the ACESM VDC for Tenant-B.
  - Tenant-A uses WCCPv2 for traffic interception because they have control over the core-layer switches (CORE-1A and CORE-2A), which supports WCCPv2. For more details on configuring WCCPv2 in the NX7K switches (CORE-1A and CORE-2A), see the Cloud Interception with VRF-Aware WCCP section in Chapter 6.
  - Tenant-B uses the ACESM VDC for traffic interception instead of WCCPv2 because they do not have control over the core-layer switches. For more details on configuring ACESM VDC and traffic interception, see the Interception at the Services Aggregation Layer section in Chapter 6.
  - The pair of WAN optimizers that is allocated to each tenant, logically forms a WAN optimizer cluster for HA/resiliency purposes.
  - In the design, the WAN optimizers are virtual appliances running on VMs over UCS or generic servers. They can be physical appliances as well. However, virtual appliances are easier to provision and have better scalability as compared to physical appliances in the context of cloud IaaS.
  - The IaaS provider will only provision these WAN optimizers with the minimal configurations. The tenants will have to administer their respective pair of WAN optimizers themselves and extend on the existing configurations (including HA configurations) when necessary. The tenants will also have to configure the respective interception mechanisms (WCCPv2 for Tenant-A and ACESM for Tenant-B) to redirect the correct application traffic flows (APP1 to APP2 for Tenant-A and APP1 to APP4 for Tenant-B) for optimization.

NOTE:

Although VRF-aware WCCPv2 is supported on the Nexus 7000 switches, it is not required in the design because a specific VDC on the core-layer switches has already been allocated to Tenant-A. In other words, the WCCPv2 configuration for Tenant-A on the core-layer switches, CORE-1A and CORE-2A, can revert to the usual global IPv4 address space.

- HSRP setup:
  - Tenant-A will have to configure CORE-1A as the active HSRP peer and CORE-2A as the standby HSRP peer.
  - The IaaS provider has configured CORE-1 as the active HSRP peer and CORE-2 as the standby HSRP peer for Tenant-B.
- Network Analysis Module (NAM) and Intrusion Detection System Services Module (IDSM-2) on SC-1 and SC-2 (not shown in diagram for brevity):
  - Implement ERSPAN source sessions on the NX1KV switches in the virtual access layer (see Figure 9.18). The ERSPAN source sessions GRE-encapsulate and forward mirrored traffic (from VLANs 101, 102, 201, and 202) to corresponding ERSPAN destination sessions on SC-1 and SC-2. The ERSPAN destination sessions perform GRE-decapsulation and forward the mirrored traffic to the respective NAMs and IDSMs. For more details on the ERSPAN configurations, see the ERSPAN Design Study section.
  - In this example, the NAM and IDSM are used by the IaaS provider for internal auditing and security monitoring. They are transparent to the tenants.

WAN module high-level design

The WAN module extends what we have designed thus far over the WAN to the remote branch offices (RBOs) of Tenant-A and Tenant-B. At this point in time, remote access through the Internet for Tenant-A and Tenant-B mobile users is not a top priority. Therefore, this is not included in this design study. The primary urgency from the IaaS provider (IT management) of Enterprise "M" is to ensure that the service-oriented infrastructure (SOI) is ready for the cloud IaaS trial launch on the two remote branch sites. Figure 9.26 depicts the high-level view of the WAN module design that comprises the peering layer and the next-generation (next-gen) WAN layer.

The high-level WAN module design illustrated in Figure 9.26 has the following components:

- Four Cisco 7600 Series routers at the enterprise DC:
  - DC-PE1 and DC-PE2 that form the peering layer.
  - DC-P1 and DC-P2 that form the DMVPN hub (head-end) routers.
- Three Cisco 2821 ISRs at the tenant RBOs:
  - TA-PE1 and TA-PE2 at Tenant-A RBO.
  - TB-PE1 at Tenant-B RBO.
  - These branch routers are provisioned and managed by the IaaS provider.
- Hub-and-spoke DMVPN configurations:

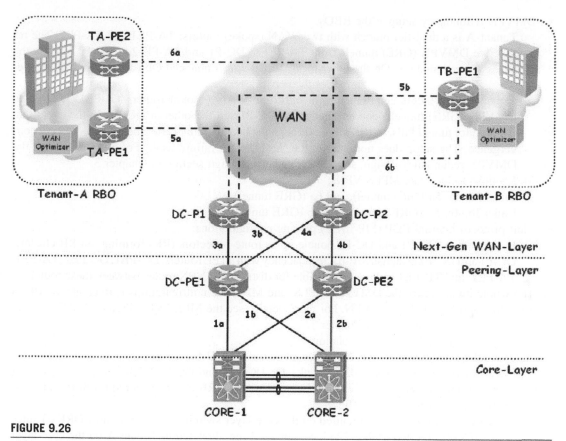

FIGURE 9.26

High-level WAN module design

- DC-P1 and DC-P2 are the DMVPN hub routers. DC-P1 is the primary hub and DC-P2 is the backup.
- TA-PE1, TA-PE2, and TB-PE1 are the spoke routers.
- Links 5a and 5b from DC-P1 to TA-PE1 and TB-PE1, respectively, are the primary (active) GRE tunnels.
- Links 6a and 6b from DC-P2 to TA-PE2 and TB-PE1, respectively, are the backup (standby) GRE tunnels.
- IPSec is enabled for these GRE tunnels.
- In the design, the GRE tunnels are maintained in active/standby state by controlling the route metrics. This reduces the load on the spoke routers, allows the hub routers to be better engineered for steady-state performance, and provides a more deterministic traffic path behavior. For more details on the DMVPN configurations, see the DMVPN Overview and the MPLS VPN over DMVPN sections in Chapter 3.

- DMVPN redundancy setup at the RBOs:
  - Tenant-A is a dual-tier branch with two WAN (spoke) routers: TA-PE1 and TA-PE2. The respective DMVPN (GRE) tunnels from TA-PE1 to DC-P1 and TA-PE-2 to DC-P2 provide the necessary redundancy. On the other hand, HSRP with Enhanced Object Tracking (EOT) between TA-PE1 and TA-PE2 provides the network resiliency for the end-users in this branch.
  - Tenant-B is a single-tier branch with only one WAN (spoke) router, TB-PE1. It has two DMVPN (GRE) tunnels, one terminating at DC-P1 and the other at DC-P2. In the event that the primary tunnel fails, traffic will go through the backup tunnel after the routing protocol convergence. The setup does not cater to the WAN router failure itself. For more details on the DMVPN redundancy design, see the Redundancy Design section in Chapter 3.
- MPLS links to facilitate MPLS VPNs:
  - Links 3a, 4a, 5a (GRE tunnel), and 6a (GRE tunnel)
  - Links 3b, 4b, 5b (GRE tunnel), and 6b (GRE tunnel)
- Multiprotocol internal BGP (MP-iBGP) peering configurations:
  - In the design, DC-P1 and DC-P2 double up as route-reflectors (RR) forming an RR cluster.
  - DC-P1 and DC-P2 establish MP-iBGP adjacency with all PE routers, DC-PE1, DC-PE2, TA-PE1, TA-PE2, and TB-PE1 and are responsible for distributing VPN routes between these routers.
- The whole intention for the DMVPN, MPLS, and MP-iBGP configurations is to create an MPLS VPN for each tenant over DMVPN. For more details, see the MPLS VPN Prelude and the MPLS VPN over DMVPN sections in Chapter 3.
- VRF configurations for L3 path isolation:
  - Two VRFs are created: VRF-A for Tenant-A and VRF-B for Tenant-B.
  - Links 1a, 1b, 2a, and 2b are 802.1q trunks. On DC-PE1 and DC-PE2, VRF-A is configured for those subinterfaces carrying Tenant-A's traffic, while VRF-B is configured for those subinterfaces carrying Tenant-B's traffic.
  - No VRF-A configuration is required on the core-layer switches (CORE-1 and CORE-2) since VDCs (CORE-1A and CORE-2A) have already been allocated to Tenant-A on the core-layer switches. For more details, see the Fabric Module High-Level Design section.
  - VRF-B needs to be configured on CORE-1 and CORE-2 for Tenant-B. In this case, the core-layer switches are essentially acting as multi-VRF routers.
  - Over at the RBOs, only VRF-A needs to be configured on TA-PE1 and TA-PE2. Likewise, only VRF-B is required on TB-PE1.
- Last but not least, a WAN optimizer (Riverbed Steelhead appliance SH-1050-H) is leased by the IaaS provider to each tenant at their respective RBOs. In this case, the tenants will have to decide on the appropriate placement of the WAN optimizer and configure the relevant traffic interception and redirection mechanisms themselves.

Design comments

It is always a challenge to achieve a perfect "10" design. A good design is often subject to different requirements from the technical and nontechnical perspectives. These design studies attempt to do both. On the one hand, we want to avoid bombardment with bothersome details. On the other, we want to make the design comprehensive and concise. A high-level design helps you to grasp the overall cloud IaaS design strategy.

We started with the virtual access layer, which happens to be the initial stage of virtualization, and worked our way through the compute submodule, the storage module, the fabric module, the services aggregation layer, and, finally, all the way to the remote branches with the WAN module.

All these should help you fathom the fundamental concepts toward building a successful service-oriented infrastructure (SOI) for cloud IaaS provisioning.

SUMMARY

In this chapter, there is a series of design studies to ensure that you have exposure to the consolidation techniques, the virtualization strategies, and the construction of the SOI, leading to the deployment of private cloud computing and the provisioning of cloud IaaS offerings.

The first design study involves the virtual access layer as it happens to be the front-end of server virtualization. Next, ERSPAN is briefly covered to gain visibility into network flows that are obscured by the virtual access layer. A simple WAN optimization study is covered next. This is followed by a unified fabric design study that illustrates the unification of the DC LAN and DC SAN with FCoE at the physical access layer. We then move on to examine the ToR architecture as an enabler toward a "rack-and-roll" server deployment model, vPC as an enhancement to STP, and FCIP as a robust SAN extension technique over the WAN. The final design study is the grand finale where all the bits and pieces that have been covered are now assembled together as the big picture (or the overall map) for the construction of the SOI, so that cloud IaaS can be provisioned over it.

Our private cloud computing journey has finally come to an end. Before closing, we would like to thank you for enduring this long and occasionally rough voyage with us. We hope that what has been covered in this book will be useful in your upcoming cloud computing technical pursuits.

The end *is always a* new beginning.
—**Captain Cloud in *Get Crazy***

Acronyms and Abbreviations

1GE	1 Gigabit Ethernet
10GE	10 Gigabit Ethernet
AAA	Authentication, Authorization and Accounting
ACE	Application Control Engine
ACESM	Application Control Engine Service Module
ACK	Acknowledge
ACL	Access Control List
ACN	Assignment Change Number
ADM	Add/Drop Multiplexer
AH	Additional Header
AHS	Additional Header Segment
AFID	Autonomous Fabric ID
ANSI	American National Standards Institute
API	Application Programming Interface
APP	Application
ARP	Address Resolution Protocol
AS	Autonomous System
ASIC	Application Specific Integrated Circuit
ASLR	Address Space Layout Randomization
ASR1K	ASR 1000 Router
ATM	Asynchronous Transfer Mode
B2B	Buffer-to-Buffer
BA	Bridge Assurance
BB_Credit	Buffer-to-Buffer Credit
BC	Business Continuity
BF	Build Fabric
BGP	Border Gateway Protocol
BH	Basic Header
BIOS	Basic Input/Output System
BLSR	Bidirectional Line Switch Ring
BPDU	Bridge Protocol Data Unit
BVI	Bridge-group Virtual Interface
BW	Bandwidth

C	Customer
CAPEX	Capital Expenditures
CAST	Alyssa P Hacker and Ben Bitdiddle
Cat6K	Catalyst 6500
CDB	Command Descriptor Block
CDP	Cisco Discovery Protocol
CE	Customer Edge
CEF	Cisco Express Forwarding
CFS	Cisco Fabric Services
CHAP	Challenge Handshake Authentication Protocol
CIA	Confidentiality, Integrity, and Availability
CIFS	Common Internet File System
CIMP	Cloud Infrastructure Management Platform
CLI	Command Line Interface
CN	Change Number
CNA	Converged Network Adapter
CP	Congestion Point
CPP	Control Path Processor
CPU	Central Processing Unit
CRC	Cyclic Redundancy Check
CsC	Carrier support Carrier
CUG	Closed User Group
CWDM	Course Wavelength Division Multiplexing
CWM	Congestion Window Monitoring
CoS	Class of Service
D_ID	Destination ID
DAI	Dynamic ARP Inspection
DAS	Direct Attached Storage
DC	Data Center
DCB	Data Center Bridging
DCBX	Data Center Bridging Exchange
DCNM	Data Center Network Manager
DCU	Dispersion Compensation Unit
DDR3	Double-Data-Rate 3
DH-CHAP	Diffie Hellman Challenge Handshake Authentication Protocol
DHCP	Dynamic Host Control Protocol
DiffServ	Differentiated Services
DIMM	Dual Inline Memory Module
DMVPN	Dynamic Multipoint Virtual Private Network
DMZ	Demilitarized Zone
DoS	Denial-of-Service
DPC	Data Path Controller
DPI	Deep Packet Inspection

DR	Disaster Recovery
DSCP	Differentiated Services Code Point
DST_VIF	Destination Virtual Interface Identifier
DVS	Distributed Virtual Switch
DWDM	Dense Wavelength Division Multiplexing
DWRR	Deficit Weighted Round Robin
E2E	End-to-End
E-CE	Enterprise Customer Edge
E-PE	Enterprise Provider Edge
E_Port	Expansion Port
EDFA	Erbium-Doped Fibre Amplifier
ELP	Exchange Link Parameters
ENode	End Node
EOF	End-of-Frame
EOT	Enhanced Object Tracking
ERSPAN	Encapsulated Remote Switched Port Analyzer
ESC	Exchange Switch Capabilities
ESCON	Enterprise System Connection
Eth	Ethernet
ETS	Enhanced Transmission Selection
ETSI	European Telecommunications Standards Institute
EUI	Extended Unique Identifier
F_Port	Fabric Port
FAIS	Fabric Application Interface Standard
FC	Fibre Channel
FC-BB	Fibre Channel Backbone
FC-SP	Fibre Channel Security Protocols
FCC	Fibre Channel Congestion Control
FCF	FCoE Forwarder
FCIP	Fibre Channel over IP
FCIP_DE	FCIP Data Engine
FCIP_LEP	FCIP Link End Point
FCNS	Fibre Channel Name Server
FCP	FC Protocol
FCS	Frame Check Sequence
FCoE	Fibre Channel over Ethernet
FCoE_LEP	FCoE Link End Point
FC_ID	Fibre Channel Identifier
FC-MAP	FCoE MAC Address Prefix
FDISC	Discover Fabric Service Parameters
FEC	Forwarding Equivalence Class
FEX	Fabric Extender
FICON	Fibre Connection

FIP	FCoE Initialization Protocol
FLOGI	Fabric Login
FM	Fabric Manager
FPMA	Fabric Provided MAC Address
FQDN	Fully Qualified Domain Name
FSF	FCIP Special Frames
FSPF	Fabric Shortest Path First
FTP	File Transfer Protocol
FWSM	Firewall Service Module
GBIC	Gigabit Interface Converter
Gbps	Gigabits per second
GE	Gigabit Ethernet
GFP	Generic Framing Procedure
GLBP	Gateway Load Balancing Protocol
GRE	Generic Routing Encapsulation
GUI	Graphical User Interface
HA	High Availability
HAL	Hardware Abstraction Layer
HBA	Host Bus Adapter
HBH	Hop-By-Hop
HIA	Here_I_Am
HOL	Head-Of-Line
HSRP	Hot Standby Router Protocol
HTML	Hypertext Markup Language
HTTP	Hypertext Transfer Protocol
HTTPS	Hypertext Transfer Protocol Secure
IaaS	Infrastructure-as-a-Service
ICMP	Internet Control Message Protocol
ID	Identifier
IETF	Internet Engineering Task Force
iFCP	Internet Fibre Channel Protocol
IFT	Isolated Fabric Topology
IGMP	Internet Group Management Protocol
IGP	Interior Gateway Protocol
IKE	Internet Key Exchange
INCITS	International Committee for Information Technology Standards
I/O	Input/Output
IP	Internet Protocol
IPC	Inter Processor Communication
IPPCP	IP Payload Compression
IPS	Intrusion Protection System
IPSec	Internet Protocol Security
IQN	iSCSI Qualified Name

IRB	Integrated Routing and Bridging
iSCSI	Internet Small Computer System Interface
ISL	Inter-Switch Link
ISO	International Organization for Standardization
ISR	Integrated Services Router
IS-IS	Intermediate System to Intermediate System
iSNS	Internet Storage Name Service
ISU	I_See_You
IT	Information Technology
ITU	International Telecommunication Union
ITU-T	ITU Telecommunication Standardization Sector
IVR	Inter-VSAN Routing
JBOD	Just a Bunch of Disks
JPEG	Joint Photographic Experts Group
L1	Layer 1
L2	Layer 2
L2MP	L2 Multi-Path
L2TPv3	Layer 2 Tunneling Protocol version 3
L3	Layer 3
LACP	Link Aggregation Control Protocol
LAN	Local Area Network
LB	Load-Balancing
LBA	Logical Block Address
LCAS	Link Capacity Adjustment Scheme
LDP	Label Distribution Protocol
LER	Label Edge Router
LSP	Label Switched Path
LSR	Label Switch Router
LU	Logical Unit
LUN	Logical Unit Number
LZ	Lempel-Ziv
LZS	Lempel-Ziv-Stac
MAC	Media Access Control
MAC-DA	MAC Destination Address
MAC-SA	MAC Source Address
MAN	Metro Area Network
MAPI	Messaging Application Programming Interface
MCN	Membership Change Number
MEC	Multichassis EtherChannel
mGRE	Multipoint GRE
MITM	Man-In-The-Middle
MP-BGP	Multiprotocol BGP
MP-eBGP	Multiprotocol external BGP

MP-iBGP	Multiprotocol internal BGP
MPLS	Multiprotocol Label Switching
MSFC	Multilayer Switch Feature Card
MTU	Maximum Transmission Unit
MWS	Maximum Window Size
N_Port	Node Port
NAA	Network Address Authority
NAM	Network Analysis Module
NBAR	Network Based Application Recognition
NAS	Network-Attached Storage
NAT	Network Address Translation
NFS	Network File System
NHRP	Next Hop Resolution Protocol
NIC	Network Interface Card
NIST	National Institute of Standards and Technology
NOC	Network Operations Center
NPIV	N_Port ID Virtualization
NP_Port	Proxy N_Port
NSV	Not-So-VRF
nWWN	Node World Wide Name
NX	No Execute
NX1KV	Nexus 1000V
NX2K	Nexus 2000
NX5K	Nexus 5000
NX7K	Nexus 7000
N_Port	Node Port
OADM	Optical Add Drop Multiplexer
OAM&P	Operations, Administration, Maintenance and Provisioning
OC	Optical Carrier
OPEX	Operation Expenditures
OS	Operating System
OSPF	Open Shortest Path First
OUI	Organization Unique Identifier
OVF	Open Virtualization Format
OX_ID	Originator Exchange ID
P2P	Point-to-Point
P	Provider
PaaS	Platform-as-a-Service
PBR	Policy-based Routing
PC	Personal Computer
PDAs	Personal Digital Assistant
PDP	Policy Decision Point
PDU	Protocol Data Unit

PE	Provider Edge
PEP	Policy Enforcement Point
PE_Port	Physical E_Port
PFC	Priority-based Flow Control
PFC3	Policy Feature Card 3
PF_Port	Physical F_Port
PG	Priority Group
PGID	Priority Group ID
PLM	Product Lifecycle Management
PMTU	Path MTU
PMTUD	Path MTU Discovery
PNG	Portable Network Graphics
PN_Port	Physical N_Port
Po	Port Channel
POI	Point-of-Interception
PPMN	Path-Protected Mesh Network
PPRC	Peer-to-Peer Remote Copy
PVLAN	Private VLAN
pWWN	Port World Wide Name
QoS	Quality of Service
QCN	Quantized Congestion Notification
R2T	Ready to Transfer
R_RDY	Receiver Ready
R_T_TOV	Receiver Transmitter Time-Out Value
RA	Redirect_Assign
RAID	Redundant Array of Independent Disks
RAM	Random Access Memory
RAS	Reliability, Availability and Serviceability
RBO	Remote Branch Office
RCF	Reconfigure Fabric
RD	Route Distinguisher
RDBMS	Relational Database Management System
RDM	Raw Device Mapping
RDP	Remote Desktop Protocol
RIPv2	Routing Information Protocol version 2
RP	Reaction Point
RPO	Recovery Point Objective
RQ	Removal_Query
RR	Route Reflector
RU	Rack Unit
RSP	Response
RTO	Recovery Time Objective
RTT	Round-Trip Time

RX_ID	Responder Exchange ID
S_ID	Source ID
SaaS	Software-as-a-Service
SACK	Selective Acknowledgment
SAN	Storage Area Network
SCSI	Small Computer System Interface
SDH	Synchronous Digital Hierarchy
SDR	Scalable Data Referencing
SFP	Small Form-Factor Pluggable
SG	Service Group
SLA	Service Level Agreement
SLB	Server Load-Balancer
SLPv2	Service Location Protocol version 2
SMB	Small to Medium Business
SME	Small and Medium Enterprise
SNIA	Storage Networking Industry Association
SOAP	Simple Object Access Protocol
SOF	Start-of-Frame
SOI	Service-Oriented Infrastructure
SONET	Synchronous Optical Networking
SP	Service Provider
SPAN	Switched Port Analyzer
SPKM	Simple Public Key Mechanism
SPMA	Server Provided MAC Address
SRC_VIF	Source Virtual Interface Identifier
SRDF	Symmetrix Remote Data Facility
SRP	Secure Remote Password
SSH	Secure Shell
SSO	Stateful Switchover
STP	Spanning Tree Protocol
SVI	Switch Virtual Interface
SW_ILS	Switch Internal Link Services
TCO	Total Cost of Ownership
TFO	Transport Flow Optimization
TCP	Transmission Control Protocol
TDM	Time-Division Multiplexing
TLV	Type-Length-Value
TMN	Telecommunication Management Network
TOE	TCP Offload Engine
ToR	Top-of-Rack
TPM	Trusted Platform Module
TRILL	Transparent Interconnection of Lots of Links
TXT	Trusted Execution Technology

UCS	Unified Computing System
UCSM	UCS Manager
UFT	Unified Fabric Topology
ULP	Upper Level Protocol
UPSR	Unidirectional Path Switch Ring
URL	Uniform Resource Locator
UUID	Unique User ID
VC	Virtual Circuit
VCAT	Virtual Concatenation
VCI	Virtual Circuit Identifier
VDC	Virtual Device Context
VDI	Virtual Desktop Infrastructure
vDS	vNetwork Distributed Switch
VEM	Virtual Ethernet Module
VE_Port	Virtual E_Port
vEth	Virtual Ethernet
VFC	Virtual Fibre Channel
VF_Port	Virtual F_Port
VIM	Virtual Infrastructure Methodology
VIP	Virtual IP
VLAN	Virtual LAN
VM	Virtual Machine
VMFS	Virtual Machine File System
VMM	Virtual Machine Monitor
VN	Virtual Network
VNTag	Virtual NIC Tag
VN_Port	Virtual N_Port
VOA	Variable Optical Attenuator
vPC	Virtual Port Channel
vPC HM	vPC Host Mode
VPI	Virtual Path Identifier
VPN	Virtual Private Network
VRF	Virtual Routing and Forwarding
VRRP	Virtual Router Redundancy Protocol
VSAN	Virtual SAN
VSB	Virtual Service Blade
VSG	Virtual Security Gateway
VSI	Virtual Storage Infrastructure
VSM	Virtual Supervisor Module
vSS	vNetwork Standard Switch
VSS	Virtual Switching Systems
WAAS	Wide Area Assplication Services
WAN	Wide Area Network

WCCP	Web Cache Communication Protocol
WCCPv2	Web Cache Communication Protocol version 2
WDM	Wavelength Division Multiplexing
WKP	Well-Known Port
WSDL	Web Services Description Language
WWN	World Wide Name
WWW	World Wide Web
XFER_RDY	Transfer Ready
XML	Extensible Markup Language

References

References to other resources in this book are provided here, organized by chapter, in the event that you want to delve more deeply into a subject. In addition, for selected chapters we have provided bibliography for further reading.

Introduction and About the Authors

[1] Smoot, S. R. (1998). Maximizing Perceived Quality Given Bit-Rate Constraints in MPEG Encoding Through Content-Adaptivity. (Doctoral dissertation). University of California at Berkeley (NRLF). (T7.6.1998 S666).
[2] Tan, N. K. (1999). Configuring Cisco Routers for Bridging, DLSw+, and Desktop Protocols. McGraw-Hill.
[3] Tan, N. K. (2003). Building VPNs with IPSec and MPLS. McGraw-Hill Professional.
[4] Tan, N. K. (2004). MPLS for Metropolitan Area Networks. Auerbach Publications.
[5] Thomas, T. M., Aelmans, A., Houniet, F., and Tan, N. K. (2000). Building Scalable Cisco Networks. McGraw-Hill.

Chapter 1

[1] RAID, http://en.wikipedia.org/wiki/RAID.
[2] Cloud Computing - A Primer Part 1, http://www.cisco.com/web/about/ac123/ac147/archived_issues/ipj_12-3/123_cloud1.html.
[3] The NIST Definition of Cloud Computing, http://csrc.nist.gov/groups/SNS/cloud-computing/cloud-def-v15.doc.
[4] CIA Triad, http://en.wikipedia.org/wiki/CIA_triad#Key_concepts.
[5] Sandbox, http://en.wikipedia.org/wiki/Sandbox_(computer_security).

Bibliography

E.G. Nadhan, Service-Oriented Cloud Computing Infrastructure, HP Technology Forum & Expo, 2009.
Energy-Efficient Unified Fabrics: Transform the Data Center Infrastructure with Cisco Nexus Series, http://www.cisco.com/en/US/prod/collateral/switches/ps9441/ps9670/white_paper_c11-508518.pdf.

Chapter 2

[1] AMD-V, http://en.wikipedia.org/wiki/AMD-V#AMD_virtualization_.28AMD-V.29.
[2] Xen, http://en.wikipedia.org/wiki/Xen.
[3] Hyper-V, http://en.wikipedia.org/wiki/Hyper-V.
[4] Virtual Networking Features of the VMware vNetwork Distributed Switch and Cisco Nexus 1000V Switches, http://www.vmware.com/files/pdf/technology/cisco_vmware_virtualizing_the_datacenter.pdf.
[5] NX-OS, http://en.wikipedia.org/wiki/NX-OS.
[6] ISO file, http://en.wikipedia.org/wiki/Iso_file.
[7] Open Virtualization Format, http://en.wikipedia.org/wiki/Open_Virtualization_Format.
[8] Cisco Discovery Protocol, http://en.wikipedia.org/wiki/Cisco_Discovery_Protocol.

[9] Internet Group Management Protocol, http://en.wikipedia.org/wiki/IGMP.

[10] Stateful Switchover, http://www.cisco.com/en/US/docs/ios/12_0s/feature/guide/sso120s.html.

[11] VMware Virtual Infrastructure Methodology, http://www.vmware.com/pdf/vim_datasheet.pdf.

[12] Extensible Markup Language, http://en.wikipedia.org/wiki/XML.

[13] Encapsulated Remote Switched Port Analyzer, http://www.cisco.com/en/US/docs/switches/datacenter/nexus1000/sw/4_2_1_s_v_1_4/system_management/configuration/guide/n1000v_system_9span.html#wp1054701.

[14] Universally Unique Identifier, http://en.wikipedia.org/wiki/Uuid.

[15] Bridge Protocol Data Unit, http://en.wikipedia.org/wiki/BPDU#Bridge_Protocol_Data_Units_.28BPDUs.29.

[16] Logical Block Address, http://en.wikipedia.org/wiki/Logical_block_addressing.

[17] Command Descriptor Block, http://en.wikipedia.org/wiki/SCSI_CDB.

[18] ASIC, http://en.wikipedia.org/wiki/Application-specific_integrated_circuit.

[19] Cisco Storage Services Module, http://www.cisco.com/en/US/prod/collateral/modules/ps5991/ps6293/product_data_sheet0900aecd802496f7_ps5991_Products_Data_Sheet.html.

[20] EMC Invista, http://en.wikipedia.org/wiki/EMC_Invista.

[21] Transparent Interconnect of Lots of Links, http://en.wikipedia.org/wiki/TRILL_(Computer_Networking).

[22] Intermediate System to Intermediate System, http://en.wikipedia.org/wiki/IS-IS.

[23] Bisectional Bandwidth, http://en.wikipedia.org/wiki/Bisection_bandwidth.

[24] Hot Standby Router Protocol, http://en.wikipedia.org/wiki/Hot_Standby_Router_Protocol.

[25] Virtual Routing and Forwarding, http://en.wikipedia.org/wiki/VRF.

[26] Gratuitous ARP, http://en.wikipedia.org/wiki/Address_Resolution_Protocol#ARP_announcements.

[27] Robert W. Kembel, Fibre Channel: A Comprehensive Introduction, Northwest Learning Associates, Inc., December 7, 2009.

[28] Deficit-Weighted Round Robin, http://en.wikipedia.org/wiki/Deficit_Weighted_Round_Robin.

[29] Head-of-Line Blocking, http://en.wikipedia.org/wiki/Head-of-line_blocking.

[30] Cyclic Redundancy Check, http://en.wikipedia.org/wiki/Cyclic_redundancy_check.

Bibliography

Cisco Nexus 1000V Series Switches Deployment Guide, Version 2, http://www.cisco.com/en/US/prod/collateral/switches/ps9441/ps9902/guide_c07-556626.html.

Cisco Service Delivery Center Infrastructure 2.1 Design Guide, http://www.cisco.com/en/US/solutions/ns340/ns394/ns50/net_design_guidance0900aecd806fe4bb.pdf.

Data Center Design with VMware ESX 4.0 and Cisco Nexus 5000 and 1000V Series Switches, http://www.cisco.com/en/US/prod/collateral/switches/ps9441/ps9670/C07-572832-00_VMware_ESX4_Nexus_DG.pdf.

Data Center Bridging, http://www.cisco.com/en/US/solutions/collateral/ns340/ns517/ns224/ns783/at_a_glance_c45-460907.pdf.

Evolving Data Center Architectures: Meet the Challenge with Cisco Nexus 5000 Series Switches, http://www.cisco.com/en/US/solutions/collateral/ns340/ns517/ns224/ns783/white_paper_c11-473501.html.

Deploying 10 Gigabit Ethernet with Cisco Nexus 5000 Series Switches, http://www.cisco.com/en/US/prod/collateral/switches/ps9441/ps9670/white_paper_c27-489248_ns783_Networking_Solutions_White_Paper.html.

Data Center Top-of-Rack Architecture Design, http://www.cisco.com/en/US/prod/collateral/switches/ps9441/ps9670/white_paper_c11-522337.html.

FC-BB-5, http://www.t11.org/ftp/t11/pub/fc/bb-5/09-056v5.pdf.

S. Gai, C. DeSanti, I/O Consolidation in the Data Center, Cisco Press, September 18, 2009.

An Introduction to Fibre Channel over Ethernet, and Fibre Channel over Convergence Enhanced Ethernet, http://www.redbooks.ibm.com/redpapers/pdfs/redp4493.pdf.

R.W. Kembel, Fibre Channel over Ethernet (FCoE), Northwest Learning Associates, Inc., January 1, 2010.

Additional Bibliography for Chapter 2

VMware Infrastructure 3 in a Cisco Network Environment, http://www.cisco.com/application/pdf/en/us/guest/netsol/ns304/c649/ccmigration_09186a00807a15d0.pdf.

Cisco Nexus 1000V System Management Configuration Guide, http://www.cisco.com/en/US/docs/switches/datacenter/nexus1000/sw/4_2_1_s_v_1_4/system_management/configuration/guide/n1000v_system.html.

Cisco Nexus 1000V High Availability and Redundancy Configuration Guide, http://www.cisco.com/en/US/docs/switches/datacenter/nexus1000/sw/4_2_1_s_v_1_4/high_availability/configuration/guide/n1000v_ha_cfg.html.

Designing Cisco Storage Networking Solutions (DCSNS), v3.0, Student Courseware, Cisco Training.

Chapter 3

[1] Closed User Group, http://en.wikipedia.org/wiki/Closed_User_Group_(CUG).
[2] Virtual Private Network, http://en.wikipedia.org/wiki/Vpn.
[3] Routing Information Protocol, Version 2, http://en.wikipedia.org/wiki/RIPv2.
[4] Open Shortest Path First, http://en.wikipedia.org/wiki/Ospf.
[5] Border Gateway Protocol, http://en.wikipedia.org/wiki/Bgp.
[6] Generic Routing Encapsulation, http://en.wikipedia.org/wiki/Generic_Routing_Encapsulation.
[7] Time-Division Multiplexing, http://en.wikipedia.org/wiki/Time-division_multiplexing.
[8] Asynchronous Transfer Mode, http://en.wikipedia.org/wiki/Asynchronous_Transfer_Mode.
[9] Synchronous Optical Networking, http://en.wikipedia.org/wiki/Synchronous_optical_networking.
[10] Multiprotocol Label Switching, http://en.wikipedia.org/wiki/Multiprotocol_Label_Switching.
[11] Dynamic Multipoint Virtual Private Network, http://en.wikipedia.org/wiki/Dmvpn.
[12] Carrier Supporting Carrier, http://www.cisco.com/en/US/docs/ios/12_0st/12_0st14/feature/guide/csc.html.
[13] Layer 2 Tunneling Protocol Version 3, http://en.wikipedia.org/wiki/L2TPv3.
[14] Label Distribution Protocol, http://en.wikipedia.org/wiki/Label_Distribution_Protocol.
[15] Multiprotocol Extensions for BGP-4, http://tools.ietf.org/html/rfc4760.
[16] Internet Protocol Security, http://en.wikipedia.org/wiki/Ipsec.
[17] Internet Key Exchange, http://en.wikipedia.org/wiki/Internet_Key_Exchange.
[18] Virtual Router Redundancy Protocol, http://en.wikipedia.org/wiki/Vrrp.
[19] Gateway Load Balancing Protocol, http://en.wikipedia.org/wiki/GLBP.
[20] Enhanced Object Tracking, http://www.cisco.com/en/US/docs/ios/12_2t/12_2t15/feature/guide/fthsrptk.html.

Bibliography

Data Center Service Integration: Service Chassis Design Guide, http://www.cisco.com/en/US/docs/solutions/Enterprise/Data_Center/dc_servchas/service-chassis_design.html.

V. Moreno, K. Reddy, Network Virtualization, Cisco Press, July 29, 2006.

Network Virtualization—Path Isolation Design Guide, http://www.cisco.com/en/US/docs/solutions/Enterprise/Network_Virtualization/PathIsol.html.

Next-Generation Enterprise MPLS, VPN-Based WAN Design and Implementation Guide, http://www.cisco.com/en/US/docs/solutions/Enterprise/WAN_and_MAN/ngwane.pdf.

Service Module Design with ACE and FWSM, http://www.cisco.com/application/pdf/en/us/guest/netsol/ns376/c649/ccmigration_09186a008078de90.pdf.

Designing Cisco Network Service Architectures (ARCH), v2.0, Student Courseware, Cisco Training.

Chapter 4

[1] V. Jacobson, R. Braden, TCP extensions for long-delay paths, IETF RFC 1323, http://www.ietf.org/rfc/rfc1072.txt, 1988.

[2] M. Mathis, J. Semke, J. Mahdavi, T. Ott, Macroscopic behavior of the TCP congestion avoidance algorithm, Computer Commun. Rev. 27 (1977) 67–82.

[3] J. Ziv, A. Lempel, Compression of Individual Sequences via Variable-Rate Coding, IEEE Transactions on Information Theory (1978).

[4] Squid Configuration Directives, http://www.squid-cache.org/Doc/config/.

[5] Microsoft® Exchange 2010®/Outlook 2010 Performance with Riverbed® WAN Optimization, Riverbed White Paper (2011).

[6] V. Jacobson, M. Karels, Congestion Avoidance and Control, Proc. Sigcomm '88 Symp 18 (4) (1988) 314–329.

[7] S. Floyd, HighSpeed TCP for Large Congestion Windows, IETF RFC 3649, (2003), http://www.ietf.org/rfc/rfc3649.txt.

[8] S. Floyd, Limited Slow-Start for TCP with Large Congestion Windows, IETF RFC 3742, (2003), http://www.ietf.org/rfc/rfc3742.txt.

[9] High-Speed TCP for Long Fat Networks, Riverbed White Paper (2010).

[10] Citrix Branch Repeater VPX 5.6, Citrix Product Manual, http://support.citrix.com/product/brrepeat/vVPX5.6/#tab-docCitrix.

[11] Cisco Wide Area Application Services Configuration Guide, Cisco Product Guide, http://www.cisco.com/en/US/docs/app_ntwk_services/waas/waas/v401/configuration/guide/intro.html.

[12] Riverbed Cloud Services Deployment Guide, Riverbed Product Manual, http://support.riverbed.com, 2001.

Chapter 5

Bibliography

BRKAPP-2021, Deploying and Troubleshooting Web Cache Communication Protocol (WCCP) for WAN Acceleration, Security and Content Delivery, Cisco Live 2010 Presentation.

Cisco WAAS Deployment Using Web Cache Communication Protocol, version 2 (WCCPv2), Cisco Public White Paper.

Configuring WCCP, http://www.cisco.com/en/US/partner/docs/ios/ipapp/configuration/guide/ipapp_wccp_ps6441_TSD_Products_Configuration_Guide_Chapter.html.

PBR Support for Multiple Tracking Options, http://www.cisco.com/en/US/partner/docs/ios/iproute_pi/configuration/guide/iri_prb_mult_track_ps6441_TSD_Products_Configuration_Guide_Chapter.html.

Web Cache Communication Protocol V2.0, https://tools.ietf.org/html/draft-wilson-wrec-wccp-v2-00.

Chapter 6

Bibliography

Administration Guide, Cisco ACE Application Control Engine Module, http://www.cisco.com/en/US/docs/interfaces_modules/services_modules/ace/vA4_1_0/configuration/administration/guide/admgd.html.

Cisco Nexus 7000 Series NX-OS Unicast Routing Configuration Guide, http://www.cisco.com/en/US/docs/switches/datacenter/sw/5_x/nx-os/unicast/configuration/guide/l3_cli_nxos.html.

Cisco Nexus 7000 Series NX-OS Virtual Device Context Configuration Guide, http://www.cisco.com/en/US/docs/switches/datacenter/sw/5_x/nx-os/virtual_device_context/configuration/guide/vdc_nx-os_cfg.html.

Cisco Virtual Wide Area Application Services: Cloud-Ready WAN Optimization Solution, http://www.cisco.com/en/US/prod/collateral/contnetw/ps5680/ps11231/solution_overview_c22-620028.html.

Cisco Virtual Wide Area Application Services: Technical Overview, http://www.cisco.com/en/US/prod/collateral/contnetw/ps5680/ps11231/technical_overview_c17-620098.html.

MPLS VPN VRF Selection Using Policy Based Routing, http://www.cisco.com/en/US/docs/ios/12_2s/feature/guide/fs_pbrsv.html#wp1043334.

Getting Started Guide, Cisco ACE Application Control Engine Module, http://www.cisco.com/en/US/docs/interfaces_modules/services_modules/ace/vA4_1_0/configuration/getting/started/guide/ACE_GSG.html.

Routing and Bridging Guide, Cisco ACE Application Control Engine Module, http://www.cisco.com/en/US/docs/interfaces_modules/services_modules/ace/vA4_1_0/configuration/rtg_brdg/guide/rtbrgdgd.html.

Security Guide, Cisco ACE Application Control Engine Module, http://www.cisco.com/en/US/docs/interfaces_modules/services_modules/ace/vA4_1_0/configuration/security/guide/securgd.html.

Server Load-Balancing Guide, Cisco ACE Application Control Engine Module, http://www.cisco.com/en/US/docs/interfaces_modules/services_modules/ace/vA4_1_0/configuration/slb/guide/slbgd.html.

Virtualization Guide, Cisco ACE Application Control Engine Module, http://www.cisco.com/en/US/docs/interfaces_modules/services_modules/ace/vA4_1_0/configuration/virtualization/guide/virtgd.html.

Designing Data Center Application Services (DCASD), v2.0, Student Courseware, Cisco Training.

Implementing Data Center Application Services (DCASI), v2.0, Student Courseware, Cisco Training.

Chapter 7

[1] Dense Wavelength Division Multiplexing, http://en.wikipedia.org/wiki/Wavelength-division_multiplexing#Dense_WDM.

[2] Coarse Wavelength Division Multiplexing, http://en.wikipedia.org/wiki/Wavelength-division_multiplexing#Coarse_WDM.

[3] Synchronous Digital Hierarchy, http://en.wikipedia.org/wiki/Synchronous_Digital_Hierarchy.

[4] Fabric Shortest Path First, http://en.wikipedia.org/wiki/FSPF.

[5] Enterprise System Connection, http://en.wikipedia.org/wiki/ESCON.

[6] Fiber Connection, http://en.wikipedia.org/wiki/FICON.

[7] Gigabit Interface Converter, http://en.wikipedia.org/wiki/Gbic.

[8] Small Form-Factor Pluggable Transceiver, http://en.wikipedia.org/wiki/Small_form-factor_pluggable_transceiver.

[9] Generic Framing Procedure, http://en.wikipedia.org/wiki/Generic_Framing_Procedure.

[10] 8b/10b Encoding, http://en.wikipedia.org/wiki/8B/10B.

[11] Internet Fibre Channel Protocol, http://en.wikipedia.org/wiki/IFCP.

[12] R.W. Kembel, Fibre Channel Switched Fabric, Northwest Learning Associates, Inc., December 7, 2009.

[13] Fibre Channel Network Protocols, http://en.wikipedia.org/wiki/Fibre_Channel_network_protocols.

[14] Path MTU Discovery, http://en.wikipedia.org/wiki/Path_MTU_Discovery.

[15] IP Payload Compression Using LZS, http://tools.ietf.org/html/rfc2395.

[16] Service Location Protocol, http://en.wikipedia.org/wiki/Service_Location_Protocol.

[17] Internet Storage Name Service, http://en.wikipedia.org/wiki/ISNS.

[18] World Wide Port Name, http://en.wikipedia.org/wiki/World_Wide_Port_Name.

Bibliography

Card Protection, http://www.cisco.com/en/US/docs/optical/15000r9_1/15454/sdh/reference/guide/454e91_card-protection.html.

Circuits and Tunnels, http://www.cisco.com/en/US/docs/optical/15000r6_0/15327/reference/guide/2760circ.html.

Cisco MDS 9000 Family CLI Configuration Guide, http://www.cisco.com/en/US/docs/storage/san_switches/mds9000/sw/rel_3_x/configuration/guides/cli_3_3/clibook.html.

Cisco MDS 9000 Family Cookbook, http://www.cisco.com/en/US/docs/storage/san_switches/mds9000/sw/rel_3_x/cookbook/MDScookbook31.pdf.

Designing Cisco Storage Networking Solutions (DCSNS), v3.0, Student Courseware, Cisco Training.

Fibre Channel Extension over Metropolitan DWDM, http://www.cisco.com/en/US/prod/collateral/optical/ps5725/ps2011/prod_white_paper0900aecd80181093.html.

Fibre Channel over IP, http://en.wikipedia.org/wiki/FCIP.

Fibre Channel over SONET/SDH, http://www.cisco.com/en/US/products/hw/modules/ps2710/products_white_paper09186a00801b97b3.shtml.

J.L. Hufferd, iSCSI: The Universal Storage Connection, Addison-Wesley Professional, November 15, 2002.

Implementing Advanced Cisco Storage Networking Solutions (IASNS), v3.0, Student Courseware. Cisco Training.

Implementing Cisco Storage Networking Solutions (ICSNS), v3.0, Student Courseware, Cisco Training.

Internet Small Computer System Interface, http://en.wikipedia.org/wiki/ISCSI.

SAN Extension over SONET/SDH Networks, http://www.cisco.com/en/US/products/hw/optical/ps2006/products_qanda_item09186a00801b97a4.shtml.

Storage Extension over Optical, http://www.cisco.com/en/US/prod/collateral/optical/ps5725/ps2011/ps2014/prod_presentation09186a008033a36a.ppt.

Chapter 8

[1] Trusted Execution Technology, http://en.wikipedia.org/wiki/Trusted_Execution_Technology.

[2] DDR3 SDRAM, http://en.wikipedia.org/wiki/Ddr3.

[3] Dual In-Line Memory Module, http://en.wikipedia.org/wiki/Dimm.

[4] Network Operations Center, http://en.wikipedia.org/wiki/Network_operations_center.

[5] Open Compute Project, http://opencompute.org/.

Bibliography

Cisco Nexus 1000V Layer 2 Switching Configuration Guide, http://www.cisco.com/en/US/docs/switches/datacenter/nexus1000/sw/4_2_1_s_v_1_4/layer_2_switching/configuration/guide/n1000v_l2.html.

Cisco Nexus 1000V Security Configuration Guide, http://www.cisco.com/en/US/docs/switches/datacenter/nexus1000/sw/4_2_1_s_v_1_4/security/configuration/guide/n1000v_security.html.

A. Clemm, Network Management Fundamentals, Cisco Press, December 1, 2006.

Cloud Computing, A Primer Part 2, http://www.cisco.com/web/about/ac123/ac147/archived_issues/ipj_12-4/124_cloud2.html.

Cloud Computing Overlay for Unified Service Delivery: Delivering Infrastructure-as-a-Service, http://www.cisco.com/en/US/solutions/collateral/ns341/ns525/ns951/solution_overview_c22-539404.html.

K. Corbin, et al., NX-OS and Cisco Nexus Switching, Cisco Press, June 20, 2010.

Deploying Secure Multi-Tenancy into Virtualized Data Centers, http://www.cisco.com/en/US/docs/solutions/ Enterprise/Data_Center/Virtualization/securecldeployg.html.

Designing Secure Multi-Tenancy into Virtualized Data Centers, http://www.cisco.com/en/US/docs/solutions/ Enterprise/Data_Center/Virtualization/securecldg.html.

DMZ Virtualization Using VMware vSphere 4 and the Cisco Nexus 1000V Virtual Switch, http://www.cisco.com/ en/US/prod/collateral/switches/ps9441/ps9902/dmz_virtualization_vsphere4_nexus1000V.pdf.

S. Gai, et al., Cisco Unified Computing System (UCS), Cisco Press, June 11, 2010.

Chapter 9

[1] Simple Object Access Protocol, http://en.wikipedia.org/wiki/Simple_Object_Access_Protocol.

[2] Web Services Description Language, http://en.wikipedia.org/wiki/Web_Services_Description_Language.

[3] Case Study: Hydro-Québec, Riverbed White Paper, http://www.riverbed.com/us/assets/media/documents/ case_studies/CaseStudy-Riverbed-Hydro-Quebec.pdf, 2011.

[4] Using Cisco Fabric Services, http://www.cisco.com/en/US/docs/switches/datacenter/nexus5000/sw/ configuration/guide/fm/cfs.pdf.

[5] World Wide Name, http://en.wikipedia.org/wiki/World_Wide_Name.

Bibliography

Cisco MDS 9000 Family CLI Configuration Guide, http://www.cisco.com/en/US/docs/storage/san_switches/ mds9000/sw/rel_3_x/configuration/guides/cli_3_3/clibook.html.

Cisco MDS 9000 Family Cookbook, http://www.cisco.com/en/US/docs/storage/san_switches/mds9000/sw/ rel_3_x/cookbook/MDScookbook31.pdf.

Cisco Nexus 1000V Interface Configuration Guide, http://www.cisco.com/en/US/docs/switches/datacenter/ nexus1000/sw/4_2_1_s_v_1_4/interface/configuration/guide/n1000v_if.html.

Cisco Nexus 1000V Port Profile Configuration Guide, http://www.cisco.com/cn/US/docs/switches/datacenter/ nexus1000/sw/4_2_1_s_v_1_4/port_profile/configuration/guide/n1000v_port_profile.html.

Cisco Nexus 1000V Series Switches Deployment Guide Version 2, http://www.cisco.com/en/US/prod/collateral/ switches/ps9441/ps9902/guide_c07-556626.html.

Cisco Nexus 1000V System Management Configuration Guide, http://www.cisco.com/en/US/docs/switches/ datacenter/nexus1000/sw/4_2_1_s_v_1_4/system_management/configuration/guide/n1000v_system.html.

Cisco Nexus 2000 Series Fabric Extender Software Configuration Guide, http://www.cisco.com/en/US/docs/ switches/datacenter/nexus2000/sw/configuration/guide/Cisco_Nexus_2000_Series_Fabric_Extender_- Software_Configuration_Guide_Release_4_2_chapter3.html.

Cisco Nexus 5000 Series NX-OS Layer 2 Switching Configuration Guide, http://www.cisco.com/en/US/docs/ switches/datacenter/nexus5000/sw/layer2/502_n2_1/b_Cisco_n5k_layer2_config_gd_rel_502_N2_1.html.

Cisco Nexus 5000 Series NX-OS SAN Switching Configuration Guide, http://www.cisco.com/en/US/docs/ switches/datacenter/nexus5000/sw/san_switching/502_n2_1/b_Cisco_n5k_nxos_sanswitching_config_ guide_rel502_n2_1.html.

Cisco Nexus 5000 Series NX-OS System Management Configuration Guide, http://www.cisco.com/en/US/docs/ switches/datacenter/nexus5000/sw/system_management/502_n2_1/b_Cisco_n5k_system_mgmt_cg_rel_502_ n2_1.html.

Cisco Nexus 7000 Series NX-OS Interfaces Configuration Guide, http://www.cisco.com/en/US/docs/switches/ datacenter/sw/5_x/nx-os/interfaces/configuration/guide/if_cli.html.

Cisco Nexus 7000 Series NX-OS Layer 2 Switching Configuration Guide, http://www.cisco.com/en/US/docs/switches/datacenter/sw/5_x/nx-os/layer2/configuration/guide/b_Cisco_Nexus_7000_Series_NX-OS_Layer_2_Switching_Configuration_Guide_Release_5.x.html.

Data Center Design with VMware ESX 4.0 and Cisco Nexus 5000 and 1000V Series Switches, http://www.cisco.com/en/US/prod/collateral/switches/ps9441/ps9670/C07-572832-00_VMware_ESX4_Nexus_DG.pdf.

Data Center Top-of-Rack Architecture Design, http://www.cisco.com/en/US/prod/collateral/switches/ps9441/ps9670/white_paper_c11-522337.html.

Deploying 10 Gigabit Ethernet with Cisco Nexus 5000 Series Switches, http://www.cisco.com/en/US/prod/collateral/switches/ps9441/ps9670/white_paper_c27-489248_ns783_Networking_Solutions_White_Paper.html.

Implementing Cisco Storage Networking Solutions (ICSNS), v3.0, Student Courseware, Cisco Training.

Next-Generation Enterprise MPLS VPN-Based WAN Design and Implementation Guide, http://www.cisco.com/en/US/docs/solutions/Enterprise/WAN_and_MAN/ngwane.pdf.

Unified Fabric White Paper—Fibre Channel over Ethernet (FCoE), http://www.cisco.com/en/US/docs/solutions/Enterprise/Data_Center/UF_FCoE_final.pdf.

Index

Note: Page numbers followed by *b* indicate boxes and *f* indicate figures.

Printed and bound by CPI Group (UK) Ltd, Croydon, CR0 4YY

03/10/2024

01040310-0004